Library of Congress
Subject Headings

Library of Congress Subject Headings

Principles and Application

Fourth Edition

Lois Mai Chan

Library and Information Science Text Series

LIBRARIES UNLIMITED
A Member of the Greenwood Publishing Group
Westport, Connecticut • London

Ess Ess Publications
4837/24, Ansari Road
Darya Ganj
New Delhi-110 002
Phones: 41563444, 23260807
Fax: 011-41563334
E-mail: info@essessreference.com
www.essessreference.com

Library of Congress Cataloging-in-Publication Data

Chan, Lois Mai.
Library of Congress subject headings : principles and application / by Lois Mai Chan.—
4th ed.
p. cm. — (Library and information science text series)
Includes bibliographical references and index.
ISBN 1-59158-154-0 — ISBN 1-59158-156-7 (pbk. : alk. paper)
1. Subject headings, Library of Congress. I. Title. II. Series.
Z695.Z8L5226 2005
025.4'9—dc22 2004063837

British Library Cataloguing in Publication Data is available.

Library of Congress Catalog Card Number: 2004063837

ISBN: 978-81-7000-516-2

First Indian Imprint 2007

Libraries Unlimited, 88 Post Road West, Westport, CT 06881
A Member of the Greenwood Publishing Group, Inc.
www.lu.com

Ess Ess Publications
4837/24, Ansari Road, Darya Ganj
New Delhi-110002
Phones : 41563444, 23260807 Fax : 011-41563334
E-mail : info@essessreference.com
www.essessreference.com

Printed by Ritomate International, Noida Special Economic Zone, India. www.ritomate.com

In memory of

Kar K. and Sau N. Mark

Contents

Part 2
Application

Part 3
Current and Future Prospects

Preface

This fourth edition of *Library of Congress Subject Headings: Principles and Application* reflects the changes in the continuing development of the Library of Congress Subject Headings (LCSH) system since the third edition appeared in 1995. Since that date, use of LCSH has expanded considerably. It is now the most comprehensive nonspecialized controlled vocabulary in the English language; and, in many respects, the system has become a de facto standard for subject cataloging and indexing in circumstances far beyond those for which it was originally designed.

During the past decade, the information retrieval environment has undergone enormous changes. In many respects, these changes have been reflected in the revision and continuing development of the LC subject headings system. Another change that has affected the system is that in the same decade the use of LCSH has extended far beyond the United States. It has been adopted, translated, or adapted for use in the catalogs of libraries in many countries around the world, and many more are considering doing the same. Furthermore, LCSH is now used not only as a major subject access tool in library catalogs and national bibliographies but also as a means for enhancing subject access to information beyond the library community.

Like its previous editions, this edition attempts to shed light on the current state of the LCSH system. The book is divided into three parts. Part 1 gives a brief history of the system, analyzes its principles, and describes its provisions for vocabulary and subject authority control. Historical reviews (highlights) are included because they shed light on current practice and provide the background for understanding the theoretical assumptions that have governed how LCSH has developed. Part 2 deals with the Library of Congress's subject cataloging policies, exemplified by LC subject headings extracted from the Library's MARC records. With the aim of describing and illuminating current LC subject cataloging practice, it treats the assignment of subject headings in general and also discusses how particular types of materials are handled. New to this edition are discussions and examples of the subject cataloging of various types of electronic resources and interactive media. Part 3 discusses LCSH in the global context of the networked environment; it has been completely rewritten, drawing on recent literature on the subject. Part 3 also includes a chapter on FAST (Faceted Application of Subject Terminology), the LCSH-based controlled vocabulary designed for electronic resources that is currently under development at OCLC Online Computer Library Center.

In order to avoid confusing "what is" with "what ought to be," my own opinions are largely limited to parts 1 and 3 of the book.

The appendices contain sample Library of Congress MARC records; lists of the most frequently used free-floating subdivisions; lists of general reference sources to be consulted in establishing headings; MARC 21 coding for subject data; and the rules for the abbreviation, capitalization, and punctuation of Library of Congress subject headings. A glossary and a bibliography appear at the end of the book.

All the subject headings cited in this edition have been verified in the *Library of Congress Authorities* database, and cataloging examples—the majority dated since 2002—are taken from the Library of Congress Online Catalog and reflect current LC cataloging policies as of 2004. Except for the subject authority records in chapter 7, examples in the text do not contain MARC 21 codes because many prospective readers of this book are not MARC 21 users. Examples of LC bibliographic records with MARC 21 codes are included in appendix A. Throughout the book, boldface type is used to indicate valid LC subject headings, and italics signifies unauthorized terms or obsolete headings.

A premise underlying the preparation of this edition (and earlier ones) is that an understanding of both the principles and the rules of application of the current system is essential for those applying LCSH in libraries as well as for those seeking to improve or adapt the system or the vocabulary for use in different information retrieval environments. The book is primarily intended for library and information professionals, library and information science educators, and advanced students; library technicians, paraprofessionals, and beginning students may also find it helpful. Comments received on previous editions indicate that, in addition, many outside of the library field have also found the book useful.

I am indebted to many individuals for their help in the preparation of this edition. I wish to acknowledge the assistance given by the following: Lynn El-Hoshy and Geraldine E. Ostrove, subject specialists at the Library of Congress, for answering numerous questions regarding application of LCSH, heading revisions, music cataloging, and recent policy changes; Marie E. Whited, Yale Law Library, for her help with the section on law; Theodora Hodges for her invaluable editorial assistance and for preparing the index; Nicole M. Montgomery for bibliographic assistance; and Jennifer K. Nelson for proofreading.

PART 1

PRINCIPLES, FORM, AND STRUCTURE

1 Introduction

It was more than one hundred years ago, in the summer of 1898, that the Library of Congress (LC) decided that its card catalog should be in dictionary form—in other words, a catalog in which author, title, and subject entries were interfiled in alphabetical order. For the topical entries in the new catalog, the Library began work on a list of preferred terms to be used as subject headings. This list was to grow into what we now know as the Library of Congress subject headings (LCSH) system. Its base is a continuously maintained, controlled-vocabulary list of headings and subdivisions, enhanced with lead-in terms (i.e., *see* references to preferred terms), cross references to related terms, tracers, and, in some cases, directions for application. The list is now available in electronic form and can be accessed online, and it is also published regularly in print format under the title *Library of Congress Subject Headings* (*LCSH*). Furthermore, the Library keeps up a program that notifies system users of additions and changes in the list as well as provides them with other information important to using the list appropriately.

Although LCSH was originally intended as a tool for use with the Library's own collections, it now serves a much wider audience, becoming the de facto standard for subject cataloging and indexing in circumstances far beyond those for which it was originally designed.[1] Generally referred to as LCSH,[2] it is now one of the two standard systems used for the subject cataloging of general collections in American libraries. (The other is the *Sears List of Subject Headings*, a simpler list developed for small and medium-sized libraries.[3]) Thus, LCSH has become an important subject access tool both within the Library of Congress and outside. Most of the cataloging records provided by major bibliographic utilities and services such as OCLC Online Computer Library Center and RLIN (Research Libraries Information Network) carry LC subject headings, and most of the individual libraries in the United States use them for subject cataloging. Furthermore, a number of commercial retrieval services such as DIALOG carry the LC MARC file, bringing LC subject cataloging to their subscribers, along with flexible and powerful search capabilities.

Internationally, LCSH has also gained wide acceptance. Over the years, many libraries in other countries have adopted or adapted LCSH, using it as is or as a model for developing controlled vocabularies for use in their own catalogs.[4] For example, the Bodleian Library at the University of Oxford has been using LCSH for many years, and the British Library has included LC subject headings in MARC records since 1995. *Canadian Subject Headings* (CSH),[5] the system used by most Canadian libraries, is "largely based on *LCSH* in its underlying principles of organization, structure and vocabulary and is specifically designed as an adjunct list to be used in tandem with *LCSH*."[6] *Répertoire de vedettes-matière* (RVM),[7] a French adaptation of both LCSH and CSH, is used in Francophone Canada. RVM, in turn, served as the basis of the subject indexing system RAMEAU used by libraries in France, Belgium, and Switzerland.[8] Other countries that have adopted or adapted controlled vocabularies based on LCSH include Brazil,[9] the Czech Republic, Iran,[10] Lithuania, Malaysia, Portugal,[11] and Sweden.

One factor in the system's popularity here and abroad may be that for most of its history the Library of Congress has made its cataloging data available to other institutions, initially through catalog cards and later through MARC records and various electronic LCSH products. Probably another is LC's policy of ongoing updates.

Since the mid-1990s, there has been a surge of new metadata schemas designed for the description and representation of electronic resources in various information communities, including libraries, museums, visual arts collections, government information systems, geospatial data systems, and so on. For subject access, most of them recommend the use of controlled vocabulary in addition to keyword searching. Many of them list LCSH as one of the possible choices for subject vocabulary.

In most cases, growth such as has occurred for LCSH is considered a mark of a system's success. Yet it is generally acknowledged by information professionals that LCSH is far from a perfect system. It shows considerable internal inconsistency, and it still exhibits certain characteristics that cater more to manual than to online systems. Nevertheless, LCSH has clearly demonstrated its versatility in a wide range of conditions and is not only holding its own but is growing in popularity. The system is constantly updated; even so, there seems no question that more changes are in order, perhaps even far-reaching ones. Major changes, many would claim, are long overdue. However, to be effective, any changes designed to enhance a system must take into account all the ramifications affecting the current system. It is therefore appropriate here that we take a new look at the principles on which LCSH was based and that have governed its development for more than a century. We turn first to the early history of LCSH for the insights it can provide into its current structure. Next we examine other factors that have influenced its development and are reflected in current policies. Finally, we look at some of the problems inherent in designing any thesaurus or subject headings list intended for general use.

HISTORY

The Beginnings

Shortly after the Library of Congress moved from the Capitol to its new building in 1897, its officials faced the question of how the collection should be organized. One major decision, made in late 1897, was to establish a new classification system. Another, made in 1898, was to adopt the dictionary form for the main catalog. Charles A. Cutter's *Rules for a Dictionary Catalog*[12] had been published in 1876 and by 1898 was in its third edition; the dictionary catalog was well on its way to becoming the predominant catalog form in American libraries. The move of the Library of Congress to such a catalog, plus the effect of its practice of selling its printed cards, put the Library at the forefront of the development of both American cataloging practice in general and the use of the dictionary arrangement as a catalog form in particular. Indeed, according to J. C. M. Hanson, the first chief of the Catalogue Division, one of the Library's reasons for adopting the dictionary form for the catalog was "a desire to be in a position to cooperate with the largest possible number of American libraries."[13]

As the Library's subject headings came to be used more and more widely, many librarians asked that its headings list be published. This was done, under the title *Subject Headings Used in the Dictionary Catalogues of the Library of Congress,*[14] which first appeared in 1914. There has been a continuing series of editions ever since (with a title change to *Library of Congress Subject Headings* at the eighth edition in 1975).

The development of the list was the responsibility of the staff of the Library's Catalogue Division. Hanson and Charles Martel, whose tours of duty as virtually successive chiefs of the division spanned the years 1897 to 1930, have been formally recognized as the individuals who provided its initial guiding principles. In the introduction to the fourth edition (1943), David Judson Haykin, then chief of the Library's Subject Cataloging Division, presented his view of the origin of the list:

> There was not, to begin with, a scheme or skeleton list of headings to which additions could be made systematically, completing and rounding out a system of subject headings for a dictionary catalog. Such a scheme could not have been devised at the time the Library's dictionary catalogs were begun, because there was no solid body of doctrine upon which it would be based; the guiding principles which were then in print for all to read and apply were very meager and concerned themselves with the form of headings and their choice. They did not provide the theoretical basis for a system of headings.[15]

Actual work on the new subject catalog began simultaneously with the printing of the first author cards in July 1898,[16] when it was found necessary to begin an authority list of subject headings. Haykin's earlier quoted statement that there was not a "skeleton list of headings to which additions could be made systematically" might give the impression that the Library of Congress list was begun *in vacuo*. In fact, a list of subject headings had been published a few years earlier by the American Library Association;[17] this list was conceived as an appendix to Cutter's rules and was designed for use by small and medium-sized public libraries.[18] In a paper presented at the American Library Association (ALA) Conference in 1909, Hanson recounted the beginning of the compilation of the Library of Congress list:

> While it was recognized that the A.L.A. list of subject headings had been calculated for small and medium sized libraries of a generally popular character, it was nevertheless decided to adopt it as a basis for subject headings with the understanding, however, that considerable modification and specialization would have to be resorted to.... New subjects as they came up for discussion and decision were noted on slips and filed. If the subject had already been adopted by the A.L.A. committee, i.e., had appeared as a regular printed heading on the List, a check mark was added to indicate regular adoption by the Library of Congress.[19]

Hanson also indicated that other works were consulted in addition to the ALA list. These included the Dewey classification and the Expansive classification, the Harvard list of subjects, the New South Wales subject index, Forescue's subject index, and numerous other catalogs, bibliographies, encyclopedias, and dictionaries.

At the time that LC was making its first decisions on how to structure its dictionary catalog, Cutter's *Rules for a Dictionary Catalog* had been in circulation for more than twenty years and was well regarded in the profession. Indeed, among those interested in subject access provisions, it has been generally accepted ever since that Charles Cutter's work on subject headings was seminal to that aspect of the field. One would therefore expect it to have had considerable influence on what the LC did in setting up headings for its new catalog. Thus, it is of considerable interest to realize how little acknowledgment was made of Cutter's work—at the time, or even many decades later. As quoted above, Haykin talked about the inadequate theoretical basis of "guiding principles then in print" as late as 1943; in his *Subject Headings: A Practical Guide*,[20] which was published in 1951 and acknowledged as the official guide in subsequent editions of the list, there are only a few passing references to Cutter's rules. Furthermore, Cutter was never mentioned in the preface or introduction to any of the list's many editions. When recognition did come, many years later in 1970, it was still not in an official statement from LC, but in a paper presented at an international symposium by Richard S. Angell when he was chief of the Subject Cataloging Division:

> The final formulation of Cutter's objectives and rules was taking place at the same time that the Library of Congress was expanding and reorganizing the collections at the turn of the century. His work had a considerable influence on the founders of the Library of Congress catalog.[21]

Nevertheless, as we shall see in later chapters, Cutter's influence is quite obvious in Haykin's discussion of the fundamental concepts of Library of Congress subject headings: the reader as the focus, unity, usage, and specificity. Furthermore, Cutter's subject heading principles are even now reflected in LCSH, in spite of the many modifications and compromises that have been made in the face of practical demands. As Francis Miksa put it, LCSH is a reflection of Cutter's principles "interpreted through Haykin."[22]

Editions and Versions of the Subject Headings List

Almost from the beginning, the Library of Congress took on the responsibility of giving other libraries an account of its cataloging practices. One channel for such information has been the introductions to new editions of the list; another has been auxiliary publications bearing on the lists themselves and on subject headings practice. Auxiliary publications are discussed briefly below, for the information they convey on the development of the system.

Preparation for publishing the list began in 1909 and, as mentioned above, the first edition appeared in 1914 under the title *Subject Headings Used in the Dictionary Catalogues of the Library of Congress*. Since the eighth edition in 1975, the title has been *Library of Congress Subject Headings*. Until 1988, the list was revised and published at five- to nine-year intervals, but it is now kept current continuously, with a new print version published annually. LCSH is kept up to date by means of *LC Subject Headings Weekly Lists*, included in each issue of *Cataloging Service Bulletin* and available at the Library's web site.[23]

Following are highlights in the development of the list:

1914 (1st edition)—Included *see* and *see also* references as well as the list itself.

1943 (4th edition)—Included a separate list of *refer from* tracers.

1948 (5th edition)—Incorporated *refer from* references into main list; introduced symbols to denote type of reference.

1966 (7th edition)—Began to be produced using an automated system, making supplements easier.

1975 (8th edition)—Reflected title change to *Library of Congress Subject Headings*. Included a long introduction featuring subdivision practice, plus a separate list of headings for children's literature.

1986 (10th edition)—Became available also in an electronic version called *SUBJECTS*, now a part of the authority database called *Library of Congress Authorities*.

1988 (11th edition)—Issued annually from this edition on.

Currently, the electronic version of LCSH is also available in *Classification Web*, a web-based tool that includes both LCSH and the Library of Congress Classification with links between many subject headings and their corresponding classification numbers. However, because many catalogers and subject searchers still find it easier to use the printed list than to go online, *LCSH* (the print version) remains useful even in situations with online access to LCSH.

In this book, the following terms are used to refer to the various versions:

LCSH = the Library of Congress Subject Headings system in general and the list in whatever form

Library of Congress Subject Headings (LCSH) = the print version

Library of Congress Authorities = a database mounted on the LC web site (http://authorities.loc.gov) that allows browsing, display, and downloading of authority records for subject, name, title, and name/title combinations

Auxiliary Publications

Not all information needed for the application of LCSH appears in *Library of Congress Subject Headings* or its other versions. Many headings and subdivisions appear elsewhere, as do many of the Library's policies and instructions on using LCSH. Publications related to LCSH and its application began appearing in 1906 and continue to the present day. The most important is *Subject Cataloging Manual: Subject Headings* (SCM), which first appeared in 1984 and is now in its fifth edition.[24] It is kept current with semiannual updates. Other helpful publications—all issued on a regular basis—are listed below:

Cataloging Service Bulletin (published quarterly, contains lists of subject headings of current interest, and revised subject headings and information about changes in policy, headings, subdivisions)

Free-Floating Subdivisions: An Alphabetical Index (published annually, lists all subdivisions designated as *free-floating*, a term referring to form and topical subdivisions that may be assigned by subject catalogers under designated subjects without their usage being formally authorized)

LC Subject Headings Weekly Lists (available at the Library's web site (http://lcweb.loc.gov/catdir/cpso/cpso.html#subjects); contains new and revised headings approved at weekly editorial meetings)

Library of Congress Subject Headings: Principles of Structure and Policies for Application: Annotated Version[25] (commissioned and published by the Library of Congress; outlines the structural principles of LCSH and policies on its application, extracted from various LC documents relating to LCSH)

ASSUMPTIONS ABOUT FUNCTION

The features of any indexing system, both in terms of structure and rules of application, reflect what the designers of the system believe it should do for its users; different notions of a system's purpose lead to different results. Since the late nineteenth century, many statements of what a subject catalog should accomplish have been published, and some of them have been received with considerable acclaim. When one analyzes the question of what these statements call for in practical terms, however, one finds a vague picture that at best reflects conflicting demands on the catalog.

Cutter's 1876 statement of "objects" is still cited often as an articulation of the functions of subject entries:

1. To enable a person to find a book of which . . . the subject is known [and]
2. To show what the library has . . . on a given subject [and] in a given kind of literature.[26]

When Cutter was writing, his context was books and libraries, and his access system was a card catalog. But his comments can be generalized to a wider milieu: for "book" read "library material" or "information resources"; for "library has" read "what is available." Cutter's two points are impressive in the simplicity of their wording. However, to the extent that their meaning can be assumed, they make different demands on an access system. His first point calls for a subject catalog to be simply a tool for identifying and retrieving specific known items, to be a finding list for users who have a particular item in mind, and to enable them to use a subject term for access. His second point, on the other hand, calls for collocation of material by subject and by genre—a much more demanding task because it requires dealing with groups of entries together rather than with individual items.

Seventy-five years later, in the mid 1950s, Jesse H. Shera and Margaret Egan spelled out eight "objectives for any form of subject cataloging."[27] They called for access by subject to all relevant materials, at any level of analysis, under precisely phrased controlled-vocabulary headings that are further differentiated by subheadings. They also called for a supporting structure of cross references from variant terms and to affiliated subject fields (affiliated in several different ways), plus information that would allow patrons to make selections based on various criteria. Writing when they did, Shera and Egan recognized that it was impractical for all of their objectives to be met, and that limitations of personnel and finance would force modifications.[28]

Both the Cutter and Shera/Egan statements were well received when they appeared, yet both statements were too vague to be useful when considered as guides to policy making. What is meant by the phrases "of which the subject is known" and "what the library has on a subject" or by Shera and Egan's statements about "all relevant materials," "affiliations among subject fields," or "criteria for selection"? How far should cross references go in showing affiliations among subjects? To what units should subject cataloging apply: books, parts of books, series, individual titles in series, serials, journal articles, nonprint materials of various types? How exhaustive should the subject analysis be: many headings per item to cover all concepts, or one or two—ideally one—to summarize its content? Such questions were raised periodically in the decades following Shera's and Egan's work. But within the library profession, except for general agreement on using headings to summarize content, there has been little consensus on how best to answer them.

One point is especially worth making about these function statements. Only the one from Shera and Egan stresses the importance of cross references—what is called syndetic structure—in a controlled-vocabulary system. Yet both Cutter's recommendations and the first edition of LCSH included *see* and *see also* references, and by 1988 LCSH had moved to using BT (broader term), NT (narrower term), and RT (related term at same level) references instead of all-purpose *see also* references. Obviously, since its inception the Library of Congress has thought of its system as incorporating not only vocabulary control but syndetic information.

In 1990, almost forty years after the statement of function by Shera and Egan, the Library of Congress commissioned and published a document that put forth, in summary, the principles of structure and policies of implementation governing LCSH. The document began with a statement acknowledging that the Library saw the system not only as a tool for its own use but as a subject retrieval system that could serve the whole information community:

> The Library of Congress subject headings system serves both internal and external needs:
>
> > (1) As a controlled vocabulary for subject cataloging of the Library of Congress collection:
> >
> > > The Library of Congress Subject Headings system was originally designed as a controlled vocabulary for representing the subject and form of the books and serials in the Library of Congress collection, with the purpose of providing subject access points to the bibliographic records contained in the Library of Congress catalogs.
> >
> > (2) As a controlled vocabulary for use in subject cataloging and indexing by other libraries or indexing agencies:
> >
> > > As an increasing number of other libraries have adopted the Library of Congress subject headings system, it has become a tool for subject indexing of library catalogs in general. In recent years, it has also been used as a tool in a number of online bibliographic databases outside of the Library of Congress.[29]

DELIBERATIONS ON A CODE FOR LCSH

Many information professionals believe that the inconsistencies and irregularities that have crept into LCSH over the years are due to the fact that the system has grown by accretion without the guidance of a specific code or body of rules. It is clear that although the basic principles of the dictionary catalog laid down by Cutter and reinterpreted by Haykin have been adhered to in general, they have often been compromised in the face of practical constraints or considerations. In some cases, too, the same principles have been interpreted differently on different occasions. As a result, over the years there has been repeated interest in the question of formulating a code for subject cataloging that corresponds to the one for descriptive cataloging. Since Cutter, the only codification of subject heading practice for dictionary catalogs has appeared in Italian, in the Vatican Library's *Rules for the Catalog of Printed Books*, completed in the 1930s and translated into English in 1948.[30] In essence, the subject headings portion of that code reflected the practice of the Library of Congress at the time the Vatican code was drafted, that is, in the 1930s.

In this country, for many years the closest thing to a set of rules for subject headings since Cutter was Haykin's *Subject Headings: A Practice Guide* (1951). Haykin's work was officially acknowledged as a statement of principles for the choice and form of headings and references. It contains an account and exposition of Library of Congress practice, with occasional apologetics, but is not cast in the form of a code. Besides, although Haykin's work was a full and consistent treatment of the practice and guiding principles in operation at that time, it was written more than fifty years ago; since that time there have been many changes in both the theory and practice of subject analysis.

In the 1950s, perhaps in response to the realization that Haykin's work was not prescriptive, there was an intensified call for a code. Carlyle Frarey's survey of catalog use studies[31] and other works on subject headings in the 1940s had caught the attention of the retrieval community and could have laid the groundwork for a code. Haykin himself apparently began work on a code in the late 1950s. However, his work was not completed, and the remains of his attempt exist only in an unpublished document entitled "Project for a Subject Heading Code."[32] Furthermore, in the ensuing years there has been no formal effort by the Library of Congress either to continue Haykin's project or to begin anew.

In the late 1980s, there was a renewed call for a subject cataloging code, both at professional meetings and in the literature.[33] However, neither the Library of Congress nor the American Library Association took any official action. In 1990, perhaps in response to pressure, the document mentioned earlier, *Library of Congress Subject Headings: Principles of Structure and Policies for Application,* was published, a work that represents an effort to articulate the principles of LCSH and the Library's application policies. On the international front, the International Federation of Library Associations and Institutions

(IFLA) published a document entitled *Principles Underlying Subject Heading Languages*,[34] a broad statement regarding the construction and application of subject headings.

In the current environment, more and more retrieval options are available to library users and other information consumers than previously, and advances in system design—such as automatic term truncation and switching, and prompts on refining searches—have increased the likelihood of successful searches. At the same time, online catalog use studies indicate that, although subject searches make up the greatest portion of all searches,[35] users still have difficulties searching by subject even in online catalogs.[36] Given that fact, and the problems with precision in keyword searching, perhaps it is more important than ever to understand and examine our current subject headings system for clues to potential improvement.

IMPACT OF THE INTERNET AND THE WORLD WIDE WEB

The situation for subject access has changed dramatically with the emergence of the Internet and the World Wide Web as well as with the attendant burgeoning of metadata schemas for providing access to the huge store of information that is available there. In this new environment, traditional subject access systems face a major challenge, one that goes to the heart of information retrieval: Can a controlled vocabulary system, particularly one such as is reflected in *Library of Congress Subject Headings,* play a helpful role in the digital age? Many think yes; many others are doubtful. Whatever the answer, it will affect the library and information community profoundly. This matter will be addressed in depth in part 3 of this book.

CONCLUSION

The Library of Congress subject headings system is extensive and complex, not only as a controlled vocabulary per se but in the rules governing how subject catalogers and indexers should apply its provisions. For this reason particularly, applying LCSH successfully requires careful training in all aspects of the system, both in terms of its structure and application. Accordingly, this book was originally conceived as a tool to aid in such training. It examines in depth the basic principles underlying LCSH in light of the literature on subject access in general and on LCSH in particular, and it describes, with copious examples, the policies of its application at the Library of Congress. Now in its fourth edition, this book has proved useful as an education and training tool, not only for new users of the system but for experienced LCSH users, who have welcomed it as a review tool and a source of information about recent changes to the list and to its application. It is hoped that this edition will fulfill the same needs.

It should be clear from the thrust of much of this chapter, however, that the book has a secondary purpose. It has been pointed out that recent changes in the information retrieval environment—particularly the burgeoning of the World Wide Web and the Internet—have led to a strong demand from the information community for better subject access to web resources. One potential solution is greater use of controlled vocabulary as a query expansion device or as a means to provide richer subject access points in metadata records. Given its size and subject range, LCSH is a prime candidate to be the basis for such a tool. The phrase "as a basis" is of prime importance here: LCSH as it stands is too cumbersome, with too many intricate rules for forming subject strings, for it to be effective in dealing with the enormous scope of web resources. A new system, FAST (Faceted Application of Subject Terminology), based on LCSH vocabulary but with a simpler syntax that makes it easier to apply, has been under development at OCLC Online Computer Library Center and will be tested to ascertain whether, indeed, the LCSH vocabulary can be useful in the web environment. There is a risk with such an operation, however, that simplification could destroy much of the system's retrieval strength. This risk is lowered if those working on modification fully understand all of the strengths and weaknesses of the current system. It is here we find the book's secondary purpose: to help information professionals review and strengthen their knowledge of LCSH as a whole. This book begins with a history of LCSH and then focuses on its fundamental principles of structure and application.

NOTES

1. J. C. M. Hanson, "The Subject Catalogs of the Library of Congress," *Bulletin of the American Library Association* 3 (1909): 385-97; Lois Mai Chan, "Still Robust at 100: A Century of LC Subject Headings," *The Library of Congress Information Bulletin* 57(8) (August 1998): 200.

2. In this text, the term "LCSH" is used to refer to the Library of Congress's subject headings *system*; the title of the print version of the subject headings list is given as *Library of Congress Subject Headings*.

3. *Sears List of Subject Headings*, 18th ed., ed. Joseph Miller and Joan Goodssell (New York: H. W. Wilson, 2004).

4. Robert P. Holley, "Report on the IFLA Satellite Meeting 'Subject Indexing: Principles and Practices in the 90's,' August 17-18, 1993, Lisbon, Portugal," in *Cataloging & Classification Quarterly* 18(2) (1993): 87-95; and *Subject Indexing: Principles & Practices: Proceedings of the IFLA Satellite Meeting held in Lisbon, Portugal, 17-18 August 1993, and sponsored by the IFLA Section on Classification and Indexing and the Instituto da Biblioteca Nacional e do Livro, Lisbon, Portugal*, ed. Robert P. Holley, Dorothy McGarry, Donna Duncan, and Elaine Svenonius, UCBIM Publications—New Series, vol. 15 (München: K. G. Saur, 1995).

5. *Canadian Subject Headings* (Ottawa: National Library of Canada, 1978-).

6. Alina Schweitzer, "A Balancing Act Between Conformity and Divergence: Subject Access to Library Materials in Canada," in *Subject Indexing: Principles & Practices in the 90's.*

7. *Répertoire de vedettes-matière* (Ottawa: Bibliothèque nationale du Canada, 1976-).

8. Suzanne Jouguelet, "Evolution des pratiques d'indexation par sujets en France," in *Subject Indexing: Principles & Practices in the 90's.*

9. Eugénio Decourt & Sónia Maria Guerreiro Pacheco, "Subject Access in the Brazilian Library Network BIBLIODATA CALCO," in *Subject Indexing: Principles & Practices in the 90's.*

10. Poori Soltani, "Major Subject Access in Iran," in *Subject Indexing: Principles & Practices in the 90's.*

11. Inês Lopes, "Subject Indexing in Portuguese Libraries: A New Approach with SIPORbase," in *Subject Indexing: Principles & Practices in the 90's;* and Chan, "Still Robust at 100."

12. Charles A. Cutter, *Rules for a Dictionary Catalog*, 4th ed. rewritten (Washington, D.C.: Government Printing Office, 1904).

13. Hanson, "Subject Catalogs," 387.

14. Library of Congress, Catalog Division, *Subject Headings Used in the Dictionary Catalogues of the Library of Congress* (Washington, D.C.: Government Printing Office, Library Branch, 1910–1914).

15. Library of Congress, Subject Cataloging Division, *Subject Headings Used in the Dictionary Catalogs of the Library of Congress*, 4th ed., ed. Mary Wilson MacNair (Washington, D.C.: U.S. Government Printing Office, 1943), iii.

16. Hanson, "Subject Catalogs," 387.

17. *List of Subject Headings for Use in Dictionary Catalogs*, prepared by a Committee of the American Library Association (Boston: Published for the ALA Publishing Section by the Library Bureau, 1895; 2nd ed. rev., 1898; 3rd ed. rev., 1911).

18. Carlyle J. Frarey, *Subject Headings, The State of the Library Art* (New Brunswick, N.J.: Graduate School of Library Science, Rutgers—The State University, 1960), vol. 1, part 2, 17.

19. Hanson, "Subject Catalogs," 387, 391.

20. David Judson Haykin, *Subject Headings: A Practical Guide* (Washington, D.C.: Government Printing Office, 1951).

21. Richard S. Angell, "Library of Congress Subject Headings—Review and Forecast," in *Subject Retrieval in the Seventies: New Directions: Proceedings of an International Symposium*, ed. Hans (Hanan) Wellisch and Thomas D. Wilson (Westport, Conn.: Greenwood Publishing, 1972), 143.

22. Francis Miksa, *The Subject in the Dictionary Catalog from Cutter to the Present* (Chicago: American Library Association, 1983), 365.

23. http://lcweb.loc.gov/catdir/cpso/cpso.html#subjects

24. Library of Congress, Office of Subject Cataloging Policy, *Subject Cataloging Manual: Subject Headings*, 5th ed., 2000 cumulation (Washington, D.C.: Cataloging Distribution Service, Library of Congress, 2000).

25. Lois Mai Chan, *Library of Congress Subject Headings: Principles of Structure and Policies for Application: Annotated Version*, prepared by Lois Mai Chan for the Library of Congress, Advances in Library Information Technology, No. 3 (Washington, D.C.: Cataloging Distribution Service, Library of Congress, 1990).

26. Cutter, *Rules for a Dictionary Catalog*, 12.

27. Jesse H. Shera and Margaret Egan, *The Classified Catalog: Basic Principles and Practices* (Chicago: American Library Association, 1956), 10.

28. Shera and Egan, *The Classified Catalog*, 10.

29. Chan, *Library of Congress Subject Headings*, 1.

30. Vatican Library, *Rules for the Catalog of Printed Books*, trans. from 2nd Italian ed. by Thomas J. Shanahan, Victor A. Schaefer, and Constantin T. Vesselowsky, and ed. Wyllis E. Wright (Chicago: American Library Association, 1948).

31. Carlyle J. Frarey, "Studies of Use of the Subject Catalog: Summary and Evaluation," in *Subject Analysis of Library Materials*, ed. by Maurice F. Tauber (New York: School of Library Service, Columbia University, 1953), 147-165.

32. David Judson Haykin, "Project for a Subject Heading Code" (unpublished manuscript, revised, Washington, D.C., 1957), 10pp.

33. William E. Studwell, "The 1990s: Decade of Subject Access: A Theoretical *Code* for LC Subject Headings Would Complete the Maturation of Modern Cataloging," *American Libraries* 18 (December 1987): 958; and William E. Studwell, "On the Conference Circuit: The Subject Heading *Code*: Do We Have One? Do We Need One?" *Technicalities* 10 (October 1990): 10-15.

34. *Principles Underlying Subject Heading Languages (SHLs)*, ed. Maria Inês Lopes and Julianne Beall, Working Group on Principles Underlying Subject Heading Languages, approved by the Standing Committee of the IFLA Section on Classification and Indexing (München: K. G. Saur, 1999).

35. Karen Markey, *Subject Searching in Library Catalogs before and after the Introduction of Online Catalogs.* OCLC Library, Information, and Computer Science Series 4 (Dublin, Ohio: OCLC, 1984), 77.

36. Karen Markey Drabenstott and Diane Vizine-Goetz, *Using Subject Headings for Online Retrieval: Theory, Practice, and Potential* (San Diego: Academic Press, 1994), 124.

2 Basic Principles

INTRODUCTION

Since the mid 1980s, the Library of Congress has published two documents on its subject headings system that draw together information previously scattered among various sources. These documents are *Subject Cataloging Manual: Subject Headings*[1] and *Library of Congress Subject Headings: Principles of Structure and Policies for Application.*[2] Until the appearance of these publications, persons interested in understanding the principles that underlie the Library of Congress subject headings system had to infer them from a variety of sources: Library of Congress practice and policy statements; Cutter's writings; statements by Haykin and other chiefs of the Subject Cataloging Division; Haykin's 1951 book, *Subject Headings: A Practical Guide*;[3] and the system itself.

This chapter elaborates the principles governing the formation of topical subject headings as they are articulated in the LC documents. Topical headings are those representing concepts, objects, or forms. Proper names are also used as subject headings. Personal, corporate, and geographic headings representing jurisdictions are governed by *Anglo-American Cataloguing Rules.*[4] Proper name headings are discussed in chapter 4. This chapter examines the principles governing the formation of topical headings in light of past and current literature on subject analysis. In the literature, the terms most commonly used to denote the various principles are *user* and *usage, literary warrant, uniform and unique headings, internal consistency, stability, specificity, direct entry, coextensivity, and precoordination* and *postcoordination.* These are discussed below.

THE USER AND USAGE

From the early days of the catalog on, meeting the needs of the user has been deemed the most important function of the catalog. For Cutter, this was the foremost principle in cataloging. In the preface to the fourth edition of *Rules for a Dictionary Catalog* he states:

> The convenience of the public is always to be set before the ease of the cataloger. In most cases they coincide. A plain rule without exceptions is not only easy for us to carry out, but easy for the public to understand and work by. But

> strict consistency in a rule and uniformity in its application sometimes lead to practices which clash with the public's habitual way of looking at things. When these habits are general and deeply rooted, it is unwise for the cataloger to ignore them, even if they demand a sacrifice of system and simplicity.[5]

Haykin calls this guiding principle "the reader as a focus":

> [T]he reader is the focus in all cataloging principles and practice. All other considerations, such as convenience and the desire to arrange entries in some logical order, are secondary to the basic rule that the heading, in wording and structure, should be that which the reader will seek in the catalog, if we know or can presume what the reader will look under. To the extent that the headings represent the predilection of the cataloger in regard to terminology and are dictated by conformity to a chosen logical pattern, as against the likely approach of the reader resting on psychological rather than logical grounds, the subject catalog will lose in effectiveness and ease of approach.[6]

What this principle means is self-evident, but how to make it operational is not. The problem lies in the difficulty of delineating or typifying the user.

Cutter did not appear to have difficulty knowing users and usage. In his study on the subject, Francis Miksa offers this explanation: "For Cutter . . . the public was notably regular in its habits. In fact, he spoke of the habits of the public as being prominent enough to be observed and in a certain sense charted."[7] Users of libraries in Cutter's time probably were relatively homogeneous, as Miksa suggests, and fairly easily defined. However, the continuing emphasis on the "convenience of the public" in the face of changing historical contexts has made it difficult to define a "typical user." As users became more diversified, questions concerning them are constantly being asked: Who is the user? Is there such a thing as a typical user? Many writers on the subject catalog have pointed out this issue. Two particularly cogent comments follow:

> Marie Louise Prevost (1946): "What is the 'public' which we, in general libraries, serve through the catalog? Children, young people, adults; the expert, the inept, the illiterate, the savant; scientists, artists, authors, teachers and—librarians. Once the diverse nature of the users of the catalog is recognized, it becomes a patent absurdity to speak of cataloging according to the 'public' mind as if that mind were a single entity."[8]

> Paul S. Dunkin (1969): "Is there such a creature as 'the public,' or are there many publics, each with its individual varieties and needs? Studies will, no doubt, continue as long as cash can be found to pay for them. Suppose some study were to succeed; suppose it were to show that there is only one user and to identify that user and his needs and habits. Would we dare to build a catalog around those habits and needs? Perhaps not. Habits and needs change; this year's man will not be the same man next year. A catalog built on this year's public's habits and needs might hinder next year's public."[9]

Over the years, there have been numerous studies of catalog users in general, and of use of the subject catalog in particular. Yet few of these studies made it clear who and what kind of person this user was who supposedly held such powerful sway over the form and shape of the catalog. Nevertheless, the policy of the "convenience of the public" continued to operate, apparently based on the premise that catalogers understand who users are and how they behave. Since the 1980s, however, the online public access catalog has afforded a powerful new tool for documenting and tracking catalog use, and a series of studies have been carried out.[10] From these studies, profiles of users and of user searching behavior have begun to emerge. One significant finding is that a majority of users use the online catalog for subject searching.[11] Another is that, although catalog users remain diverse in their backgrounds, needs, and habits, many of them share a common characteristic: most have difficulty with the subject searching process in online catalogs.[12] With the evolution of the online catalog and integrated systems, the question of success or failure in subject retrieval has become an even more complex matter than one of subject vocabulary alone. Some of the more recent studies have also focused on systems design for more effective subject retrieval in the online catalog.[13]

Related to the question of user needs is the issue of linguistic usage. LC's policy states: "User needs are best met if headings reflect current usage in regard to terminology. Thus, terms in current use are selected in establishing new subject headings."[14] The desirability of this policy has long been recognized. In naming the subjects in the catalog, Cutter proposed that the usage of the public be the guiding principle:

> General rules, always applicable, for the choice of names of subjects can no more be given than rules without exception in grammar. Usage in both cases is the supreme arbiter, the usage, in the present case, not of the cataloger but of the public in speaking of subjects.[15]

Haykin phrases the principle of usage in similar terms:

> The heading chosen must represent common usage or, at any rate, the usage of the class of reader for whom the material on the subject within which the heading falls is intended. Usage in an American library must inevitably mean current American usage. Unless this principle is adhered to faithfully most readers will not find the material they desire under the heading which first occurs to them, if they find it at all.[16]

At the same time, almost from the beginning there has been general agreement that "common usage" is not always easy to determine.

Basically, there are two different approaches to the problem of meeting user needs. The first, proposed by Cutter and seconded by Haykin, is to prefer usage over logic or philosophy as the supreme arbiter in the choice of form and language. The second is to develop a system that adheres to logic and strictly formed principles and assume that the user can learn a logical and consistent system. Strong arguments can be brought forward to support either approach. A system based on the usage of the public is considered more "user friendly." However, there are problems. For one, given the growing number of people who use libraries and other information sources, particularly the World Wide Web, term usage today is even more diverse than it was when Prevost and Dunkin were voicing their objections to making the approach of "the public" a primary guide for subject cataloging. Practices vary from user to user and cannot be easily and clearly articulated. Thus it is difficult to maintain their consistency. For another, because of recent technological developments in cataloging, it is necessary to have a system that can be easily adapted to machine manipulation; in this context, there is an increasing demand for consistency and uniformity, both goals that can be achieved through the second approach. In the case of the Library of Congress subject headings list, the question of which approach to take in further development is particularly relevant because the list itself, which was originally designed for the Library's own collection and its own users, now also serves as a subject access tool for a variety of libraries and other retrieval systems, including many outside the United States. This is significant because features and characteristics that have been developed to meet the demands of a large general research collection are not always suitable in other contexts.

LITERARY WARRANT

Early decisions about the basic source of the concepts represented in LCSH had an important influence on the nature of the list. Writers on controlled-vocabulary subject access systems frequently point out that there are two fundamentally different ways to build such a system: from the top down, so to speak, that is, deciding what topics constitute the universe of discourse and what terms and inter-connectors should be used to represent them; and from the bottom up, that is, looking at what is written and selecting terms and inter-connectors based on what is found in the literature. The latter approach is known as building on literary warrant, a concept first put forward by E. Wyndham Hulme.[17] It was literary warrant that governed construction of both the Library of Congress classification and LCSH. The subject headings list was developed in especially close connection with the Library's collection; it was not conceived at the outset as, nor has it ever been intended to be, a comprehensive system covering the universe of knowledge. The policy of literary warrant is stated in the preface to the early editions of the headings list: "The list covers subjects in all branches of knowledge so far as the cataloguing of the corresponding classes of books in the Library of Congress progressed."[18]

Systems based on literary warrant grow mainly by accretion. As time passes, logic and consistency suffer in spite of conscientious maintenance efforts. As early as 1943, in the preface of the fourth edition of *Subject Headings*

Used in the Dictionary Catalogs of the Library of Congress, Haykin notes certain inconsistencies in the list and attributes them to the way the list grew: "The failures in logic and consistency are, of course, due to the fact that headings were adopted in turn as needed, and that many minds participated in the choice and establishment of headings."[19]

A further result of any list's growth by literary warrant is that it reflects the nature and size of the collection it was designed to serve; for LCSH, the collection is that of the Library of Congress. LCSH has been criticized for showing a strong American bias; this bias simply reflects the fact that the de facto national library of the United States is naturally heavily oriented toward American materials. In recent years, this bias has lessened because of the headings contributed by other libraries, particularly participants of the SACO (Subject Authority Cooperative Program) project of PCC (Program for Cooperative Cataloging), based on the needs of their own collections. The application of LCSH to web resources provides yet another dimension of literary warrant. In recent years, the Library of Congress has added many headings and subdivisions to accommodate electronic resources

UNIFORM HEADING

It has long been a tenet of subject cataloging practice that, in order to show what a library has on a given subject, each subject should be represented in the catalog under only one name and one form of that name. Uniformity of terms was considered a remedy for the scattering that resulted from the earlier practice of catchword title entry, in which entry was made under a term used by the author of the work being cataloged. A true subject heading gathers all works on the same subject together, regardless of the author's choice of terminology. Haykin called this the principle of unity: "A subject catalog must bring together under one heading all the books which deal principally or exclusively with the subject."[20]

The English language is rich in synonyms derived from different linguistic traditions. Many things are called by more than one name, and many concepts can be expressed in more than one way. Even within one country, variant names for the same object or concept often occur in different geographic areas. There are also many near-synonyms that are so close in meaning that it is impractical to establish them as separate subject headings. In all these cases, one of the several possible terms is chosen as the subject heading. If the term chosen appears in different forms or spellings, only one form is used.

However, it should be noted that the objective of listing all works on the same subject together can also be achieved by listing all works on that subject under each synonymous term. In other words, if a collection has twenty items on a subject that can be expressed with five different terms, it is possible to list all the items repeatedly under each of the five possible headings. However, although this was physically possible, it was not economically feasible in the card catalog, and even in the online catalog the practice causes problems because of the difficulty in maintaining consistency. Thus, the principle of uniform headings is still honored, with choices among candidate expressions conforming as far as possible to prevailing usage.

In establishing a subject heading, three choices are often required: name (term or term string for the entity or concept), form (grammatical construction), and entry element. When a subject has more than one name, one must be chosen as the heading to represent all materials on that subject, regardless of authors' usage. For example, in LCSH, the heading **Ethics** was chosen from among *Ethics, Deontology, Ethology, Moral philosophy, Moral science, Morality,* and *Morals.* Similarly, **Oral medication** was chosen in preference to *Drugs by mouth, Medication by mouth,* and *Peroral medication.* Frequently, a word may be spelled in different ways, for example, *Esthetics* or *Aesthetics, Hotbeds* or *Hot-beds, Marihuana* or *Marijuana.* Again, only one of the spellings is used as the valid heading.

Another choice is needed when the name chosen for a heading can be expressed in grammatically different forms, that is, as a phrase, a term with a qualifier, or a term with a subdivision or subdivisions. For example, a choice must be made between *Surgical diagnosis* and *Surgery–Diagnosis* and between *Cookery (Shrimp)* and *Cookery–Shrimp.*

A further decision about the entry element may also be necessary if the term contains two or more elements and both or all could possibly serve as an entry point, for example:

Cookery–Shrimp
Shrimp–Cookery

Diagnosis, Surgical
Surgical diagnosis

Plants, Effect of light on
Effect of light on plants
Light on plants, Effect of

The decision about the entry element used to be extremely important in the context of the manual catalog in which each heading was accessed by the first word only. In an online catalog, however, word order has little bearing on access and retrieval, although it is still important in index display and browsing.

In LCSH a heading in the form of a phrase may be established either in its natural word order or in the inverted form, but not both. In this type of heading, the principle of uniform heading is observed almost without exception. In other forms of headings, particularly headings with subdivisions, exceptions to the practice of uniform heading are sometimes made, particularly when the two components of a heading are equally significant, for example:

United States–Foreign relations–France

France–Foreign relations–United States

These are "duplicate headings" in the true sense of the term; they are identical or reciprocal in wording, though with different entry elements. Such duplicate entries were needed in the manual catalog to provide additional access points. Again, the need disappears in online catalogs with search options of any sophistication, but the practice continues to a limited extent. However, no new reciprocal headings of this type are being established.

Perhaps the major choice in establishing new headings is the choice among candidate synonyms. As stated earlier, the guiding principle in the choice has been "current American usage."[21] Cutter, Haykin, and other writers have also offered general guidelines[22] regarding choice of terms in the following categories: synonymous terms, variant spellings, English and foreign terms, technical (or scientific) and popular terms, and obsolete and current terms.

Choice among Synonymous Terms

LC's guideline regarding choice among synonyms states:

> When an object or concept may be expressed by synonyms, the term chosen as the heading is the one that represents the best possible balance among the criteria of being unbiased, familiar to users, and unambiguous in meaning (having fewest meanings other than the sense in which it is used).[23]

Near-synonymous terms also present a problem. Thelma Eaton notes: "Much more of a problem than synonyms are the near-synonymous terms. . . . There are other subjects that are not exactly the same, but they are closely related and it is easy to put them together under one heading."[24] Cutter's instruction concerning near-synonymous terms is: "In choosing between two names not exactly synonymous, consider whether there is difference enough to require separate entry; if not, treat them as synonymous."[25] In LCSH, there are many examples of near-synonyms treated as synonyms. For example, *Theological education* is treated as a synonym of **Religious education**, and *Freedom* is treated as a synonym of **Liberty**.

Choice between Variant Spellings

A special case of synonymy is variation in spelling. Needless to say, a current spelling is preferred to an obsolete one at the time of establishing a heading. If one or more spellings of the same word are equally current, the one most familiar to the largest numbers of users, based on reference sources, is chosen. For variant spellings that are in use concurrently, American spellings are preferred, for example, **Labor** instead of *Labour*; **Catalog** instead of *Catalogue*. In other cases, the choice follows *Webster's Third New International Dictionary*, for example, **Aesthetics** instead of *Esthetics*; **Archaeology** instead of *Archeology*.

Choice between English and Foreign Terms

The choice between an English and a foreign term would appear to be obvious: A system designed to serve English-speaking users should naturally rely on English terms. Yet there are exceptions. Cutter's rule concerning language states: "When possible let the heading be in English, but a foreign word may be used when no English word expresses the subject of a work."[26] Haykin states the rule as follows:

> Foreign terms should be used only under the following conditions: (1) when the concept is foreign to Anglo-American experience and no satisfactory term for it exists, e.g., *Reallast, Précieuses*; and (2) when, especially in the case of scientific names, the foreign term is precise, whereas the English one is not, e.g., *Ophiodon elongatus*, rather than *Buffalo cod* or *Blue cod*; *Pityrosporum ovale*, rather than *Bottle bacillus*. Terms of foreign origin, which retain their foreign form, but which have been incorporated into the English vocabulary are, of course, to be regarded as English words, e.g., *Terrazzo, Sauerkraut*.[27]

The Library of Congress chooses English terms as a matter of general policy. However, the foreign term is chosen if (1) there is no English term for the concept and the concept is normally expressed in foreign terms even in English-language works and reference sources, for example, **Bonsai**; **Coups d'état**; **Opéra comique**; or (2) based on proper research, no citation to the concept can be found in any English-language work or reference sources, and the concept appears to be unique to the language in question, for example, **Waqf**. [28]

Choice between Scientific (or Technical) and Popular Terms

On the choice between a scientific or popular term for a concept or entity, Cutter states:

> A natural history society will of course use the scientific name, a town library would equally of course use the proper name—**Butterflies** rather than **Lepidoptera, Horse** rather than **Equus caballus**. But the scientific may be preferable when the common name is ambiguous or of ill-defined extent.[29]

Haykin echoes Cutter's comment:

> Whether a popular term or a scientific one is to be chosen depends on several considerations. If the library serves a miscellaneous public, it must prefer the

> popular to the scientific term. It may even prefer it, if the proper term is commonly used in the professional or scientific literature; in speaking of the genus bee in general, for example, even the scientists will use the term "bee" rather than *Apis*. However, the popular term must be precise and unambiguous.[30]

On another occasion, Haykin further explains:

> The choice is not difficult because, obviously, in a catalog intended for a miscellaneous public the popular term must be used as the kind most likely to be resorted to by the largest group of users, whereas scientific terms, although usually more precise in their meanings, will be sought by the specialist in each field and are, therefore, suitable for a special library catalog.[31]

The user is the focus in both Cutter's and Haykin's statements. Both allow that the choice must be different in a general library serving a general public from that in a special library serving specialists. In LCSH popular terms are generally used if they are in common use and unambiguous, for example, **Cockroaches** instead of *Blattaria*; **Lizards** instead of *Lacertilia*. However, for animals and plants, while the common name in popular use is preferred, the Latin name is chosen if the common name represents several levels (species, genus, family); if it is not in general lay usage; or if the organism occurs only in a foreign country or countries.[32]

Choice between Obsolete and Current Terms

In establishing a new heading, a current term is easily chosen over an obsolete term, provided that one is clearly more current than another. The only problem is, how does one recognize an obsolete term? Personal knowledge of the language is a help but not always a reliable guide. Frequently, outside sources must be consulted. Dictionaries seem to be the natural tool. Haykin, however, notes that dictionaries do not usually indicate a choice on the basis of currency.[33] He recommends periodicals as the "surest sources" of usage because they carry the most current literature on various subjects. However, in dealing with new subjects, a heading is needed immediately, often before its terminology is settled, as recognized in the *Subject Cataloging Manual*:

> Headings are usually established to reflect current American usage for a concept, but sometimes no consensus has yet developed among the authorities in a given field as to the proper terminology for the concept. When establishing a new heading in such a situation, conduct authority research . . . and then make an intuitive judgment based on available evidence (in some cases only the work being cataloged) by selecting elements that will allow the heading to express what is intended and at the same time serve as a retrieval term in the system.[34]

A new invention or concept is sometimes called different names by different people, and the cataloger is in the position of having to choose among several possible names without much help or guidance from outside sources. One example was the choice of *Electronic calculating-machines* as the heading for computers when they first appeared, a heading that was later replaced by **Computers**.

The ideal of currency in a catalog or index requires that terminology be updated when it is no longer current. Haykin points out the need for constant revision:

> [The cataloger] must use the term in the sense in which it is currently used, regardless of the older literature in and out of the catalog. This leads inevitably to a policy of constant change in order to maintain the catalog up to date. To put this policy into effect the cataloger must substitute the latest heading for the one which is obsolescent or obsolete and must refer the reader to the current heading from the headings which have fallen into disuse.[35]

Until the mid 1970s the Library of Congress had been rather conservative in revising obsolete headings; indeed, in the 1960s and 1970s, outdated terminology was the most criticized aspect of the list, much more so than its structural aspects. An example of such criticism was Sanford Berman's analysis of subject headings relating to people.[36] In recent years, the Library of Congress has been much more responsive to changing language usage, in part because computer technology has greatly facilitated modifications.

UNIQUE HEADING

A corollary to the principle of uniform heading is the principle of *unique heading,* that is, the idea that each heading should represent only one subject. This principle specifically addresses the issue of homographs. To minimize irrelevant documents in the retrieval process, words that are spelled the same but have different meanings must be distinguished. Cutter's rule states: "Carefully separate the entries on different subjects bearing the same name, or take some other heading in place of one of the homonyms."[37] Frequently, "some other heading" may not be available. In such a case, a qualifier is added to differentiate between the homographs, for example, **Cold**; **Cold (Disease)** and **Rings (Algebra)**; **Rings (Gymnastics)**, so that each heading represents only one subject or concept.

SPECIFIC ENTRY AND COEXTENSIVITY

Specific and Direct Entry

In general, each subject in LCSH is represented by the most specific, or precise, term that names the subject, rather than a broader or generic term that encompasses the subject. In other words, the term used to represent a subject is coextensive with the subject. In rare cases, a broader term may be used when the most specific term is considered too narrow and therefore not likely to be sought by catalog users.

In the literature, the concepts of specificity (or specific entry) and direct entry are almost always addressed together. For that reason, they are discussed together here. It is worth noting, however, that the two concepts are quite different in nature. Specificity is a many-faceted notion, used in talking about terms themselves and about the match between the meaning of a given term and the content of the document to which it is applied. The concept of directness involves the way a heading of given specificity is presented, either by itself or in context. An entry with the heading **Monkeys** is a direct entry, while an entry with the equally specific form *Chordata–Vertebrates–Mammals–Primates–Monkeys* is a typical indirect entry one would find in a classed catalog. The difference between the concepts of specificity and directness is not always recognized, a fact that often makes it difficult to ferret out what writers mean when they talk about specificity and direct entry.

Cutter explains the rule of specific entry in the following terms: "Enter a work under its subject-heading, not under the heading of a class which includes the subject . . . . Put Lady Cust's book on 'The cat' under **Cat** not under **Zoölogy** or **Mammals**, or **Domestic animals**; and put Garnier's 'Le fer' under **Iron**, not under **Metals** or **Metallurgy**."[38] The Vatican code states the principle of specific entry in these terms: "Works are recorded under their specific subjects, and not under the names and designations of the classes and disciplines to which they belong, e.g., **Poll-tax**, not **Taxation** or **Finance**."[39]

From these statements and examples, it would appear that the difference between the classed catalog and the dictionary catalog in the treatment of the subject Cats represents a choice between **Zoology** and **Cats** as the subject heading. This is, in fact, not the case. In a classed catalog, the heading for a book on cats would presumably be *Zoology–Vertebrates–Mammals–Domestic animals–Cats*, and not **Zoology** alone. In terms of the degree of specificity, this heading is as specific as the heading **Cats**. The real difference is in the choice of the entry element, or the access point in the catalog. In a classed catalog, in order to find the subject Cats, the user must look under **Zoology** (or in an accompanying index), whereas in the dictionary catalog, the subject is listed under **Cats** without intervening elements. This is what is meant by direct entry: The user looks directly under the term that specifically describes the topic rather than under a broader term that includes the specific term as a subdivision.

It should be noted that to achieve the benefit of direct access in the catalog, the advantages of subject collocation must be abandoned. However, in the course of the development of the dictionary catalog in American libraries, there seems to have been a consistent desire to have the best of both worlds, to maintain some of the advantages of the classed catalog in grouping related subjects together. This was especially true in the earlier stages when users as well as makers of subject headings were still accustomed to the classed catalog. As a result, many headings that are characteristic of a classed catalog were introduced into dictionary catalogs over the years.

In the online catalog and in other computerized systems in which keyword searching is common, the entry element is not an issue in retrieval but is still important in the display of results. In retrieval, any of the words except stop words can be used to retrieve a heading, but in browsing, the left-most word, that is, the entry element, determines the order of the display.

Concept of Specificity

There is another source of difficulty with the principle of specific entry beyond the fact that it is often confused or fused with the notion of direct entry. This difficulty comes in defining the very concept of specificity. From Cutter on, there have been various attempts at a definition.

Cutter: "Enter a work under its subject-heading, not under the heading of a class which includes that subject."[40]

Haykin: "The heading should be as specific as the topic it is intended to cover. As a corollary, the heading should not be broader than the topic."[41]

Oliver Linton Lilley, in an inquiry into the meaning and nature of specificity, identifies at least four types of relationships that determine its nature:

1. Specificity is in part a function of a particular subject area.
2. Specificity is in part a function of a particular library.
3. Specificity is in part a function of a particular book.
4. Specificity is in part a function of a searcher's exact need in a particular moment of time.[42]

Later writers on subject analysis continue to search for a workable definition of specificity. Among the more successful attempts are the studies by John Balnaves and Elaine Svenonius. Balnaves summarizes five interrelated but distinguishable aspects of the term:

1. The manner in which one term can be said to be subordinate to, and more specific than another in a hierarchical arrangement of terms . . .
2. The extent to which a characteristic which distinguishes a document class is precisely labelled by a descriptor . . .

3. The extent to which each descriptor provides direct access to the file for the class of documents which it labels . . .
4. The extent to which each descriptor is a precise and exact label for the smallest class to which a document belongs . . .
5. The extent to which descriptors are assigned to classes to which parts of documents belong, as well as to classes to which the whole document belongs.[43]

His final conclusion is: "Whatever improves precision is specificity."

Svenonius identifies seven types of specificity. They are, in summary:

(i) Formal Specificity: Specificity can be defined in terms of the logical relation of class inclusion.

(ii) Extensional Specificity: In ordinary language the specificity relation (regarded as inclusion) is used with logical precision when it holds between classes that can be clearly defined in extensional or referential terms.

(iii) Phrase-length Specificity: One extension of the inclusion relation into the domain of non-referential language is when specification is regarded as modifying. There are exceptions but generally it holds that a word modified is more specific than the word unmodified.

(iv) Coercive Specificity: The specificity relation can be defined more or less well by enumerating all the pairs of objects (words) between which the relation is supposed to hold.

(v) Componential Specificity: A quantitative measure of specificity has been developed by Thyllis Williams. Roughly, the specificity of a word is proportional to the complexity of its dictionary definition, where definition complexity is understood in terms of both the descriptive components and the syntax of the definition.

(vi) Consensus Specificity: Presumably there exists some partial consistency in different people's opinions about specificity, a consensus whose bounds are unknown but which might be measurable using sociolinguistic experimental methods.

(vii) Operational Specificity: Operational specificity is defined in the context of indexing, or assigning subject headings to books in a library. The operational specificity of an index term is the number of books in the collection indexed by the term. Operational specificity is decidedly relative, but it is so in a clear, mathematically measurable way. Its relativity reflects the very legitimate variability not of "specific," but of "specific (precise) enough for some purpose." Further, the definition of operational specificity

> goes some way to make explicit the concept of specificity as it is understood in the application of the specific entry principle. It does this insofar as the function of the principle is to regulate the number of entries that accumulate under any one heading. Moreover, an operational definition of specificity is useful in that it provides a method for systematically varying indexing specificity. That is, the definition makes it possible to approach experimentally the question: "How specific is specific?"[44]

Although these writers differ in their approaches and definitions of the concept of specificity, there appears to be a certain degree of agreement that specificity is a relative term and must be viewed in a particular context. The term takes on different meanings depending on the context. Some of the common frames of reference in which the concept of specificity has been defined are discussed below.

(1) *Specificity in relation to the hierarchical structure of a particular indexing language.* This is sometimes referred to as term specificity, or what Metcalfe calls "subject specification."[45] The specificity of a term is defined in relation to other terms in the same indexing language. In this context, the indexing term on a lower level of a hierarchical chain is said to be more specific than one on a higher level. Thus, the relationship between general and specific terms is similar to that of broad and narrow terms (or broad and close, with regard to classification). In such a context, **Cats** is more specific than **Mammals**, which in turn is more specific than **Vertebrates**. Although the specificity of a term can be easily ascertained in a two-dimensional hierarchical chain containing single-concept terms, problems arise when multidimensional hierarchies containing complex terms are involved. For example, it can be easily recognized that **Stomach** is more specific than **Digestive organs**, and that **Ulcers** is more specific than **Diseases**. It is not easy, however, to determine whether **Stomach–Diseases** or **Digestive organs–Ulcers** is the more specific term. In such cases, the notions of specificity and generality become difficult to define.

Another problem relating to term specificity is how to determine the optimal level of specificity in a particular indexing language. On this question, F. W. Lancaster makes the following observation:

> However often a term is used in indexing, it is unjustified if, over a two-year period (for instance), it has never been used in searching. This might indicate that the term is unnecessarily specific, but indexers use it because it is available and documents exist on the specific topic. Even so, requests are never made this specifically in the particular subject area, so a term at this level of specificity is redundant.[46]

An alternative to relying on frequency of use in searching as the criterion of term specificity is to view specificity in terms of frequency of application in indexing, as suggested by G. Salton and C. S. Yang:

> Term specificity . . . may be assumed to be related to the number of documents to which a given term is assigned in a given collection, the idea being that the smaller the document frequency, that is, the more concentrated the assignment of a term to only a few documents in a collection, the more likely it is that a given term is reasonably specific.[47]

In her discussion of "operational specificity," Svenonius puts forth a similar view: "The operational specificity of an index term or subject heading is defined as the number of items in the collection indexed by the term, that is the number of postings made to the term; or in other words, the specificity of a term is its frequency of occurrence."[48] In this sense, the specificity of any term is relative to a particular collection of documents. As pointed out by Angell, the level of specificity should be determined "by the characteristics of the demands which are made upon an information system in a particular application or installation."[49]

(2) *Specificity in regard to literary warrant.* One can also think of specificity in terms of how closely the terms in the thesaurus or subject headings list match the topics in the collection being indexed. This type of specificity certainly holds for the match between LCSH and the Library of Congress collection. The selection of terms for LCSH, in fact, has from the beginning been based on what has been needed to catalog the collection at the Library of Congress. New headings are established as they are required in cataloging new books added to the Library's collection, and subdivisions are often developed because of the large number of postings under a particular heading in the catalog. However, as LCSH has been adopted by many other libraries and its use extended beyond the library catalog into the Internet and the World Wide Web, determining the optimal degree of specificity poses a unique problem for those responsible for its development and maintenance. Because the list has become so widely used, it must now try to perform the impossible task of being all things to all people. The various demands placed on the system by different classes of users are often incompatible and even conflicting. As a result, it has been difficult to achieve a consistent and uniform level of specificity throughout the system.

(3) *Specificity in relation to the document being indexed.* In this case, a specific heading is one that coincides with, or corresponds to, the content of the document being represented. Metcalfe uses the term *document specification*[50] for this aspect of specificity. Another term often used now to express this aspect of specificity is *coextensivity*. The degree to which this kind of specificity is achieved is partly the function of the indexing language and partly that of application in the indexing process. In this respect, the specificity of a particular indexing term is viewed in relation to the document to which it is assigned, not to its place in the hierarchical structure of the indexing language. A specific heading is not necessarily a narrow one, nor a general heading always a broad one. In other words, *general* is not synonymous with *broad*, nor *specific* with *narrow*. For example, the heading **Zoology** is generally considered broad, and the heading **Cats** narrow. The heading **Zoology** is general when applied to a work about

cats. However, for a work on zoology, the heading **Zoology** becomes as specific as the heading **Cats** is for a work about cats. On the other hand, the heading **Cats** when applied to a work about Siamese cats is a general heading. In this context, a specific heading is one that corresponds to the content of the document to which it is applied, while a general heading is one that represents the class to which the subject content of the document is subordinate. Library of Congress's views on this matter appear in the following statements:

> The heading that represents precisely the subject content of the work is assigned as the primary subject heading, unless such a heading does not exist and cannot be established.[51]

> Specificity is not a property of a given subject heading; instead, it is a relative concept that reflects the relationship between the subject heading and the work to which it is applied. For example, a seemingly broad heading like **Psychology** is specific when it is assigned to an introductory textbook on psychology.[52]

Whether coextensivity is always desirable is open to debate. There seems to be a general assumption that perfectly coextensive headings should be used if possible. However, in practice this assumption has not always held. In fact, Haykin goes so far as to say that, "there are limits to the principle of specificity . . . beyond which its application does not appear to serve the best interest of the reader."[53] The answers to the coextensivity question must necessarily vary with regard to the nature and extent of the collection and the needs of the users. At the Library of Congress, attempts are generally made to achieve coextensivity by assigning specific headings whenever they are available, by creating such headings when they are not, or by assigning several separate headings (each broader than the content of the document being cataloged) in order to cover various aspects of a complex subject. (This last practice is discussed further in chapter 8.)

(4) *Specificity with regard to the depth of indexing*. Frequently, the term *specificity* is used to refer to depth of indexing. Indexing may be at the document level (summarization), where the subject headings represent the overall content of the document, or it may be at a deeper (unit or chapter) level, where the terms chosen represent the individual components. Depth indexing results in a large number of headings assigned to each document to cover the individual parts or units within the document. The number of terms assigned depends primarily on indexing policy, not on the nature of the indexing language; the same thesaurus or subject headings list can in most cases be used either way. The degree of the depth of indexing is generally determined by the demands of the users and, not infrequently, by the availability of personnel and resources. The Library of Congress generally follows a policy of summarization rather than indexing in depth. (This aspect of Library of Congress practice is discussed in detail in chapter 8.)

INTERNAL CONSISTENCY

It has been an almost tacit assumption from the beginning that a subject catalog should be internally consistent. Predictability is an essential factor in successful subject retrieval, and predictability is higher if, under analogous circumstances, a given heading pattern recurs throughout the system. Thus consistency as well as stability is a factor in end-user ease of consultation. At the thesaurus construction stage, taking internal consistency as a goal calls for the use of similar forms and structures in headings for similar topics.

Svenonius, in a discussion on the design of controlled vocabularies, notes a problem with this approach: "Consistency considerations, introduced often for the sake of structure, primarily affect term form and frequently conflict with the dictates of common usage."[54] As mentioned earlier, Cutter and Haykin both claim that, for subject headings, general usage should take precedence over logic and consistency; in so doing, they seem to be deviating from the prior claim of logical consistency and arguing for exceptions. Haykin also, in a different source,[55] justifies "failures in logic and consistency" by the fact that headings were adopted over time, and that many minds participated in their choice.

At the Library of Congress, wherever feasible, attempts are made to maintain consistency in form and structure among analogous headings through the use of recurring patterns.[56] This is not always possible, however, because for any new heading under consideration, analogous headings may show different patterns. This happens often, especially when a complex heading is proposed. To date, no systematic effort has been made to revise existing headings to ensure that analogous headings always show the same grammatical structure and form.

STABILITY

Stability is one principle underlying LCSH that receives little attention in the literature but still must be kept in mind by anyone studying the system with an eye to the future. That principle calls for maintaining as much stability in the system as is compatible with the need to keep it responsive to changing conditions.

In respect to other institutions using LCSH, having stability as a goal means that change is gradual enough that these institutions are not often faced with changes that place large demands on their personnel and other resources, either in learning what is new or in doing whatever is necessary to bring existing provisions into conformity. Even simply mapping old headings onto new ones, and vice versa, is a labor-intensive operation, requiring resources that may not easily be spared. In respect to users of LCSH and other LCSH-based retrieval tools, keeping LCSH relatively stable means that, once they become familiar with the system, end-users are not faced upon further use with something that has changed drastically and must be relearned. For them, "convenience of the user" requires that remembered search patterns still work.

As can be seen, stability and responsiveness to changed circumstances are conflicting goals and must be carefully balanced. During the process of revision, in the excitement of developing a system that is fully up to date and easy to maintain as such, it is easy to overlook the advantages of system stability. The expected benefits of each proposed change must be carefully assessed, and the cost of implementation and its end-user inconvenience (if any) must be taken into account. Almost always, changes are improvements, and worth their costs. Still, it can be a mistake not to calculate those costs from all perspectives.

PRECOORDINATION AND POSTCOORDINATION

Generally, the content of a document falls into one of the following categories:

1. a single object or concept, or single objects or concepts treated separately in a work, for example, *Children; Children* and *Young adults*
2. an aspect(s) of an object or concept, for example, *Health care for children; Reading interests of children; Crimes against children*
3. two or more objects or concepts treated in relation to each other, for example, *Children in popular culture; Effects of violence on children*

It is clear from this list that except for single objects or concepts, document content cannot always or even often be represented by single terms or simple adjectival phrases. When this is the case, specificity must be achieved by other means. In this context, Mortimer Taube identified two types of specificity: "the specificity of a specific word or phrase and whatever degree of subdivision is allowed" and "the specificity achieved by the intersection, coordination, or logical product of terms of equal generality."[57]

The first category in the list above (single object or concept) presents a problem only when a document treats a topic at a deeper level of specificity than is allowed for in the indexing vocabulary, or when users are not expected to approach the system at such a level of specificity. Frequently with the second category (aspects) and always with the third category (relationships), a single term is not sufficient; so, in order to achieve the specificity required, two or more terms must be used. In many cases, a phrase is used to combine two or more general terms, either of which is broader than the resulting heading, for example, *Intelligent testing for children; Fertilization of flowers*; *Effect of light on plants*. Another way to represent complexity is to use two or more separate terms without indicating the nature of their relationship; for example, a document might be assigned the two headings *Flowers* and *Fertilization*. Such an approach leaves it to searchers to track down documents indexed with terms reflecting all the aspects of the topics that interest them.

The two different approaches are called *precoordination* and *post-co ordination*. In a precoordinate system, multiple terms representing a topic and its aspects are precombined in the source vocabulary or by the cataloger or indexer at the time of cataloging or indexing, using prepositions or other devices (punctuation or the structure of the string) to show how the terms are interrelated. In a postcoordinate system, terms for the main subject and its aspects are simply listed separately. Searchers combine the terms at the point of retrieval. Most modern indexing systems are postcoordinate. LCSH, like many systems originating from the manual environment, is basically precoordinate. Precoordinate headings, when available, are assigned to works on complex subjects, and new precoordinate headings are constantly being established. On the other hand, because no system can be totally precoordinate, catalogers at the Library of Congress often take a postcoordinate approach.

There have been complex headings in the Library of Congress list since the early editions. However, because policies regarding their formation have varied, the list as a whole shows many inconsistencies in this regard. A statement from the Library of Congress acknowledges this: "Although LCSH is primarily a precoordinate system, practice under many headings requires postcoordination in order to achieve specificity. There are numerous cases in which we do not combine elements in the heading itself or in subdivisions in order to be specific. Decisions can be determined by looking at LC cataloging."[58]

Precoordination

In a precoordinate system, the combination of multiple topics or facets may take place either when the heading enters the vocabulary or when it is assigned to a document. In the former approach, called *enumeration,* complex headings are listed in full; in the latter, called *synthesis*, individual terms are listed separately to be combined by the cataloger or indexer as needed.

Enumeration

In early editions of *Library of Congress Subject Headings*, almost all precoordinate headings were enumerated (that is, appeared as such) in the list. Over the years, however, the Library of Congress has taken an increasingly analytico-synthetic approach, through subdivisions and phrase patterns that subject catalogers or indexers may freely combine, within guidelines and as appropriate. Enumerated complex headings in LCSH show the following patterns. Some are relatively simple:

- Adjectival phrases

Chuckwagon racing
Energy labeling
Plant inspection
Wildlife recovery

- Phrases containing conjunctions or followed by etc. (representing partial synonymy)

  Bear deterrents and repellents
  Camp sites, facilities, etc.
  Decoration and ornament
  Lacquer and lacquering

- Phrases containing conjunctions (representing relationships)

  Children and terrorism
  Computers and college students
  Libraries and the unemployed
  Mass media and gays

- Phrases containing prepositions

  Discrimination against people with disabilities
  Internet in library reference services
  Oil pollution of groundwater
  Recorders (2) with plucked instrument ensemble

- Headings with subdivisions

  Library users–Japan
  Life skills–Testing
  Mars (Planet)–Water
  Sound recordings–Remixing

- Combinations of the forms above

  Arts and crafts gardens–United States
  Clocks and watches in art
  Illumination of books and manuscripts
  Newly independent states–Diplomatic and consular services

- Highly complex and specific combinations, for instance:

  Concertos (Bandoneon with chamber orchestra)–Solo with piano
  Ex-concentration camp inmates–Return visits to concentration camp sites
  Jewish religious education of children with disabilities
  Magnetic memory (Computers)–Testing–Computer programs
  University and colleges–Employees–Labor unions–Law and legislation

When dealing with complex subjects for which there are precoordinate headings, cataloging consists of finding the best match between the work being cataloged and the available precombined headings.

Synthesis

When a precoordinate heading that would suit a particular work is not enumerated in LCSH, a heading may be synthesized by combining elements according to appropriate procedures. Especially since the mid-1970s, the Library of Congress has relied more on synthesis than enumeration for precoordinate complex headings. This development is consistent with the progress taking place in the field of indexing. As Svenonius states, "Probably the most significant development in index language construction in the twentieth century is the move from largely enumerative index languages to largely synthetic ones."[59]

Synthesis in LCSH is achieved mainly through the use of free-floating subdivisions, a device that allows the combination of a main term with terms representing common aspects of subjects without requiring that each combination be authorized. Typically, such synthesized headings do not appear in the list. Thus, many highly complex headings appear in bibliographic records but not in *Library of Congress Subject Headings*, for example:

France–History–Revolution, 1789-1799–Literature and the revolution

Lawyers–United States–Discipline–Cases

Social sciences–Study and teaching (Graduate)–United States

Teenagers–Books and reading–United States

Synthesis renders a precoordinate subject indexing system much more flexible because it allows many more possible combinations than an enumerative system can accommodate. However, LCSH is not totally synthetic, as are some systems. There are stringent limits regarding how elements may be combined, and in learning to use the system a great deal of effort must be spent on recognizing them. Synthesis of subject strings is discussed in detail in chapter 5.

An important factor in synthesizing precoordinate headings is the order, called *citation order*, in which terms are combined in headings. Over the years, the increasing reliance on synthesis in LCSH has not been accompanied by well-established citation order rules. One difficulty is that different citation orders for the same terms may result in headings with different meanings, for example, **Science–Indexes–Periodicals** (meaning a journal of scientific indexes), and **Science–Periodicals–Indexes** (meaning an index to scientific journals).

In 1991, the Library of Congress took a step toward normalization of the use of subdivisions. The Subject Subdivisions Conference was held in Airlie, Virginia, to discuss the future of subdivisions in the LCSH system. From this conference emerged six recommendations, the first of which concerns a fixed citation order for combining subdivisions.[60] The question of citation order is discussed in detail in chapter 5.

Postcoordination

In cataloging a work on a complex subject for which there is no coextensive heading in LCSH and for which one cannot be synthesized, the subject cataloger at the Library of Congress may either propose a new heading as required for the work being cataloged (a procedure currently preferred) or choose to use several existing headings, that is, take the postcoordinate approach, if the topic in question appears to be new but is judged to be not yet discrete and identifiable,[61] for example:

Title: *Intercultural competence : interpersonal communication across cultures*
SUBJECTS:
Intercultural communication.
Interpersonal communication–United States.
Communicative competence–United States.

In dealing with a complex subject for which no single heading exists, it is sometimes difficult to predict whether the Library of Congress will take the precoordinate or the postcoordinate approach. Catalogers outside the Library of Congress, not knowing whether the Library of Congress will create a specific heading for the complex subject—and, if so, which form it will take—tend to assign several existing headings to cover the various elements or aspects treated in the document. For example, LCSH contains the heading **Nuns as public school teachers**, but no single heading *Public school teachers*. Until such a heading is established—a likely occurrence when a subject cataloger at the Library of Congress encounters a work on that subject—subject catalogers outside the Library of Congress will probably assign such a work two headings, **Public schools** and **Teachers**. Currently, with the exception of free-floating subdivisions and phrases, there are yet no established guidelines stating when terms may be combined to form precoordinate headings and when the cataloger should take the postcoordinate approach. Catalogers either follow existing patterns or determine each case as the question arises.

LC policies regarding the synthesis and assignment of subject headings are discussed in detail with examples in part 2 of this book.

NOTES

1. Library of Congress, Cataloging Policy and Support Office, *Subject Cataloging Manual: Subject Headings*, 5th ed., 2000 cumulation (Washington, D.C.: Library of Congress, 2000).

2. Lois Mai Chan, *Library of Congress Subject Headings: Principles of Structure and Policies for Application: Annotated Version*, prepared by Lois Mai Chan for the Library of Congress, Advances in Library Information Technology, No. 3 (Washington, D.C.: Cataloging Distribution Service, Library of Congress, 1990).

3. David Judson Haykin, *Subject Headings: A Practical Guide* (Washington, D.C.: Government Printing Office, 1951), 7.

4. *Anglo-American Cataloguing Rules*, 2nd ed., 2002 rev., prepared under the direction of the Joint Steering Committee for Revision of AACR, a committee of the American Library Association, the Australian Committee on Cataloguing, the British Library, the Canadian Committee on Cataloguing, Chartered Institute of Library and Information Professionals, the Library of Congress (Chicago: American Library Association, 2002).

5. Charles A. Cutter, *Rules for a Dictionary Catalog*, 4th ed., rewritten (Washington, D.C.: Government Printing Office, 1904), 6.

6. Haykin, *Subject Headings*, 7.

7. Francis Miksa, *The Subject in the Dictionary Catalog from Cutter to the Present* (Chicago: American Library Association, 1983), 74.

8. Marie Louise Prevost, "An Approach to Theory and Method in General Subject Heading," *Library Quarterly* 16 (April 1946): 140.

9. Paul S. Dunkin, *Cataloging U.S.A.* (Chicago: American Library Association, 1969), 141-142.

10. Carol A. Mandel and Judith Herschman, "Subject Access in the Online Catalog" (a Report prepared for the Council on Library Resources, August 1981); Charles R. Hildreth, *Online Public Access Catalogs: The User Interface* (Dublin, Ohio: OCLC, 1982); Joseph R. Matthews, Gary S. Lawrence, and Douglas K. Ferguson, eds., *Using Online Catalogs: A Nationwide Study* (New York: Neal-Schuman, 1983); Karen Markey, *The Process of Subject Searching in the Library Catalog* (Dublin, Ohio: OCLC, 1983); Markey, *Subject Searching in Library Catalogs: Before and After the Introduction of Online Catalogs* (Dublin, Ohio: OCLC, 1984); Karen Markey Drabenstott and Diane Vizine-Goetz, *Using Subject Headings for Online Retrieval: Theory, Practice, and Potential* (San Diego: Academic Press, 1994).

11. Markey, *Subject Searching in Library Catalogs*, 77.

12. Drabenstott and Vizine-Goetz, *Using Subject Headings for Online Retrieval*, 124.

13. Christine L. Borgman, "Why Are Online Catalogs Still Hard to Use?" *Journal of the American Society for Information Science* 47 (July 1996): 493-503; Karen Markey Drabenstott and Marjorie S. Weller, "Failure Analysis of Subject Searches in a Test of a New Design for Subject Access to Online Catalogs: ASTUTE Experimental Catalog Use at Earlham College and the University of Michigan-Dearborn," *Journal of the American Society for Information Science* 47 (July 1996): 519-537.

14. Chan, *Library of Congress Subject Headings: Principles of Structure and Policies for Application*, 2.

15. Cutter, *Rules for a Dictionary Catalog*, 69.

16. Haykin, *Subject Headings*, 8.

17. E. Wyndham Hulme, "Principles of Book Classification," *Library Association Record* 13 (1911): 445-447.

18. Library of Congress, Catalog Division, *Subject Headings Used in the Dictionary Catalogues of the Library of Congress*, 3rd ed., ed. Mary Wilson MacNair (Washington, D.C.: U.S. Government Printing Office, 1928), iii.

19. Library of Congress, Subject Cataloging Division, *Subject Headings Used in the Dictionary Catalogs of the Library of Congress*, 4th ed., ed. Mary Wilson MacNair (Washington, D.C.: U.S. Government Printing Office, 1943), iii.

20. Haykin, *Subject Headings*, 7.

21. Library of Congress, *Subject Cataloging Manual*, H187.

22. In the choice of proper names, the problem is more than one of usage alone. Since most proper names used as subject headings also serve as main and added entries, a coordination between descriptive cataloging and subject cataloging is necessary. The choice and forms of proper names are discussed in chapter 4.

23. Chan, *Library of Congress Subject Headings: Principles of Structure and Policies for Application*, 7.

24. Thelma Eaton, *Cataloging and Classification: An Introductory Manual*, 4th ed. (Ann Arbor, Mich.: Edwards Brothers, 1967), 156.

25. Cutter, *Rules for a Dictionary Catalog*, 70.

26. Cutter, *Rules for a Dictionary Catalog*, 69.

27. Haykin, *Subject Headings*, 9.

28. Library of Congress, *Subject Cataloging Manual*, H315.

29. Cutter, *Rules for a Dictionary Catalog*, 70.

30. Haykin, *Subject Headings*, 9.

31. David Judson Haykin, "Subject Headings: Principles and Development," in *The Subject Analysis of Library Materials*, ed. Maurice F. Tauber (New York: School of Library Service, Columbia University, 1953), 50.

32. Library of Congress, *Subject Cataloging Manual*, H1332.

33. Haykin, *Subject Headings*, 8.

34. Library of Congress, *Subject Cataloging Manual*, H187.

35. Haykin, *Subject Headings*, 8.

36. Sanford Berman, *Prejudices and Antipathies: A Tract on the LC Subject Heads Concerning People*, 1993 ed. (Jefferson, N.C.: McFarland, 1993).

37. Cutter, *Rules for a Dictionary Catalog*, 71.

38. Cutter, *Rules for a Dictionary Catalog*, 66.

39. Vatican Library, *Rules for the Catalog of Printed Books*, trans. from 2nd Italian ed. by Thomas J. Shanahan, Victor A. Schaefer, and Constantin T. Vesselowsky, and ed. Wyllis E. Wright (Chicago: American Library Association, 1948), 250.

40. Cutter, *Rules for a Dictionary Catalog*, 66.

41. Haykin, *Subject Headings*, 9.

42. Oliver Linton Lilley, "How Specific Is Specific?" *Journal of Cataloging and Classification* 11 (1955): 4-5.

43. John Balnaves, "Specificity," in *The Variety of Librarianship: Essays in Honour of John Wallace Metcalfe*, ed. W. Boyd Rayward (Sydney: Library Association of Australia, 1976), 54-55.

44. Elaine Svenonius, "Metcalfe and the Principles of Specific Entry," in *The Variety of Librarianship: Essays in Honour of John Wallace Mercalfe*, ed. W. Boyd Rayward (Sydney: Library Association of Australia, 1976), 186-187.

45. John W. Metcalfe, *Subject Classifying and Indexing of Libraries and Literature* (Sydney: Angus and Robertson, 1959), 278.

46. F. W. Lancaster, *Vocabulary Control for Information Retrieval*, 2nd ed. (Arlington, Va.: Information Resources Press, 1986), 108.

47. G. Salton and C. S. Yang, "On the Specification of Term Values in Automatic Indexing," *Journal of Documentation* 29 (December 1973): 352.

48. Svenonius, "Metcalfe and the Principles of Specific Entry," in *The Variety of Librarianship,* 183.

49. Richard S. Angell, "Standards for Subject Headings: A National Program," *Journal of Cataloging and Classification* 10 (October 1954): 193.

50. Metcalfe, *Subject Classifying and Indexing of Libraries and Literature*, 278.

51. Chan, *Library of Congress Subject Headings: Principles of Structure and Policies for Application*, 34.

52. Library of Congress, *Subject Cataloging Manual*, H180.

53. Haykin, *Subject Headings*, 10.

54. Elaine Svenonius, "Design of Controlled Vocabularies," in *Encyclopedia of Library and Information Science*, ed. Allen Kent (New York: Marcel Dekker, 1990), vol. 45, suppl. 10, 87.

55. Library of Congress, *Subject Headings Used in the Dictionary Catalogs of the Library of Congress*, 4th ed., iii.

56. Chan, *Library of Congress Subject Headings: Principles of Structure and Policies for Application*, 4.

57. Mortimer Taube, "Specificity in Subject Headings and Coordinate Indexing," *Library Trends* 1 (October 1952): 222.

58. Material distributed at Regional Institutes on Library of Congress Subject Headings.

59. Svenonius, "Design of Controlled Vocabularies," 88.

60. Subject Subdivisions Conference (1991: Airlie, Va.), *The Future of Subdivisions in the Library of Congress Subject Headings System Report from the Subject Subdivisions Conference*, ed. Martha O'Hara Conway (Washington, D.C.: Library of Congress, Cataloging Distribution Service, 1992), 6.

61. Library of Congress, *Subject Cataloging Manual*, H187.

3 Forms of Main Headings

INTRODUCTION

Main headings used in the Library of Congress (LC) subject headings system fall into two main categories: topical/form headings and name headings. Most headings in the first category represent objects or concepts; a small number of them represent forms or genres. Headings containing proper names, on the other hand, may also be assigned as subject headings to works discussing individual persons, corporate bodies, places, and other entities bearing proper names. With few exceptions, these name headings are not listed in LCSH but are found in the name authority file or constructed by the cataloger according to *Anglo-American Cataloguing Rules*. In the print version of *Library of Congress Subject Headings*, terms authorized for use as subject headings are printed in boldface type. In MARC records, they are indicated by appropriate field tags.

Both topical/form and name headings may be extended by subdivisions. Proper names used in subject headings are treated in chapter 4, and subdivisions are discussed in chapter 5. This chapter discusses the terminology and syntax of topical/form headings.

FUNCTIONS OF LIBRARY OF CONGRESS SUBJECT HEADINGS

The functions of Library of Congress subject headings may be divided into the following three categories: topical, bibliographic form, and artistic or literary form.

A topical heading represents the subject content of a work. The overwhelming majority of subject headings assigned to bibliographic records belong to this category. For example, a work about clinical chemistry is assigned the heading **Clinical chemistry**; a work on the process of arriving at decisions for action is assigned the heading **Decision making**.

In contrast, some headings indicate the bibliographic form of a work rather than its subject content. Most of these are assigned to works not limited to any particular subject or to works on very broad subjects, for example, **Encyclopedias and dictionaries**; **Almanacs**; **Yearbooks**; **Devotional calendars**. There are relatively few headings of this type. Such form headings are often assigned to works discussing the particular forms, for example, a work about compiling almanacs. In these cases, no attempt is made to distinguish works *in* the forms from works *about* the forms.

Some headings representing bibliographic forms are used only as topical headings and are not assigned to individual specimens of the form. For example, the heading **American periodicals** is assigned only to works *about* American periodicals, not to publications such as *Atlantic Monthly*.

Many headings indicate the artistic or literary genre of the work. They are used extensively in the fields of literature, art, and music. In these fields, the forms of the works are considered of greater importance than their subject content. Examples of this type of heading are:

Painting, Chinese
Short stories
Suites (Wind ensemble)

In some cases, a distinction is made between works about a particular genre and works about that genre, for example, **Short stories** (as a collection); **Short story** (as a literary form). Detailed discussions on headings for art, literature, and music are presented in chapter 10.

SYNTAX

Topical headings in the Library of Congress system represent a mixture of natural and artificial forms of the English language. All headings consist of nouns or noun-equivalents. They display a variety of syntax, a term defined by Elaine Svenonius as "the order in which individual vocabulary elements of the language are concatenated to form larger expressions."[1] Single nouns, adjectival phrases, and prepositional phrases are based on natural forms and word order. On the other hand, headings with qualifiers, headings with subdivisions, and inverted headings are special formations that are not used in everyday speech.

Traditionally, forms of subject headings have been viewed in terms of their grammatical or syntactical structure, that is, the way words are put together to form phrases or sentences. Charles A. Cutter names the following categories of subject headings in a dictionary catalog: a single word; a noun preceded by an adjective; a noun preceded by another noun used like an adjective; a noun connected with another by a preposition; a noun connected with another by "and;" and a phrase or sentence.[2] In the Library of Congress system, the sentence form mentioned by Cutter is not used. David Judson Haykin identifies seven forms used in *Library of Congress Subject Headings*: noun headings, adjectival headings, inverted adjectival headings, phrase headings, inverted phrase headings, compound headings, and composite forms.[3] Richard S. Angell categorizes the forms as follows:

> Headings proper have the grammatical form of noun or phrase, the principal types of the latter being adjective-noun, phrases containing a preposition, and phrases containing a conjunction. Phrases may be in normal direct order of words, or inverted.
>
> Headings are amplified as required by 1) the parenthetical qualifier, used principally to name the domain of a single noun for the purpose of resolving homographs; and 2) the subdivision, of which there are four kinds: topic, place, time and form.[4]

The use of nonverbal symbols in conjunction with the words in a heading is relatively simple in the Library of Congress system. The comma is used to separate a series of parallel terms and to indicate an inverted heading, for example, **Law reports, digests, etc.** and **Art, Mexican**. Parentheses are used to enclose qualifiers, for example, **Shutouts (Sports)**. The dash is the signal for subdivision, for example, **Education–Aims and objectives.** The period is used to separate a subheading from the main heading and only appears in a name heading, a uniform title, or a name-title heading used as a subject heading:

United States. Air Force
Bible. N.T. Gospels
Aristotle. Poetics

In the bibliographic record, each heading or heading string, that is, combination of a main heading and one or more subdivisions, is followed by a period. For details of punctuation, see appendix J of this book.

Most topical headings represent single concepts or objects. Compound headings contain more than one concept or object, some expressing an additive relationship, others representing phase relationships (such as cause and effect, influence, bias, etc.) between concepts and objects. Still other headings represent a particular aspect of a subject, such as form, place, time, process, or property.

Because headings in LCSH have been created over many years by different individuals, often under different policies, the form of the headings is sometimes inconsistent, even among similar types of headings. As a result, in some cases there does not seem to be a relationship between grammatical form and semantic function. A heading representing an aspect of a subject is usually in the form of a subdivided heading, but it may also appear as an adjectival phrase (direct or inverted), a prepositional phrase (direct or inverted), or a heading with a qualifier, for example:

Plant inspection
Fertilization of plants

Plants, Effect of solar radiation on
Cookery (Sausages)

As mentioned above, such inconsistencies and variations reflect the different policies adopted over a period of more than a century. Some aspects of the problem are discussed below.

SINGLE-CONCEPT HEADINGS

Single-concept headings appear in the form of single-word terms or multiple-word terms.

Single-Word Headings

The simplest form of main heading is a noun or substantive, which represents a single object or concept, for example:

Catalogs
Bioinformatics
Chemistry
Democracy
Moneylenders
Pleasure
Women

When adjectives and participles are chosen, they are used as substantives or noun-equivalents:

Advertising
Aged
Poor
Sick

In the past, the definite article was used in some cases (e.g., *The arts*, *The West*) but not in others, even when grammatical usage would require it. To facilitate machine filing, a decision was later made that no new subject heading was to be established with "the" in the initial position. Many of the original headings with an initial "the" have been converted to the current form:

Original form	*Converted form*
The arts	**Arts**
The Many (Philosophy)	**Many (Philosophy)**
The One (Philosophy)	**One (The One in philosophy)**
The West	**West (U.S.)**

In cases where the definite article is retained for semantic or grammatical reasons, the heading is inverted, for example, **State, The**; **Comic, The**.

In general, the plural form of a noun is used for denoting a concrete object or a class of people, for example, **Airplanes**; **Apples**; **Castles**; **Teachers**. This is not a rigid rule, and there are exceptions. Headings that represent biological species are generally in the singular, for example, **Coconut palm**; **Japanese macaque**; **Rhesus monkey**; headings for higher levels are almost always in the plural, for example, **Palms**; **Macaques**; **Monkeys**. However, headings for domestic animals that are raised as livestock or kept as pets, as well as cultivated plants, are often in the plural form, for example, **Cats** and **Potatoes**.[5] In cases where both the singular and the plural forms of a noun have been established as headings, they represent different subjects: Usually the singular form represents a concept or abstract idea and the plural a concrete object, for example, **Essay** (as a literary form); **Essays** (for a collection of specimens of this literary form). However, in newly established headings, this distinction is no longer made. Another way of distinguishing between the concept and the specimens is to use the phrase form in one of the headings, for example, **Biography** (for collective biographies); **Biography as a literary form**.

In headings for art, the former practice of using the singular, for example, *Painting*, to represent technique, aesthetics, history, etc. and the plural, for example, *Paintings*, for the art works treated collectively, has been discontinued. Currently the singular noun, for example, **Painting**; **Sculpture**, is used to represent both the activity and the object.[6]

Multiple-Word Headings

When a single object or concept cannot be properly expressed by a single noun, a phrase is used. Multiword terms appear in the form of adjectival or prepositional phrases.

Adjectival Phrase Headings

The most common phrase headings consist of a noun or noun phrase with an adjectival modifier. The modifier takes one of the following forms:

• Common adjective

Automotive computers
Digital art
Financial writers
Universal design

- Common noun

  Budget surpluses
  Computer software developers
  Information literacy
  Space flights
  Web portals

- Ethnic, national, or geographical adjective

  American drama
  Jewish chants

- Other proper adjective

  Brownian movements
  Newtonian telescopes

- Present or past participle

  Laminated plastics
  Self-organizing maps
  Working poor

- Common noun in the possessive case

  Carpenters' squares
  Children's festivals
  Women's music

- Proper noun in the possessive case

  Halley's comet

- Proper noun

  New Age movement
  Norway lobster
  Toyota automobiles

- Combination

  Veteran-owned business enterprises
  Pressure-sensitive adhesives
  Rapid eye movement sleep
  Uninhabited combat aerial vehicles

Prepositional Phrase Headings

Prepositional phrases are used in single-concept headings when the concept is generally expressed in the English language in the form of a prepositional phrase, for example:

Balance of power
Boards of trade
Figures of speech
Right to housing
Spheres of influence
Stories without words
Willingness to pay

In the past, a large number of headings in the form of **[Class of people] as [another class of people]**, for example, *Children as actors; Women as diplomats*; etc., represented the role of a certain class of people in an activity or profession. Many of these have been converted to phrase headings such as **Child actors**; **Women diplomats**; **Women soccer players**, etc. Currently, headings in the form of **[Class of people] as [another class of people]** are established for the following categories only: (1) Classes of persons involving two professions, for example, **Artists as teachers**; **Physicians as musicians**; etc.; (2) Occupational groups in non-work-related activities.[7]

Choice between Nouns and Phrases

No satisfactory solution has yet been offered to the problem of what choice to make between a noun and a phrase when both represent the same object or concept, although Cutter states that, in general, phrases "shall when possible be reduced to their equivalent nouns, as **Moral philosophy** to **Ethics** or to **Morals**; **Intellectual** or **Mental philosophy** to **Intellect** or **Mind**."[8] However, he also recognizes the difficulty in applying such a rule:

> In reducing, for instance, Intellectual philosophy or Moral philosophy, will you say Mind or Intellect, Morals or Ethics? And the reader will not always know what the equivalent noun is,—that Physics = Natural philosophy, for example, and Hygiene = Sanitary science. Nor does it help us at all to decide whether to prefer Botanical morphology or Morphological botany.[9]

In LCSH, the choice in such cases often depends on the judgment of the cataloger who, in proposing the heading, tries to take prevailing usage into account. The same holds for the choice among different types of phrases.

Choice among Different Types of Phrases

In his rules, Cutter gives examples of the same subject named in different ways:[10]

Capital punishment
Death penalty
Penalty by death

Floral fertilization
Flower fertilization
Fertilization of flowers

He feels that there is no way to formulate an absolute rule to ensure consistency in the choice, and that the best rule of thumb is, "when there is any decided usage (i.e., custom of the public to designate the subjects by one of the names rather than by the others) let it be followed." Here Cutter immediately recognizes a difficulty: "As is often the case in language, usage will be found not to follow any uniform course." As a result of this difficulty as reflected in LCSH, there is little uniformity regarding the choice among different types of phrases.

MULTIPLE-CONCEPT HEADINGS

Multiple-concept headings appear as compound phrases, prepositional phrases, or subject heading strings consisting of a main heading with one or more subdivisions.

Compound Phrases

Compound phrase headings, consisting of two or more nouns, noun phrases, or both, with or without modifiers, connected by the word *and*, the word *or*, or the word *etc.*, serve various purposes:

(1) to express a reciprocal relationship between two general topics discussed at a broad level from the perspectives of both topics,[11] for example:

Art and technology
Education and state
Internet and teenagers
Library and labor unions
Literature and society
Television and children
Women and peace

(2) to connect subjects that are often treated together in works because they are similar, opposite, or closely associated, for example:

Boats and boating
Bolts and nuts
Coopers and cooperage
Children's encyclopedias and dictionaries
College student newspapers and periodicals
Debtor and creditor
Emigration and immigration

Good and evil
Lamp-chimneys, globes, etc.
Open and closed shelves
Stores or stock-room keeping

Library of Congress policy regarding headings of this type has varied over the years, with current policy requiring the establishment of a separate heading for each of the elements. Many previously established headings of this type have been replaced by separate headings; for example, the heading *Textile industry and fabrics* was replaced by the two headings **Textile fabrics** and **Textile industry**, and the heading *Bicycles and tricycles* was replaced by the two headings **Bicycles** and **Tricycles.**

(3) to connect two nouns when one serves to define the other, more general noun, for example:

Forces and couples
Force and energy

Prepositional Phrase Headings

Prepositional phrase headings consisting of nouns, noun phrases, or both, with or without modifiers, and connected by one or more prepositions, are used to express complex relationships between topics, for example:

Care of sick animals
Child sexual abuse by clergy
Counseling in elementary education
Federal aid to youth services
Fertilization of plants by insects
Taxation of bonds, securities, etc.
Teacher participation in curriculum planning

Free-Floating Phrase Headings

In addition to the prepositional phrase headings listed in LCSH, there are a number of phrases that can be combined with valid headings to form new headings, without being officially established or displayed in LCSH. These phrases are referred to as "free-floating." Free-floating phrase headings are used extensively in headings relating to music and in geographic headings referring to metropolitan areas, city regions, suburban areas, and suburban regions associated with geographic features,[12] for example:

Quartets (Clarinet, flute, computer, double bass)
Los Angeles Region (Calif.)

Previously, headings in the form of **[Topic] in art** and **[Topic] in literature** were free-floating phrase headings. This is no longer the case; they are no longer freely combined by catalogers when needed. Many headings in these forms have been converted to **Main heading–Subdivision**, and others are now established individually, for example:

Chapels in art
Christian saints in literature

Choice between Phrase Headings and Headings with Subdivisions

Many phrase headings represent an aspect or facet of a subject that could be represented by a subdivided heading,[13] for example, **Cataloging of art**, instead of *Art–Cataloging*. Haykin recognizes the problem of having to choose among forms that have equal standing in current usage, such as *Stability of ships*; *Ships' stability*; *Ships–Stability*, but offers no solution.[14] In LCSH, any of three forms may have been chosen with regard to individual headings:

Squares, Tables of
Factor tables
Multiplication–Tables

According to current Library of Congress policy, headings describing certain kinds of relationships are constructed with the use of standardized subdivisions such as **[Main topic]–Effect of [topic] on**; **[Main topic]–[Topic] influences**; **[Main topic]–Psychological aspects**; **[Main topic]–Social aspects**; etc.[15]

Furthermore, many phrase headings established earlier have been converted to the subdivided form:

Original form	*Converted form*
Social science research	**Social sciences–Research**
Teachers, Certification of	**Teachers–Certification**

However, in many cases, a new phrase heading is constructed when the cataloger who proposes the heading believes that the concept is very well known by the public in the phrase form, for example:

Library orientation for engineering students
{instead of *Engineering students–Library orientation*}
Television broadcasting of court proceedings
{instead of *Court proceedings–Television broadcasting*}

It has been noted that, because of the lack of specific and consistent rules regulating the choice of forms over the years, and because a large number of people have participated in establishing headings, many inconsistencies exist in LCSH. A few have already been resolved. The publication of *Subject Cataloging*

Manual: Subject Headings,[16] which began in 1984 and is now in its fifth edition, represents an attempt to regularize new heading formation to a greater degree than ever before. As older headings are revised to make them conform to new heading patterns, the system as a whole has improved, not only for catalogers who apply the subject headings, but also for end-users who use them for searching.

SEMANTICS

The principle of unique headings requires that each heading represent only one subject. The problem of polysemy or homographs is resolved in part by using *qualifiers*,[17] added for the purpose of disambiguation. A qualifier is a word or phrase enclosed within parentheses following the heading. Examples are:

Heliosphere (Astrophysics)
Heliosphere (Ionosphere)

Iris (Eye)
Iris (Plant)

Ordination (Buddhism)
Ordination (Liturgy)

Rings (Algebra)
Rings (Gymnastics)

A qualifier may also be used to provide context for obscure or technical terms, in which case it usually takes the form of the name of a discipline, of a category, or of a kind of thing, for example:

Assemblage (Art)
Boundary layer (Meteorology)
Charge transfer devices (Electronics)
Consumption (Economics)
Correlation (Statistics)
Golden age (Mythology) in literature
Guo (The Chinese word)
Open plan (Building)
Résumés (Employment)
Spectral theory (Mathematics)
Streaming technology (Telecommunications)

Over the years, parenthetical qualifiers have been added to subject headings for various purposes: (1) to distinguish between homographs, for example, **Pool (Game)**; **Cold (Disease)**; **Rape (Plant)**; (2) to clarify the meaning of an obscure or foreign term, for example, **Extra Hungariam non est vita (The Latin phrase)**; (3) to limit the meaning of a heading in order to render it more specific, for example, **Olympic games (Ancient)**; (4) to indicate the genre of a proper name, for example, **Banabans (Kiribati people)**; **DECSYSTEM-20 (Computer)**; (5) to designate a special application of a general concept, for example, **Cookery (Fish)**; and (6) to specify the medium of performance in music headings, for example, **Concertos (Violin)**.

In rare cases, a heading may contain two qualifiers, for example, **Profession (in religious orders, congregations, etc.) (Canon law).** In some cases, it is not clear why the qualified form instead of a phrase form or subdivided form was used, or why the qualifier was used at all, for example, **Profession (in religious orders, congregations, etc.)**; **Programming languages (Electronic computers)**. In many cases, another form could have achieved the desired purpose, for example, *Cookery–Fish*; *Ancient Olympic Games* (or *Olympic games, Ancient*).

The practice in regard to qualifiers, as with so many other features of LCSH, has not been consistent. In 1978, the Library of Congress began to develop guidelines[18] regarding the use of qualifiers. The parenthetical qualifier is to be used (a) to specify the intended meaning of the term if several dictionary definitions exist, (b) to resolve ambiguity if the main heading is similar in construction to other existing or possible headings, and (c) to make an obscure term more explicit. Current practice follows these guidelines.[19] The parenthetical qualifier is no longer used to designate a special application of a general concept. For this purpose, the following forms are used instead:

- Headings with subdivisions (preferred form)

  Geography–Network analysis
  {not *Network analysis (Geography)*}
  Public health–Citizen participation
  {not *Citizen participation (Public health)*}

- Adjectival phrase headings

  Industrial design coordination
  {not *Designs (Industrial publicity)*}

- Prepositional phrase headings

  Information theory in biology
  {not *Information theory (Biology)*}
  Anesthesia in cardiology
  {not *Anesthesia (Cardiology)*}
  Abandonment of automobiles
  {not *Automobiles–Abandonment*}

INVERTED HEADINGS

In the past, many phrase headings were established in the inverted form in order to bring a significant word into a prominent position as the entry element, a practice that resulted in better collocation of related topics, for example:

Calendar, Celtic
Chemistry, Organic
Education, Higher
Philosophy, Modern
Quotations, American

Because LCSH was originally designed for the card catalog, each record contained only a few access points and was filed in the catalog only under the first word. The choice of the word to be used as the entry element in a phrase heading was therefore an important consideration. In a manual catalog, or in a single-entry listing or display, each subject heading was accessible only under the first word. The inverted form of a heading such as **Insurance, Life** serves the purpose of collocating entry elements in cases where using natural word order—for instance, *Life insurance*—would scatter similar headings such as *Property insurance, Unemployment insurance,* etc. In online retrieval systems with keyword searching capability, the entry element is less of an issue, affecting browsing and display, but less so retrieval. Therefore, newly established headings are in the direct form, except where a pattern of inverted headings already exists among similar headings. Nonetheless, while many of the inverted headings have been converted to the direct form in recent years, many still exist. For this reason, an understanding of the background and rationale for inverted headings may be in order.

Since there were no specific guidelines, nor discernible patterns, for inverting headings in the past, there is no way to predict the form of a heading in LCSH, as the following headings demonstrate:

Bessel functions
Functions, Abelian
Abelian groups
Groups, Multiply transitive

Agricultural chemistry
Environmental chemistry
Nuclear chemistry
Chemistry, Analytic
Chemistry, Organic
Chemistry, Technical

To normalize word order, the Library of Congress made the decision in 1983 to create most new headings in direct form in natural word order.[20] However, because of the large number of headings already established in the inverted form, it was decided to retain such headings in the following categories:

(1) headings modified by language, nationality, or ethnic groups:

Art, American
Authors, Spanish
Economic assistance, Emirian
Folk literature, Scottish Gaelic
Porcelain, Chinese

(2) headings qualified by time period:

Logic, Ancient
Philosophy, Medieval
History, Modern

(3) headings with qualifiers for artistic or musical style:

Art, Baroque
Bronzes, Renaissance
Drawing, Rococo

(4) headings for types of fossils:

Footprints, Fossil
Trees, Fossil

(5) music headings with the following qualifiers:

[...], Arranged
[...], Sacred
[...], Secular
[...], Unaccompanied

(6) battles (see discussion in Chapter 4)

(7) geographic headings (see discussion in Chapter 4)

(8) names of fictitious and legendary characters (see discussion in Chapter 4)

(9) royal houses, etc. (see discussion in Chapter 4)

However, there are a number of exceptions:

(A) headings containing modifiers designating language, nationality, or ethnic groups followed by the terms below are established in natural word order:

[...] diaries
[...] drama
[...] drama (Comedy)
[...] drama (Tragedy)
[...] drama (Tragicomedy)
[...] essays
[...] farces
[...] fiction
[...] imprints
[...] language
[...] letters
[...] literature
[...] newspapers
[...] periodicals
[...] philology
[...] poetry
[...] prose literature
[...] wit and humor
[...] wit and humor, Pictorial

(B) topical headings modified by ethnic groups in the United States are established in natural word order:

African American artists
Japanese American women
Italian American art

Until all inverted headings are converted to natural word order, users and catalogers should be aware of the patterns of existing inverted headings in LCSH.

NOTES

1. Elaine Svenonius, *The Intellectual Foundation of Information Organization* (Cambridge, Mass.: MIT Press, 2000), 58.

2. Charles A. Cutter, *Rules for a Dictionary Catalog*, 4th ed., rewritten (Washington, D.C.: Government Printing Office, 1904), 71-72.

3. David Judson Haykin, *Subject Headings: A Practical Guide* (Washington, D.C.: Government Printing Office, 1951), 21-25.

4. Richard S. Angell, "Library of Congress Subject Headings—Review and Forecast," in *Subject Retrieval in the Seventies: New Directions: Proceedings of an International Symposium*, ed. Hans (Hanan) Wellisch and Thomas D. Wilson (Westport, Conn.: Greenwood Publishing, 1972), 144.

5. Library of Congress, Cataloging Policy and Support Office, *Subject Cataloging Manual: Subject Headings*, 5th ed., 2000 cumulation (Washington, D.C.: Library of Congress, 2000), H1332.

6. Library of Congress, *Subject Cataloging Manual*, H1250.

7. Library of Congress, *Subject Cataloging Manual*, H360.

8. Cutter, *Rules for a Dictionary Catalog*, 72.

9. Cutter, *Rules for a Dictionary Catalog*, 74.

10. Cutter, *Rules for a Dictionary Catalog*, 74.

11. Library of Congress, *Subject Cataloging Manual*, H310.

12. Library of Congress, *Subject Cataloging Manual*, H362, H1917.5.

13. Subdivisions are discussed in detail in chapter 5.

14. Haykin, *Subject Headings*, 23.

15. Library of Congress, *Subject Cataloging Manual*, H310.

16. Library of Congress, *Subject Cataloging Manual.*

17. Library of Congress, *Subject Cataloging Manual*, H357.

18. "Parenthetical Qualifiers in Subject Headings," *Cataloging Service Bulletin* 1 (Summer 1978): 15-16.

19. Library of Congress, *Subject Cataloging Manual*, H357.

20. Library of Congress, *Subject Cataloging Manual*, H306.

4 Proper Name Headings

INTRODUCTION

In the LCSH system, proper names may be assigned as main subject headings, as parts of subject strings, or as subdivisions. The term *proper name* includes personal names, names of corporate bodies, names of conferences and meetings, geographic names, names of works established as uniform titles, and names of individual entities. In the past, most of these headings were not printed in *Library of Congress Subject Headings*. This policy was changed in 1976; since the tenth edition, the list has included many name headings used as subject headings, but generally not those used as headings in descriptive cataloging as well.

At the Library of Congress, headings for proper names that have been or are likely to be used in descriptive cataloging, such as headings for persons, corporate bodies, jurisdictions, uniform titles, and names of certain types of entities,[1] are established by descriptive catalogers according to *Anglo-American Cataloguing Rules*, 2nd edition, 2002 revision (*AACR2R*).[2] A few of these are included in LCSH for the purpose of displaying special subdivisions or unique references, or to serve as pattern headings.[3] Also omitted from LCSH are free-floating phrase headings such as those for regions of geographic features, regions of cities, and metropolitan areas. Authority records for both name and subject headings are kept in the file called *Library of Congress Authorities* (http://authorities.loc.gov).

PERSONAL NAMES

Names of Individual Persons

Names of individual persons are used as subject headings for biographies, eulogies, festschriften, criticisms, bibliographies, and literary works in which the persons figure. At the Library of Congress, to ensure that the same form of a personal name is used for both author and subject, headings consisting of names of persons are established according to *AACR2R*. Following are some examples of personal name headings:

Alexander, the Great, 356-323 B.C.
Ambrose, Saint, Bishop of Milan, d. 397
Aristotle
Byron, George Gordon Byron, Baron, 1788-1824
Catherine II, Empress of Russia, 1729-1796
Charlemagne, Emperor, 742-814
Columbus, Christopher
Devonshire, Andrew Robert Buxton Cavendish, Duke of, 1920-
Franz Joseph I, Emperor of Austria, 1830-1916
John Paul II, Pope, 1920-
Kennedy, John F. (John Fitzgerald), 1917-1963
Madonna, 1958-
Nicholas, of Cusa, Cardinal, 1401-1464

Subdivisions used under name headings are discussed in chapter 5.

Names of Families, Dynasties, Royal Houses, Etc.

The heading for a family appears in the form of **[Proper name] family**, for example, **Bush family**. The older form with a qualifier, for example, *Smith family (William Smith, 1669-1743)*, has been discontinued. No effort is made to distinguish between families with the same surname. The heading **Kennedy family**, for example, is used for works about any family with the surname Kennedy. Examples of family name headings include:

Adams family
Bailly family
Cook family
Koch family

If the same family has been known by different names, the most common form of the name is chosen as the heading, with cross-references from other forms. Variants are usually determined from the work being cataloged and from standard reference works. Another source of variants is references to surnames already used as headings.

Similar family names from different ethnic backgrounds and family names that have been changed as the result of emigration are established as separate headings, connected by related references.

Names of dynasties and royal houses are established in the following forms: **[Name] dynasty** (for non-European royal houses); **[Name], House of** (for European royal houses). Dates indicating the span of years of a particular dynasty are added to the heading whenever possible. Examples include:

Hoysala dynasty, ca. 1006-ca. 1346
Habsburg, House of
Saxe-Coburg-Gotha, House of
Vasa, House of
Orange-Nassau, House of

USE references are made from variant forms of the name, and *BT* (broader term) references are made from appropriate history headings for dynasties and from **[Country (or region)]–Kings and rulers** for royal houses. A discussion and examples of cross references appear in chapter 6.

Headings for individually named houses of dukes, counts, or earls are established in the form of **[Name], [Title of rank in English] of**, for example:

Celje, Counts of
Derby, Earls of
Leinster, Dukes of

Headings for other aristocratic or noble families are established in the form of **[Name] family**, for example:

Tokugawa family

Names of Mythological, Legendary, or Fictitious Characters

Names of mythological, legendary, or fictitious characters are not covered by *AACR2R*. However, they are often required as subject headings. Headings for mythological characters that are not gods or goddesses are established in the form of **[Name of character] ([Ethnic adjective] mythology)**, for example:

Draupadī (Hindu mythology)
Lilith (Semitic mythology)

The qualifier **(Legendary character)** is used with headings for legendary characters:

Aeneas (Legendary character)
Anansi (Legendary character)
Brer Rabbit (Legendary character)
Hamlet (Legendary character)
Pecos Bill (Legendary character)
Robin Hood (Legendary character)
Roland (Legendary character)

The qualifier **(Fictitious character)** is used with names of characters of literary or artistic invention, as opposed to legendary characters originating from legends, myths, or folklore. Examples of headings for fictitious characters include:

Bond, James (Fictitious character)
Holmes, Sherlock (Fictitious character)
Potter, Harry (Fictitious character)
Tarzan (Fictitious character)

Names of comic characters are also established in the form of **[Name of character] (Fictitious character)**, for example:

Felix the Cat (Fictitious character)
Snoopy (Fictitious character)
Spiderman (Fictitious character)

Biblical figures are established with appropriate qualifiers, for example:

Abraham (Biblical patriarch)
Eve (Biblical figure)
Moses (Biblical leader)

Names of Gods and Goddesses

Names of gods and goddesses are established in the form of **[Name of god or goddess] ([Ethnic adjective] deity)**, for example:

Amon (Egyptian deity)
Apollo (Greek deity)
Xuantian Shangdi (Chinese deity)

Previously, names of gods and goddesses of classical mythology were usually established only in the Latin form, with *see* references from the names of their Greek counterparts. Charles A. Cutter defends the use of the Latin form for the reasons "(1) that the Latin names are at present more familiar to the majority of readers; (2) that it would be difficult to divide the literature, or if it were done, many books must be put both under **Zeus** and **Jupiter**, **Poseidon** and **Neptune**, etc., filling considerable room with no practical advantage."[4] This policy has been changed. The current policy[5] requires that the heading be established as required by the work being cataloged, for example:

Hermes (Greek deity)
Cacus (Roman deity)

When equivalencies can be determined between Greek and Roman gods and goddesses, reciprocal *RT* (related term) references are made between them.

Minerva (Roman deity)
  RT Athena (Greek deity)

Athena (Greek deity)
  RT Minerva (Roman deity)

NAMES OF CORPORATE BODIES

Works related to the origin, development, activities, and functions of individual corporate bodies are assigned subject headings under their names. Like personal name headings, headings for corporate bodies are established according to *AACR2R*.

Corporate bodies include public and private organizations, societies, associations, institutions, government agencies, commercial firms, churches, and other groups identified by a name, such as conferences and exploring expeditions. Examples of corporate names used as subject headings are given below. Some of the headings are qualified by generic terms or names of places, as required by *AACR2R* and Library of Congress descriptive cataloging policies.[6]

Arthur M. Sackler Gallery (Smithsonian Institution)
Cleveland Browns (Football team : 1999)
Colonial Williamsburg Foundation
Conference on Security and Cooperation in Europe. Follow-up Meeting (3rd : 1986 : Vienna, Austria)
First Baptist Church (Charleston, S.C.)
Golden State Warriors (Basketball team)
Library of Congress. Cataloging Policy and Support Office
Metropolitan Museum of Art (New York, N.Y.)
Michigan. Dept. of State
Queen Elizabeth (Ship)
Rand Corporation
United Nations. Armed Forces
Teens (Musical group)

The forms of geographic names used as qualifiers are discussed on pages 72–73.

Name Changes in Corporate Bodies

When the name of a corporate body is changed, successive entries (that is, the practice, in cataloging, of establishing both former and later names as valid headings) are established according to *AACR2R*. However, for subject cataloging purposes, successive headings for the same corporate body are not assigned to the same work, even if it covers the history of the body under different names;[7] instead, cross references are used to link the successive names. This usage is indicated in the name authority records.

OTHER INDIVIDUAL ENTITIES BEARING PROPER NAMES

In addition to the proper names discussed above, many other individual entities that bear proper names also serve as subject headings. Headings for which there are no provisions in *AACR2R* are established and displayed in LCSH. Some of the categories are given below with examples.

Animals[8]

Subject headings are required for works about individual animals. The heading consists of the name of the animal qualified by type of animal, with a cross reference from the broader, generic term, for example:

Man o' War (Race horse)
BT Horses

Princess (Cat)
BT Cats

Squirt (Dolphin)
BT Dolphins

Historical Events

Historical events identified by specific names are entered under their names, usually accompanied by dates:

Anthracite Coal Strike, Pa., 1887-1888[9]
Gettysburg, Battle of, Gettysburg, Pa., 1863
Longshoremen's Strike, San Francisco, Calif., 1934
Canadian Invasion, 1775-1776
Canadian Spy Trials, Canada, 1946
King Philip's War, 1675-1676
Louisiana Purchase

Northwestern Conspiracy, 1864
Persian Gulf War, 1991
September 11 Terrorist Attacks, 2001
Verdun, Battle of, Verdun, France, 1940
Watergate Affair, 1972-1974
World War, 1939-1945

Names of other events may also be used as headings, for example:

Brighton Run (Antique car race)
National Book Week

Prizes, Awards, Scholarships, Etc.

Individual prizes, awards, scholarships, and so on, are represented by specific headings:

Congressional Award
Erasmus Prize
Father of the Year
International Simón Bolívar Prize
Maryland Hunt Cup
Nobel Prizes

Holidays, Festivals, Etc.

Examples of headings for holidays, festivals, etc., are:

All Saints' Day
Ascension Day
Bastille Day
Christmas
Feast of Fools
Good Friday
Hanukkah
Memorial Day
Mid-autumn Festival
Ramadan
Thanksgiving Day

Ethnic Groups, Nationalities, Tribes, Etc.

Headings for ethnic, national, or tribal groups are established in the form of their appropriate names, for example, **Arabs**; **Chinese**; **Indians of North America**; **Italians**; **Jews**; **North Africans**; **Nzakara (African people)**; etc.

Until 1981, many headings for individual nationalities living outside of their native countries were established in the form of *[National group] in [Place]*,[10] for example, *Poles in Austria*; *Russians in France*. All such headings in LCSH have been converted to the form of **[National group]–[Place]**, for example, **Poles–Austria**; **Russians–France**; **Americans–Foreign countries**.

Headings for groups of individual nationalities living within the United States as permanent residents or naturalized citizens are established in the composite form **[Qualifier designating country of origin] Americans**, for example, **Italian Americans**; **Japanese Americans**. These headings may be further subdivided by locality, for example:

Italian Americans–New York (State)–New York
Japanese Americans–California–San Francisco

Headings such as **Japanese–United States** and **Germans–United States** are used for aliens living in the United States, students from abroad, etc. For groups of Americans already identified with ethnic groups whose names are in composite form, for example, French Canadians in the United States, headings such as **French Canadians–United States**, etc., are used instead of *French Canadian Americans*, etc.

For a specific nationality living outside of the United States, headings of the type **[Nationality]–[Place]** are used whether these people reside in the country permanently or temporarily. Examples are:

Italians–Foreign countries {for Italians in several countries}
Germans–France
Japanese–China–Manchuria
North Africans–Belgium

Religions, Philosophical Systems, Etc.

Examples of headings for individual religions, philosophical systems, etc., are:

Buddhism
Christianity
Confucianism
Islam
Neoplatonism

Objects Bearing Proper Names

Specific name headings are also established for objects bearing proper names, for example:

Bury Saint Edmunds Cross
Hazard Analysis and Critical Control Point (Food safety system)

GEOGRAPHIC NAMES

Geographic names[11] are used widely in both subject and descriptive cataloging. As subject headings, they may be the main heading or part of a heading phrase, they may be used as subdivisions (discussed in detail in chapter 5), or they may figure as qualifiers. Examples include:

Norway–Description and travel
Paris (France) in motion pictures
Library finance–United States
Building permits–Belgium
First Baptist Church (Bloomington, Ill.)

Names of countries and political or administrative divisions within countries such as provinces, states, cities, and towns are referred to as jurisdictional names. Such names are used very often in descriptive cataloging as entries in and of themselves, as parts of corporate names, or as additional designations or qualifiers. Such headings are established according to the provisions of *AACR2R* for geographic names. Other geographic names, such as those for natural features and man-made structures associated with places, are referred to as non-jurisdictional names. With few exceptions, non-jurisdictional headings are established and maintained in LCSH. Attempts are made to ensure compatibility with *AACR2R* whenever possible.

The following sections discuss general aspects of geographic heading formation and usage. Because the distinction between jurisdictional and non-jurisdictional names comes into the discussion at many points, the first two sections extend, and give examples for, the brief definitions presented above. Later sections treat language, choice of entry element, qualifiers, free-floating phrase headings, and changes of name. A final section deals with categories of geographic headings that require special treatment.

Jurisdictional Headings

Entities that can be called jurisdictions include countries, principalities, territories, states, provinces, counties, administrative districts, cities, archdioceses, and dioceses. When names for these entities figure in subject headings, the *AACR2R* forms are used. Examples of jurisdictional names are:

Bavaria (Germany)[12]
Berlin (Germany)
Bourbon County (Ky.)
Brittany (France)
Dorset (England)
Glasgow (Ky.)
Glasgow (Scotland)
Great Britain
London (England)
Ontario
Pennsylvania
Provence (France)
Sardinia (Kingdom)
Vienna (Austria)

Some of the examples above include a qualifier enclosed in parentheses. Geographic qualifiers will be discussed in detail later in this chapter.

Non-Jurisdictional Headings[13]

Many headings for geographic areas or entities are not jurisdictional units. As noted above, these headings are established in LCSH, with the exception of those formed by using free-floating terms (a matter that is covered later in this chapter). Types of places with non-jurisdictional names include:

archaeological sites, historic cities, etc.
areas and regions (when not free-floating)
canals
dams
extinct cities (pre-1500)
farms, ranches, gardens
forests, grasslands, etc.
geographic features (e.g., caves, deserts, non-jurisdictional islands, lakes, mountains, plains, ocean currents, rivers, seas, steppes)
geologic basins , geologic formations, etc.
mines
parks, reserves, refuges, recreation areas, etc.
reservoirs
roads, streets, trails
valleys

Examples of headings for non-jurisdictional place names are:

130 Bush Street (San Francisco, Calif.)
Africa, Southern
Arroyo Hondo Site (N.M.)
Big Cypress National Preserve (Fla.)
Big Sur Coast National Scenic Area (Calif.)
Black Hills National Forest (S.D. and Wyo.)
Box Canyon Falls (Colo.)
Buffalo Rock State Park (Ill.)
Gateway National Recreation Area (N.J. and N.Y.)
Grand Canyon (Ariz.)
Gulf Region (Tex.)
Harry S. Truman National Historic Site (Mo.)
Himalaya Mountains
Knossos (Extinct city)
Lehigh Canal (Pa.)
Maryland Route 202 (Md.)
Missouri River
Oregon National Historic Trail
North End (Boston, Mass.)
Saint Point Magnuson Park (Seattle, Wash.)
Tahoe, Lake (Calif. and Nev.)
Willapa Bay (Wash.)

Language

The language of jurisdictional names is determined by *AACR2R* and *Library of Congress Rule Interpretations (LCRI).*[14] The English form of the name, particularly a conventional name, is preferred, unless there is no English name in common use. Examples include:

South America
{not Sudamerica; America del sur}
Germany
{not Deutschland}
Spain
{not España}
Bavaria (Germany)
{not Bayern}
Vienna (Austria)
{not Wien}

The vernacular form is chosen when there is no English form in general use or when the vernacular form is widely accepted in English-language works, for example, **Rio de Janeiro (Brazil)**. In determining the language of a non-jurisdictional name to be used in a heading, the Library of Congress usually relies on the following sources for names of places in the United States: the Geographic Names Information System (GNIS; http://geonames.usgs.gov/) and U.S. Geological Survey (U.S. Board on Geographic Names (BGN) domestic names system). The decisions made by BGN are evaluated in connection with other reference sources used as authorities for establishing geographic names (see appendix E for a list of these authorities) to determine if there are any conflicts with existing headings and to aid in the preparation of cross references. For places in other countries, the GEONET Names Server (GNS) of the Defense Mapping Agency (the BGN foreign names system) (http://earth-info.nima.mil/gns/html/) is consulted.

Naturally, for places in English-speaking regions, English names are used. For places in non-English-speaking regions, on the other hand, a choice must often be made between English and vernacular names. In cases where the BGN has approved both an English and a vernacular form of a name, the English form is chosen as the heading.[15] In certain cases, even when the name approved by BGN is in the vernacular form, an English name is used in the heading if it is a conventional name justified by reference sources.[16] Based on these policies, the following forms are used in subject headings:

Japanese Alps (Japan)
{not Nihon arupusu}
Rhine River
{not Rhein}
West Lake (China)
{not Hsi-hu}

The vernacular form of the name is chosen if (1) the entity in question is best known by its vernacular name among English-speaking users; or (2) the entity in question is a man-made or designated area, such as a park, garden, reserve, street, or road. When the vernacular name is chosen as the heading for a non-jurisdictional entity, the generic term in the name is translated into English, unless the generic term in vernacular form is better known in the English-speaking world or is an integral part of the conventional name:

Fontainebleau, Forest of (France)
{not Forêt de Fontainebleau (France)}
Steinhuder Lake (Germany)
{not Steinhuder Meer (Germany)}
Rio de la Plata (Argentina and Uruguay)
{not Plate River (Argentina and Uruguay)}

Maderanertal (Switzerland)
{not Maderaner Valley (Switzerland)}
Tien Shan
{not Tien Mountains}

Vernacular names in non-Roman scripts are transliterated according to Library of Congress transliteration tables. Note, however, that transliteration conventions are subject to change according to accepted usage. For example, for names in the Chinese script, the Library previously used the Wade-Giles Romanization, but switched to the pinyin system in 2000:[17]

Beijing (China)
{not Peking (China) or Peiping (China)}
Qinling Mountains (China)
{not Ch'in-ling Mountains (China)}

Entry Element

When a geographic name contains more than one word, there is also the problem of choice of entry element. With few exceptions, names of political jurisdictions generally appear in their natural word order, without inversion, for example, **South Africa**; **North Carolina**; **Lake Forest (Ill.)**. This holds true even for names of foreign places beginning with an article, for example, **El Salvador**.

Initial articles in non-jurisdictional foreign geographic names for places located in English-speaking countries are retained. The heading is inverted for English names, however, if the name begins with the article "The" as an integral part of the name.[18] Examples include:

El Dorado Lake (Kan.)
El Rancho Gumbo (Mont.)
Mall, The (Washington, D.C.)

Initial articles in non-jurisdictional geographic names for places located in non-English-speaking countries are omitted unless the initial article is *the* and forms an integral part of the name. In such cases, the heading is inverted:

Bierzo (Spain)
{not El Bierzo (Spain)}
Sound, The (Denmark and Sweden)
{not The Sound (Denmark and Sweden)}

In general, whenever the name of a natural feature begins with a generic term followed by a proper name in a later position, the inverted form is used. In such cases, the proper name is used as the entry word:

Berkeley, Vale of (England)
Blanc, Mont (France and Italy)
Dover, Strait of
Hood, Mount (Or.)
Mexico, Gulf of
Superior, Lake
Tiberias, Lake (Israel)

In a small number of cases in which a foreign-language generic term has little generic significance for most English-speaking users, and when the vernacular form is well known, the direct form is retained:

Costa del Sol (Spain)

Geographic names that contain adjectives indicating directions or parts, and that are not considered proper names, are generally inverted:

Africa, East
Africa, Central
Africa, North
Alps, Eastern
Asia, Central
Asia, Southeastern
California, Southern
Tennessee, East

However, the following examples show geographic names that are proper names in direct order:

Central America
East End (Long Island, N.Y.)
South China Sea
West Indies
East Asia
South Asia

Qualifiers[19]

For jurisdictional names, qualifiers are added to geographic names according to *AACR2R*. A parenthetical qualifier is frequently added to a geographic name to identify it more clearly or to distinguish it from another place or places with the same name. Qualifiers added to non-jurisdictional names are formulated in a way compatible with jurisdictional names where feasible.

For geographic names, three types of qualifiers are used: generic (e.g., **Lake George (N.Y.: <u>Lake</u>)**, geographic (e.g., **Saint-Dizier (France)**; **Athens**

(Ga.)), and type-of-jurisdiction (e.g., **New York (State)**; **Mexico (Viceroyalty)**). The qualifier is placed within parentheses after the name. If two or more types of qualifiers are required for a heading, they are enclosed within a single set of parentheses and separated by the sequence space-colon-space. Examples include:

Naples (Italy)
Naples (Kingdom)
Piedmont (Principality)
Savoy (Duchy)
Indian River (Fla. : Lagoon)
Union (Berks County, Pa. : Township)
Cape of Good Hope (South Africa : Cape)
Dolores River (Colo. and Utah)
Mackinac Island (Mich. : Island)

The name of a city used as a qualifier takes the form of the established heading for the city reformulated by (a) placing it within a single set of parentheses, (b) separating the city name from the name of its own larger qualifying jurisdiction with a comma, and (c) omitting any additional information that is part of the established heading for the city unless there is a conflict. Examples include:

Florence (Italy)	{form of main heading for city}
(Florence, Italy)	{form when used as qualifier}
Richmondville (N.Y.)	{form of main heading for city}
(Richmondville, N.Y.)	{form when used as qualifier}
Black Creek (Wis. : Village)	{form of main heading for city}
(Black Creek, Wis.)	{form when used as qualifier}

The following discussion treats current Library of Congress policies regarding different types of qualifiers for geographic headings: generic, geographic, and political or type-of-jurisdiction.

Generic Qualifiers

Many natural features contain generic terms as an integral part of their names, for example:

Mississippi River Valley
Rocky Mountains

When there are two or more geographic entities with the same name, and the conflict cannot be resolved by the geographic qualifiers, a generic qualifier is added in parentheses, even if it repeats a generic term in the place name, for example:

Baja California (Mexico : Peninsula)
Baja California (Mexico : State)
Baja California (Mexico : Territory)

Cold Lake (Alta.)
Cold Lake (Alta. : Lake)

Grand Island (N.Y. : Island)
Grand Island (N.Y. : Town)

Geographic Qualifiers

Geographic qualifiers for jurisdictional headings are formulated according to *AACR2R*. They are used when it is appropriate to add the name of a place to a heading as shown below.

Names used as geographic qualifiers include those of countries, regions, provinces, states, islands, counties, and cities. Names of continents are not used as qualifiers; nor are names of sections within cities (e.g., Brooklyn, Georgetown, etc.), except in cases of conflict.

The following discussion of geographic qualifiers for jurisdictional headings is based on *AACR2R* and on Library of Congress policies regarding options in *AACR2R*; the discussion of geographic qualifiers for non-jurisdictional headings is based on policies established by the Cataloging Policy and Support Office of the Library of Congress and published in *Subject Cataloging Manual: Subject Headings* and *Cataloging Service Bulletin.*

(1) *Geographic qualifiers for jurisdictional headings.* According to Rule 23.4 in *AACR2R*, the name of a larger place is added as a qualifier to the name of a place other than a country or, in certain cases, a state or province.[20] In general, all places below the national level require qualifiers, with the following exceptions to which *no* geographic qualifiers are added:

states of Australia, Malaysia, and the United States

provinces of Canada

Serbia and Montenegro

parts of the British Isles: England, the Republic of Ireland, Northern Ireland, Scotland, Wales, the Isle of Man, the Channel Islands

the city of Jerusalem

Vatican City

Examples include:

New South Wales
Vermont
Pinang
Ontario
Scotland
Jerusalem

In accordance with *AACR2R*, the qualifier, when required, is the name of a country, for example, **Paris (France)**; **Tokyo (Japan)**; **Rome (Italy)**; **Leipzig (Germany)**; **Seoul (Korea)**; **Hyesan-si (Korea)**. (Note that the qualifier **(Korea)** is used for places in both North and South Korea.)

However, there are a number of notable exceptions. As noted above, for places in the United States, Canada, Australia, Great Britain, Malaysia, Serbia and Montenegro, the primary qualifiers are the first-order political divisions of the appropriate countries; the same holds true for places located on certain islands or island groups. The types of qualifiers used with jurisdictional headings are listed below:

Heading Being Established	***Qualifier***
Cities, counties, etc.	
in United States	Name of state
in Canada	Name of province
in Australia	Name of state
in Northern Ireland	Northern Ireland
in Malaysia	Name of state
in Serbia and Montenegro	Name of republic
Cities in the British Isles (except Northern Ireland)	Name of region, or island area, or constituent country
All places below the national level on an island or island group[21] in countries other than those listed	Name of island or island group
All other places below the national level	Name of country

Appendix F of this book provides a list of qualifiers for exceptional countries. Examples of headings with geographic qualifiers include:

Aberdeen (Scotland)
Bourbon County (Ky.)
Cairo (Egypt)

Dorset (Vt. : Town)
Dorset (England)
Edinburgh (Scotland)
Georgetown (Washington, D.C.)
Kiev (Ukraine)
Nagasaki-ken (Japan)
Newcastle (N.S.W.)
{not Newcastle (Australia)}
North Holland (Netherlands)
Oxford (England)
Palma de Mallorca (Spain)
San Francisco (Calif.)
Belgrade (Serbia)
Budva (Montenegro)
Toronto (Ont.)
Washington (D.C.)

Note that the names of many of the first-order political jurisdictions and some of the countries are abbreviated according to *AACR2R* when used as primary qualifiers but are spelled out in full when used as main headings:

Minnesota {the state}
Duluth (Minn.)

Alberta {the province}
Edmonton (Alta.)

A list of first-order political divisions and their appropriate abbreviations appears in appendix F.

If the name of a larger place used as a qualifier has changed, the current name is used:

Kinshasa (Congo)
{not Kinshasa (Zaire)}

(2) *Geographic qualifiers for non-jurisdictional headings.* In general, the Library of Congress also follows *AACR2R* in establishing non-jurisdictional headings. However, there are a number of variations because of the unique nature of non-jurisdictional headings. The variations and situations not covered by *AACR2R* are discussed below.

(a) *Entities located wholly within a single country or first-order political division.* The qualifier used is the same as that used for jurisdictional headings, for example:

Atlantic Coast (Suriname)
Box Canyon Falls (Colo.)
Great Barrier Reef (Qld.)
Asama Mountain (Japan)
Lake District (England)
Tay River (Scotland)

(b) *Entities located in two jurisdictions.* For an entity located in two jurisdictions, the names of both are added as qualifiers. The names are added in alphabetical order unless the entity is located principally in one of the jurisdictions, which will then be the one listed first. For a river, however, the place of origin is always listed first:[22]

Everest, Mount (China and Nepal)
Neusiedler Lake (Austria and Hungary)
Wye, River (Wales and England)
Black Creek (N.M. and Ariz.)

This policy, however, does not apply to international bodies of water, which are not qualified unless there is a conflict:

Bering Strait
English Channel

(c) *Entities located in more than two jurisdictions.* For an entity that spreads over three or more jurisdictions, no qualifier is added unless there is a conflict or the name is ambiguous, for example:

Appalachian Region
Gaza Strip
Caribbean Sea
Amazon River
West (U.S.)

(d) *Conflicts between geographic entities.* In cases of conflicts between headings representing the same type of geographic entity, one or more narrower jurisdictions are added, followed by a comma, before the regular qualifier within the same set of parentheses, for example:

Pelican Lake (Otter Tail County, Minn.)
Pelican Lake (Saint Louis County, Minn.)

Rio Negro (Amazonas, Brazil)
Rio Negro (Brazil and Uruguay)

If the conflict involves a river located in more than two jurisdictions, a qualifier containing the name of the jurisdiction in which the river originates and the name of the jurisdiction where the mouth is located is added. In this case, the two names are joined with a hyphen instead of with *and:*

Paraná River (Brazil-Argentina)
Paraná River (Goiás, Brazil)

Red River (Tex.-La.)
Red River (China and Vietnam)

If the conflict exists between headings representing different types of geographic entities, a generic qualifier is added after the regular qualifier in the same set of parentheses and separated by the sequence space-colon-space:

Mecklenburg (Germany : Castle)
Mecklenburg (Germany : Region)

Cape of Good Hope (South Africa) {the city}
Cape of Good Hope (South Africa : Cape)

(e) *Individual non-jurisdictional islands or island groups.*[23] Individual non-jurisdictional islands or island groups that lie near a land mass and are under its jurisdiction, as well as individual islands that form part of a jurisdictional island cluster, are qualified by the name of the country or first-order political division:

Aegina Island (Greece)
Elizabeth Islands (Mass.)
Hawaii Island (Hawaii)
Izu Islands (Japan)
Nantucket Island (Mass.)
Santa Catalina Island (Calif.)
{not Santa Catalina Island (Channel Islands, Calif.)}

The name of the city is used as the qualifier if the island is a city section or if the city name is needed to resolve a conflict, for example:

Ile de la Cité (Paris, France)

If the island does not lie near its controlling jurisdiction, but is part of an island group, the name of the island group is used as the qualifier, for example:

Palma (Canary Islands)
Madeira (Madeira Islands)

Pulap Island (Micronesia)
Rota Island (Northern Mariana Islands)
Shortland Islands (Solomon Islands)

Qualifiers are not used with isolated islands or island groups that are not associated with a mainland country, or with islands that comprise more than one autonomous jurisdiction:

Borneo
Islands of the Pacific
Midway Islands

(f) *Natural features within cities.* Lakes, hills, etc., located within cities are qualified by the name of the larger jurisdiction rather than by the name of the city, except in cases of conflict, for example:

Corpus Christi, Lake (Tex.)
West Lake (China)

(g) *Other entities within cities.* For headings of city districts, quarters, sections, and other entities located within a city (such as buildings, parks, streets, plazas, bridges, monuments, etc.), see discussion and examples later in this chapter.

(h) *Entities on islands.* Headings for entities on islands are qualified by the name of the island established either as a jurisdictional or non-jurisdictional heading:

Lincoln Downs Brook (R.I.)
Hellshire Hills (Jamaica)
Teide, Pico de (Tenerife, Canary Islands)
Werner Mountain (Greenland)

Headings for entities on islands in Hawaii, Japan, or New Zealand are qualified by **(Hawaii)**, **(Japan)**, or **(N.Z.)**, instead of the names of the individual islands, which are used only in cases of conflict. Examples include:

Kaneohe Bay (Hawaii)
Fuji, Mount (Japan)
Taupo, Lake (N.Z.)
Kailua Bay (Hawaii Island, Hawaii)
Kailua Bay (Oahu, Hawaii)

(i) *Other qualifiers.* Places in Antarctica are qualified by **(Antarctica)**, and places on the moon are qualified by **(Moon)**, for example:

Transantarctic Mountains (Antarctica)
Victoria Land (Antarctica)
Mare Crisium (Moon)

Type-of-Jurisdiction Qualifiers

When two or more places belonging to different types of jurisdictions bear the same name, a qualifier indicating the type of jurisdiction is added in accordance with *AACR2R.* The type-of-jurisdiction qualifier follows the geographic qualifier if there is one. Since headings for all modern cities now carry geographic qualifiers, the qualifier *(City)* used with some of the pre-1981 headings, for example, *New York (City)*; *Rome (City)*, is no longer used. The type-of-jurisdiction qualifier is usually an English term, if available. The vernacular term is used when there is no equivalent in English. Examples include:

Québec (Province)
Québec (Québec)

Naples (Italy)
Naples (Kingdom)

Poznán (Poland : Voivodeship)
Poznán (Poland)

The type-of-jurisdiction qualifier is omitted when the name of the jurisdiction itself is used as a qualifier:

Washington (State) {form of heading}
(Wash.) {form when used as qualifier}

Micronesia (Federated States) {form of heading}
(Micronesia) {form when used as qualifier}

Arequipa (Peru : Dept.) {form of heading}
(Arequipa, Peru) {form when used as qualifier}

Free-Floating Phrase Headings Involving Names of Places

A number of free-floating terms and phrases may be combined with certain types of geographic names to form valid headings. The term "free-floating" means that a word or phrase may be combined with a valid main heading without its usage being formally authorized. Headings resulting from free-floating combinations generally do not appear in LCSH.

(1) *Geographic regions.* The word **Region** may be added on a free-floating basis to a valid heading for a geographic feature (including parks, roads, mines, etc., but not islands, river valleys, or watersheds) to form the heading for a region:[24]

Geographic heading	*Heading for region*
Caspian Sea	**Caspian Sea Region**
Death Valley (Calif. and Nev.)	**Death Valley Region (Calif and Nev.)**
Mammoth Cave National Park Region (Ky.)	**Mammoth Cave National Park Region (Ky.)**
Rocky Mountain National Park (Colo.)	**Rocky Mountain National Park Region (Colo.)**

Regions that are well known by alternative name forms, as well as those having unique names, are established under those names instead of names constructed as above:

Caribbean Area
{not *Caribbean Sea Region*}
Mediterranean Region
{not *Mediterranean Sea Region*}
Sierra Nevada Region (Calif. and Nev.)
{not *Sierra Nevada Mountains Region (Calif. and Nev.)*}
Black Country (England)
Midlands (England)
Innviertel (Austria)
Texas Hill Country (Tex.)

When the name of a region in a country or first order political division consists of a directional qualifier such as "eastern" or "southern," and the name of the country or division, the geographic qualifier is omitted:

Italy, Southern
California, Southern

The terms *Watershed*, *Delta*, and *Estuary* were previously free-floating. Their use as free-floating elements has been discontinued; all headings for watersheds, deltas, and estuaries are now established and displayed in *LCSH*, for example:

Potomac River Estuary
Po River Delta (Italy)
Chesapeake Bay Watershed
Madison River Watershed (Wyo. and Mont.)

(2) *River regions*. A river region differs from a river in that the region includes the drainage basin and other adjacent territories beyond the basin. Headings for river regions[25] or watershed regions are formed by adding the free-floating term **...Region** to the river name, rather than the name of the valley or watershed, for example:

Danube River Region
{not *Danube River Valley Region* or *Danube River Watershed Region*}
Potomac River Region
{not *Potomac River Valley Region* or *Potomac River Watershed Region*}

(3) *Valley regions.* Headings for valley regions[26] not associated with a river are formed by adding the free-floating term **...Region** to the name of the valley, for example:

Death Valley (Calif. and Nev.)
Death Valley Region (Calif. and Nev.)

(4) *Metropolitan areas and city regions.* These are discussed in the section "Areas Associated with Cities" below.

Changes of Name

Names of places change frequently. Library of Congress policy requires that only the latest name of a political jurisdiction that has one or more earlier names be used in subject headings. In such cases, a decision must be made about which name to use as a subject heading. There are two types of changes, linear name changes and mergers and/or splits. Following is a discussion of Library of Congress policies regarding changes of names used in subject cataloging.

Linear Name Changes[27]

When the name change of a country, state, city, etc., does not affect its territorial identity, all new subject entries are made under the new name—with *USE* reference(s) from earlier name(s)—regardless of the period covered by the works being cataloged, and all subject entries under the old name are changed to the new name. Examples of linear name changes include:

Former name(s)	*Latest name*
Gold Coast	**Ghana**
British Honduras	**Belize**
Ceylon	**Sri Lanka**
Northern Rhodesia	**Zambia**
Southern Rhodesia	**Zimbabwe**

While both the earlier and later names are used as valid headings for main entries and added entries in descriptive cataloging, only the latest name is used in subject entries, both as a main heading and as a geographic qualifier, for example, **Boma (Congo)** instead of *Boma (Zaire)*.[28]

The practice of using a uniform heading as the subject entry for a place regardless of name changes has the advantage of collocating material about a particular place. The policy is, however, at variance with descriptive cataloging practice, as *AACR2R* specifies successive entries rather than a uniform heading for works issued under different names of a government.

Merger and/or Split[29]

When the change of name involves substantial territorial changes as a result of mergers or splits, various headings are assigned depending on the area and the time period covered in the item. The general policy is to assign headings corresponding to the physical extent of the area discussed in the work being cataloged.

Mergers

When two or more jurisdictions undergo mergers, headings for both the premerger jurisdictions and the postmerger jurisdiction may be used as subject headings. The subject headings assigned to works involving places that have undergone mergers depend on the time period covered (i.e., prior to or after the merger) and whether the area discussed in the work corresponds to the *pre*- or *postmerger* jurisdiction.

An example of a merger is the joining of the Territory of Papua and the Territory of New Guinea, in 1945, to form the administrative unit of the Territory of Papua and New Guinea, which became self-governing in 1973 under the name Papua-New Guinea. The following headings are assigned to works about this place as appropriate:

Papua
New Guinea (Territory)
Papua New Guinea

Splits

When a jurisdiction undergoes a split, headings for both the *presplit* jurisdiction and the *postsplit* jurisdictions may be used as subject headings. The subject headings assigned to works involving places that have undergone a split depend on the area and time period covered in the work being cataloged, and on whether the name of the earlier jurisdiction is retained by the later jurisdiction.

An example of a split is the two Koreas:

Korea
Korea (North)
Korea (South)

An example of a split and merger is Germany:[30]

Germany
Germany (East)
Germany (West)
Germany

Geographic Headings Requiring Special Treatment

Some types of geographic headings are given special treatment because of their unique nature. These include names of ancient or early cities and of archaeological sites; areas associated with cities; entities within cities; parks, reserves, etc.; and other man-made structures associated with places.

Extinct Cities and Archaeological Sites[31]

Previously, the names of ancient or early cities and of archaeological sites were not listed in LCSH. However, since 1976, newly established headings in this category have been included in LCSH. Because cities that went out of existence before the creation of modern states (ca. AD 1500) are rarely required for descriptive cataloging, these headings are generally established as subject headings. If there is evidence that the exact original site of the ancient or early city has been continuously or recurrently occupied up until modern times, however, the heading established for the modern city is used, for example:

London (England) {instead of *Londinium*}
Vienna (Austria) {instead of *Vindobona*}

General guidelines for establishing ancient or early cities that no longer exist are described below.

(1) Use the form of the name most commonly found in standard reference sources (encyclopedias, gazetteers, etc.).

(2) Add the qualifier **(Extinct city)** to a city in Europe, Africa, or Asia if it existed only before medieval times. Examples include **Pompeii (Extinct city)** and **Troy (Extinct city)**. The name of the larger jurisdiction in which the city would be located today is added if there are two or more cities by the same name, for example, **Thebes (Egypt : Extinct city)** and **Thebes (Greece)**.

Cities of the Americas that ceased to exist by 1500 are treated as archaeological sites, for example, **Chichén Itzá Site (Mexico)**.

(3) When the name of an extinct city is used as a qualifier for another heading, the qualifier **(Extinct city)** is omitted, for example:

Angkor (Extinct city)	{heading for city}
Angkor Wat (Angkor)	{form used as qualifier}
Memphis (Extinct city)	{heading for city}
Temple of Hathor (Memphis)	{form used as qualifier}

(4) For an archaeological site, the heading is established on the basis of the work being cataloged. The term **Site** and the appropriate geographic qualifier are added to the name. Examples include:

Cobá Site (Mexico)
Copan Site (Honduras)
Duke I Site (Tenn.)
Fourth of July Valley Site (Colo.)
Masada Site (Israel)

If the site is located in a modern city, the name of the city is used as the qualifier, for example:

Roman Forum Site (London, England)
Lewis-Weber Site (Tucson, Ariz.)
Kami Site (Osaka, Japan)

If the site is a named cave or mound, the name of the cave or mound is used as the site name, for example:

Texcal Cave (Mexico)
Shanidar Cave (Iraq)

Areas Associated with Cities[32]

There are four kinds of headings that designate the various areas associated with an individual city, as shown in these examples based on Chicago:

Chicago (Ill.)
Chicago Metropolitan Area (Ill.)
Chicago Suburban Area (Ill.)
Chicago Region (Ill.)

In terms of territory, these four types of headings have been defined as follows:

(1) **[City name]**: the city jurisdiction itself.

(2) **[City] Metropolitan Area**: a designated area consisting of the city itself and those densely populated territories immediately surrounding it that are socially and economically integrated with it.

(3) **[City] Suburban Area**: the territory associated with the city, including neighboring residential areas lying outside the city and nearby smaller satellite jurisdictions, but not the city itself.

(4) **[City] Region**: an area including the city itself and its surrounding territory, the exact size and boundaries of which are indefinite and may vary according to the work being cataloged.

The phrases **Metropolitan Area**, **Suburban Area**, and **Region** are free-floating; they may he combined with the name of a city and its qualifier to form valid headings. Headings for metropolitan and suburban areas and city regions are qualified in the same manner as cities, for example:

Boston Suburban Area (Mass.)
Pensacola Metropolitan Area (Fla.)
Montréal Metropolitan Area (Québec)
Binghamton Metropolitan Area (N.Y.)
{not Binghamton Metropolitan Area (N.Y. and Pa.)}.
Binghamton Region (N.Y.)
Jerusalem Region

Metropolitan and suburban areas and regions associated with the cities of Washington, D.C., and New York are not qualified even though the headings for the cities are, thus:

New York Metropolitan Area
Washington Suburban Area

A metropolitan or suburban area, or a region involving two cities, is represented by two separate headings, for example:

Dallas Metropolitan Area (Tex.)
Fort Worth Metropolitan Area (Tex.)
{not Dallas-Fort Worth Metropolitan Area (Tex.)}

Names of metropolitan and suburban areas and city regions may be used as main headings or subdivisions.

Entities Within Cities[33]

Headings for districts, quarters, sections, and other man-made structures located within a city, such as buildings, streets, plazas, parks, bridges, monuments, etc., consist of the name of the entity qualified by the name of the city.

The heading for the entity is normally in the vernacular form of the country in which it is located, except for pre-1500 buildings and for structures that have well-established English names. The name of the entity is qualified by the name of the city, and the name of a borough, city section, or city district is included in the qualifier only if it is necessary to resolve a conflict between entities with identical names located in the same city. Examples include:

2040 Union Street (San Francisco, Calif.)
Adams National Historical Park (Quincy, Mass.)
Balboa Park (San Diego, Calif.)
Boulevard du Temple (Paris, France)
Brooklyn (New York, N.Y.)
Brooklyn Bridge (New York, N.Y.)
Disneyland Paris (Marne-la-Vallée, France)
Edinburgh Castle (Edinburgh, Scotland)
Fontana di Trevi (Rome, Italy)
Forbidden City (Beijing, China)
Fort Worth Water Garden (Fort Worth, Tex.)
Gateway Arch (Saint Louis, Mo.)
Glaspalast (Munich, Germany)
Golden Gate Bridge (San Francisco, Calif.)
Hauptbahnhof (Hamburg, Germany)
Hôtel de ville (Lausanne, Switzerland)
Hôtel de ville (Lyon, France)
Jaffa Gate (Jerusalem)
Library of Congress James Madison Memorial Building (Washington, D.C.)
Los Angeles Theatre (Los Angeles, Calif.)
Mount Clare (Baltimore, Md. : Building)
Park Avenue (New York, N.Y.)
Pont-Neuf (Paris, France)
Promenade du Peyrou (Montpellier, France)
Residenzschloss (Weimar, Thuringia, Germany)
Roman Forum (Rome, Italy)
Stalag 12 D (Trier, Germany : Concentration camp)
Sunset Boulevard (Los Angeles, Calif.)
Times Square (New York, N.Y.)
Western Wall (Jerusalem)
Yankee Stadium (New York, N.Y.)
Yihe Yuan (Beijing, China)

Details of buildings that bear proper names are represented by headings in the form **[Name of detail] ([Name of structure])**, for example:

Hyman Liberman Memorial Door (South African National Gallery)
Saito (Yakushiji, Nara-shi, Japan)

The names of city sections and districts may be used as main headings, but they are not used as geographic subdivisions. They are used as qualifiers only if necessary to resolve a conflict between entities with identical names located in the same city.

Parks, Reserves, Etc.

At the Library of Congress, the following types of entities are established as non-jurisdictional headings:

- public and private parks of all kinds
- nature conservation areas, natural areas, natural history reservations, nature reserves
- wild areas, wilderness areas, roadless areas
- forests forest reserves and preserves
- seashores, marine parks and reserves, wild and scenic rivers
- wildlife refuges, bird reservations and sanctuaries, game ranges and preserves. wildlife management areas
- historic sites, national monuments, etc.
- trails

Headings for individual parks, reserves, etc., including those located within cities, consist of the names of the entities with appropriate geographic qualifiers. Examples of headings for individual parks, reserves, etc., include:

Bandelier National Monument (N.M.)
Hiawatha National Forest (Mich.)
Ice Age National Scientific Reserve (Wis.)
Mount Saint Helens National Volcanic Monument (Wash.)
Naturpark Hohe Mark (Germany)
North York Moors National Park (England)
Palos Forest Preserve (Ill.)
Spruce Knob-Seneca Rocks National Recreation Area (W. Va.)
Central Park (New York, N.Y.)

Other Man-Made Structures Associated with Places Larger Than a City

Other man-made structures include physical plants, roads, bridges, monuments, etc., that are not located within a particular city. They are normally entered directly under their own names, with the addition of geographic and/or generic qualifiers as appropriate (see discussion of geographic qualifiers earlier in this chapter). Examples include:

Balmoral Castle (Scotland)
Battle Road (Mass.)
Blenheim Palace (England)
EPCOT Center (Fla.)
Great Point Light (Mass.)
Great Pyramid (Egypt)
Great Wall of China (China)
Harry S. Truman Reservoir (Mo.)
Hearst-San Simeon State Historical Monument (Calif.)
Hoover Dam (Ariz. and Nev.)
Mount Vernon (Va. : Estate)
Overland Telegraph Line (N.T. and S. Aust.)
Sturgeon Fort (Sask.)
Three Mile Island Nuclear Power Plant (Pa.)

NOTES

1. For a list of such entities, consult Library of Congress, Cataloging Policy and Support Office, *Subject Cataloging Manual: Subject Headings*, 5th ed., 2000 cumulation (Washington, D.C.: Library of Congress, 2000), H405.

2. *Anglo-American Cataloguing Rules*, 2nd ed., 2002 rev., prepared under the direction of the Joint Steering Committee for Revision of AACR, a committee of: the American Library Association, the Australian Committee on Cataloguing, the British Library, the Canadian Committee on Cataloguing, Chartered Institute of Library and Information Professionals, the Library of Congress (Chicago: American Library Association, 2002).

3. Categories of unprinted headings are listed in chapter 8.

4. Charles A. Cutter, *Rules for a Dictionary Catalog*, 4th ed. (Washington, D.C.: Government Printing Office, 1904), 69.

5. Library of Congress, *Subject Cataloging Manual*, H1636.

6. *Library of Congress Rule Interpretations*, 2nd ed., [editor, Robert M. Hiatt ; formulated by the Office for Descriptive Cataloging Policy, Library of Congress], (Washington, D.C. : Cataloging Distribution Service, Library of Congress, 1989-)

7. For the assignment of subject headings to works about a corporate body, see chapter 9.

8. Library of Congress, *Subject Cataloging Manual*, H1332.

9. For instruction concerning the forms of headings for strikes, consult the note under the heading **Strikes and lockouts** in LCSH.

10. Library of Congress, *Subject Cataloging Manual*, H1919.5.

11. Library of Congress, *Subject Cataloging Manual,* H690-H1055.

12. The formations **Berlin (Germany : East)** and **Berlin (Germany : West)** are used only as parts of headings for corporate bodies located in the former East or West Berlin, for example, **Berlin (Germany : East). Magistrat; Berlin (Germany : West). Landesausgleichsamt.**

13. Library of Congress, *Subject Cataloging Manual*, H690.

14. *Library of Congress Rule Interpretations.*

15. Library of Congress, *Subject Cataloging Manual*, H690.

16. Library of Congress, *Subject Cataloging Manual*, H690.

17. Library of Congress, *Subject Cataloging Manual*, H690.

18. Library of Congress, *Subject Cataloging Manual*, H690.

19. Library of Congress, *Subject Cataloging Manual*, H810.

20. *Anglo-American Cataloguing Rules*; chap. 23, 3-6.

21. Library of Congress, *Subject Cataloging Manual*, H807.

22. Library of Congress, *Subject Cataloging Manual*, H800.

23. Library of Congress, *Subject Cataloging Manual*, H807; H810, pp. 5-6.

24. Library of Congress, *Subject Cataloging Manual*, H760.

25. Library of Congress, *Subject Cataloging Manual*, H800, p. 7.

26. Library of Congress, *Subject Cataloging Manual*, H800, p. 8.

27. Library of Congress, *Subject Cataloging Manual*, H708.

28. Information concerning such subject cataloging usage is carried in field 667 in the MARC 21 format for authority records.

29. Library of Congress, *Subject Cataloging Manual*, H710.

30. Library of Congress, *Subject Cataloging Manual*, H945.

31. Library of Congress, *Subject Cataloging Manual*, H715, H1225.

32. Library of Congress, *Subject Cataloging Manual*, H790.

33. Library of Congress, *Subject Cataloging Manual*, H720, H1334.

5 Subdivisions

INTRODUCTION

In the Library of Congress subject headings system, a main heading may be subdivided by one or more elements called *subdivisions*. The concept embodied in the subdivision usually reflects a secondary emphasis with relation to the topic of the main heading.[1] Subdivisions are used extensively to subarrange a large file or to bring out aspects of a topic.

The decision as to whether to subdivide a subject depends to a large extent on one's perception of the purpose of subdivision. If subdivision is used solely as a means of subarrangement, as David Judson Haykin believed,[2] it is called for only if there is a substantial amount of material on a subject. But if subdivision is used for the purpose of rendering a heading more specific, which is by and large the current philosophy of the Library of Congress, a heading is subdivided whenever documents that focus on a specific aspect of the subject exist in the collection. In other words, the decision is based on literary warrant. The subdivided heading thus serves to maintain coextensivity between the heading and the document, as stated in the current policy: "Assign subdivisions to reflect the contents of the work without regard to the size of the file under the basic heading."[3]

There are four types of subdivisions in the Library of Congress subject headings system: topical, geographic, chronological, and form. Topical subdivisions have always been used to achieve specificity as well as to provide for subarrangement. Current policy requires the use of form subdivisions when applicable and appropriate. On the other hand, chronological subdivisions are still used mainly as a device for subarranging large files. As a result, many subjects, such as **Satire, English**, are not subdivided by period, even though they lend themselves to chronological treatment. Likewise, the histories of many small countries or principalities, for example, **Liechtenstein** and **Monaco**, are not divided chronologically. In the past, geographic subdivisions were also used mainly as a means of subarrangement. This is why some headings are still not subdivided by place even though library materials on the subject limited to a certain locality exist. Recent years witnessed a trend toward greater use of geographic subdivision even where the size of the file would not require it; the criterion followed now is suitability of geographic qualification to the literature of the subject.

TOPICAL SUBDIVISION

A topical subdivision represents an aspect of the main heading other than space, time, or form. Examples of topical subdivisions are:

Auditing–Standards
Cats–Behavior therapy
France–Foreign relations
Geology–Mathematics
Venice (Italy)–Buildings, structures, etc.

In general, topical subdivisions are not used to bring out hierarchically related topics, that is those representing *genus–species, class–subclass,* or *whole–part* relationships. In LCSH, with few exceptions, topical subdivisions bring out aspects dealing with objects, processes, actions, and properties relating to the main heading. For example, the relationship between the main heading and the topical subdivision in headings such as **Heart–Diseases** or **Agriculture–Taxation** is not that of genus–species or whole–part type. Haykin notes: "CONSTRUCTION INDUSTRY–TAXATION is another way of saying 'taxation of the construction industry', and obviously not 'taxation as a division of the subject CONSTRUCTION INDUSTRY'."[4] He states that topical subdivision is used "only where the broad subject forms part of the name of the topic and a convenient phrase form sanctioned by usage is lacking, or, for the purpose of the catalog, where it is desirable to conform to an existing pattern."[5] For example, *legal research* is a commonly accepted phrase, while *physical research* is not. Therefore, the headings that were established for these subjects are **Legal research** and **Physics–Research**. However, in order to ensure greater uniformity, current policy requires the use of the form **[Topic]–Research** for newly established headings.

In LCSH, topical subdivisions are most often used to bring out aspects or facets of the main subject, such as concepts, methods, or techniques,[6] rather than to indicate its kinds or parts. Nonetheless, a small number of headings characteristic of classed entries have been introduced into the list. The following example is of the genus–species type:

Shakespeare, William, 1564-1616–Characters–Children

In this example, the genus–species relationship occurs between the subdivision and the sub-subdivision. While these headings bring together all types of characterization in Shakespeare's works, the practice results in inconsistency because this form is not used regularly with similar or related headings, for example:

Children in literature
{not Literature–Characters–Children}

In the example above, the principle of specific entry is observed.

There are also a small number of headings of the whole-part type, for example:

Airplanes–Motors–Carburetors
Airplanes–Motors–Mufflers
Airplanes–Wings

The purpose of this form is subject collocation, that is, the grouping of different parts of an airplane together. Again, there is the problem of maintaining consistency and predictability in similar headings. Although **Motors** and **Wings** are entered as subdivisions under **Airplanes**, other parts of the airplane are entered in the direct form: **Ailerons**; **Flaps (Airplanes)**; **Tabs (Airplanes)**. Fortunately, references are made from the forms not used, and the user is guided to the forms used:

Aircraft carburetors
USE **Airplanes–Motors–Carburetors**

Airplanes–Flaps
USE **Flaps (Airplanes)**

GEOGRAPHIC SUBDIVISION

Many subjects lend themselves to geographic treatment. When the geographic aspect of the subject is of significance, geographic (also called place or local) subdivisions are often used.

In LCSH, not all headings may be subdivided geographically; the designation *(May Subd Geog)* following a heading is used to indicate that the heading may be subdivided by place. Previously, only topics that lent themselves particularly well to geographic treatment and those headings under which there was a large file of material could be so divided. Current policy allows a greater degree of geographic subdivision; all newly established headings for subjects that can be treated from a geographic point of view are subdivisible by place. The designation *(Not Subd Geog)* follows headings on which the Library of Congress has made a decision not to subdivide by place, for example, **Applegate family** *(Not Subd Geog)*. Headings without either designation are currently not subdivided by place but may be so in the future.

For a given place, when the inverted form is used in the main heading, the same form is generally used when the place appears as a subdivision under other headings:

Asia, Southeastern–Economic conditions
Social service–Asia, Southeastern
Africa, Northeast–Strategic aspects
United States–Relations–Africa, Northeast

There are two forms of geographic subdivision: direct and indirect. In direct geographic subdivision, the name of the place in question immediately follows a topical main heading or topical subdivision, for example, **Art–California**. In indirect geographic subdivision—the form used with local places—the name of a larger geographic place is interposed between the topical element and the local place in question, for example, **Art–France–Normandy**. With the exception of Antarctic regions and the names of certain island groups, no geographical name higher than the level of a country is used as an interposing element, and none below the level of a city is used as a geographic subdivision. Furthermore, no geographic subdivision may contain more than two levels of geographic elements, for example:

Music–Europe
Music–Germany
{not *Music–Europe–Germany*}

Music–Germany–Bavaria
Music–Germany–Munich
{not *Music–Germany–Bavaria–Munich*}

The following sections discuss direct and indirect geographic subdivision in detail. The procedures described below represent current Library of Congress policy regarding geographic subdivision.[7]

Direct Subdivision

If the place in the geographic subdivision is at the country level or above, the name of the place follows the main heading or main heading–topical subdivision combination immediately, for example:

Benedictine nuns–Europe
Catholic Church–Belgium
Economic stabilization–Middle East
Geology–Antarctica
Monarchy–Great Britain
Peace Corps (U.S.)–Ghana
Post-communism–Former Soviet republics
Soil chemistry–Arctic regions
Teachers–Training of–United States

In addition, the types of places listed below also follow the topical element directly:

(1) the first-order political divisions of the following three countries:[8]

Country	*First-order divisions*	*Examples*
Canada	provinces	**Ontario**; **Alberta**
Great Britain	constituent countries	**England**; **Scotland**
United States	states	**Alaska**; **Montana**

For a complete list of the first-order political divisions of these countries, see appendix F. Examples of headings with direct geographic subdivisions include:

Agricultural administration–Alberta
Castles–Scotland
Palaces–England
Architecture–Massachusetts
Glaciers–Alaska

(2) places located in more than a single country (or in more than one first-order political division of the three exceptional countries listed above), including:

places located in the three exceptional countries noted above, for example, **Southern States**; **New England**

historical kingdoms, empires, etc., for example, **Holy Roman Empire**

geographic features and regions, such as continents and other major regions, bodies of water, mountain ranges, etc., for example, **Europe**; **Great Lakes**; **West (U.S.)**; **Mexico, Gulf of**; **Rocky Mountains**; **Nile River Valley**

In such cases, any geographic qualifier normally accompanying the name is retained. For a discussion of qualifiers for geographic names, see chapter 4. Examples include:

Earth movements–Sierra Nevada (Calif. and Nev.)
Oceanography–Baltic Sea
Art–Mediterranean Region

(3) the cities[9] Washington, D.C., and Jerusalem, for example:

Education–Washington Metropolitan Area
Historic buildings–Washington (D.C.)
Armenians–Jerusalem

Vatican City[10] is also used without interposing elements, for example:

Christian art and symbolism–Vatican City

(4) Islands or island groups[11] of the following types:

(a) Islands or island groups located some distance away from the controlling jurisdiction, for example:

Crabs–Easter Island
Meteorology–Falkland Islands
Mollusks–Galapagos Islands

(b) Islands or island groups that are autonomous or comprise more than one autonomous jurisdiction, for example:

Zoology–Borneo
Natural history–Hispaniola
Botany–Islands of the Pacific

(c) Names of individual Caribbean islands south of the Virgin Islands. These islands are assigned directly after the heading regardless of their present political status, the reason being that most individual Caribbean islands can be associated with several different island groups and that most of these islands have achieved independence or are likely to do so in the future. Examples of such headings include:

Ethnology–Grenada
{not *Ethnology–West Indies–Grenada*}
Marine algae–Bonaire
{not *Marine algae–Netherlands Antilles–Bonaire*}

All other places below the country level are entered indirectly.

Indirect Subdivision

When a heading is subdivided by a place within a country, the name of the relevant country or of the first-order political division (in Canada, Great Britain, or the United States) is interposed between the subject heading and the name of any subordinate political, administrative, or geographical division. Although the interposition of the name of the larger geographic entity renders the heading a blatantly classed entry, the benefit of collocating materials relating to the larger area has been considered important enough by the Library of Congress to suspend the principle of specific and direct entry.

General Procedure for Indirect Subdivision

Places below the national level are normally assigned indirectly. With the exceptions noted above, a heading is subdivided locally by interposing the name of the country between the heading and the name of any geographic entity contained wholly within the country. These geographic entities include:

- subordinate political jurisdictions, such as provinces, districts, counties, cities, etc.
- historic kingdoms, principalities, etc.
- geographic features and regions, such as mountain ranges, bodies of water, lake regions, watersheds, metropolitan areas, etc.
- islands situated within the territorial limits of the country in question

Examples:

Agriculture–Brazil–Paraná (State)
Architecture–Belgium–Flanders
Architecture, Gothic–Germany–Bavaria
Elephants–Tunisia–Carthage (Extinct city)
Excavations (Archaeology)–Greece–Athens
Geology–Turkey–Taurus Mountains
Spanish language–Dialects–Spain–Leon (Kingdom)
Upper class–France–Aix-en-Provence

The local place name used in an indirect subdivision is not qualified by the name of a larger geographic entity if the qualifier (abbreviated or spelled out) is the same as the interposing element:

Paris (France)
Art–France–Paris
{not *Art–France–Paris (France)*}

Vienna (Austria)
Music–Austria–Vienna

Okeechobee, Lake (Fla.)
Eutrophication–Florida–Okeechobee, Lake
{not *Eutrophication–Florida–Okeechobee, Lake (Fla.)*}

Chicago Suburban Area (Ill.)
Reference services (Libraries)–Illinois–Chicago Suburban Area

If the geographic entity in question is below the level of a first-order political division of Canada, Great Britain, or the United States, it is entered as a sub-subdivision under the name of the first-order political division. In other words, the names of the first-order political divisions instead of the names of the countries are used as interposing elements:

Architecture–British Columbia–Vancouver
Architecture–England–Cambridge
Art, American–Illinois–Chicago
Cliff-dwellings–Colorado–Mesa Verde National Park

If the name of the local place is in the form of the name of the country (or the name of a first-order political division in Canada, Great Britain, or the United States) followed by an adjectival qualifier, no interposing element is required:

Nutrition surveys–Italy, Southern
{not *Nutrition surveys–Italy–Italy, Southern*}

Hot tubs–California, Southern
{not *Hot tubs–California–California, Southern*}

It should be noted that, for Canada, Great Britain, and the United States, the first-order political divisions used in indirect subdivision represent the same geographic level as the qualifiers used in establishing geographic headings according to the current *Anglo-American Cataloguing Rules* (*AACR2R*):

Vancouver (B.C.)–Buildings, structures, etc.
Architecture–British Columbia–Vancouver

Cambridge (England)–Social conditions
Social classes–England–Cambridge

It may therefore appear that *AACR2R* governs subject cataloging policies for indirect subdivision. This is in fact not the case; the coincidence is limited to the three countries just mentioned. This fact should be borne in mind particularly in dealing with places in Australia, Malaysia, and Serbia and Montenegro; places within these countries are assigned through the names of the countries rather than through the first-order political divisions, for example:

Kosovo (Serbia)–Ethnic relations
Albanians–Serbia and Montenegro–Kosovo (Serbia)–History

Sydney (N.S.W.)–Buildings, structures, etc.
Architecture–Australia–Sydney (N.S.W.)

In the examples above, the qualifiers **(Serbia)** and **(N.S.W.)** are retained in the local subdivisions because they differ from the interposing elements.

In the case of a single island that is part of an island group located some distance away from its controlling jurisdiction, the name of the island group of which it is a part is interposed, for example:

Water-supply–Canary Islands–Tenerife

An island that is part of a jurisdiction is divided indirectly through the country or first-order political division,[12] for example:

Beaches–New York (State)–Long Island

When areas associated with cities are used as geographic subdivisions, they are assigned indirectly (with the exceptions noted below) through the jurisdiction in which the city proper is located, even if the area or region spreads over more than one jurisdiction, for example, **Minorities–Missouri–Saint Louis Metropolitan Area**. By way of exception, areas and regions associated with New York City, Washington, D.C., and Jerusalem are used as direct subdivisions, for example, **Minorities–New York Metropolitan Area**; **Minorities–Washington Suburban Area**; **Minorities–Jerusalem Region**.

No level lower than that of a city or town is used in an indirect subdivision.[13] Thus, *Tourist trade–California–Chinatown (San Francisco)* is not a valid heading. Such a topic can, however, be expressed by assigning two headings, such as **Tourism–California–San Francisco** and **Chinatown (San Francisco, Calif)**.

Changes of Name or Jurisdiction

As discussed in chapter 4, when the name of the place in question has changed during the course of its existence, the latest name is always used in the heading, regardless of the form of the name or period covered in the work being cataloged. For example, as a subject heading or geographic subdivision, **Zimbabwe** is used instead of *Southern Rhodesia*.

If a region or jurisdiction has existed under various sovereignties in its history, the name of the country currently in possession of the place is interposed, regardless of past territorial arrangements described in the work cataloged, as long as the region or jurisdiction is now wholly contained in that country:

Title: *Constructing class and nationality in Alsace, 1830-1945* / David Allen Harvey. 2001.
SUBJECTS:
Working class–France–Alsace–History.
Group identity–France–Alsace–History.

Extinct cities are assigned indirectly through the appropriate modern jurisdiction, for example:

Excavations (Archaeology)–Turkey–Troy (Extinct city)

Summary of Procedures for Geographic Subdivision

Because of the complexity of geographic subdivision, the following summary of guidelines for direct and indirect geographic subdivision may be helpful.

(1) Direct subdivision

(a) Countries or places not wholly within a country

–France; **–Europe**; **–Himalaya Mountains**;
–Andes Region; **–Bering Sea**; **–Pacific Ocean**

(b) Place in two or more countries

–Gobi Desert (Mongolia and China)

(c) First-order political divisions (provinces, constituent countries, and states) in Canada, Great Britain, and the United States

–British Columbia; **–Scotland**; **–Illinois**

(d) Places in two or more first order political divisions in Canada, Great Britain, and United States

–Death Valley (Calif. and Nev.); **–Rocky Mountains**

(e) Places with names containing the name of a country or a first-order political division in inverted form

–California, Southern; **–Italy, Northern**;
–Tennessee, East

(f) Two exceptional cities:

–Washington (D.C.); **–Jerusalem**

(g) **–Vatican City**

(h) Islands at a distance from "owning" land mass

–Falkland Islands

(2) Indirect subdivision

(a) Places within a country, assigned indirectly through the name of the country or through the first-order political divisions of Canada, Great Britain, and United States; only two levels permitted:

–France–Paris; **–Argentina–Buenos Aires**
–Italy–Rome; **–Illinois–Chicago**; **–British Columbia**
–Vancouver; **–Scotland–Edinburgh**

(b) Metropolitan areas

–Massachusetts–Boston Metropolitan Area

If in several states, divided through the state the city is in.

(c) Islands in a group distant from "owners," assigned indirectly through the island group.

–Canary Islands–Las Palmas

(d) Islands close to owning jurisdiction, assigned indirectly through country or first-order political division:

–New York (State)–Long Island

(e) Latest form of name used in cases of name changes

–Sri Lanka– {not *–Ceylon–* }; **–Zimbabwe–** {not *–Rhodesia, Southern–* }

(f) Present territory used as interposing element in cases of territorial changes

(g) Qualifier for local place name omitted if the same as interposing element

(3) City sections not used in geographic subdivision, the lowest level being the city

(4) Citation orders of local subdivision

[Topical main heading–Geographic subdivision –Topical subdivision–Chronological subdivision –Form subdivision]

or

[Topical main heading–Topical subdivision–Geographic subdivision–Chronological subdivision–Form subdivision]

(5) Indirect subdivision involving places in Malaysia, Serbia and Montenegro, and Australia not affected by *AACR2R* rules for qualifiers

CHRONOLOGICAL SUBDIVISION

A chronological subdivision brings out the time period of the subject represented by the main heading. Such a subdivision may follow the main heading directly or appear after another subdivision, for example, after the subdivision **–History**. Not all headings are subdivided chronologically. For the most part, chronological subdivision is used with main headings that lend themselves to chronological treatment, most frequently in the social sciences or arts and humanities, and particularly in history. The chronological subdivisions used under a heading either correspond to epochs generally recognized in the literature of the field or represent spans of time frequently treated in books. Formerly, many chronological subdivisions used in cataloging did not appear in the printed list. This policy was changed in 1975, and now all established chronological subdivisions appear in *LCSH.*

General Principles of Chronological Subdivision

A chronological subdivision under a heading denotes a certain point in time or a span of time. The division into chronological periods varies according to place and to subject: scholarly consensus is the general guide.

Chronological subdivisions under the history of a given country are not always mutually exclusive. As Haykin pointed out, "the presence in the catalog of broad subdivisions does not preclude the use of subdivisions covering events or lesser epochs falling within the broad period."[14] For example:

France–History–1789-
–Revolution, 1789-1793
–1789-1815
–1789-1900

In application, however, a broad chronological subdivision and a more specific chronological subdivision falling within it are not usually assigned to the same work.

In chronological subdivisions under the name of a country that has undergone one or more name changes, the latest name of the country is used as the main heading; occasionally, this practice produces anachronistic headings, for example, **United States–History–Colonial period, ca. 1600-1775**. In this respect, the advantage of collocating the history of a particular country under the same heading has outweighed logical considerations.

Chronological subdivisions under subjects other than places are usually mutually exclusive:

English literature–Middle English, 1100-1500
–Early modern, 1500-1700
–18th century
–19th century
–20th century
–21st century

Corporate headings for chiefs of state that are used as main or added entries, for example, *Great Britain. Sovereign (1558-1603 : Elizabeth)*, are not used as subject headings except when they are needed as name–title subject entries.

For a work about the reign or administration of a chief of state, a counterpart in the form of **[Name of jurisdiction]–History–[Chronological subdivision]** is used, for example:

United States–History–1969-
Great Britain–History–Elizabeth, 1558-1603

One peculiarity in the treatment of wars and battles has been pointed out by Haykin.[15] Wars, other than civil wars, are entered under their own names with references from the names of participating countries, followed by the appropriate periods of their history and from variant names that have been applied to the wars:

Austro-Prussian War, 1866
{with USE references from the following:
Austria–History–War with Prussia, 1866
Austro-German War, 1866
Prussia (Germany)–History–War with Austria, 1866
Seven Weeks' War}

Spain–History–Civil War, 1936-1939

Exceptions are made for wars, other than those of worldwide scope, in which the United States (or the American colonies) participated; these are entered under **United States**:

United States–History–Queen Anne's War, 1702-1713
{with USE reference from the following:
{Queen Anne's War, 1702-1713}

United States–History–Tripolitan War, 1801-1805
{with USE references from the following:
Barbary War, 1801-1805
Tripoline War, 1801-1805
Tripolitan War, 1801-1805}

World War, 1914-1918

Battles, on the other hand, are entered under their own names rather than under the war headings, with cross references from the latter:

Galveston, Battle of, Galveston, Tex., 1863
Waterloo, Battle of, Waterloo, Belgium, 1815

Forms of Chronological Subdivisions

Before describing the various forms of chronological subdivisions, it is important to note that chronological subdivision is not the only device in the Library of Congress system for representing the chronological aspects of a topic. Some main headings, particularly in the fields of art and literature, denote both subject and chronological characteristics; their most common form is an inverted adjectival phrase:

Art, Ancient
Art, Gothic
Art, Renaissance
Art, Rococo
Art, Romanesque
Baroque literature
Literature, Medieval
Literature, Modern

There are several different forms for true chronological subdivisions. Furthermore, different forms may appear under the same heading, depending on which form is most appropriate for representing a particular period.

(1) A main heading may be followed by a subdivision containing the beginning and ending dates or the beginning date alone (also called an open-ended date):

Egypt–Economic conditions–332 B.C.-640 A.D.
Japan–Economic conditions–1989-
United States–Social life and customs–1865-1918
World politics–1945-

(2) A main heading may be followed by a subdivision containing the name of a monarch, a historical period, or an event, followed by dates:

Christian art and symbolism–Medieval, 500-1500
English drama–Restoration, 1660-1700
German poetry–Middle High German, 1050-1500
China–History–Ming dynasty, 1368-1644
Germany–History–Ferdinand I, 1556-1564
Germany–History–Unification, 1990
Japan–History–Meiji period, 1868-1912
United States–History–King William's War, 1689-1697
United States–History–Colonial period, ca. 1600-1775
United States–History–Revolution, 1775-1783

This form is mostly used with the subdivision **–History** under names of places. The same periods, when applied under topical subdivisions such as **–Foreign relations** and **–Politics and government**, usually appear without the descriptive terms or phrases:

Great Britain–History–Puritan Revolution, 1642-1660
Great Britain–Politics and government–1642-1660

Great Britain–History–Victoria, 1837-1901
Great Britain–Foreign relations–1837-1901

(3) A main or subdivided heading may be followed by the name of the century as a subdivision, for example:

English language–21st century
Europe, Eastern–Church history–20th century
Netherlands–Church history–17th century

This form of chronological subdivision is usually adopted when there is no distinctive name for the period or event, when a longer period of time than a single event or movement has to be covered, or when only very broad chronological subdivisions are required.

(4) A main heading may be followed by a chronological subdivision constructed with the preposition "to" followed by a date, for example:

Great Britain–Civilization–To 1066
Sicily (Italy)–Politics and government–To 1282
Rome–History–To 510 B.C.

This type of chronological subdivision usually appears as the first of the chronological subdivisions under a subject or place. It is used when the beginning date is uncertain or cannot be determined.

(5) A main heading may be followed by a subdivision in the form **–Early works to [date]**. While chronological subdivisions usually indicate the periods covered in works, this type of chronological subdivision represents the date of publication, for example, **Aeronautics–Early works to 1900**; **Geometry–Early works to 1800**. This type is used most frequently with headings in scientific or technical fields, because scholars often want to separate recently published works from earlier literature.

FORM SUBDIVISION

Haykin defines the term *form subdivision* and explains its nature and function in the following terms: "Form subdivision may be defined as the extension of a subject heading based on the form or arrangement of the subject matter in the book. In other words, it represents what the book is, rather than what it is about, the subject matter being expressed by the main heading."[16]

Form subdivisions include those that indicate either the physical or the bibliographical form of a work, for example, **–Bibliography**; **–Maps**; **–Encyclopedias**; **–Pamphlets**; **–Periodicals**; **–Pictorial works**; **–Software**. They may follow any type of main heading or heading string, for example:

Art, Medieval–Congresses
Cosmology–Encyclopedias
Great Britain–History–Civil War, 1642-1649–Pamphlets
Minorities–Massachusetts–Bibliography

By tradition, certain subdivisions that indicate intended audiences, form of presentation, or authors' approaches to their subjects are also considered to be form subdivisions, for example, **–Juvenile literature**; **–Anecdotes**; and **–Biography**.

Form subdivisions appear under all types of headings, including topical, geographic, corporate, and personal name headings. One area still not fully developed in regard to form subdivisions is nonprint media. In the treatment of subject content, there should not be any difference between print and nonprint materials. Since the main difference between them is the physical format or media, it would appear that using form subdivisions indicating the media to bring out the differences would be appropriate. In practice, however, there are relatively few subdivisions representing nonprint media in LCSH so far. Those that exist include:

–Databases
–Juvenile films
–Juvenile software
–Juvenile sound recordings
–Microform catalogs
–Software
–Sound recordings for foreign speakers
–Video catalogs
–Video recordings for foreign speakers

Distinction between Form and Topical Subdivisions

Many form subdivisions are used to represent both works *in* the form and works *about* the form;[17] in the latter case, they function as topical subdivisions. For example, in **Medicine–Periodicals**, meaning a general medical journal, the subdivision indicates the bibliographic form; whereas in **Medicine–Periodicals–History**, the subdivision **–Periodicals** is part of the subject. In other words, it is the function of the subdivision in a string that determines whether a subdivision is a topical or form subdivision.[18]

The different MARC 21 codes for topical (subfield x) and form (subfield v) subdivisions, implemented by the Library of Congress in 1999, help distinguish between the two types of subdivisions. In environments where topical and form subdivisions are not distinguished by codes or labels (for example, subfield codes), the identification of form subdivisions is often by context. For the cataloger, the question is: Where does one look for guidance when applying two or more subdivisions in the same heading? There are several sources of and methods for finding information:

Subject Cataloging Manual: Subject Headings (SCM)

Free-floating Subdivisions: An Alphabetical Index (FFS)

Patterns discerned in assigned heading strings in LC MARC records

Subdivision authority records

The test of what the work "is" versus what the work is "about" to determine the appropriate category of subdivision

The "reading backwards" or "from right to left" test to determine the proper order of subdivisions within the string, for example:

Art–Bibliography–Periodicals {a serially issued art bibliography}
Art–Periodicals–Bibliography {a bibliography of art journals}

Academic achievement–Periodicals–Indexes
{an index to a journal or journals on academic achievement, the subdivision **–Periodicals** being topical}

Universities and colleges–Finance–Periodicals
{a journal on higher education finance, the subdivision **–Periodicals** being form in this case}

FREE-FLOATING SUBDIVISIONS[19]

Definition and Application

At the Library of Congress, each time a subdivision is used under a heading for the first time, its usage must be established editorially, that is, authorized, in the same manner that a new heading is established. (This procedure is described in chapter 7.) There are, however, certain exceptions to this pattern of practice. A number of subdivisions, generally of wide application, have been designated as "free-floating." A free-floating subdivision is defined as a "form or topical subdivision that may be used under designated subjects without the usage being established editorially, and, as a consequence, without an authority record being created for each main heading/subdivision combination that might be needed."[20] As a result, many subject strings found in bibliographic records do not appear in LCSH.

Although the official designation of a large number of subdivisions as free-floating did not take place until 1974, limited use of such subdivisions dates back to the second edition (1919) of *Subject Headings Used in the Dictionary Catalogues of the Library of Congress*, in which certain form subdivisions were omitted from the printed list but used in cataloging. In the fourth edition, the concept of pattern headings—meaning the use of certain headings as patterns or models for subdivisions for headings in the same subject category—was introduced through the inclusion of the headings for four persons (Lincoln, Napoleon, Shakespeare, and Washington) as patterns for personal name headings. In subsequent editions, common form subdivisions and pattern headings continued to expand until 1974, when a large number of commonly used subdivisions were declared free-floating.

The increased use of free-floating subdivisions and pattern headings has contributed to the transformation of LCSH from a basically enumerative system into an increasingly analytico-synthetic one. In a way, these subdivisions are analogous to the standard subdivisions in the *Dewey Decimal Classification*, which reflect the principle of facet analysis and provide for greater freedom in synthesis.

Most of the **[Heading]–[Free-floating subdivision]** combinations are constructed by the cataloger as needed. Some combinations appear in LCSH because they require unique cross references or serve as examples.

In application, although free-floating subdivisions may be assigned freely by catalogers, they should not be used without regard for appropriateness or established principles governing the use of a particular subdivision. In determining the appropriateness of using a free-floating subdivision for the first time under a subject heading, the following considerations should be borne in mind.

(1) *Correct usage.* The cataloger should consider the compatibility of the subdivision with the subject heading to which it is to be attached. Many free-floating subdivisions have restricted usage; they are used under specific types of main headings or in specific circumstances. Information regarding their proper usage is found in three sources: scope notes and general references in LCSH, free-floating lists and instructions in *Subject Cataloging Manual: Subject Headings*, and the publication *Free-Floating Subdivisions: An Alphabetical Index.*[21] Any limitations in scope and application accompanying the subdivision should be observed.

(2) *Conflict.* Before assigning a free-floating subdivision, the cataloger should first determine whether the use under consideration conflicts with a previously established heading. If there is a conflict, the subdivision should not be assigned. Frequently, a phrase heading already exists that carries the same meaning as the heading with the subdivision being considered. For example, since the heading **Library administration** already exists, the subdivision **–Administration** should not be used under **Libraries**. Further examples are **Electronic apparatus and appliances** instead of *Electronics–Equipment and supplies*; **Christmas music** instead of *Christmas–Songs and music*.

Categories of Free-Floating Subdivisions

There are five categories of free-floating subdivisions. These are discussed below.

Free-Floating Form and Topical Subdivisions of General Application

A large number of common subdivisions have been designated free-floating. They include common form subdivisions that can be used under virtually all types of headings and common topical subdivisions that are widely used across many subject areas or disciplines. Some of them are further subdivided by other form, topical, or, in a few cases, chronological sub-subdivisions. Usage of these subdivisions is explained in the scope notes that appear in the lists of free-floating subdivisions in the *Subject Cataloging Manual,* as well as in the introduction to the print version of *Library of Congress Subject Headings* and under individual entries in *LCSH.*

Many of the free-floating subdivisions listed under pattern headings may be further subdivided by place, as instructed by the designation *(May Subd Geog)* after the subdivision.

Free-Floating Subdivisions under Specific Types of Headings

The Library of Congress has developed separate lists of free-floating subdivisions used under headings of various types, for example, classes of persons, ethnic groups, corporate bodies, names of persons, names of places, etc. (For selected lists[22] of these subdivisions, see appendices B through D.) Among these, subdivisions used under the names of persons and places merit special attention.

Free-Floating Subdivisions under Individual Name Headings

(1) *Persons.*[23] Headings for individual persons may be subdivided by the terms appearing in the list of free-floating subdivisions used under names of persons.

Previously, a number of personal name headings were designated as pattern headings for subdivisions in several broad categories of persons: rulers and statesmen, musicians, philosophers, founders of religions, and literary authors. Free-floating subdivisions were established in separate lists and printed in *Library of Congress Subject Headings* under these pattern name headings. Until 1998, a separate list existed for free-floating subdivisions under individual literary authors. The separate lists of free-floating subdivisions used under personal names have since been consolidated into one list for all personal headings, including those of literary authors.

The following examples show combinations of personal name headings with free-floating subdivisions:

Alexander, the Great, 356-323 B.C.–Friends and associates
Kennedy, John F. (John Fitzgerald), 1917-1963–Assassination
Mozart, Wolfgang Amadeus, 1756-1791–Homes and haunts

The list of free-floating subdivisions used under headings for persons appears in appendix C of this book. Among the subdivisions listed, four relate the person to specific disciplines, fields, or topics:

–Career in [specific field or discipline]
–Contributions in [specific field or topic]
–Knowledge–Agriculture, [America, etc.]
{Represents the person's knowledge of a particular topic as well as the person's educational background in a specific topic.}
–Views on [specific topic]

These subdivisions are to be completed on a free-floating basis, for example:

Jefferson, Thomas, 1743-1826–Career in agriculture
Jefferson, Thomas, 1743-1826–Contributions in architecture
Debussy, Claude, 1862-1918–Knowledge–Literature
John Paul II, Pope, 1920--Views on Judaism

(2) *Families.* A list of free-floating subdivisions used under names of families appears in *Subject Cataloging Manual: Subject Headings.*[24] Examples include:

–Archives
–Art patronage
–Correspondence
–Directories
–Homes and haunts
–Photograph collections
–Political activity
–Registers

(3) *Corporate bodies.*[25] Free-floating subdivisions appearing in this list may be used under headings for individual corporate bodies covering a large variety of types: businesses and corporations, nonprofit institutions, voluntary associations, cultural institutions, religious organizations, political parties, fraternal groups, labor organizations, professional societies, clubs, international agencies, government agencies on all levels, etc. Also included are individual exhibitions, fairs, expositions, etc. However, types of organizations, individual corporate bodies covered by pattern headings, such as individual educational institutions and legislative bodies, are excluded; so are jurisdictions covered in the list for places. Examples of free-floating subdivisions under names of individual corporate bodies include:

–Buildings
–By-laws
–Corrupt practices
–Officials and employees

In addition to the subdivisions appearing in the list *Free-Floating Subdivisions: Corporate Bodies*, additional or varying subdivisions may be found in lists of pattern headings for specific types of corporate bodies such as individual educational institutions, legislative bodies, military services, etc.

Free-Floating Subdivisions under Headings for Classes of Persons and Ethnic Groups

Although many of the free-floating subdivisions used under headings for classes of persons and those for ethnic groups are similar, they are established in two separate lists because each category has certain unique subdivisions not applicable to the other.[26] Examples:

[Classes of persons]–Bonding
–Conduct of life
–Medals

[Ethnic groups]–Agriculture
–Census
–Missions

Free-Floating Subdivisions under Geographic Headings

The following lists of free-floating subdivisions have been designated for use with different types of geographic headings:

(1) *Subdivisions used under headings for places.* These subdivisions may be used, within stated limitations, under the following types of geographic name headings that have been established either as valid *AACR2R* name headings or as subject headings: continents; regions; islands; countries; states, provinces, and equivalent jurisdictions; counties and other local jurisdictions larger than cities; metropolitan areas, suburban areas, and regions based on names of cities; cities; extinct cities; city sections, districts, or quarters. Examples of headings include:

Antarctica–Description and travel
Asia–Foreign relations–United States
Athens (Greece)–Antiquities
Bermuda Islands–History–Sources
Boston (Mass.)–Officials and employees–Salaries, etc.
Carthage (Extinct city)–Social life and customs
Elephants–Tunisia–Carthage (Extinct city)
Hong Kong (China)–Description and travel
Rive gauche (Paris, France)–Description and travel
Washington Suburban Area–Intellectual life

For a complete listing, see appendix D in this book. Appropriate subdivisions from this list may also be used under headings for geographic features or for regions based on geographic features, for example, **Indian Ocean Region–Emigration and immigration–History–Congresses.**

(2) *Subdivisions used with names of bodies of water.*[27] These subdivisions may be used under names of individual bodies of water, including rivers, man-made lakes, reservoirs, and canals, for example:

Colorado River (Colo.-Mexico)–Navigation
Suez Canal (Egypt)–Water-rights

However, this list does not apply to generic headings for types of bodies of water such as **Lakes; Saline waters; Sounds (Geomorphology)**.

Free-Floating Form and Topical Subdivisions Controlled by Pattern Headings[28]

Some subdivisions are of common application under headings in a particular subject category. In order to avoid repeating these subdivisions under each heading in that category, they are listed under one or occasionally several representative headings, which then serve as patterns for subdivision. Subdivisions under pattern headings then become free-floating and can be used with all headings of the same subject category, if appropriate, and when there is no conflict. For example, the heading **German language–Grammar, Historical** is a valid heading, even though it does not appear in LCSH, because the subdivision **–Grammar, Historical** appears under the pattern heading **English language**.

Table 5.1 shows the pattern headings designated by the Library of Congress, last updated in 2002.[29] Lists of free-floating subdivisions under many of the pattern headings listed in this table appear in *Subject Cataloging Manual: Subject Headings*. Where there is a discrepancy or conflict between the subdivisions appearing in one of these lists and those listed under the pattern heading in *Library of Congress Subject Headings*, the source that bears a later date has precedence since it represents more recent revisions.

Table 5.1. Pattern Headings (Updated as of 2002)*

Subject Field	*Category*	*Pattern Heading(s)*	
RELIGION	Religious and monastic orders	Jesuits	H1186
	Religions	Buddhism	H1185
	Christian denominations	Catholic Church	H1187
	Sacred works (including parts)	Bible	H1188

Subject Field	*Category*	*Pattern Heading(s)*	
HISTORY AND GEOGRAPHY	Colonies of individual countries	Great Britain–Colonies	H1149.5
	Legislative bodies (including individual chambers)	United States. Congress	H1155
	Military services (including armies, navies, marines, etc.)	United States–Armed Forces	H1159
		United States. Air Force	
		United States. Army	
		United States. Marine Corps.	
		United States. Navy	
	Wars	World War, 1939-1945	H1200

Subject Field	*Category*	*Pattern Heading(s)*	
SOCIAL SCIENCES	Industries	Construction industry Retail trade	H1153
	Types of educational institutions	Universities and colleges	H1151.5
	Individual educational institutions	Harvard University	H1151
	Legal topics	Labor laws and legislation	H1154.5

Subject Field	*Category*	*Pattern Heading(s)*	
THE ARTS	Art	Art, Italian Art, Chinese Art, Japanese Art, Korean	H1148
	Groups of literary authors (including authors, poets, dramatists, etc.)	Authors, English	H1155.2
	Literary works entered under author	Shakespeare, William, 1564-1616, Hamlet	1155.6
	Literary works entered under title	Beowulf	H1155.8
	Languages and groups of languages	English language French Language Romance languages	H1154
	Literatures (including individual genres)	English literature	H1156
	Musical compositions	Operas	H1160
	Musical instruments	Piano Clarinet	H1161

Subject Field	*Category*	*Pattern Heading(s)*	
SCIENCE AND TECHNOLOGY	Land vehicles	Automobiles	H1195
	Materials	Concrete Metals	H1158
	Chemicals	Copper Insulin	H1149
	Organs and regions of the body	Heart Foot	H1164
	Diseases	Cancer Tuberculosis	H1150
	Plants and crops	Corn	H1180
	Animals	Fishes Cattle	H1147

*Library of Congress, *Subject Cataloging Manual: Subject Headings,* H1146.

It should be noted that free-floating subdivisions that may be used with headings controlled by pattern headings are not limited to those appearing in the pattern headings lists. Many of the free-floating form and topical subdivisions of general application discussed earlier, although not listed under pattern headings, may also be applied as appropriate.

Birds–Poetry

{ **–Poetry** is a general free-floating subdivision, although it is not listed under either the heading **Birds** or the pattern heading for animals, **Fishes**}

German language–Periodicals
English language–Rhetoric–Study and teaching–United States
Spanish language–Semantics–Bibliography

Free-Floating Chronological Subdivisions

In general, chronological subdivisions are not free-floating because period divisions are unique under individual topics and regarding specific places. An exception is the chronological subdivisions found in the list of free-floating subdivisions of general application. These are broad chronological subdivisions used as sub-subdivisions under the free-floating subdivision **–History**:

–History–To 1500
–Modern period, 1500-
–16th century
–17th century
–18th century
–19th century
–20th century
–21st century

Their use is restricted to topical headings to which the free-floating subdivision **–History** can be assigned appropriately. However, they are not used with headings that begin with the name of a region, country, etc. For example, *America–History–19th century* is not a valid heading. Chronological subdivisions under headings for places are enumerated in LCSH.

In addition, a limited number of free-floating chronological subdivisions are included under the pattern headings for music compositions and under certain headings in literature.

Subjects or Topics as Free-Floating Subdivisions

According to Library of Congress practice, under certain headings names of subjects may be assigned as subdivisions whenever appropriate without establishing the usage editorially. These headings are indicated in different ways:

(1) by means of a "multiple" subdivision, such as:

Baptism–Anglican Communion, [Catholic Church, etc.]
English language–Dictionaries–French, [Italian, etc.]
Mysticism–Brahmanism, [Judaism, Nestorian Church, etc.]

The following headings may be generated from headings with the multiple subdivisions listed above:

Baptism–Church of England
French language–Dictionaries–Sango
Mysticism–Eastern Orthodox Church

Further details on multiple subdivisions are given in chapter 8.

(2) with an instructional scope note, such as:

Subject headings
This heading may be further subdivided by subject, e.g., Subject headings–Aeronautics

Instructional scope notes of this type should not be confused with general SA (*see also*) references, which do not necessarily indicate free-floating status of a subdivision.

In addition to the free-floating subdivisions discussed above, LCSH includes a number of free-floating words or phrases used in combination with geographic names to form complex main headings. Such phrase headings are discussed in chapter 4.

ORDER OF SUBDIVISIONS

In the early stages of the development of LCSH, subdivisions were relatively simple. Usually, a subject was divided by a form, chronological, place, or topical aspect. Gradually, more and more subdivisions were introduced, and various kinds of subdivisions were sanctioned as applicable to the same heading to form a string of terms. Furthermore, in many cases, more than one subdivision of the same kind may now be used under a particular heading. The string in some cases can be quite elaborate, for example:

United States–History–Civil War, 1861-1865–Secret service –Juvenile literature
Mathematics–Study and teaching (Secondary)–Illinois–Chicago Metropolitan Area–Evaluation–Statistics.

To ensure consistency in application, the citation order, that is, the order in which multiple elements in a heading string are arranged, becomes an important issue. Library of Congress practices regarding citation order are discussed below.

Order of Main Heading and Subdivision

In the formation of headings with numerous subdivisions, the order of elements in the string is important. Until recently, there were few stated instructions concerning this order. Most modern classification schemes contain such instructions, called citation formulae. However, in assigning subject headings, catalogers often have had to rely on arrangements already established in the list as a guide: New headings were generally established according to existing patterns. Even so, what was done over the years was not always consistent. Thus, there is considerable variation on this score in LCSH as it stands now.

The matter is not simply a question of the optimal order of subdivisions under a heading. When a subject for which a heading is to be devised contains a topical element and another element representing place or another topical aspect, it is often necessary to determine which is to be the main heading and which the subdivision, in other words, which should be the entry element.

Topic versus Form

On the whole, the topic serves as the main heading, with the form as a subdivision, for example, **Chemistry–Bibliography**; **Library science–Periodicals**. However, there are a few exceptions to this pattern, for example, **Reference books–Chemistry**.

Topic versus Period

Like the form subdivision, the chronological division does not usually stand alone without first conceding the subject. Rather, topics are divided by time periods, for example, **Drama–18th century**. There is, however, an exception to this pattern: Widely used names of historical periods may appear as main headings. In such cases, they are not usually subdivided by topic, although they are often subdivided by form of material, for example, **Renaissance–Juvenile literature**; **Middle Ages–Bibliography**.

Topic versus Topic

In LCSH, the term representing a concrete subject generally serves as the main heading, and the term indicating an action as the subdivision; the usage is similar to the key system/action arrangement in many indexing systems. This concrete/action citation order is in line with established theories of facet analysis and synthesis, which have been expounded over time by Julius O. Kaiser (concrete/process),[30] Marie Louise Prevost (noun rule),[31] Brian C. Vickery (substance/action),[32] S. R. Ranganathan (personality/energy),[33] Derek Austin (key system/action),[34] and E. J. Coates (thing/action).[35] In LCSH, this citation pattern of concrete/action is generally observed, for example:

Kidneys–Surgery
Kidneys–Diseases–Diagnosis
Automobiles–Taxation

However, there are occasional exceptions, for example:

Advertising–Cigarettes
Classification–Books

Topic versus Place

Place names are used widely as subdivisions under a topic to indicate the geographical aspect from which a subject is treated, just as chronological and form subdivisions show time and literary approach or physical form. In contrast with period or form, place may also be the main subject of a work, particularly in the fields of history and geography. In many fields of the social sciences, in fact, place may be considered of greater significance than topic even when it is not featured as such. In such cases, a place name may be used as the main heading, with subdivisions for topical and other elements as appropriate, for example, **United States–History**; **United States–Social life and customs**. In some cases, the distinction or emphasis is not so obvious, as in works on geology.

Because of the principle of uniform heading, catalogers do not have the option to use reciprocal place/topic and topic/place headings for the same concept. What principles can they then follow in reaching a decision whether to favor place or topic?

In an attempt to solve the topic/place problem, Coates proposes ranking the main areas of knowledge according to the extent to which they appear to be significantly conditioned by locality: (1) geography and biological phenomena, (2) history and social phenomena, (3) language and literature, (4) fine arts, (5) philosophy and religion, (6) technology, and (7) phenomena of physical sciences. He suggests that subjects near the top of this list be entered under the place subdivided by the subject and those at the bottom be treated in reverse, but he recognizes that the "problem is at what point in the middle of the list should the change be made."[36]

LCSH, as it stands now, reflects these difficulties. Some headings are in the form of topics subdivided by place, while others have place names subdivided by topics. As there have been no clear-cut criteria for determination, it is difficult for users or catalogers to predict which form should be used in each case. Fortunately, the list of free-floating subdivisions under place names (see appendix D) indicates which topics are used as such. Furthermore, for each topic used as a subdivision under place names, a cross reference is given under the name of the topic in LCSH:

Boundaries
SA *subdivisions* Boundaries *under names of countries, states, etc.*
Travel
SA *subdivisions* Description and travel *under names of countries, cities, etc.*

As was seen to be the case for other entry element questions, the choice of the order of elements in a subdivided heading is not as important in most online systems as it is for card catalogs or printed indexes. In online systems where main heading and subdivision are equally accessible, the terms arranged in either order, **[Topic]–[Place]** or **[Place]–[Topic]**, are retrievable. Nevertheless, it still has an effect on the browsing of index display.

Order of Subdivisions under the Same Main Heading

When there are two or more subdivisions under the same main heading, the citation order can affect the meaning. As an example, take the two pairs of headings:

Science–Study and teaching–History
{meaning a history of science education}
Science–History–Study and teaching
{meaning study and teaching of science history}

It is clear that each of these headings represents a distinct subject. The citation order should be determined by the meaning of the string. However, a predetermined order facilitates heading construction and consistency among catalogers. For this consideration, and in the interest of facilitating machine validation of subject headings, the Subject Subdivisions Conference,[37] also known as the Airlie House Conference, recommended that, in the case of a topical main heading with numerous subdivisions, a consistent citation order be established in the following form: *[Topic]–[Place]–[Chronology]–[Form]*.

Currently, there are two basic patterns for citation order:[38]

(1) When the string begins with a geographic heading, the elements are generally arranged in the following citation order:

[Place]–[Topic]–[Time]–[Form]

For example:

England–Civilization–17th century–Sources
Great Britain–Court and courtiers–History–16th century–Sources

The subdivision **–History** is frequently used to introduce a time period; in such cases, as shown in the last example, the combination **–History–[Time]** may be considered the chronological element.

(2) When the string begins with a topical heading, the following citation order prevails:

[Topic]–[Place]–[Time]–[Form]

For example:

Nobility–Great Britain–History–16th century–Sources
Plantation life–Georgia–History–19th century–Sources

When the string contains another topical element, the elements may be arranged in one of the following two citation orders:

(A) **[Topic]–[Place]–[Topic]–[Time]–[Form]**
(B) **[Topic]–[Topic]–[Place]–[Time]–[Form]**

Currently, the choice of citation order depends on whether or not the designation *(May Subd Geog)* follows the topical subdivision in LCSH or in the free-floating subdivisions lists. When a heading contains a geographic subdivision and one or more of the other subdivisions, the geographic subdivision is normally placed between the main heading and the other subdivision(s). For example, in *LCSH:*

Education *(May Subd Geog)*
–Finance

Headings generated:

Education–Florida–Finance
Education–New Jersey–Finance–Statistics

However, many topical subdivisions are themselves further subdivided by place. In such cases, the designation *(May Subd Geog)* appears after the topical subdivision, as shown in LCSH or in various lists of free-floating subdivisions. In such cases, the geographic subdivision follows the topical subdivision. For example:

In *LCSH:*

Education *(May Subd Geog)*
–Economic aspects *(May Subd Geog)*

Headings generated:

Education–Economic aspects–Finland
Education–Economic aspects–United States

In *LCSH:*

Land titles *(May Subd Geog)*
–Registration and transfer *(May Subd Geog)*

Heading generated:

Land titles–Registration and transfer–California–Popular works

In *LCSH:*

Christian art and symbolism *(May Subd Geog)*
–Medieval, 500-1500 *(May Subd Geog)*

Heading generated:

Christian art and symbolism–Medieval, 500-1500–France–Paris –Exhibitions

Furthermore, to the basic patterns of citation order discussed above, there are minor variations when the string contains more than one subdivision of a particular type, that is, a string with more than one topical element and/or more than one form subdivision, for example:

Railroads–France–Cars–Design and construction–History –19th century–Pictorial works
Heart–Diseases–Patients–Rehabilitation–Evaluation–Congresses
United States–History–Civil War, 1861-1865–Sources–Juvenile literature–Indexes

Combinations of Two or More Form Subdivisions in the Same Heading String

Because most form subdivisions are free-floating, and in many instances the combination of two or more form subdivisions is allowed in the same heading string, the citation order sometimes presents a challenge to the cataloger. For example:

United States–History–Revolution, 1775-1783–<u>Personal narratives –Juvenile literature</u>
Great Plains–History–Sources–<u>Bibliography–Catalogs</u>

Such a practice raises two questions: (1) when may a form subdivision be further subdivided by another form subdivision, and (2) in what order should the subdivisions appear? To answer these questions, *Subject Cataloging Manual: Subject Headings* and *Free-Floating Subdivisions: An Alphabetical Index* list many precombined multiple subdivisions to assist the catalogers, for example,

–Biography–Dictionaries {–form–form}
–Dictionaries–Polyglot {–form–topic}

However, it is not practical to enumerate all possible combinations in the lists of subdivisions, so the cataloger is often required to exercise judgment in combining subdivisions based on existing patterns or on instructions given in the *Subject Cataloging Manual.*

For combinations not listed in *SCM* or *FFS*, other methods must be employed.[39] In most subject headings, the form subdivision appears as the last element, following the general pattern of subdivision order, [**Topic–Topic–Place–Time–Form**]. However, there are exceptions such as: **–Textbooks for foreign speakers–English** (–form–topic).

Another method that has been suggested is to "read backwards," or from right to left, to see if the string fits the context of the document.

Periodicals–Indexes {for an index (form) to periodicals (topic)}
Indexes–Periodicals {for a serially issued index (both being form)}

As shown in the examples above, the same subdivision can serve as either form or topic. The function and the order of the subdivisions are determined by the context.

In a few cases, works *in* a particular form and works *about* that form are represented by different subdivisions or combinations. For example, **–Abstracts** and **–Indexes** are used for works *in* those forms, while **–Abstracting and indexing** is used for works *about* the preparation of abstracts and indexes in a particular field.

NOTES

1. Lois Mai Chan, *Library of Congress Subject Headings: Principles of Structure and Policies for Application*, annotated version (Washington, D.C.: Cataloging Distribution Service, Library of Congress, 1990), 16.

2. David Judson Haykin, *Subject Headings: A Practical Guide* (Washington, D.C.: Government Printing Office, 1951), 27.

3. Library of Congress, Cataloging Policy and Support Office, *Subject Cataloging Manual: Subject Headings*, 5th ed., 2000 cumulation (Washington, D.C.: Library of Congress, 2000), H180, p. 8.

4. David Judson Haykin, "Subject Headings: Principles and Development," in *The Subject Analysis of Library Materials*, ed. Maurice F. Tauber (New York: School of Library Service, Columbia University, 1953), 51.

5. Haykin, *Subject Headings*, 36.

6. Lynn M. El-Hoshy, "Introduction to Subdivision Practice in the Library of Congress Subject Headings System," in Subject Subdivisions Conference (1991: Airlie, Va.), *The Future of Subdivisions in the Library of Congress Subject Headings System* (Washington, D.C.: Cataloging Distribution Service, Library of Congress, 1992), 117.

7. Library of Congress, *Subject Cataloging Manual*, H830.

8. For a complete list of the first-order political divisions of these countries, see appendix D.

9. Library of Congress, *Subject Cataloging Manual*, H980, H1050.

10. Library of Congress, *Subject Cataloging Manual*, H1045.

11. Library of Congress, *Subject Cataloging Manual*, H807.

12. Library of Congress, *Subject Cataloging Manual*, H807, p. 6.

13. Library of Congress, *Subject Cataloging Manual*, H830, p. 4.

14. Haykin, *Subject Headings*, 34.

15. Haykin, *Subject Headings*, 34-35.

16. Haykin, *Subject Headings*, 27.

17. El-Hoshy, "Introduction to Subdivision Practice," 117.

18. Edward T. O'Neill et al., "Form Subdivisions: Their Identification and Use in LCSH," *Library Resources & Technical Services* 45(4) (2001): 187-197.

19. Library of Congress, *Subject Cataloging Manual*, H1095.

20. Library of Congress, *Subject Cataloging Manual*, H1095, p. 1.

21. Library of Congress, *Free-floating Subdivisions: An Alphabetical Index,* prepared by Subject Cataloging Division (Washington, D.C.: Library of Congress, Cataloging Distribution Service, 1989-).

22. For complete lists, consult LC, *Subject Cataloging Manual*.

23. Library of Congress, *Subject Cataloging Manual*, H1110.

24. Library of Congress, *Subject Cataloging Manual*, H1120.

25. Library of Congress, *Subject Cataloging Manual*, H1105.

26. Library of Congress, *Subject Cataloging Manual*, H1100, H1103.

27. Library of Congress, *Subject Cataloging Manual*, H1145.5.

28. Library of Congress, *Subject Cataloging Manual*, H1146-1200.

29. Library of Congress, *Subject Cataloging Manual*, H1146.

30. Julius O. Kaiser, *Systematic Indexing*, The Card System Series, vol. 2 (London: Pitman, 1911), 300-303.

31. Marie Louise Prevost, "An Approach to Theory and Method in General Subject Headings," *Library Quarterly* 16 (1946): 140-151.

32. Brian C. Vickery, "Systematic Subject Indexing," *Journal of Documentation* 9(1) (1953): 48-57.

33. S. R. Ranganathan, *Elements of Library Classification*, 3rd ed. (Bombay: Asia Publishing House, 1962), 82-89.

34. Derek Austin, *PRECIS: A Manual of Concept Analysis and Subject Indexing*, 2nd ed., with assistance from Mary Dykstra (London: The British Library, Bibliographic Services Division, 1984), 107-121.

35. E. J. Coates, *Subject Catalogues: Headings and Structure* (London: Library Association, 1960, reissued with new preface 1988), 50-58.

36. Coates, *Subject Catalogues*, 61.

37. Subject Subdivisions Conference, *The Future of Subdivisions in the Library of Congress Subject Headings System*, 6.

38. Library of Congress, *Subject Cataloging Manual*, H860; H1075, pp. 4-6.

39. O'Neill et al., "Form Subdivisions," 189.

6 Cross References

INTRODUCTION

In LCSH, and in most controlled vocabularies that adhere to the principle of uniform heading, a given subject is represented by only one valid heading or term. Users, however, cannot always be expected to know which of several synonyms or near-synonymous terms, or which of several possible forms, has been chosen as the valid heading. Furthermore, under the principle of specific and direct entry, material on a given subject is listed under a specific term even though many users may look for it under a broader or more general term. Finally, users need to be made aware of headings that are related to the subject being sought. Therefore, it is in the best interest of users if the system provides linkages between related terms and between terms that are not used as headings to those that are. Both objectives are achieved by means of cross references. In retrieval, cross-references carry a great deal of the burden of leading users to desired information.

Three types of relationships are represented in the cross-reference structure of LCSH: equivalence, hierarchical, and associative. These relationships are expressed in terms of USE and UF (Used for), BT (Broader term) and NT (Narrower term), RT (Related term), and SA (See also) references. Each reference links a term or heading with another heading or with a group of headings. Before the eleventh edition (1988) of *Library of Congress Subject Headings*, the symbols *see*, *x* (*see from*), *sa* (*see also*), and *xx* (*see also from*) were used.

EQUIVALENCE RELATIONSHIPS[1]

References among equivalent terms serve to link those not used as headings to the term chosen as the valid heading. Such references allow the user to access materials on a particular subject by inputting (or looking under) any term that is synonymous with the uniform heading under which all such materials are listed. In LCSH, a USE reference guides the user from a term that is not used as a heading to the term that is. USE references are made from synonymous terms, variant spellings, alternative forms, different entry elements, opposite terms, and "overly" narrow terms. Thus, USE references provide an entry vocabulary for the system. Each subject heading, by itself, enables retrieval of a subject through one term only, while a subject heading with, for example, four USE references allows retrieval through five different terms. In other words, the user is able to access the subject through any of five possible synonymous or variant terms instead of one.

In some online systems, such referencing is automatic and transparent; searchers inputting any one of a number of equivalent terms can retrieve all of the material the system has on the topic to which the term refers. No matter how sophisticated the system, however, this can only happen if equivalent terms are linked at both thesaurus construction and system design stages.

The following discussion focuses on term relationships in LCSH, but the concept can be applied equally to other situations in which LCSH or a variant of it is used in indexing or cataloging. In LCSH, instructions for making USE references are given under both the unused or non-preferred term(s) and under the valid heading. The symbol UF means a USE reference is to be made from the term or terms that follow. For example:

Animal industry

UF Animal products industry
Livestock industry

Reciprocal entries appear under the UF terms:

Animal products industry
USE **Animal industry**

Livestock industry
USE **Animal industry**

In the MARC 21 format for authorities, the synonymous terms not used as headings are indicated by appropriate field tags.[2]

In most controlled vocabularies, USE references from synonymous terms and variant spellings are generally made. The other types of USE references in the Library of Congress system are provided because of the principle of uniform heading and the unique features of specific and direct entry discussed earlier.

Synonymous Terms

When a heading has been chosen from two or more synonymous terms, USE references are made from the unused terms to the heading. Charles A. Cutter's rule states: "Of two exactly synonymous names choose one and make a reference from the other."[3] In practice, this kind of reference is extended to near-synonymous terms when it is considered impractical to distinguish between them. David Judson Haykin notes that the basic significance of such references is that "the subject matter is entered not under the heading which occurred to the reader, but under the one chosen by the cataloger even when the terms are not completely synonymous."[4]

Examples of USE references from synonymous terms to the valid heading are shown below:

Appetite depressants
UF Appetite suppressing drugs

Audiobooks
UF Cassette books
Recorded books

Big bang theory
UF Big bang cosmology
Superdense theory

Child authors
UF Juvenile authors

Ethics
UF Morals

Fitness walking
UF Exercise walking
Health walking
Healthwalking

Fuzzy logic
UF Nonlinear logic

Greenhouses
UF Hothouses

Liberty
UF Emancipation
Freedom
Liberation

Oral medication
UF Drugs by mouth
Peroral medication

Overpopulation
UF Population explosion

Urban hospitals
UF City hospitals
Metropolitan hospitals

Variant Spellings

USE references are made from different spellings and different grammatical structures, as well as from canceled headings:

Aeolian harp
UF Eolian harp

Aesthetics
UF Esthetics

Airplanes
UF Aeroplanes

Archaeology
UF Archeology

Audiobooks
UF Audio books

Dialing
UF Dialling

Dogs
UF Dog

Fishing nets
UF Fish nets
Fishnets

Microcrystalline polymers
UF Microcrystal polymers
Polymer microcrystals

Seafood
UF Sea food

Abbreviations, Acronyms, Initials, Etc.

If the heading has been established in the spelled-out form, USE references from abbreviated forms are not generally made, unless such forms are well known to the general public:

Adenylic acid
UF AMP (Biochemistry)

Ammonium nitrate fuel oil
UF AN-FO
ANFO

Electronic mail systems
UF Email systems

Conversely, if the heading has been established in the form of an abbreviation, an acronym, or initials, a USE reference is regularly made from the spelled-out form:

CPR (First aid)
UF Cardiopulmonary resuscitation

MARC formats
UF Machine-Readable Cataloging formats

Different Language Terms

USE references are generally not made from equivalent terms in foreign languages to topical headings that are established in English, unless the foreign terms are well known to English-speaking users:

Carnival
UF Mardi Gras (Festival)

Free enterprise
UF Laissez-faire

USE references from vernacular names are regularly made to English-language headings representing named entities, for example:

Aizu Region (Japan)
UF Aizu-bonchi (Japan)

Cubagua Island (Venezuela)
UF Isla Cubagua (Venezuela)

Texcal Cave (Mexico)
UF Cueva del Texcal (Mexico)

Yellow River (China)
UF Huang He (China)

USE references are also made from English translations to headings established in the vernacular, for example:

Yangtze River (China)
UF Long River (China)

Popular and Scientific Terms

USE references are made from popular terms to the scientific term chosen as the heading, and from scientific terms to the popular term if the latter has been chosen as the heading:

Cockroaches
UF Blattaria
Blattoidea

Medusahead wildrye
UF Elymus caput-medusae
Taeniatherum asperum

Prosencephalon
UF Forebrain

Vitamin C
UF Ascorbic acid

Alternative Forms

Because of the principle of uniform heading, which requires that a heading appear in only one form in the catalog, references are made to an established heading from other forms of the heading likely to be consulted by users. It should be pointed out, however, that in LCSH this is true in principle but not always consistent in practice, particularly among headings established some time ago. Newly established headings show greater consistency:

Aerobic exercises
UF Aerobics

Aged–Education
UF Education of the aged

Banks and banking–Accounting
UF Bank accounting

Bacillus anthracis–Decontamination
UF Decontamination of bacillus anthracis

Federal aid to private schools
UF Private schools–Federal aid

Foreign exchange–Accounting
UF Foreign exchange accounting

Galaxies–Evolution
UF Galactic evolution

Glass–Research
UF Glass research

Cataloging of rare books
{No UF references}

Hospitals–Accounting
{No UF references}

Different Entry Elements

When a heading is inverted, a USE reference is generally provided from the direct form:

Art, Medieval
UF Medieval art

Chemistry, Organic
UF Organic chemistry

Education, Higher
UF Higher education

For inverted headings qualified by nationality, ethnic group, or language, USE references from the natural word order are always made:

Painting, Chinese
UF Chinese painting

For headings established in the direct form, USE references are made from inverted forms if they are considered to provide useful access points:

Aerospace planes
UF Planes, Aerospace

Laser fusion
UF Fusion, Laser

Mexican American arts
UF Arts, Mexican American

Popular music
UF Music, Popular

The inverted UF reference is not made if there is a BT reference that begins with the same word or words as the UF reference, for example:

Talking birds
BT Birds {the reference *UF Birds, Talking* is not made}

When a compound heading expresses a relationship between two objects or concepts, a USE reference is made from the form with the terms in reverse order:[5]

Architecture and state
UF State and architecture

Computers and college students
UF College students and computers

In cases of previously established compound headings that connect two parallel or opposite objects or concepts often treated in the same work, but not necessarily in relationship to each other, a USE reference is made from the second term in the heading:

Bear deterrents and repellents
UF Bear repellents

Cities and towns
UF Towns

Emigration and immigration
UF Immigration

Encyclopedias and dictionaries
UF Dictionaries

Compound headings of this type are no longer being established. Separate headings are made instead.

If the heading is in the form of a topic subdivided by other topic(s), a UF reference is made from the reversed form, for example:

Advertising–Newspapers
UF Newspapers–Advertising

Opposite Terms Not Used as Headings

In the past, when a heading was established under one of two opposite terms, a USE reference was made from the one not chosen:

Literacy
UF Illiteracy

Militarism
UF Antimilitarism

Temperance
UF Intemperance

This practice is now rare. Current policy is to establish each term as a separate heading when required.

Narrow Terms Not Used as Headings

When a term is considered too narrow to be useful as a separate heading, a USE reference, also called an upward reference, is sometimes made from the narrower term to a broader one that is used as a valid heading:

Church management
UF Parish management

Liberty
UF Civil liberty
Personal liberty

Pollution
UF Pollution–Control
Pollution–Prevention

Popular music
UF Popular songs
Popular vocal music

Schools–Accounting
UF High schools–Accounting
Public schools–Accounting

Occasionally a USE reference is made from a narrower term not used as a heading to a broader heading and to other related headings at the same time:

Christmas books
USE **Christmas**
Christmas–Exercises, recitations, etc.
Christmas plays
Christmas stories
Gift books

In recent years fewer and fewer upward-pointing USE references have been added to the list. Current policy favors establishing the narrower terms as separate headings.

General USE References[6]

A general USE reference, which links an unauthorized or non-preferred term to a group of related headings, is used when the relationships among terms, headings, and subdivisions are too complex to be represented with simple USE references, when it is considered impractical to list as specific references all relevant individual headings, or when it is desirable to explain free-floating subdivision usage, for example:

Ecuadorean . . .
USE *subject headings beginning with or qualified by the word* Ecuadorian

Office, Appointment to
USE *subdivision* Officials and employers–Selection and appointment *under names of countries, cities, etc. and names of individual government agencies; and subdivisions* Selection and appointment *under types of officials*

HIERARCHICAL RELATIONSHIPS[7]

A hierarchical or related term reference connects two or more terms that are both (or all) valid subject headings. Cutter's rule states: "Make references from general subjects to their various subordinate subjects and also to coordinate and illustrative subjects."[8] Haykin rephrases the rule in these terms:

> In binding related headings together the basic rule is that a "see also" reference be made from a given subject: 1) to more specific subjects or topics comprehended within it, or to an application of the subject; and 2) to coordinate subjects which suggest themselves as likely to be of interest to the user seeking material under the given heading, because they represent other aspects of the subject, or are closely related to it.[9]

In LCSH, headings related hierarchically are connected by reciprocal BT (Broader term) and NT (Narrower term) references. In earlier editions of the list, *see also* references were used to provide links among related terms, and from broader terms to narrower terms, but not vice versa. Similarly, in MARC 21 subject authority records, BT and RT references appear in the 5XX fields. NT references are generated for display in the catalog but do not appear in the authority records. In the printed list, for each BT reference, a reciprocal NT (Narrower term) reference is made under the broader heading.

Under each valid heading, other headings representing concepts on a level immediately above that heading in the hierarchy are listed as BT (Broader term), except when the heading in question represents the "top term" in the hierarchy or when the broader term cannot be readily identified. Other exceptions include headings for geographic regions, family names, and inverted headings qualified by names of languages, nationalities, ethnic groups, or terms that designate time periods, when the only appropriate BT is the identical heading without the qualifier. Headings without BT's are called "orphan" headings.[10]

When a heading belongs to more than one hierarchy, multiple BT references may be made. In complex situations such as compound headings, prepositional phrase headings, and headings with subdivisions, BT references are made in select cases, even when the relationships so expressed are not truly hierarchical.

Scholars have noted the relationship between classification and the hierarchical-reference structure in a controlled vocabulary. Similar to the structure of a classification scheme, the BT/NT references are built on hierarchical relationships among subjects. Using the subject **Cats** as an example, Phyllis A. Richmond[11] demonstrates the "hidden classification" in the cross-reference structure of LCSH. She concludes that even though the structure is imperfect and could be improved, the potential is there. In an examination of the relationship between LC subject headings and classification for Judaica, Bella Hass Weinberg[12] also notes the "hidden classification" or hierarchical structure embodied in the BT and NT references in LCSH.

The following chain of references illustrates the hierarchical principle reflected in the BT/NT references in LCSH. Although the hierarchical structure is not always as rigorous as might be expected, each term in a chain of subjects from a hierarchy in LCSH is usually connected to the one immediately above it and the one below it by BT and NT references, for example:

Chordata
NT Vertebrates

Vertebrates
BT Chordata
NT Mammals

Mammals
BT Vertebrates
NT Primates

Primates
BT Mammals
NT Monkeys

Monkeys
BT Primates
NT Cercopithecidae

Cercopithecidae
BT Monkeys
NT Macaques

Macaques
BT Cercopithecidae
NT Japanese macaque

Japanese macaque
BT Macaques

Figure 6.1 illustrates part of a classificatory structure based on the hierarchical references in LCSH. The hierarchical structure is embodied in the references, with occasional irregularities. For instance, the subject **Chordata** is not connected to any subject superordinate to it, for example, **Animals**.

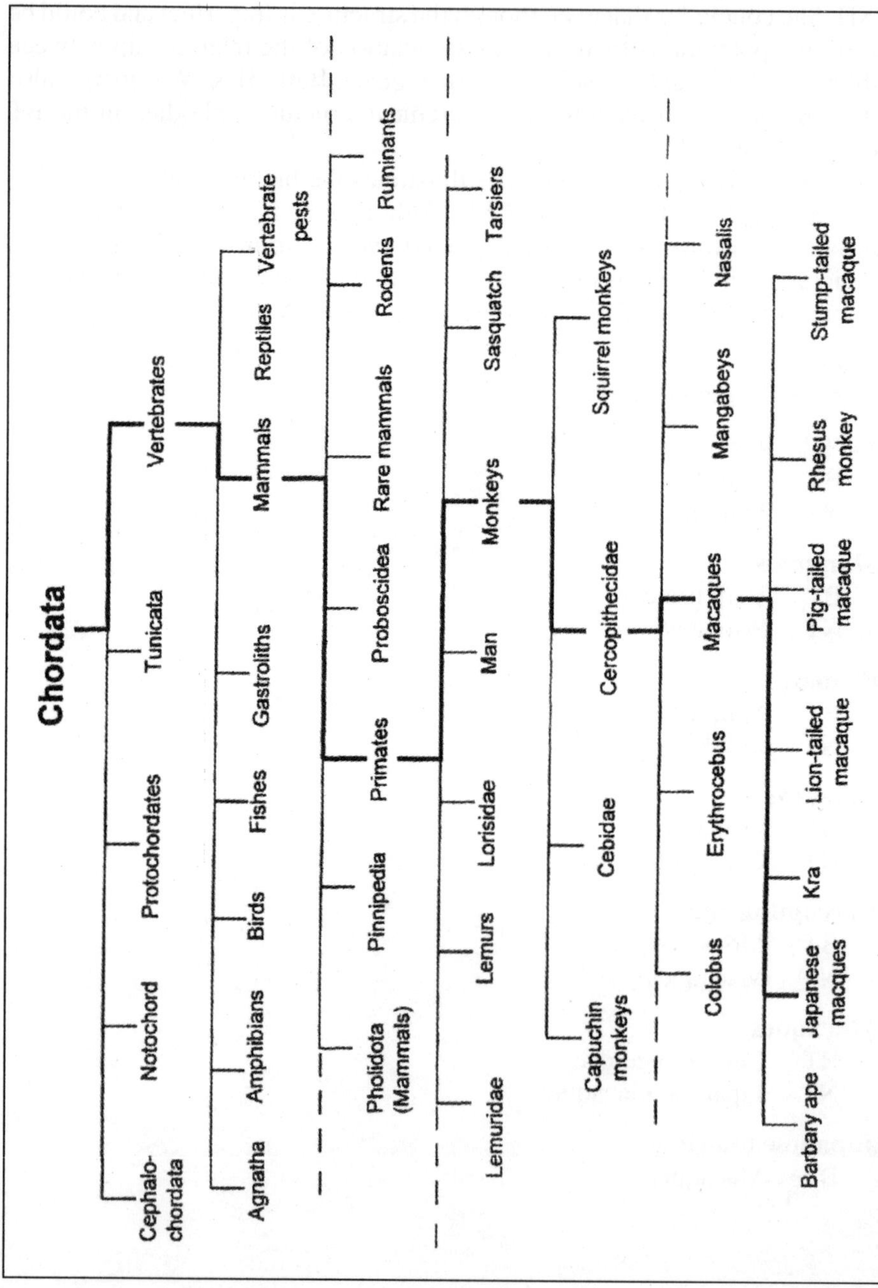

Figure 6.1 Part of a Classificatory Structure Based on the Hierarchical References in LCSH.

Theoretically, an alphabetical list of index terms with a thorough, systematically constructed network of cross-references can provide the best of both worlds by combining the advantages of the alphabetical and classified approaches. Tying a controlled vocabulary to a classificatory structure facilitates the making of proper cross references, ensuring that term relationships are well defined and represented. Many modern indexing vocabularies are built upon classified structures. An example is *Medical Subject Headings*[13] with its attendant tree structures.

In LCSH, hierarchical references are made between headings having the relationships delineated below.

(1) Genus/species (or class/class member). Examples include:

Apes
NT Gorilla

German fiction
NT Science fiction, German

Motor vehicles
NT Automobiles

Sheep dogs
NT Belgian sheepdog

The NT reference is not made, however, in cases of inverted headings qualified by names of languages, nationalities, or ethnic groups when the broader term is identical to the narrower heading without the qualifier. References such as the following are not made.

Art
NT Art, German
Art, Japanese

(2) Whole/part. Examples include:

Hand
BT Arm
NT Fingers
Palm (Anatomy)

Fingers
BT Hand
NT Finger joint
Fingernails
Thumb

When a heading belongs to more than one hierarchy, a reference is made from the next broader heading in each hierarchy:

Causeways
BT Bridges
Roads

(3) Instance (or generic topic/entity name heading).[14] Examples include:

Buildings–Texas
NT Old Stone Fort (Nacogdoches, Tex.)

Botanical gardens–California
NT Huntington Herb Garden (San Marino, Calif.)

Dwellings–Georgia
NT Chief Vann House (Spring Place, Ga.)
Plum Orchard (Ga.)
Robert Toombs House (Washington, Ga.)
Stafford Plantation (Ga.)

Mountains–France
NT Vanoise Mountains (France)

Palaces–England
NT Blenheim Palace (England)
Hampton Court (Richmond upon Thames, London, England)

Palaces–Spain
NT Alcázar (Madrid, Spain)
Alcázar (Seville, Spain)
Alhambra (Granada, Spain)

Rivers–Colorado
NT Gunnison River (Colo.)
North Platte River
Piedra River (Colo.)

Streets–France
NT Boulevard du Temple (Paris, France)

World War, 1939-1945–Campaigns–Italy
NT Cassino (Italy), Battle of, 1944

The geographic subdivision in the generic heading is at the level of the country or first-order political division in the case of Canada, Great Britain, and the United States. This level is often broader than that represented by the qualifier of the individual name heading for places in Australia, Malaysia, and Serbia and Montenegro (see discussion in chapter 4).

In contrast, subject-to-name references,[15] including personal names, corporate names, jurisdictional names, and uniform titles, are not made.

(4) Compound and complex relationships. For headings containing multiple topics or concepts, BT references are made from those topics or concepts not used as the entry element. Such topics, which often represent generic concepts with regard to the compound or complex headings, are presented in their established heading form:

Music and anthropology
BT Anthropology

Education and crime
BT Crime

Hydrogen as fuel
BT Fuel

Internet in library reference services
BT Reference services (Libraries)

Aerial photography in city planning
BT City planning

Surrealism in motion pictures
BT Motion pictures

Domestic relations (Roman law)
BT Roman law

BT references are also made from headings that correspond to subdivisions, for example, **–Contracting out**; **–Election**. For example,

County services–Contracting out
BT Contracting out

Judges–Election
BT Elections

References of this type are not made if the terms are too broad or general, such as **[Topic]–Application** and **[Topic]–Utilization**.

ASSOCIATIVE RELATIONSHIPS[16]

Related-term (RT) references are made between terms that are related other than hierarchically, that is, related topics that do not constitute a genus/species or whole/part relationship. These references appear under both headings involved:

Religion
RT Theology

Theology
RT Religion

Comprehension
RT Memory

Memory
RT Comprehension

RT references are now required in the following cases, unless they share a common BT or begin with the same word or word stem. To avoid subjective judgments in making RTs, the Library of Congress has established the following guidelines, with deliberate effort to limit their number.[17] RT references are made:

(1) to link two terms with overlapping meanings

Ships RT Boats and boating	**Boats and boating** RT Ships
Longevity RT Old age	**Old age** RT Longevity
Drugs–Overdosage RT Medication errors	**Medication errors** RT Drugs–Overdosage

(2) to link a discipline and the object studied

Earthquakes RT Seismology	**Seismology** RT Earthquakes
Epithelial cells RT Exfoliative cytology	**Exfoliative cytology** RT Epithelial cells
Entomology RT Insects	**Insects** RT Entomology

(3) to link a class of persons and their fields of endeavor, provided that the two headings do not begin with the same word stem

Physicians RT Medicine	**Medicine** RT Physicians

GENERAL SEE ALSO (SA) REFERENCES

For reasons of economy, a general SA (*See also*) reference is sometimes made from a heading to a group of headings, frequently listing one or more individual headings as examples. Such a reference serves to suggest to the user the pattern of the heading under which a particular class or group of topics is entered, to alert users of the existence of more specific headings, and to provide guidance as to the type of heading more appropriate to their search. Currently, specific references are preferred.

SA references represent an open-ended approach, in that no exhaustive list of headings referred to is given, and the user is left to formulate the terms to be searched. In the past, a type of general *see also* reference frequently used was one made from the generic heading to its members named collectively, with one or more specific examples given:

Tools
SA individual specific tools, e.g. Files and rasps; Saws

The policy of making this type of general *see also* reference has now been largely abandoned by the Library of Congress[18] in favor of making specific references, for example:

Tools
NT Agricultural implements
Artists' tools
Axes
Carpentry–Tools

Still, there are situations in which it is impractical or redundant to make specific references. In such cases, general *see also* references are still being made. Currently there are six types of such references:[19]

(1) General SA references to headings beginning with the same word or word stem:

Heart
SA *headings beginning with the words* Cardiac *or* Cardiogenic

(2) General SA references to name headings:

Universities and colleges *(May Subd Geog)*
SA *headings beginning with the word* College; *and names of individual institutions*

(3) General SA references to subdivisions under subject headings (general)

Abbreviations *(May Subd Geog)*
SA *subdivision* Abbreviations *under subjects, e.g.* Associations, institutions, etc.–Abbreviations; Law–Abbreviations

(4) General SA references to subdivisions under pattern headings

Exercise
SA *subdivision* Exercise *under individual animals and groups of animals, e.g.* Cattle–Exercise; Pets–Exercise; *and types of exercise, e.g.* Fencing; Rowing; Running

(5) General SA references to subdivisions under name headings

Birthplaces *(May Subd Geog)*
SA *subdivision* Birthplace *under names of individual persons*

(6) General SA references to subdivisions under place names

Economic history (*Not Subd Geog*)

SA *subdivision* Economic conditions *under names of countries, cities, etc., and under classes of persons and ethnic groups*

According to current policy, SA references are made only when a subdivision is free-floating. However, a number of SA references to non-free-floating subdivisions were made in the past and remain in LCSH. Therefore, the presence of such a reference does not necessarily indicate the free-floating status of a particular subdivision.

CROSS-REFERENCES FOR PROPER NAME HEADINGS

Certain types of name headings require special cross references. These are discussed below.

Personal Names

Individual Persons

Cross references for headings of individual persons are made according to *AACR2R* and maintained in name authority records. Examples include:

Lewis, C. S. (Clive Staples), 1898-1963
See references from:
Lewis, Jack, 1898-1963
Hamilton, Clive, 1898-1963
Clerk, N. W., 1898-1963
Lewis, Clive Staples, 1898-1963

Onassis, Jacqueline Kennedy, 1929-
See references from:
Kennedy, Jacqueline Bouvier, 1929-
Kennedy, Jackie, 1929-
Onassis, Jackie, 1929-
Bouvier, Jacqueline, 1929-
Jackie, 1929-

For contemporary authors or authors with separate bibliographic identities who have multiple headings, only the "basic heading" established according to *Library of Congress Rule Interpretations*[20] is used as the subject heading for works about the person, for example:

Twain, Mark, 1835-1910
For works of this author entered under other names, search also under Clemens, Samuel Langhorne, 1835-1910, Snodgrass, Quintus Curtius, 1835-1910

Clemens, Samuel Langhorne, 1835-1910
Works by this author are usually entered under Twain, Mark, 1835-1910. For a listing of other names used by this author, search also under Twain, Mark, 1835-1910[21]
SUBJECT USAGE: This heading is not valid for use as a subject. Works about this person are entered under Twain, Mark, 1835-1910[22]

Snodgrass, Quintus Curtius, 1835-1910
Works by this author are usually entered under Twain, Mark, 1835-1910. For a listing of other names used by this author, search also under Twain, Mark, 1835-1910
SUBJECT USAGE: This heading is not valid for use as a subject. Works about this person are entered under Twain, Mark, 1835-1910

References for headings of fictitious and mythological characters are established and maintained in LCSH. UF and RT references are made from variant names and different entry elements. Examples include:

Potter, Harry (Fictitious character)
UF Harry Potter (Fictitious character)

Randolph, Snooky (Fictitious character)
UF Snooks (Fictitious character)
UF Snooky (Fictitious character)

Zeus (Greek deity)
BT Gods, Greek
RT Jupiter (Roman deity)

Family Names

For headings of family names, UF references are made for different spellings not used as valid headings, and RT references are made to and from each known variant of the family name that has been established as a valid heading:

Adams family
UF Adam family
Adamson family
Addams family
Adems family
Adom family
RT Ade family

Goodenough family
UF Goodenow family
Goodnough family

Cook family
RT Koch family

Koch family
RT Cook family

Gregory family
RT McGregor family

McGregor family
RT Gregory family

Dynasties[23]

For royal houses, USE references are made from variant forms of the name, and *BT* references are made from appropriate history headings for dynasties and from **[Country, Country of origin** or **Country most closely identified with royal house]–Kings and rulers**. Examples include:

Hoysala dynasty, ca. 1006-ca. 1346
BT India–Kings and rulers

Habsburg, House of
UF Austria, House of
Hapsburg, House of
BT Austria–Kings and rulers

Saxe-Coburg-Gotha, House of
UF Coburg, House of
BT Bavaria (Germany)–Kings and rulers

Savoy, House of
BT Italy–Kings and rulers

Houses of Dukes, Counts, or Earls

For names of houses of dukes, counts, or earls, UF references from variant names, forms, and entry elements are made, as well as BT references from **Nobility –[Country]**. Examples include:

Leinster, Dukes of
UF Dukes of Leinster
BT Nobility–Ireland

Masino, Counts of
UF Counts of Masino
BT Nobility–Italy

Derby, Earls of
UF Earls of Derby
BT Nobility–Great Britain

Corporate Names

Like headings for individual persons, headings for individual corporate bodies are established according to *AACR2R* and maintained in name authority records.

For corporate bodies that have changed their names, successive headings, that is, headings under both earlier and later names, are made, for example:

American Library Association. Information Science and Automation Division
Search also under the later heading:
Library and Information Technology Association (U.S.)

Library and Information Technology Association (U.S.)
Search also under the earlier heading:
American Library Association. Information Science and Automation Division

For discussions on the use of earlier and later name headings in cataloging, see chapters 4 and 9.

Geographic Names

Jurisdictional Names

Jurisdictional headings and cross references are made according to the provisions of *AACR2R* and maintained as name headings in the authority file. Examples include:

Austria
See references from:
Ostmark
Alpen- und Donau-Reichsgaue
Ausztria
Österreich
See also references from:
Austro-Hungarian Monarchy
Holy Roman Empire

George Town (Pinang)
See references from:

Georgetown (Pinang)
George Town, Pulau Pinang
Pinang (Pinang)
Penang (Pinang)
George Town (Malaysia)

Non-Jurisdictional Names[24]

Non-jurisdictional headings and cross references are established and listed in *LCSH*. UF references are made from variant (including former) names, different language forms, and different entry elements. If appropriate, BT references are made from generic headings subdivided by country or first-order political division to specific non-jurisdictional geographic headings, for example:

Berkeley, Vale of (England)
UF Vale of Berkeley (England)
BT Valleys–England

Bierzo (Spain)
UF El Bierzo (Spain)

Costa del Sol (Spain)
UF Sol, Costa del (Spain)
BT Coasts–Spain

Cumberland River (Ky. and Tenn.)
BT Rivers–Kentucky
BT Rivers–Tennessee

El Rancho Gumbo (Mont.)
UF Rancho Gumbo (Mont.)
BT Ranches–Montana

Gallipoli Peninsula (Turkey)
UF Gelibolu Peninsula (Turkey)
BT Peninsulas–Turkey

Geysers, The (Calif.)
UF Big Geysers (Calif.)
The Geysers (Calif.)
BT Geysers–California

Mojave Desert (Calif.)
UF Mohave Desert (Calif.)
BT Deserts–California

Mississippi River
BT Rivers–United States
NT Mississippi Embayment

Pompeii (Extinct city)
UF Pompei (Extinct city)
Pompeii (Ancient city)
BT Extinct cities–Italy
Italy–Antiquities

Texas Panhandle (Tex.)
UF Panhandle (Tex. : Region)

If the feature is located in more than three countries or first-order political divisions of the United States, Canada, or Great Britain, the generic heading in the BT references is subdivided by an appropriate broader geographic name:

Ohio River
BT Rivers–United States

Alps
BT Mountains–Europe

Changes in Geographic Names

In the case of name changes from mergers or splits in which different names of the same place are used as headings for works covering different periods, RT references are made between the successive (i.e., earlier and later) headings. These references are traced in the name authority records but do not necessarily appear in LCSH. Following are examples of changes in jurisdictional names:

Germany
(Subject usage: This heading is used for the region and country before or during World War II; the postwar zones of occupation collectively; East and West Germany collectively during the period 1949-1990; or the reunified Germany since 1990.)
UF Federal Republic of Germany
Weimar Republic
Etc.
RT Germany (East)
Germany (West)
Etc.

Germany (East)

(Subject usage: This heading is used for works on the eastern part of Germany before 1949; the Russian occupation zone; the German Democratic Republic 1949-1990; or the eastern part of reunified Germany since 1990.)

UF Democratic German Republic
East German Democratic Republic
East Germany (Democratic Republic)
Eastern Germany
Germany (Democratic Republic)
Germany (Democratic Republic, 1949-)
Germany (East)
Etc.

RT Germany
Germany (West)
Etc.

Germany (West)

(Subject usage: This heading is used for works on the western part of Germany before 1949; the United States, British, and French occupation zones; the German Federal Republic 1949-1990; or the western part of reunified Germany since 1990.)

UF Federal Republic of Germany
German Federal Republic
Germany (Federal Republic, 1949-)
Germany (West)
West Germany (1949-1990)
Western Germany
Etc.

RT Germany
Germany (East)
Etc.

Headings for Other Named Entities and Events

Appropriate cross references are made for headings of other types of named entities and events. Examples include:

London and Port Stanley Railway

BT Railroads–Canada

London Bridge (London, England)

BT Bridges–England

Persian Gulf War, 1991
UF Desert Storm, Operation, 1991
Gulf War, 1991
Operation Desert Storm, 1991
War in the Gulf, 1991
RT Iraq-Kuwait Crisis, 1990-1991
BT Iraq–History–1958-
Persian Gulf Region–History
United States–History, Military–20th century

United States–History–King George's War, 1744-1748
UF Governor Shirley's War
King George's War, 1744-1748
BT Austrian Succession, War of, 1740-1748
Indians of North America–Wars–1600-1750
NT Minas (N.S.) Expedition, 1747

World War, 1914-1918
UF European War, 1914-1918
First World War, 1914-1918
Great War, 1914-1918
World War 1, 1914-1918
World War I, 1914-1918
World War One, 1914-1918
BT History, Modern–20th century
NT Schlieffen Plan

CONCLUSION

Cross references provide a useful structure of relationships among subject headings. In practice, however, it has not been demonstrated that the effectiveness and usefulness of these references have been fully realized in actual use. In many libraries, it is a question whether all appropriate references have been provided in the catalog. To ensure that all the suggested references are made requires a great deal of effort and time. At a time when fast cataloging is a top priority and online cataloging is often performed by technicians at the terminal, one wonders how many libraries are actually able to follow up on all references each time a new heading is introduced into the catalog or a new reference has been suggested by the Library of Congress. On the other hand, both the principle of specific entry and the principle of uniform heading rely heavily on cross references for subject collocation. Omission or negligence in the provision of cross references reduces access points and greatly lessens the effectiveness of LCSH as a tool for subject retrieval. Because online catalogs vary in their provision of extensive browsing capability, it is particularly important to provide cross references that can link the user's input terms to those used in subject access fields in bibliographic records.

Together, different kinds of references enhance access points and help users navigate their searches through terms that are related hierarchically or otherwise. The importance of cross references cannot be overemphasized. Neglecting cross references greatly compromises the effectiveness of a controlled vocabulary.

NOTES

1. Library of Congress, Cataloging Policy and Support Office, *Subject Cataloging Manual: Subject Headings*, 5th ed., 2000 cumulation (Washington, D.C.: Library of Congress, 2000), H373.

2. In the MARC 21 authorities format, the synonymous terms not used as headings are included in the 4XX fields, cf. *MARC 21 Format for Authority Data: Including Guidelines for Content Designation*, prepared by Network Development and MARC Standards Office (Washington, D.C.: Cataloging Distribution Service, Library of Congress, 1999).

3. Charles A. Cutter, *Rules for a Dictionary Catalog*, 4th ed., rewritten (Washington, D.C.: Government Printing Office, 1904), 70.

4. David Judson Haykin, *Subject Headings: A Practical Guide* (Washington, D.C.: Government Printing Office, 1951), 14.

5. Library of Congress, *Subject Cataloging Manual*, H310.

6. Library of Congress, *Subject Cataloging Manual*, H374.

7. Library of Congress, *Subject Cataloging Manual*, H370, H375.

8. Cutter, *Rules for a Dictionary Catalog*, 79.

9. Haykin, *Subject Headings*, 14.

10. Library of Congress, *Subject Cataloging Manual*, H370.

11. Phyllis Allen Richmond, "Cats: An Example of Concealed Classification in Subject Headings," *Library Resources & Technical Services* 3 (Spring 1959): 102-112.

12. Bella Hass Weinberg, "The Hidden Classification in Library of Congress Subject Headings for Judaica," *Library Resources & Technical Services* 37 (October 1993): 369-379.

13. *Medical Subject Headings* (Bethesda, Md.: U.S. Department of Health and Human Services, Public Health Service, National Institutes of Health, National Library of Medicine, 1960-).

14. Forms of name headings and their qualifiers are discussed in detail in chapter 4.

15. Examples of subject-to-name references included:

Architects, British
SA Wren, Sir Christopher, 1632-1723

Soft drink industry-Great Britain
SA Schweppes (Firm)

International airports-New York (State)
SA John F. Kennedy International Airport
Television programs-Canada
SA Connections (Television program)
Confucianism-Sacred books
SA Shih san ching

16. Library of Congress, *Subject Cataloging Manual*, H370.

17. Library of Congress, *Subject Cataloging Manual*, H370, pp. 11-12.

18. "General See Also References," *Cataloging Service Bulletin* 19 (Winter 1982): 15.

19. Library of Congress, *Subject Cataloging Manual*, H371.

20. *Library of Congress Rule Interpretations,* 2nd ed. [editor, Robert M. Hiatt; formulated by the Office for Descriptive Cataloging Policy, Library of Congress], (Washington, D.C.: Cataloging Distribution Service, Library of Congress, 1989-), 22.2B, 2.

21. On an LC name authority record, this note is found in field 663.

22. In an LC name authority record, this note is found in field 667.

23. Library of Congress, *Subject Cataloging Manual*, H1574.

24. Library of Congress, *Subject Cataloging Manual*, H690.

7 Subject Authority Control and Maintenance

INTRODUCTION

In the Library of Congress subject cataloging system using the controlled vocabulary LCSH, only authorized terms are valid for use as subject headings.[1] Among the principles governing LCSH is that of specificity, which requires that a heading or headings closest to the contents of the work being cataloged be assigned. As knowledge grows, new subjects—for which no adequate subject headings yet exist—are constantly emerging. Therefore, any topic encountered in cataloging, but not yet represented in LCSH, may be proposed as a new subject heading so long as it represents a "discrete, identifiable concept."[2] Furthermore, because terminology also changes, and because the list must reflect current usage in order to be effective, modifications of established headings may also be proposed.

Developing and maintaining a list of controlled vocabulary is often referred to as thesaurus construction and maintenance. The vehicle for thesaurus construction and maintenance at the Library of Congress is an editorial group within the Cataloging Policy and Support Office (CPSO), which meets weekly. Attendants at the weekly meetings include the editor of LCSH (serving as the team leader of the Subjects Headings Editorial Team), an assistant editor of LCSH (responsible for processing the weekly list), a subject cataloging policy specialist, a representative from the Cooperative Cataloging Team (representing SACO, the subject authority component of the PCC), and any interested LC catalogers, visitors, etc. The group considers all proposals for changes: additions to, alterations in, or deletions of existing headings, heading/subdivision combinations, cross references, or free-floating subdivisions. For new headings, the group deliberates on terminology (wording), cross references, scope notes, compatibility with descriptive headings (if applicable), and conformity to existing patterns and broad policies governing LCSH. A new heading or changed heading that has been approved by this group is said to be "editorially established".

New headings proposed and examined at each editorial meeting are generally of five types: headings representing new objects or concepts, combinations (coordinations) of existing headings, new subdivisions under existing headings, new free-floating subdivisions, and cross references. Headings proposed for revision and updating are handled in the same way; they must be reviewed by the editorial group before they are formally established in their new form. Guidelines for establishing new headings are given in the *Subject Cataloging Manual: Subject Headings.*[3]

After each weekly editorial meeting, all new and revised headings are placed in a weekly list and posted to the CPSO web site (http://lcweb.loc.gov/catdir/cpso/wlsabt.html). They are then incorporated into the authority file and included in the next edition of *Library of Congress Subject Headings.*

ESTABLISHING NEW HEADINGS[4]

Procedure

Most proposals for new subjects originate with catalogers, who recognize the need for a new or changed heading in the course of their everyday work. When a subject that is not yet represented in LCSH is found in a work being cataloged, the cataloger usually proposes a new heading. A new subject heading may also be proposed for a topic needed as a BT reference for an existing heading, in order to complete its hierarchical chain.

Until 2003, catalogers at the Library of Congress were responsible for proposing new or changed subject headings as needed in cataloging the Library's collections. In 2003, the Program for Cooperative Cataloging (PCC) established the SACO Program to enable librarians from PCC member libraries to propose new and changed LC subject headings. Members of SACO may submit subject heading proposals to the Library of Congress for review and approval. Over the past decade, many new headings were established and existing headings changed as a result of SACO activities.

Authority Research

In proposing a new subject heading, and as preparation for the authority record that will be made if the heading is approved, catalogers have to do considerable research. Catalogers proposing new headings must document all the elements that apply to the proposal at issue. Their first step is the identification of a new concept in a work being cataloged. This concept is then verified in reference sources. If the proposed heading is analogous to an existing heading or a pattern, the existing heading or pattern may be cited as one of the authorities on which the proposed heading is based.

Sources consulted as authorities for establishing new headings are recorded in the proposed authority record, regardless of whether the term sought appears in them or not. To guard against later duplication of effort, that is, checking the same source again, information on such "empty" sources is particularly important in cases where the cataloger fails to find the term in question in any likely source outside the work being cataloged.

The most frequently consulted sources[5] include the following:

- the work being cataloged
- existing LC subject headings, which may serve as patterns for the proposed heading
- records in LC's MARC database
- general dictionaries, especially *Webster's Third New International Dictionary* (Web. 3), which is always cited when applicable
- general encyclopedias, for example, *Americana*, *Britannica*, *Collier's*, etc.
- general indexes and thesauri, for example, *New York Times Index*, *Legislative Indexing Vocabulary* (LIV), *Readers' Guide*, etc.
- titles in the LC MARC database
- bibliography in the work being cataloged
- topical reference sources and other authoritative works in the field in question, if the topic is peculiar to a particular discipline

For certain categories of headings, subject catalogers have been instructed to consult specific references. For a list of these sources, see appendix E. When needed, Library of Congress catalogers may also consult appropriate individuals or agencies by telephone.

Authority Records

LCSH is kept up to date through the creation and maintenance of subject authority records, which are kept in the authority file—the set of current authority records. After editorial approval, an authority record is prepared for each new heading that has been established. For a changed heading, the existing authority record is updated. The new and revised authority records are then entered into the Library of Congress authority database.

A subject authority record contains information regarding the following aspects of the subject heading:

- exact form of the approved subject heading
- scope note, if appropriate
- instruction for geographic subdivision and Library of Congress classification number(s), if any
- references: UF, BT, RT, and general references

- authorities or sources consulted in determining the choice of the heading and references

Following are examples of subject authority records retrieved from the online system of the Library of Congress. Each record shows the established heading, cross references, the authorities consulted, and notes. Details of the MARC 21 Authority Format regarding subject authority records are shown in appendix G. Following are the legends of the most frequently used MARC 21 codes for subject authority records:

010 __ |a ***Library of Congress control number***
040 __ |a ***Cataloging source***
053 __ |a ***Library of Congress classification number***
073 __ |a ***Subdivision usage***
150 __ |a ***Heading (Topical term)***
180 __ |a ***General subdivision***
181 __ |a ***Geographic subdivision***
182 __ |a ***Chronological subdivision***
185 __ |a ***Form subdivision***
450 __ |a ***See from tracing (Topical term)***
451 __ |a ***See from tracing (Geographic name)***
451 __ |a ***See from tracing***
480 __ |a ***See from tracing (General subdivision)***
481 __ |a ***See from tracing (Geographic subdivision)***
482 __ |a ***See from tracing (Chronological subdivision)***
485 __ |a ***See also from tracing (Form subdivision)***
550 __ |a ***See also from tracing (Topical term)***
  __ |w g ***(Broader term)***
  __ |w h ***(Narrower term)***
551 __ |a ***See also from tracing (Geographic name)***
  __ |w g ***(Broader term)***
  __ |w h ***(Narrower term)***
580 __ |a ***See also from tracing (General subdivision)***
  __ |w g ***(Broader term)***
  __ |w h ***(Narrower term)***
581 __ |a ***See also from tracing (Geographic subdivision)***
  __ |w g ***(Broader term)***
  __ |w h ***(Narrower term)***
582 __ |a ***See from tracing (Chronological subdivision)***
585 __ |a ***See also from tracing (Form subdivision)***
667 __ |a ***Nonpublic general note, including note regarding subject usage***
670 __ |a ***"Source data found" note***
675 __ |a ***"Source data not found" note***
680 __ |a ***Public general note***
681 __ |a ***Subject example tracing note***

• *Topics in social sciences*:

LC Control Number: sh2001010959
HEADING: Space tourism
010 __ la sh2001010959
040 __ la DLC lb eng lc DLC
150 __ la Space tourism
551 __ lw g la Outer space lx Civilian use
550 __ lw g la Tourism
670 __ la Work cat.: 2001008069: Dennis Tito, first space tourist, 2003.
670 __ la LC database, Dec. 14, 2001 lb (Space tourism)
670 __ la George Washington University, Space Tourism Initiative website, Dec. 14, 2001.
675 __ la Janes aerospace dict.; la SAE dict. of aerosp. eng.

LC Control Number: sh2003003061
HEADING: Direct democracy
010 __ la sh2003003061
040 __ la DLC lb eng lc DLC
150 __ la Direct democracy
450 __ la Direct legislation
550 __ lw g la Democracy
550 __ la Referendum
670 __ la Encyc. Britannica lb (direct democracy)
670 __ la World Book encyc. lb (direct democracy)
670 __ la National Initiative for Democracy Web site lb (direct democracy)
670 __ la WWW, April 15, 2003 lb (direct democracy; direct legislation)
680 __ li Here are entered works on a form of government in which the people govern themselves under procedures of majority rule rather than by electing representatives.

LC Control Number: sh2003006425
HEADING: Worksite schools
010 __ la sh2003006425
040 __ la NvLN lb eng lc DLC
150 __ la Worksite schools
550 __ lw g la Public schools
550 __ la Industry and education
670 __ la Work cat.: Dietz, D. Worksite schools : a study of cooperation between public education and private, 2001 lb (unpublished thesis)
680 __ li Here are entered works on public schools located on the private property of a host corporation and usually deriving a significant portion of their upkeep from the host corporation.

• *Topics on contemporary public affairs and events*

LC Control Number: sh2001000147
HEADING: September 11 Terrorist Attacks, 2001
010 __ |a sh2001000147
040 __ |a DLC |b eng |c DLC |d DLC
053 _0 |a HV6432.7
150 __ |a September 11 Terrorist Attacks, 2001
450 __ |a 9/11 Terrorist Attacks, 2001
450 __ |a 911 Terrorist Attacks, 2001
450 __ |a Attack on America, 2001 (September 11 Terrorist Attacks)
410 2_ |a Pentagon (Va.) |x Terrorist Attack, 2001
450 __ |a Pentagon-World Trade Center Terrorist Attacks, 2001
450 __ |a Sept. 11 Terrorist Attacks, 2001
450 __ |a September 11 Terror Attacks, 2001
450 __ |a September 11 Terrorism, 2001
450 __ |a Terrorist Attacks, September 11, 2001
410 2_ |a World Trade Center (New York, N.Y.) |x Terrorist Attack, 2001
450 __ |a World Trade Center-Pentagon Terrorist Attacks, 2001
550 __ |w g |a Hijacking of aircraft |z United States
550 __ |w g |a Terrorism |z United States
670 __ |a New York Times, Sept. 12, 2001 |b (terrorist attacks; Sept. 11 terrorist attacks)
670 __ |a New York Times on the Web, Sept. 12-17, 2001 |b (terrorist attacks; attack on America; Sept. 11 terrorist attacks; Sept. 11 terror attacks; Sept. 11 terrorism)
670 __ |a Washington Post, Sept. 12, 2001 |b (terrorist attacks; attack on America; Sept. 11 terrorist attacks)
670 __ |a NBC News television broadcasts, Sept. 11-17, 2001 |b (attack on America)
670 __ |a Alltheweb search, Oct. 5, 2001 |b (911 terrorist attacks; 9/11 terrorist attacks)
680 __ |i Here are entered works on the attacks by terrorists on the World Trade Center in New York City and the Pentagon outside Washington, D.C., using three hijacked commercial jetliners, and on the crash of a fourth hijacked jetliner in a rural area of Pennsylvania on September 11, 2001.

• *Topics in humanities*

LC Control Number: sh2002002658
HEADING: Cool jazz
010 __ |a sh2002002658
040 __ |a DLC |b eng |c DLC
150 __ |a Cool jazz
450 __ |a Cool jazz |z United States
550 __ |w g |a Jazz
670 __ |a Work cat.: 2002070036: Bebop to cool, 2002.

670 __ |a New Grove jazz: |b Cool jazz (diverse styles of modern jazz variously perceived as subdued, understated, or emotionally cool; players themselves often voiced distaste for the label; most saxophonists were disciples of Lester Young; a number of trumpeters drew on the style of Miles Davis; cool drummers played more quietly and conservatively than other modern jazz drummers; no well-defined cool jazz piano style)

LC Control Number: sh2002004251
HEADING: Projection art
010 __ |a sh2002004251
040 __ |a DLC |b eng |c DLC
150 __ |a Projection art
450 __ |a Projected art works
450 __ |a Projected images (Art)
450 __ |a Projection pieces (Art)
450 __ |a Projection works (Art)
450 __ |a Projections (Art)
550 __ |w g |a Environment (Art)
550 __ |w g |a Light art
670 __ |a Work cat.: 82060044: Projections, 1982: |b introd. (projection art, projected art work)
670 __ |a Projected images, 1974 |b (text: environmental works that depend upon specific light sources for their existence)
670 __ |a AAT |b (projections; UFs projected images, projection pieces, projection works)
675 __ |a Grove dict. of art
680 __ |i Here are entered works on environmental art created totally or partially by using still or moving projected light images.

• *Topics in science and technology*

LC Control Number: sh 95000713
HEADING: Computer network resources
010 __ |a sh 95000713
040 __ |a DLC |c DLC |d DLC |d WaU
150 __ |a Computer network resources
360 __ |i subdivision |a Computer network resources |i under subjects
450 __ |a Internet resources
550 __ |w g |a Electronic information resources
550 __ |a Uniform Resource Identifiers
670 __ |a Work cat.: 95002183: Rosenfeld, L. Internet compendium subject guides to social sciences, business and law resources, 1995.
680 __ |i Here are entered works on computer network resources available for research in various fields. Works on methodologies for conducting research projects using the Internet are entered under |a Internet research. |i Works

on using various Internet tools and search engines effectively to find information are entered under |a Internet searching.
681 __ |i Notes under |a Internet research; Internet searching

LC Control Number: sh 99005116
HEADING: Web portals
010 __ |a sh 99005116
040 __ |a DLC |b eng |c DLC
150 __ |a Web portals
450 __ |a Internet portals
450 __ |a Portals (World Wide Web)
550 __ |w g |a Web sites
550 __ |a Web search engines
670 __ |a Work cat.: 97077803: Official Excite Internet yellow pages, 1999.
670 __ |a Info Trac business index July 9, 1999 |b (Web portals, portals, sites that sell themselves as starting points for World Wide Web browsing; Yahoo, Lycos, Excite biggest ones; often started as search engines, but now have in addition topically arranged direct links to sites on topics of interest to most browsers, and may also offer e-mail, calendar, or other services to users; often supported by advertising; special, topical portals with direct links only to a single topic or few related topics are also called vertical portals or simply hubs)
670 __ |a WWW through AltaVista July 9, 1999 |b ("Web portal", 5118 hits, conforming to Info Trac meaning; "internet portal", 4756 hits, many conforming to Info Trac meaning of "Web portal," and many meaning "Internet gateway," or networking connectivity)
680 __ |i Here are entered works on web sites that offer themselves as starting points for web browsing, usually offering topically arranged direct links to sites of general interest as well as a search engine, and sometimes also offering electronic mail or other services.

LC Control Number: sh2003005956
HEADING: Flip chip technology
010 __ |a sh2003005956
040 __ |a ArU |b eng |c DLC
150 __ |a Flip chip technology
450 __ |a Flip chip devices
550 __ |w g |a Electronic packaging
670 __ |a Work cat.: Sur, R. Low cost flip chip technology for high density solder bumps, 2002.
670 __ |a Quach, H.A. Flip chip on flexible substrate packaging technology for power electronics, 2000.
670 __ |a Compendex, March 28, 2003 |b (flip chip technology, flip chip devices, flip chip construction)
670 __ |a INSPEC thesaurus |b (flip chip devices)
670 __ |a Google search, March 27, 2003 |b (flip chip technology)
675 __ |a Electrical engineering handbook, 1997; |a ASTI

LC Control Number: sh2001002661
HEADING: Sound recordings Remixing
010 __ |a sh2001002661
040 __ |a DLC |b eng |c DLC |d PPi
150 __ |a Sound recordings |x Remixing
550 __ |w g |a Arrangement (Music)
550 __ |w g |a Electronic composition
550 __ |w g |a Sound |x Recording and reproducing
550 __ |a Remixes
550 __ |a Turntablism
670 __ |a Work cat.: 00100535: Gerrish, B.M. Remix, c2001: |b subtitle (the electronic music explosion) p. 36 (Remixing is the art of creating an alternate version of a song or instrumental piece. Early methods such as manual tape splicing and live mixing have given way to a dazzling array of digitally based tools)
670 __ |a New Grove, 2nd ed. WWW site, Oct. 15, 2001 |b (remix: recording produced by combining sections of existing recorded tracks in new patterns and with new material; found in many different types of popular music, but most usually associated with club dance music)
670 __ |a Am. heritage dict., 4th ed. |b (remix. tr. v. -mixed, -mixing, -mixes. To recombine (audio tracks or channels from a recording) to produce a new or modified audio recording; "remixed a popular ballad and turned it into a dance hit")

LC Control Number: sh2002000809
HEADING: Genomics
010 __ |a sh2002000809
040 __ |a DLC |b eng |c DLC
053 _0 |a QH447 |b QH447.8
150 __ |a Genomics
450 __ |a Genome research
450 __ |a Genomes |x Research
550 __ |w g |a Molecular genetics
550 __ |a Genomes
670 __ |a Work cat.: 2002067456: Campbell, A.M. Discovering genomics, proteomics, and bioinformatics, c2002.
670 __ |a MESH |b (Genomics)

- *Geographic names*

LC Control Number: n 80061023
HEADING: Belgian Congo
010 __ |a n 80061023
040 __ |a DLC |c DLC |d DLC
151 _0 |a Belgian Congo
451 _0 |w nna |a Congo, Belgian

451 _0 |a Belgian Kongo
451 _0 |a Congo belge
451 _0 |a Belgisch Congo
451 _0 |a Belga-Kongó
551 _0 |a Congo (Democratic Republic)
551 _0 |a Congo Free State
667 __ |a SUBJECT USAGE: This heading is not valid for use as a subject. Works about this place are entered under Congo (Democratic Republic)
670 __ |a Benkes, M. Belga-Kongó függetlenné válásának története, 1985: |b t.p. (Belga-Kongó)

LC Control Number: n 80061025
HEADING: Zaire
010 __ |a n 80061025 |z sh 85149553
040 __ |a DLC |c DLC |d DLC |d ICRL |d DLC |d WaU
043 __ |a f-cg---
151 __ |a Zaire
451 __ |a République du Zaïre
551 __ |a Congo (Democratic Republic)
667 __ |a Valid for the period Oct 1971-May 1997
667 __ |a SUBJECT USAGE: This heading is not valid for use as a subject. Works about this place are entered under Congo (Democratic Republic).
670 __ |a Boogaerts, M. |b Bibliographien ... 1969.
670 __ |a Foreign names info. bull., May 30, 1997 |b (former name: Zaire, Republic of [conventional]; République du Zaïre [French]; new name: Congo, Democratic Republic of the [conventional]; République démocratique du Congo [French])

LC Control Number: n 80061022
HEADING: Congo (Democratic Republic)
010 __ |a n 80061022
040 __ |a DLC |b eng |c DLC |d DLC |d OCl |d InU |d DLC-S |d WaU |d FU |d WaU
043 __ |a f-cg---
151 __ |a Congo (Democratic Republic)
451 __ |a Congo (Leopoldville)
451 __ |a République du Congo (Leopoldville)
451 __ |a Republic of the Congo (Leopoldville)
451 __ |a Republic of Congo (Leopoldville)
451 __ |a République démocratique du Congo
451 __ |a Democratic Republic of the Congo
451 __ |a Congo (Kinshasa)
451 __ |a RDC
451 __ |a DRC
451 __ |a Democratic Republic of Congo

551 __ |w a |a Belgian Congo
551 __ |a Zaire
667 __ |a Valid for the period July 1960-Oct. 1971 and May 1997-
670 __ |a Moniteur congolais.
670 __ |a LC manual cat. |b (hdg.: Congo (Democratic Republic); info: the Belgian Congo became independent on June 30, 1960 as the République du Congo, commonly identified as Congo (Leopoldville) at U.N. and by others to distinguish it from its neighbor Congo (Brazzaville); the previous LC hdg. Congo (Leopoldville) was changed to Congo (Democratic Republic) after the name of Leopoldville was changed to Kinshasa in July 1966; in Oct. 1971 the name of the country was changed to Zaire)
670 __ |a Foreign names info. bull., May 30, 1997 |b (former name: Zaire, Republic of [conventional]; République du Zaïre [French]; new name: Congo, Democratic Republic of the [conventional]; République démocratique du Congo [French])
670 __ |a Le DCK legue son message á la RDC, 1999: |b p. 11, passim (République Démocratique du Congo)
670 __ |a Grands lacs, 2002: |b t.p. (RDC) p. 75 (République démocratique du Congo)
670 __ |a Electoral perspectives and the process of democratisation in the DRC, 2002: |b p. 5 (Democratic Republic of Congo (DRC))
781 _0 |z Congo (Democratic Republic)

In formulating cross references, subject catalogers are instructed to ensure that the terms in the proposed USE references do not conflict with existing headings or other existing USE references, and that hierarchical and related term references connect valid headings and conform to established patterns for cross references, if any. On the proposed authority record, USED FOR references are recorded with the label UF, the labels BT and NT for hierarchical references, the label RT for related-term references, and the label SA for general see also references.

Subdivision Records[6]

Until recently, authority records have been created for main headings and precoordinated main heading–subdivision combinations only. In January 2003, Library of Congress completed a project to create subdivision authority records for more than 3,000 topical, form, and chronological free-floating subdivisions. These records contain a basic usage statement, and some contain references. Below are examples of subdivision records:

• *Topical subdivisions*

010 __|a sh 99001117
040 __|a IEN |b eng |c DLC |d DLC
073 __|a H 1147 |a H 1164 |a H 1180 |z lcsh
180 __|x Abnormalities
480 __|w nne |x Abnormities and deformities
480 __|x Deformities
667 __|a Further subdivide by subdivisions used under diseases.
680 __|i Use as a topical subdivision under individual animals and groups of animals, individual plants and groups of plants, and individual organs and regions of the body.

010 __|a sh 00005894
040 __|a IEN |b eng |c DLC
073 __|a H 1095__|a H 1105__|a H 1153__|a H 1159 |z lcsh
180 __|x Inventory control
480 __|x Control, Inventory
667 __|a Do not subdivide geographically under names of individual corporate bodies and military services.
680 |i Use as a topical subdivision under names of individual corporate bodies and military services, and under types of industries, organizations, and facilities.

• *Chronological subdivisions*

010 __|a sh2002012473
040 __|a IEN |b eng |c DLC |d DLC
073 __|a H 1148__|a H 1156__|a H 1160 |z lcsh
182 __|y 17th century
680 __|i Use as a chronological subdivision under headings for art and art forms of all nations, regions, and ethnic groups, except those headings for art and art forms of China, Japan, and Korea. Also use under forms and types of musical compositions and headings for drama.

• *Geographic subdivisions*

The Library of Congress does not routinely create subdivision records for geographic names. Instead, the subdivision forms of geographic names are recorded in 781 linking fields added to subject authority records for geographic headings, and in the future, to name authority records for geographic headings. Following is one of the few geographic subdivision records that the Library of Congress has created.

010 __|a sh 99001185
040 __|a IEN |b eng |c DLC |d DLC
073 __|a H 1095__|a H 1103__|a H 1154__|a H 1156__|a H 1159 |z lcsh
181 __|z Foreign countries

680 __|i Use as a geographic subdivision under ethnic groups, individual languages, individual literatures, military services, and types of publications qualified by language or nationality.

• *Form subdivisions*

010 __|a sh 99001772
040 __|a IEN |b eng |c DLC
073 __|a H 1095__|a H 1100__|a H 1103__|a H 1105__|a H 1140__|a H 1153 |zlcsh
185 __|v Telephone directories
485 __|w nne |v Directories |v Telephone
585 __|w g |v Directories
680 __|i Use as a form subdivision under names of countries, cities, etc., individual corporate bodies, classes of persons, ethnic groups, and types of organizations and industries.

Separate records are created for subdivisions that can function as either topical or form subdivisions:

010 __|a sh 99001647
040 __|a IEN |b eng |c DLC |d DLC
073 __|a H 1095 |z lcsh
185 __|v Periodicals
485 __|v Journals (Periodicals)
485 __|w nne |v Societies, periodicals, etc.
485 __|w nne |v Yearbooks
680 __|i Use as a form subdivision under subjects for periodicals on those subjects.
010 __|a sh 99002086
040 __|a DLC |b eng |c DLC |d DLC
073 __|a H 1095 |z lcsh
180 __|x Periodicals
480 __|x Journals (Periodicals)
480 __|w nne |x Societies, periodicals, etc.
480 __|w nne |x Yearbooks
680 __|i Use as a topical subdivision under subjects for works about periodicals on those subjects.

Subdivision records that include topical and form elements are tagged for the function that the subdivision in the first subfield performs. Additional subfields are coded for their specific functions.

010 __|a sh2003003679
040 __|a DLC |b eng |c DLC |d DLC
073 __|a H 1095 |z lcsh
180 __|x Periodicals |v Indexes
585 __|w g |v Indexes

680 __|i Use this subdivision combination as a form subdivision under subjects for indexes to periodicals on those subjects.

010 __|a sh 00007748
040 __|a IEN |b eng |c DLC
073 __|a H 1140 |z lcsh
180 __|x Climate |v Observations
585 __|w g |v Observations
680 __|i Use this subdivision combination as a form subdivision under names of countries, cities, etc.

REVISING AND UPDATING HEADINGS AND SUBDIVISIONS

A subject heading standing by itself fulfills the finding function of the catalog, but only in the way it stands as part of a larger whole in relation to other entries can it fulfill the catalog's collocation function. For this latter function, there are two requirements: The heading must be compatible with analogous headings, and there must be cross references among related headings.

A major requirement in ensuring a logically structured subject catalog is reconciling the conflicts that result from heading changes. Each change of heading affects not only the actual access points under the old heading in the catalog, but also all cross references that involve that heading. The magnitude of the work involved can be enormous. When resources are limited, large-scale revision and updating can only be performed gradually.

Changes in subject headings generally fall into the following six categories:

(1) Simple one-to-one changes for the purpose of updating terminology or spelling. Examples include:

Old heading	***Current heading***
Aeroplanes	**Airplanes**
Coaches (Music)	**Vocal coaches**
Coregonus autumnalis	**Arctic cisco**
Electronic percussion instruments	**Drum machine**
Handicapped	**People with disabilities**
Machine-readable dictionaries	**Electronic dictionaries**
Story telling–Therapeutic use	**Narrative therapy**

(2) Changes in headings containing proper names to conform to *AACR2R*. Examples include:

Old heading	***Current heading***
Piha Beach (New Zealand)	**Piha Beach (N.Z.)**

(3) Changes in form or entry element. Examples include:

Old heading	***Current heading***
Art objects, Shinto	**Shinto art objects**
Fire-making	**Firemaking**
Handpress	**Hand presses**
Public libraries–Services to adults	**Adult services in public libraries**

(4) Changes resulting from splitting a compound heading, or a heading containing two or more concepts, into separate headings. Examples include:

Old heading	***Current headings***
Campanologists	**Bell ringers** **Campanologists (Bell makers)**
Heliosphere	**Heliosphere (Astrophysics)** **Heliosphere (Ionosphere)**

(5) Changes resulting from merging overlapping headings into a single heading. Examples include:

Old heading	***Current heading***
Orion (Antisubmarine aircraft) *Orion (Reconnaissance aircraft)*	**Orion (Patrol aircraft)**

(6) Changes involving subdivisions. Examples include:

Old heading	***Current heading***
Bagpipe–Reeds	**Bagpipe reeds**
Clothing trade–Employees	**Clothing workers**
Salvation (Buddhism)	**Salvation–Buddhism**

When a subject heading containing an obsolete term is updated, all existing headings containing the obsolete term are revised to reflect the current term. All cross references related to the obsolete heading are also revised. In addition, a USE reference is made from the obsolete term to the new heading.

In addition to obsolete headings, many other headings have been or are being removed from LCSH. Each time a subdivision is declared free-floating, an effort is made to remove the subdivision under existing headings in LCSH, unless the heading–subdivision combinations contain unique cross references or their own subdivisions or are used as examples.

THE AUTHORITY FILE FOR SUBJECTS

For many years, the printed version of *LCSH* served as its subject authority file. Various supplementary lists were published, and a number of card files were created and maintained for internal use by the Subject Cataloging Division. Later, a subject authority card file was set up, and, later still, the automated *Subject Authority File.*

The first application of automation to subject headings at the Library of Congress was the conversion of the subject headings list into machine-readable form to enable the Government Printing Office to print the seventh (1966) edition of *LCSH* by photocomposition. The system, used until 1985, was developed and implemented by the Library of Congress between 1969 and 1972, that is, while the list was in its seventh edition, and soon after the Library began inputting its new English-language cataloging into the MARC database. It was thus one of the earliest of the Library's automation efforts. In 1986, the conversion of subject authority records according to the specifications in the *USMARC Format for Authority Data*[7] (now the *MARC 21 Format for Authority Data*[8]) was completed, and the *Subject Authority File* was implemented. For many years, subject authority records and name authority records were kept in two separate files. They are now maintained in the same database, *Library of Congress Authorities,* which is available at the Library's web site (http://authorities.loc.gov). This database contains subject authority headings, name authority headings, title authority headings, as well as name/title authority headings. These four types of authority records may be searched separately by designating the appropriate category. In addition, the Library of Congress maintains a master database for subject headings, which contains the most up-to-date data for subject headings and is used as the basis for generating LCSH in print and other formats.

Most of the name headings may be used as subject headings. However, by policy, some name headings are not used as subject headings.[9] In other cases, the name, when used as a subject heading, is in a different form, and the information regarding subject cataloging usage is given in the authority record in a field tagged 667 in a MARC 21 authority record, for example:

100 10 |**a** Dodgson, Charles Lutwidge, |**d** 1832-1898
667 __ |**a** SUBJECT USAGE: This heading not valid for use as a subject. Works about this person are entered under Carroll, Lewis, 1832-1898.

100 10 |**a** Clemens, Samuel Langhorne, |**d** 1835-1910
667 __ |**a** SUBJECT USAGE: This heading is not valid for use as a subject. Works about this person are entered under Twain, Mark, 1835-1910

NOTES

1. Some LC MARC records contain uncontrolled subject terms coded in the 653 field. These terms are outside of the scope of LCSH; in fully cataloged MARC records, the 653 field is "used under exceptional circumstances to provide supplementary subject access from natural language terms that are not included as headings or UF references in *Library of Congress Subject Headings* because of editorial policies, do not have precise English equivalents, and do not duplicate headings in any of the other searchable fields." (Library of Congress, Cataloging Policy and Support Office, *Subject Cataloging Manual: Subject Headings*, 5th ed., 2000 cumulation (Washington, D.C.: Library of Congress, 2000), H160, p. 1.

2. Library of Congress, *Subject Cataloging Manual*, H187.

3. Library of Congress, *Subject Cataloging Manual*, H180-H400.

4. Library of Congress, *Subject Cataloging Manual*, H200.

5. Library of Congress, *Subject Cataloging Manual*, H202, p. 4.

6. Library of Congress, Cataloging Policy and Support Office, *Subdivision Records*, http://lcweb.loc.gov/catdir/cpso/subdauth.html.

7. *USMARC Format for Authority Data: Including Guidelines for Content Designation*, prepared by Network Development and MARC Standards Office. (Washington, D.C.: Cataloging Distribution Service, Library of Congress, 1987).

8. *MARC 21 Format for Authority Data: Including Guidelines for Content Designation*, prepared by Network Development and MARC Standards Office. (Washington, D.C.: Cataloging Distribution Service, Library of Congress, 1999).

9. Library of Congress, *Subject Cataloging Manual*, H430.

PART 2

APPLICATION

8 Assigning Subject Headings

INTRODUCTION

The principles, form, and structure of Library of Congress subject headings are covered in part 1 of this book. Part 2 treats the practical aspect of subject heading assignment. The discussions are based largely on information published in *Subject Cataloging Manual: Subject Headings*,[1] *Cataloging Service Bulletin*,[2] and *Free-Floating Subdivisions: An Alphabetical Index*[3]; on consultation with the staff of the Cataloging Policy and Support Office of the Library of Congress; and on examination of LC MARC records.

Effective subject cataloging depends in large part on the individuals who assign subject headings. Their familiarity with and understanding of the nature and structure of subject headings, their interpretation of a given work, and their ability to coordinate headings with that work all affect the quality and effectiveness of subject access. Were all these factors optimal for all works cataloged, the resulting records would show a high degree of uniformity and consistency—except, of course, for the dissonances that spring from changing approaches to a subject over time. But the optimum is rarely achieved, and no subject catalog is as internally consistent as one might wish. Over the years, many theorists in the field have speculated that consistency would be greater if there were a code to govern subject heading work. However, it is extremely difficult to codify the procedures for assigning subject headings to specific works because of the inevitable subjective element that operates in subject cataloging. There are naturally differences from cataloger to cataloger in interpretation of content, and sometimes even the same individual reading the same work at two different times may not make the same judgment on its content.

It may also happen that some works are cataloged under different assumptions about the appropriate depth of subject indexing than are other works in the same catalog. Depth of cataloging for a document may vary from *summarization*, which aims to express only its overall subject content, to *exhaustive* or *in-depth indexing*, which aims to enumerate all its significant concepts or aspects, or to represent individual component parts of the work. The following examples demonstrate the two approaches: summarization and exhaustive indexing.

(1) Example of summarization:

Title: *Managing the construction process : estimating, scheduling, and project control* / Frederick E. Gould. c2002.
SUBJECTS:
Building–Superintendence.

The one heading in this example summarizes the overall subject of the work. The various aspects of the management of the construction process are not represented.

(2) Examples of exhaustive cataloging:

Title: *Daily life on the old colonial frontier* / James M. Volo and Dorothy Denneen Volo. 2002.
SUBJECTS:
Frontier and pioneer life–North America.
North America–History–Colonial period, ca. 1600-1775.
Europe–Territorial expansion–Social aspects.
North America–Ethnic relations.
Indians of North America–Government relations–To 1789.
Indians of North America–First contact with Europeans.
Fur trade–Social aspects–North America–History.
France–Relations–Great Britain.
Great Britain–Relations–France.

Title: *Teaching to change the world* / Jeannie Oakes, Martin Lipton. c2003.
SUBJECTS:
Public schools–United States.
Education–Aims and objectives–United States.
Curriculum planning–United States.
Classroom management–United States.
Effective teaching–United States.
Educational change–United States.

Title: *Western historical thinking : an intercultural debate* / edited by Jhorn Rhusen. 2002.
SUBJECTS:
History–Philosophy.
Civilization, Western.
Asia–Civilization–Historiography.
History–Methodology.
Historiography.

The subject headings assigned to the works in the second group above bring out individual topics within the work in addition to the heading(s) that summarize(s) the overall content. The difference between the two sets of examples lies in the exhaustive analysis.

Another concept related to depth of cataloging is level of cataloging: whether subject headings are assigned on the basis of the overall content of an entire work or on the content of individual units (such as chapters or articles), within a work.

It is the cataloging policy of a given library or information agency that primarily governs both the depth and exhaustiveness and the level of analysis, though individual judgments may vary considerably even under a given policy. Library of Congress policy has leaned toward summarization, most particularly in its earlier years.

In situations where summarization is considered insufficient, additional subject headings may be assigned. Alternatively, terms from the work itself may be used to bring out individual topics or aspects of the work. One might, for example, augment cataloging records by additional subject access points based on words and phrases found within the table of contents of the work being analyzed. This device would increase the number of subject access points and allow for a certain degree of free-text access to terms used in the document cataloged.

The discussion in part 2 of this book is based on Library of Congress practice, and examples are taken from LC MARC records. Individual libraries may establish their own policies with regard to the exhaustiveness and levels of subject cataloging.

GENERAL CONSIDERATIONS

General Policy

The general policy of assigning subject headings at the Library of Congress is stated in *Subject Cataloging Manual: Subject Headings* in the following words: "Assign to the work being cataloged one or more subject headings that best summarize the overall contents of the work and provide access to its most important topics. *LC practice:* Assign headings only for topics that comprise at least 20% of the work."[4] This policy provides guidelines for assigning headings that are considered essential. Headings that cover the overall content are referred to as primary headings. In practice, the policy has been interpreted loosely. While most LC catalogers follow it, many have regularly assigned additional headings to enhance access.

Sources of Subject Headings Assigned to Cataloging Records

As discussed in part 1 of this book, subject headings assigned to LC MARC records are not limited to those included in LCSH. Following is a list of sources of headings that may be used as subject entries in bibliographic records.[5]

Name Headings Established According to *AACR2R* Rules

Headings established according to *Anglo-American Cataloguing Rules* (*AACR2R*) include headings for persons, for corporate bodies, and for jurisdictions, as well as for uniform titles. Most but not all of these name headings may be used as subject headings. Also, in some cases, the form of a name assigned as a subject heading may be different from the one used in descriptive cataloging; when this is the case, the form of the heading used as subject is given in field 667 of the name authority record. For examples, see chapter 7.

Headings in LCSH

LCSH, in both the print and electronic versions, contains all topical/form headings (except those formed by free-floating phrases or free-floating subdivisions) and selected proper name headings such as certain categories of geographic headings and headings for fictitious characters. The LCSH Master Database, the online version of LCSH, constitutes the most current authority for subject headings because it is brought up to date most frequently.

Headings Constructed with the Use of Free-Floating Elements

Free-floating subdivisions and other elements found in *Subject Cataloging Manual: Subject Headings* may be combined with subject or name headings. The combinations resulting from main headings and free-floating subdivisions or phrases appear in bibliographic records but are not enumerated in LCSH, except when they serve as examples or when unique cross references or further subdivisions are required.

Headings with Multiple Subdivisions[6]

Headings with "multiple" subdivisions, in the form of bracketed terms or examples following an established subdivision under a valid main heading listed in LCSH or as part of a free-floating subdivision, were introduced in the fifth edition of *LCSH* as a device to save space in the printed list. The multiple subdivisions suggest that similar subdivisions may be used under the heading or as a part of the free-floating subdivision in question. In other words, similar subdivisions have the free-floating status under that particular heading. Currently, there are five types of multiple subdivisions in LCSH:

(1) Multiple subdivisions under established headings, for example:

Subject headings–Aeronautics, [Education, Latin America, Law, etc.]
Names, Personal–Scottish, [Spanish, Welsh, etc.]

With headings like these, any topic or qualifier falling into the categories indicated in the brackets may be combined with the main heading, for example:

Subject headings–Psychology
Names, Personal–Hungarian

(2) Multiple subdivisions under pattern headings:

World War, 1939-1945–Personal narratives, American, [French, German, etc.]
English language–Dictionaries–French, [Italian, etc.]

Because the multiple subdivisions are free-floating, the following headings, though not listed in LCSH, are valid:

Korean War, 1950-1953–Personal narratives, Chinese
Chinese language–Dictionaries–Latin

(3) Multiple free-floating subdivisions under name headings, for example, **[Name of person]–Views on [specific topic]; [Place]–Foreign public opinion, Austrian, [British, etc.].**

The following headings are valid as a result:

Jefferson, Thomas, 1743-1826–Views on slavery
United States–Foreign public opinion, Russian

The practice of "multiple" headings such as *Authors, American, [English, French, etc.]*; *Coins, Arab, [Austrian, French, etc.]*, which were printed in *LCSH* until 1981, has been discontinued.

(4) Multiple subdivisions displayed by means of instructional scope notes:

Solar eclipses
Subdivided by date, for example, Solar eclipses–1854.

Scope notes, which allow for free-floating subdivision as described, should not be confused with general *see also* references, which do not necessarily authorize free-floating use of a subdivision:

Pamphlets *(May Subd Geog)*
SA *subdivision* Pamphlets *under 16th, 17th and 18th century period subdivisions of European and American history, e.g.* Germany–History–1517-1648–Pamphlets; *and under individual wars, e.g.* United States–History–Civil War, 1861-1865–Pamphlets

In this case, the subdivision **–Pamphlets** is not free-floating under period subdivisions. However, it is a free-floating subdivision under names of individual wars, because it is listed under the pattern heading for wars.

MARC Codes for Subjects

In a bibliographic record, subject headings are tagged according to the specific MARC format used. In the MARC 21 format, for instance, subject headings are coded as follows:

600 Subject added entry - Personal name
610 Subject added entry - Corporate name
611 Subject added entry - Meeting name
630 Subject added entry - Uniform title
650 Subject added entry - Topical term
651 Subject added entry - Geographic name

Each of these fields may be repeated, as there is often more than one subject entry in a given category in a particular record. For more details about the MARC 21 codes for subject, see appendix G of this book. For examples of MARC 21 coding in bibliographic records, see appendix A.

Order of Headings on Bibliographic Records[7]

In the LC MARC record, an attempt is made to match the Library of Congress Classification (LCC) number with the first subject heading(s) assigned. Both are based on the predominant topic of the work. However, it is not always possible to achieve a perfect match because LCC and LCSH often differ in specificity. When two or more headings are assigned to a bibliographic record, the following policies regarding the order of subject headings prevail:

(1) The first subject heading represents the predominant topic of the work. If the predominant topic is represented by two or more headings, these headings precede any headings for secondary topics. Among two or more predominant headings, the one more closely approximating the class number is assigned first.

In the case of individual biography, the first subject heading assigned is the personal name heading for the biographee. Those headings assigned to bring out subsidiary aspects or to reflect local interests, such as other biographical headings, extra local history headings, etc., are given last.

(2) For a work with two equally important major topics, the headings assigned to the second topic follow immediately the headings for the first topic and precede headings for secondary topics, if any.

(3) Headings for secondary topics and headings assigned as enhanced access points follow the primary headings, in no particular order.

ASSIGNING SUBJECT HEADINGS

Scope Notes

Scope notes[8] are provided under many headings in LCSH to help users determine the scope of the material covered by a particular heading and to enable catalogers to maintain consistency in the assignment of headings to works being cataloged. Scope notes generally provide information concerning one or more of the following aspects of the headings under which they appear: definition, relation to other headings, and application. Examples are given below:

(1) A single heading defined without reference to any other headings. This type of note is provided in situations in which the heading represents a concept for which the name has not yet been firmly established in usage and for which a dictionary definition is not readily available, or when reference sources consulted fail to agree completely on the meaning of the term used. It is also helpful when the LCSH term is used in a somewhat different sense than generally prevails. Examples include:

Ecocriticism *(May Subd Geog)*
Here are entered works on criticism of literature and the arts from an environmental perspective.

Reservation wage *(May Subd Geog)*
Here are entered works on the lowest wage a person is willing to accept rather than remain unemployed.

Software radio *(May Subd Geog)*
Here are entered works on wireless technology in which software changes allow a communication device to adapt to new frequencies and transmission formats.

Water efficiency *(May Subd Geog)*
Here are entered works on the relationship between the amount of water required for a particular purpose and the quantity of water used or delivered, including measures taken to achieve more efficient water use and reduced demand.

(2) A single heading described with reference to more specific headings. Notes of this type indicate the scope of a heading used in its most general sense and call attention to overlapping or more specific headings. Examples include:

Racism *(May Subd Geog)*
Here are entered works on racism as an attitude as well as works on both attitude and overt discriminatory behavior directed against racial or ethnic groups. Works limited to overt discriminatory behavior

directed against racial or ethnic groups are entered under Race discrimination. Works on racism directed against a particular group are entered under the name of the group with subdivision Social conditions, or similar subdivision, e.g. Civil rights. When the heading Racism is subdivided by place, a second subject entry is made in each case under the name of the place subdivided by Race relations.

(3) Two or more closely related or overlapping headings. Notes of this type provide contrasting information regarding the scope and usage of seemingly similar headings. Examples include:

Light art *(May Subd Geog)*
Here are entered works on art that uses light as an artistic medium. Works on the portrayal of light in art are entered under Light in art.

Light in art *(May Subd Geog)*
Here are entered works on the portrayal of light in art. Works on art that uses light as an artistic medium are entered under Light art.

First strike (Nuclear strategy)
Here are entered works on preemptive strategic nuclear attacks designed to destroy an enemy's strategic forces before they can be used against one's own strategic forces. Works on the principle that a military power, in the event of war, would not be the first to resort to the tactical or strategic use of nuclear weapons are entered under No first use (Nuclear strategy).

No first use (Nuclear strategy)
Here are entered works on the principle that a military power, in the event of war, would not be the first to resort to the tactical or strategic use of nuclear weapons. Works on preemptive strategic nuclear attacks designed to destroy the enemy's strategic forces before they can be used against one's own strategic forces are entered under First strike (Nuclear strategy).

World War, 1939-1945–Occupied territories
Here are entered works on enemy occupied territories discussed collectively. Works on the occupation of an individual country are entered under the name of the country with appropriate period subdivision, e.g., Belgium–History–German occupation, 1940-1945; Norway–History–German occupation, 1940-1945.

(4) Special instructions, explanations, referrals, etc. Notes of this type provide information about making additional entries, notices to catalog users, or generalized references. Examples include:

Developing countries *(Not Subd Geog)*

Here are entered comprehensive works on those countries having relatively low per capita incomes. This heading may be subdivided by those topical subdivisions used under names of regions, countries, etc., for example, Developing countries–Economic conditions, and may be used as a geographic subdivision under those topics authorized for local subdivision, for example, Technology–Developing countries.

Remixes *(May Subd Geog)*

Here are entered recorded musical works derived from one or more existing sound recordings through processes known as remixing. This heading is applied to sound recordings that are entirely remixes, prominently identified as remix(es), mixes, or expressions such as dance mix and club mix, but not to recordings where mix(es) means only medley, mixture, or miscellaneous.

School prose

For works limited to one school, the heading is qualified by nationality and subdivided by place, and an additional subject entry is made under the name of the school.

General versus Specific

The principle of specific entry requires that a work be assigned a specific heading that ideally represents exactly the contents of the work. This principle originated with Charles A. Cutter and has been the guiding principle of subject catalogs in this country for more than a century.

At the Library of Congress, subject catalogers are instructed to propose a new heading for each new topic encountered in cataloging but not yet represented in the subject headings list. In practice, however, there are occasions when it is considered premature or impractical to establish a new concept or topic as a heading. In such cases, the subject content of the work is brought out either through a general heading or through several related headings.

Under the policy of specific entry, the question arises whether, after assigning a specific heading such as **Cats** to a work about cats, one should also assign one or more general headings, such as **Domestic animals** and **Felis**. Normally, a general heading and a specific one comprehended within it are not assigned to a work dealing with a specific subject, unless at least 20 percent of the work is devoted to the general topic. A work on algebra is given the heading **Algebra**, not **Mathematics** as well; a work about cataloging is given the heading **Cataloging**, but not also **Library science**. Similarly, a work on algebra is not usually given additional headings for various branches of algebra. In other words, under a strict policy of specific entry, when a heading that is coextensive with the overall content of a work is assigned, neither more specific headings subsumed under the given heading nor more general headings that comprehend the given heading are assigned in addition. This strict policy of specific entry was adhered to more closely in the card catalog, in which each additional subject heading required a separate card entry.

Over the years, the Library of Congress has relaxed its general policies of not assigning a generic heading in addition to the specific heading coextensive with the content of the work. Now many works are assigned headings broader or more general than the main topic.

Conversely, there is also the question of whether, after assigning a heading representing the main topic of the work, headings representing the subtopics subsumed under the primary heading should also be assigned. The instruction given in the *Subject Cataloging Manual* states:

> Assign to a work only the headings that most closely correspond to the overall coverage of the work. Do not assign headings that represent the subtopics normally considered to be included in an assigned heading's coverage.[9]

However, there are exceptions, among which is the treatment of individual biographies, subtopics or special cases with emphasis, and doubling.

(1) Individual biographies. For individual biographies, a generic heading representing the class of persons to which the individual belongs is assigned in addition to the personal name heading. (For a more detailed discussion, see chapter 9.)

(2) Subtopics or specific cases with emphasis. When a work on a general topic devotes 20 percent or more of its space to a subtopic or a specific case used as an illustration of a principle, two headings are assigned, one to cover the overall content of the work and the other to represent the specific topic. The second heading in the following example is assigned to represent a part of the content:

Title: *Cosmology : the origin and evolution of cosmic structure* / Peter Coles, Francesco Lucchin. c2002.
SUBJECTS:
Cosmology.
Big bang theory.

The two headings are assigned even though there is an NT reference from **Cosmology** to **Big bang theory**. It is LC policy that the presence of a hierarchical reference between two headings should not preclude the use of both headings for the same work as long as the two headings represent the actual content of the work.

(3) Doubling in specific cases. The term *doubling* refers to the practice of assigning bilevel (generic and specific) headings to the same work. Bilevel headings are assigned in the cases described below.[10]

(a) If the work being cataloged deals with a topic in general and at the same time applies to a particular locality, two headings are assigned as follows:

Title: *Introduction to economic reasoning* / William D. Rohlf, Jr. 5th ed. 2002.
SUBJECTS:
Economics.
United States–Economic conditions.

(b) If the heading appropriate to the work being cataloged contains a heading in the form of **[Place]–Description and travel–Early works to 1800**, an additional heading in the form of **[Place]–History–[Chronological subdivision**, if judged to be significant] is assigned.[11]

(c) Bilevel headings are assigned by tradition to certain subjects, such as **World War, 1939-1945**; **Paleontology**.[12]

(d) Works of interest to local historians and genealogists are assigned headings of the type **[Place below the country level]–[Topic]** in addition to other appropriate headings.[13]

(e) Works discussing individual buildings or structures within a city are assigned headings in the form of **[City]–Buildings, structures, etc.** in addition to the name heading for the building or structure.[14]

(f) Frequently, when a heading assigned to a work contains a free-floating subdivision named in a multiple subdivision (see discussion in chapter 5), an additional heading representing the topic named in the subdivision is also assigned:[15]

Title: *Lebanese place-names : Mount Lebanon and North Lebanon : a typology of regional variation and continuity* / by Elie Wardini. 2002.
SUBJECTS:
Names, Geographical–Lebanon.
{Authorized by: **Names, Geographical–English, [Celtic, Latin, etc.]**}
Arabic language–Etymology–Names.
Names, Geographical–Arabic.

Title: *The ordination of women in the Orthodox Church* / Elisabeth Behr-Sigel & Kallistos Ware. c2000.
SUBJECTS:
Orthodox Eastern Church–Doctrines.
Orthodox Eastern Church–Membership.
Women in the Orthodox Eastern Church.

Women–Relgious aspects–Orthodox Eastern Church.
Ordination of women–Orthodox Eastern Church.
{Authorized by: **Ordination of women Buddhism, [Christianity, etc.]**}

(g) In addition to headings representing the central subject of the work, headings broader than or related to the central subject are sometimes assigned as additional access points.

Duplicate Entries

As discussed in chapter 2, exceptions are sometimes made to the principle of uniform heading (one topic/one heading) in cases in which two elements in a heading are of equal significance and it is therefore desirable to provide access to both. In such cases, specific instructions are given in LCSH to assign both headings to the same work, even though they consist of the same elements and have identical meanings:

Title: *U.S.-China relations in the twenty-first century : policies, prospects and possibilities* / edited by Christopher Marsh and June Teufel Dreyer. c2003.
SUBJECTS:
United States–Foreign relations–China.
China–Foreign relations–United States.
United States–Foreign relations–2001-

Duplicate entries of this type are particularly helpful in manual catalogs. They are not necessary in online catalogs due to keyword search capabilities. It is, however, helpful in online browsing of the alphabetical subject index.

Number of Headings for Each Record

It is difficult, and perhaps not practical, to regulate the number of subject headings to be assigned to each work. In general, such a decision is based on the requirements of the work in hand, with consideration given to the general policy of summarization. In the past, the Library of Congress restricted the number of headings for each record in order to save space in the card catalog, and the Library was often criticized for assigning too few headings. A study published in 1979 estimated that the average number of subject headings assigned to a Library of Congress cataloging record was fewer than two,[16] and many considered this finding an indication of deficiency in LC practice.

Over the years, particularly with the advent of the online catalog, in which additional headings do not have any significant impact on the bulk of the catalog, the Library of Congress has relaxed its rules on coextensivity and summarization. Current guidelines state:

> The number of headings that are required varies with the work being cataloged. Sometimes one heading is sufficient. Generally a maximum of six is appropriate. In special situations more headings may be required.
>
> *LC practice:* Do not assign more than ten headings to a work.[17]

As a result of this policy change, many more records carry multiple subject headings. Because these additional headings are assigned based on the judgment of individual catalogers, practice varies from case to case. The following examples show records to which multiple headings have been assigned.

Title: *Remembering the Alamo : memory, modernity, and the master symbol* / by Richard R. Flores. 2002.

SUBJECTS:

Alamo (San Antonio, Tex.)–Siege, 1836.
Alamo (San Antonio, Tex.)–Siege, 1836–Influence.
Memory–Social aspects–United States.
Symbolism–Social aspects–United States.
Popular culture–Texas.
Texas–Ethnic relations.
Whites–Texas–Social conditions.
Mexican Americans–Texas–Social conditions.
Texas–History–1846-1950.

Title: *Word, birth, and culture : the poetry of Poe*, Whitman, and Dickinson/ Daneen Wardrop. 2002.

SUBJECTS:

American poetry–19th century–History and criticism.
Childbirth in literature.
Literature and science–United States–History–19th century.
Language and culture–United States–History–19th century.
Dickinson, Emily, 1830-1886–Criticism and interpretation.
Whitman, Walt, 1819-1892–Criticism and interpretation.
Poe, Edgar Allan, 1809-1849–Poetic works.
Body, Human, in literature.
Sex in literature.

Title: *Daily life on the old colonial frontier* / James M. Volo and Dorothy Denneen Volo. 2002.

SUBJECTS:

Frontier and pioneer life–North America.
North America–History–Colonial period, ca. 1600-1775.
Europe–Territorial expansion–Social aspects.
North America–Ethnic relations.
Indians of North America–Government relations–To 1789.
Indians of North America–First contact with Europeans.

Fur trade–Social aspects–North America–History.
France–Relations–Great Britain.
Great Britain–Relations–France.

Title: *Centering ourselves : African American feminist and womanist studies of discourse* / edited by Marsha Houston, Olga Idriss Davis. c2002.
SUBJECTS:
African American women–Languages.
English language–United States–Discourse analysis.
English language–United States–Sex differences.
Feminists–United States–Languages.
Women–United States–Languages.
African Americans–Languages.
Black English.
Americanisms.

Title: *Russian politics : the post-Soviet phase* / Donald D. Barry. c2002.
SUBJECTS:
Russia (Federation)–Politics and government–1991-
Soviet Union–Politics and government–1985-1991.
Post-communism–Russia (Federation)
Democracy–Russia (Federation)
Constitutional law–Russia (Federation)
Political culture–Russia (Federation)
Russia (Federation)–Forecasting.

SPECIAL CONSIDERATIONS

As has been noted above, it is not always possible, even under a policy of summarization, to give each work a heading that is exactly coextensive with its content. Many works deal with multiple topics or complex subjects and so require more than one heading. Even works dealing with a single subject may occasionally require more than one heading. The following comments summarize subject heading assignment practice in terms of the types of documents encountered.

Works on a Single Topic

A heading that exactly represents the content, if available, is assigned to a work on a single topic:

Title: *Discover biology* / Michael L. Cain ... [et al.]. c2002.
SUBJECTS:
Biology.

Title: *Quantum mechanics* / Franz Schwabl ; translated by Ronald Kates. c2002.
SUBJECTS:
Quantum theory.

Title: *Automatic control systems* / Benjamin C. Kuo, Farid Golnaraghi. 2003.
SUBJECTS:
Automatic control.

Title: *Classics of philosophy* / [edited by] Louis P. Pojman. 2003.
SUBJECTS:
Philosophy.

Title: *Evolution of the earth* / Donald R. Prothero, Robert H. Dott. 2002.
SUBJECTS:
Historical geology.

Title: *Principles of vibration* / Benson H. Tongue. 2002.
SUBJECTS:
Vibration.

Title: *Operating system concepts* / Abraham Silberschatz, Peter Baer Galvin, Greg Gagne. c2002.
SUBJECTS:
Operating systems (Computers)

Title: *Linear algebra with applications* / Steven J. Leon. c2002.
SUBJECTS:
Algebras, Linear.

In cases where the topic of the work being cataloged is not represented in LCSH and for various reasons it is considered impractical to establish the concept as a new heading, a more general heading or several related headings, whichever designates more closely the content of the work, are assigned:

Title: *Building classroom discipline* / C.M. Charles. c2002.
SUBJECTS:
Classroom management.
School discipline.

Title: *Building self-esteem : strategies for success in school and beyond* / Bonnie J. Golden, Kay Lesh. c2002.
SUBJECTS:
College students–Psychology.
Self-esteem–Study and teaching.

Continuing education.

Title: *Giving professional presentations in the behavioral sciences and related fields : a practical guide for the novice, the nervous, and the nonchalant* / Michael J. Platow. 2002.
SUBJECTS:
Communication in the social sciences.
Public speaking.

Title: *Elementary classroom management* / Gail W. Senter, C.M. Charles. c2002.
SUBJECTS:
Classroom management.
Education, Elementary.

Multitopical Works

Works on Two or Three Topics

For a work covering two or three topics treated separately, a heading representing precisely each of the topics is assigned. The two or three specific headings are assigned in favor of a general heading if the latter includes in its scope more than three subtopics. This is called the "rule of three":[18]

Title: *The violin and viola : history, structure, techniques* / Sheila M. Nelson. c2003.
SUBJECTS:
Violin.
Viola.

Title: *Antoni Gaudí, Salvador Dalí* / [editorial coordination, Llorenç Bonet ; text, Llorenç Bonet, Cristina Montes ; translation, William Bain]. 2002.
SUBJECTS:
Gaudí, Antoni, 1852-1926.
Dalí, Salvador, 1904-

Title: *Money & banking* / David H. Friedman. 5th ed. c2003.
SUBJECTS:
Banks and banking.
Money.

Title: *Fodor's Martha's Vineyard and Nantucket.* c2003-
SUBJECTS:
Martha's Vineyard (Mass.)–Guidebooks.
Nantucket Island (Mass.)–Guidebooks.

Title: *Infants, children, and adolescents* / Laura E. Berk. 4th ed. c2002.
SUBJECTS:
Child development.

Infants–Development.
Adolescence.

Works on Four or More Topics

Some works on four topics are assigned broad headings that cover all the topics, and others are assigned individual headings:

Title: *The golden girls of MGM : Greta Garbo, Joan Crawford, Lana Turner, Judy Garland, Ava Gardner, Grace Kelly, and others* / Jane Ellen Wayne. 2003.
SUBJECTS:
Metro-Goldwyn-Mayer.
Motion picture actors and actresses–United States–Biography.
Actresses–United States–Biography.

Specific headings are preferred when the work being cataloged deals with four topics, each of which forms only a small portion of a general topic. This is called the "rule of four":[19]

Title: *The first golden age of the Viennese symphony : Haydn, Mozart, Beethoven, and Schubert* / A. Peter Brown. c2002.
SUBJECTS:
Symphony–18th century.
Symphony–19th century.
Haydn, Joseph, 1732-1809. Symphonies.
Mozart, Wolfgang Amadeus, 1756-1791. Symphonies.
Beethoven, Ludwig van, 1770-1827. Symphonies.
Schubert, Franz Peter, 1797-1828. Symphonies.
Symphonies–Analysis, appreciation.

For a work treating five or more related topics, a single generic heading that encompasses all the topics treated is used if one exists or can be established, even if the generic heading includes other topics not present in the work being cataloged:

Title: *Cape Cod, Massachusetts, local street detail : including Barnstable, Bourne, Brewster, Chatham, Dennis, Eastham, Falmouth, Harwich, Hyannis Port, Orleans, Provincetown, Sandwich, Truro, Yarmouth, Woods Hole, plus Cape Cod & vicinity, Martha's Vineyard, Nantucket, mileage & driving times map* / Rand McNally. c2003.
SUBJECTS:
Cities and towns–Massachusetts–Cape Cod–Maps.
Villages–Massachusetts–Cape Cod–Maps.
Roads–Massachusetts–Cape Cod Region–Maps.

If a generic heading does not exist or cannot be established, either several very broad headings or one or more form headings, for example, **American essays**, are assigned:

Title: *The Norton sampler : short essays for composition* / [edited by] Thomas Cooley. 6th ed. c2003.
SUBJECTS:
College readers.
English language–Rhetoric.
Essays.

Title: *One hundred great essays* / edited by Robert DiYanni. c2002.
SUBJECTS:
College readers.
English language–Rhetoric–Problems, exercises, etc.
Report writing–Problems, exercises, etc.
Essays.

Title: *The seagull reader. Essays* / edited by Joseph Kelly. c2002.
SUBJECTS:
American essays.
English essays.
College readers.

Title: *An introduction to critical reading* / [edited by] Leah McCraney. 5th ed. c2004.
SUBJECTS:
College readers.

Aspects of Main Topics

Many works treat topics with regard to one or more of their aspects, such as subtopic, time, and/or place. Others are presented in a specific form: a dictionary, an index, a manual. In most cases, these aspects are represented by subdivisions. In others, they are represented by a complex heading (a phrase heading or a heading with a qualifier) that combines an aspect with the main topic. In these cases, all the elements are precoordinated.

Subtopic

Title: *Teaching and learning elementary social studies* / Arthur K. Ellis. c2002.
SUBJECTS:
Social sciences–Study and teaching (Elementary)

Title: *Psychological foundations of sport* / edited by John M. Silva, Diane E. Stevens. c2002.
SUBJECTS:
Sports–Psychological aspects.

Title: *Stage directions guide to musical theater* / edited by Stephen Peithman and Neil Offen. c2002.
SUBJECTS:
Musical theater–Production and direction.

Title: *Natasha's dance : a cultural history of Russia* / Orlando Figes. 2002.
SUBJECTS:
Russia–Civilization.

In some cases, the subtopics in a complex subject are brought out by means of two or more headings:

Title: *Assessing and correcting reading and writing difficulties* / Thomas G. Gunning. c2002.
SUBJECTS:
Reading disability–Evaluation.
Reading–Ability testing.
Reading–Remedial teaching.
English language–Composition and exercises–Ability testing.
English language–Composition and exercises–Study and teaching.

In these cases, each of the headings assigned is broader than the subject treated in the work. Specificity is achieved only through postcoordination (i.e., combining the heading being consulted with other headings during the process of searching).

Place

The geographic aspect of a work may be brought out by means of a geographic heading or a geographic subdivision:

Title: *My blue heaven : life and politics in the working-class suburbs of Los Angeles, 1920-1965* / Becky M. Nicolaides. c2002.
SUBJECTS:
Working class–California–South Gate.
South Gate (Calif.)–Social conditions.
South Gate (Calif.)–Economic conditions.
South Gate (Calif.)–Politics and government.

Title: *Coming in from the Cold War : changes in U.S.-European interactions since 1980* / edited by Sabrina P. Ramet and Christine Ingebritsen. c2002.

SUBJECTS:

United States–Foreign relations–1981-1989.
United States–Foreign relations–Europe.
Europe–Foreign relations–United States.
Cold War.

Title: *Dolphins of Hilton Head : their natural history* / Cara M. Gubbins. c2002.

SUBJECTS:

Bottlenose dolphin–South Carolina–Hilton Head Island.

Title: *Strategies for teaching students with learning and behavior problems* / Candace S. Bos, Sharon Vaughn. c2002.

SUBJECTS:

Learning disabled children–Education–United States.
Remedial teaching–United States.
Problem children–Education–United States.

Title: *American journalism : history, principles, practices* / edited by W. David Sloan and Lisa Mullikin Parcell. c2002.

SUBJECTS:

Journalism–United States.

Time

The time, or chronological, aspect of a subject is usually brought out by means of chronological subdivision where the Library of Congress subject heading system allows it, either using chronological subdivisions enumerated under individual headings in LCSH or free-floating subdivisions in the form of **–History –16th century**; **–History–20th century**; etc., used under certain categories of headings:

Title: *Virginians at war : the Civil War experiences of seven young Confederates* / John G. Selby. 2002.

SUBJECTS:

Virginia–History–Civil War, 1861-1865.

Title: *Daily life in colonial New England* / Claudia Durst Johnson. c2002.

SUBJECTS:

New England–Social life and customs–To 1775.

Title: *Early China/ancient Greece : thinking through comparisons* / edited by Steven Shankman and Stephen W. Durrant. c2002.

SUBJECTS:

China–Civilization–To 221 B.C.

Greece–Civilization–To 146 B.C.

Title: *Riot and remembrance : the Tulsa race war and its legacy* / James S. Hirsch. 2002.

SUBJECTS:

African Americans–Oklahoma–Tulsa–History–20th century.

Tulsa (Okla.)–Race relations.

Racism–Oklahoma–Tulsa–History–20th century.

Riots–Oklahoma–Tulsa–History–20th century.

Violence–Oklahoma–Tulsa–History–20th century.

African American neighborhoods–Oklahoma–Tulsa–History–20th Century.

Two or three headings are assigned if the period covered in the work is longer than the specific periods represented in individual period subdivisions, example:

Title: *Partner to history : the U.S. role in South Africa's transition to democracy* / Princeton N. Lyman. 2002.

SUBJECTS:

United States–Foreign relations–South Africa.

South Africa–Foreign relations–United States.

Democratization–South Africa.

South Africa–Politics and government–1989-1994.

South Africa–Politics and government–1994-

Title: *Crucible of power : a history of American foreign relations to 1913* / Howard Jones. 2002.

SUBJECTS:

United States–Foreign relations–To 1865.

United States–Foreign relations–1865-1921.

If the specific heading assigned to the work treating the subject or place with respect to a period does not provide for period subdivisions, an additional, broader heading that allows for period subdivision is sometimes assigned to bring out the chronological aspect:

Title: *How firm a foundation : William Bradford and Plymouth* / John M. Pafford. c2002.

SUBJECTS:

Bradford, William, 1588-1657.

Plymouth (Mass.)–History.

Massachusetts–History–Colonial period, ca. 1600-1775.

In some cases, the time aspect of a work is ignored in cataloging if it is considered insignificant.

Form

Form subdivisions, most of which are free-floating (see chapter 5), are used when appropriate. They may be assigned under all types of headings: personal names, corporate names, meetings and conferences, uniform titles, geographic headings, and topical headings:

Title: *Remaking the concept of aptitude : extending the legacy of Richard E. Snow* / Lyn Corno ... [et al.] for the Stanford Aptitude Seminar ; edited by Lee J. Cronbach. 2002.
SUBJECTS:
Ability–Congresses.

Title: *How to make your science project scientific* / Tom Moorman. c2002.
SUBJECTS:
Science–Methodology–Juvenile literature.

Title: *Explorations in basic biology* / Stanley E. Gunstream. c2002.
SUBJECTS:
Biology–Laboratory manuals.

Title: *Hawley's condensed chemical dictionary* / revised by Richard J. Lewis, Sr. c2002.
SUBJECTS:
Chemistry–Dictionaries.

Title: *Field engineer's manual* / Robert O. Parmley, editor-in-chief. c2002.
SUBJECTS:
Civil engineering–Handbooks, manuals, etc.

When a form subdivision is used under a heading for a work assigned more than one heading, the same form subdivision should be used with all the headings if it is applicable:

Title: *Writing about music : an introductory guide* / Richard J. Wingell. c2002.
SUBJECTS:
Music–Historiography–Handbooks, manuals, etc.
Musical criticism–Authorship–Handbooks, manuals, etc.
Academic writing–Handbooks, manuals, etc.

Title: *Social security, medicare & government pensions* / by Joseph L. Matthews with Dorothy Matthews Berman. 2002.
SUBJECTS:
Social security–Law and legislation–United States–Popular works.
Medicare–United States–Popular works.
Pensions–Law and legislation–United States–Popular works.

Exceptions are naturally made for cases in which different parts of the work are in different forms:

Title: *Practical guide to humanitarian law* / Franpcoise Bouchet-Saulnier ; edited and translated by Laura Brav. c2002.
SUBJECTS:
Humanitarian law–Dictionaries.
Human rights–Dictionaries.
Treaties–Ratification–Indexes.

Multiple Aspects

Many complex subjects contain multiple aspects, or facets. These are often precoordinated in long heading strings:

Title: *Unhealed wounds : medical malpractice in the twentieth century* / Neal C. Hogan. 2003.
SUBJECTS:
Physicians–Malpractice–United States–History–20th century.

Title: *Video collection development in multi-type libraries : a handbook* / edited by Gary P. Handman. 2002.
SUBJECTS:
Libraries–United States–Special collections–Video recordings.

Title: *Irish famine : a documentary* / Colm Tóibbín and Diarmaid Ferriter. 2002.
SUBJECTS:
Ireland–History–Famine, 1845-1852.
Famines–Ireland–History–19th century.
Ireland–History–Famine, 1845-1852–Sources.
Famines–Ireland–History–19th century–Sources.

When a single heading or heading string cannot express all the aspects in the subject, multiple headings are assigned:

Title: *Data structures and problem solving using Java* / Mark Allen Weiss. c2002.
SUBJECTS:
Java (Computer program language)
Data structures (Computer science)
Problem solving–Data processing.

This approach is taken most frequently when a large number of concepts are involved:

Title: *Southern civil religions in conflict : civil rights and the culture wars* / Andrew M. Manis. 2002.

SUBJECTS:

African Americans–Civil rights–Southern States–History–20th century.
Civil rights movements–Southern States–History–20th century.
Civil religion–Southern States–History–20th century.
Baptists–Southern States–Political activity–History–20th century.
Southern States–Race relations.

Additional headings may be used to bring out other aspects of the work:

Title: *On being different : diversity and multiculturalism in the North American mainstream* / Conrad Phillip Kottak, Kathryn A. Kozaitis. 2003.

SUBJECTS:

Ethnology–North America.
Multiculturalism–North America.
Ethnicity–North America.
Minorities–North America.
Social structure–North America.
North America–Race relations.
North America–Social conditions.

Phase Relations

Many works treat subjects in relation to each other; in cataloging, most inter-subject relationships are referred to as *phase relations* and include general relations, influence, tool or application, comparison, and bias. When appropriate, headings representing such relations are assigned, if available, for example, **Body temperature–Effect of drugs on**; **Fungi in agriculture**; **Television and politics**. If such headings do not exist, LC subject catalogers may propose new headings if the relationship is considered significant, or they may use separate headings for each topic involved:

Title: *History and the Internet : a guide* / by Patrick D. Reagan. c2002.

SUBJECTS:

History–Computer network resources.
History–Computer-assisted instruction.
History–Research.
Internet.

Title: *Terrorist next door : the militia movement and the radical right* / Daniel Levitas. 2002.

SUBJECTS:

Militia movements–United States.

Radicalism–United States.
Right-wing extremists–United States.

Title: *Conflicting missions : Havana, Washington, and Africa, 1959-1976* / Piero Gleijeses. c2002.
SUBJECTS:
Cuba–Foreign relations–Africa.
Africa–Foreign relations–Cuba.
Cuba–Foreign relations–1959-
Africa–Foreign relations–1960-
United States–Foreign relations–Africa.
Africa–Foreign relations–United States.
United States–Foreign relations–1945-1989.
National liberation movements–Africa.
Cold War.

Title: *Application of abstract differential equations to some mechanical problems* / Isabelle Titeux, Yakov Yakubov. c2003.
SUBJECTS:
Operator equations.
Elasticity.

On the other hand, the level of a textbook and the intended audience (other than juvenile works) are often ignored if the work may be of interest to the general public as well:

Title: *Teaching in the secondary school : an introduction* / David G. Armstrong, Tom V. c2002.
SUBJECTS:
High school teaching–United States.
Education, Secondary–United States.

Title: *Real analysis : a first course* / Russell A. Gordon. c2002.
SUBJECTS:
Mathematical analysis.

Title: *Physics for scientists and engineers* / Paul M. Fishbane, Stephen G. Gasiorowicz, Stephen T. Thornton. 3rd ed. 2005.
SUBJECTS:
Physics.

Title: *Browsable classroom : an introduction to e-learning for librarians* / Carolyn B. Noah and Linda W. Braun. c2002.
SUBJECTS:
Libraries and distance education.
Distance education.
Internet in education.

If the work is of interest to a specific group, however, the intended audience is brought out:

Title: *Quick take off in Latin American Spanish* / Rosa Maria Martin and Martyn Ellis. 2003.
SUBJECTS:
Spanish language–Latin America–Conversation and phrase books–English.
Spanish language–Latin America–Sound recordings for English speakers.
Spanish language–Spoken Spanish.

Title: *TOEFL strategies* / Eli Hinkel. 3rd ed. 2004.
SUBJECTS:
Test of English as a Foreign Language–Study guides.
English language–Textbooks for foreign speakers.
English language–Examinations–Study guides.

Title: *America : a patriotic primer* / Lynne Cheney ; illustrated by Robin Preiss Glasser. c2002.
SUBJECTS:
United States–History–Juvenile literature.
United States–Politics and government–Juvenile literature.
English language–Alphabet–Juvenile literature.

Topics without Representation in LCSH

Even after multiple headings have been assigned to a work, all aspects of a work may still not be totally covered, for example:

Title: *Emergency broadcasting and 1930s American radio* / Edward D. Miller. 2003.
SUBJECTS:
Radio broadcasting–United States–History.
Radio broadcasting–Social aspects–United States.

In the example above, the topic "emergency broadcasting" is not represented by the subject headings assigned. The topic can only be retrieved through keyword searching in the title field.

If the topic of the work being cataloged is not represented in LCSH and cannot be established as a valid subject heading (because of various factors such as uncertain terminology), it is LC practice to assign a more general heading or several related headings, whichever designates more accurately the topic of the work in view of the various headings available.

Subject Headings Identical to Descriptive Access Points[20]

An appropriate subject heading is assigned to a work even though the heading may duplicate a main or added entry assigned in descriptive cataloging. This happens often with works entered under corporate bodies, with autobiographical works, with nontopical compilations of general laws, and with artistic reproductions with commentary. (A more detailed discussion and examples of these types of materials are in chapters 9 and 10.) It also occurs when a valid heading is identical with the title of work. Such duplicate access points were considered unnecessary in a manual dictionary catalog. They are, however, important in an online catalog because of the nature of online searching, which often focuses on the subject field only. Author and title entries are not retrieved in subject searches, only in searches for author or title; a user wanting material *about* a given corporate body, for instance, would probably not make an author search for it. The following examples illustrate duplicate access points:

Title: *George W. Bush speaks to the nation : speeches* / selected by Alan Gottlieb. 2004.
SUBJECTS:
Bush, George W. (George Walker), 1946-
Presidents–United States–Messages.
United States–Politics and government–2001-
MAIN ENTRY:
Bush, George W. (George Walker), 1946-

Title: *Boethius* / John Marenbon. 2003.
SUBJECTS:
Boethius, d. 524.
TITLE ADDED ENTRY:
Boethius

Title: *Concrete* / Sidney Mindess, J. Francis Young, David Darwin. c2003.
SUBJECTS:
Concrete.
TITLE ADDED ENTRY:
Concrete.

The discussion in this chapter concerns subject cataloging in general. In the Library of Congress subject headings system, several types of materials and special subject areas receive special or unique treatment. These are discussed in the following two chapters.

NOTES

1. Library of Congress, Cataloging Policy and Support Office, *Subject Cataloging Manual: Subject Headings*, 5th ed., 2000 cumulation (Washington, D.C.: Library of Congress, 2000).

2. *Cataloging Service Bulletin* 1-, Summer 1978-(Washington, D.C. Library of Congress, Processing Services).

3. Library of Congress, *Free-floating Subdivisions: An Alphabetical Index*, prepared by Subject Cataloging Division, 1st ed.-(Washington, D.C.: Library of Congress, Cataloging Distribution Service, 1989-).

4. Library of Congress, *Subject Cataloging Manual*, H180, p. 1.

5. Library of Congress, *Subject Cataloging Manual*, H200, p. 2.

6. Library of Congress, *Subject Cataloging Manual*, H1090.

7. Library of Congress, *Subject Cataloging Manual*, H80.

8. Library of Congress, *Subject Cataloging Manual*, H400.

9. Library of Congress, *Subject Cataloging Manual*, H180, p. 3.

10. Library of Congress, *Subject Cataloging Manual*, H870.

11. Library of Congress, *Subject Cataloging Manual*, H1530.

12. Library of Congress, *Subject Cataloging Manual*, H870.

13. Library of Congress, *Subject Cataloging Manual*, H1845.

14. Library of Congress, *Subject Cataloging Manual*, H1334.

15. Library of Congress, *Subject Cataloging Manual*, H1090.

16. Edward T. O'Neill and Rao Aluri, *Research Report on Subject Heading Patterns in OCLC Monographic Records* (Columbus, Ohio: OCLC, Inc., Research and Development Division, 1979), 7.

17. Library of Congress, *Subject Cataloging Manual*, H180, p. 2.

18. Library of Congress, *Subject Cataloging Manual*, H180, p. 4.

19. Library of Congress, *Subject Cataloging Manual*, H180, p. 4.

20. Library of Congress, *Subject Cataloging Manual*, H184.

9 Subject Cataloging of Special Types of Materials

The previous chapter discusses subject cataloging in general. In the Library of Congress subject headings system, several types of materials and special subject areas receive special or unique treatment. These are discussed in this chapter and in chapter 10.

ELECTRONIC RESOURCES

There are no specific overall guidelines or policies regarding subject headings assigned to electronic resources. There are, however, headings and subdivisions used specifically with electronic resources of various types. These are discussed with examples below.

Computer Software

The same principles for assigning subject headings in general are applied to computer software.[1] Headings for materials containing the software carry the subdivision **–Software** or **–Juvenile software**. The subdivision **–Computer programs** is used for works *about* computer software or programs.

At least one heading with the subdivision **–Software** or **–Juvenile software** is assigned to each software title to bring out the topic or genre of the software. Examples of subject headings assigned to computer software and to works about them are shown below.

Works Containing Software

Title: *Adobe GoLive* [electronic resource] : Web workgroup server CD. c2002.
SUBJECTS:
Web sites–Authoring programs–Software.

Title: *ValuSource PRO 2003* [electronic resource]. c2003.
SUBJECTS:
Business enterprises–Valuation–Software.
Valuation–Software.
Financial statements–Software.

Title: *Corel Ventura 10* [electronic resource]. c2002. [CD-ROM]
SUBJECTS:
Desktop publishing–Software.
Electronic publishing–Software.
Computer graphics–Software.

Following are examples of juvenile software:

Title: *Nickel takes on teasing* [electronic resource] : *a clickable social skill story*. c2003.
SUBJECTS:
Social skills–Study and teaching (Elementary)–Juvenile software.
Teasing–Prevention–Juvenile software.

Title: *Texas geography, history, and culture* [electronic resource]. c2002.
SUBJECTS:
Texas–Geography–Juvenile software.
Texas–History–Juvenile software.
Texas–Civilization–Juvenile software.

Works about Software

Works *about* software are assigned headings representing different types or different aspects of software. Examples:

Title: *Understanding agent systems* / Mark d'Inverno, Michael Luck. c2004.
SUBJECTS:
Intelligent agents (Computer software)

Title: *Software design : from programming to architecture* / Eric J. Braude. c2004.
SUBJECTS:
Computer software–Development.

Title: *Pattern oriented analysis and design : composing patterns to design software systems* / Sherif M. Yacoub and Hany H. Ammar. 2004.
SUBJECTS:
Computer software–Development.
Software patterns.

Works about Individual Computer Programs

Headings established in the form of the names of individual computer programs are assigned to works *about* the software, in addition to other appropriate headings.

Title: *Microsoft Access 2002 MOUS core level* / Floyd Jay Winters, Julie T. Manchester. 2003.
SUBJECTS:
Microsoft Access.
Electronic data processing personnel–Certification.
Microsoft software–Examinations–Study guides.

Title: *Microsoft Office XP step by step courseware* / Microsoft Corporation. c2004.
SUBJECTS:
Microsoft Office.
Business–Computer programs.

Title: *Linux application development for the enterprise* / Satya Sai Kolachina. 2004.
SUBJECTS:
Linux.
Application software–Development.

Title: *Next steps with SPSS* / Eric L. Einspruch. c2004.
SUBJECTS:
SPSS (Computer file)
Social sciences–Statistical methods–Computer programs.

Databases

Before May 1996, the subdivision **–Databases** was regularly used as a form subdivision for any electronic resource other than executable software. Since May 1996, the Library of Congress has tightened the definition of the term "database":

> A database is a collection of logically interrelated data stored together in one or more computerized files, usually created and managed by a database management system. The data are encoded, and each file is designed with a high-level structure for accepting, storing, and providing information on demand. Typically, there is a set of definitions for the database that describe its various data elements and a set of codes to identify each element. The database may include the database management software that created the file, or it may include only the data.[2]

As a result of this revised definition, the free-floating subdivision **–Databases** is used under subjects only when the item being cataloged fits the definition:

Title: *Census 2000. Summary file 3, Census of population and housing* [electronic resource]. [2003] [DVD-ROM]
SUBJECTS:
Housing–United States–Statistics–Databases.
Demographic surveys–United States–Databases.
United States–Census, 22nd, 2000–Databases.
United States–Population–Statistics–Databases.

Title: *Smithsonian Institution Research Information System* [electronic resource] : *SIRIS*. (Viewed on Nov. 7, 2003.)
SUBJECTS:
Smithsonian American Art Museum–Databases.
Art, American–Databases.
Portrait photography–United States–Databases.
Artists–United States–Portraits–Databases.
Art–United States–Exhibitions–Databases.
Art–Canada–Exhibitions–Databases.

Title: *FreeBooks4Doctors* [electronic resource] : *promoting free access to medical books*. 2002-
SUBJECTS:
Medical literature–Databases.
Medicine–Databases.

Title: *Oxford Latin American economic history database* [electronic resource]. 2002.
SUBJECTS:
Latin America–Economic conditions–20th century–Statistics–Databases.

Works about Databases

A work about databases[3] in general is assigned appropriate headings such as **Databases** and **Relational databases**. Examples include:

Title: *Database design using entity-relationship diagrams* / Sikha Bagui and Richard Earp. c2003.
SUBJECTS:
Database design.
Relational databases.

Title: *Database and data communication network systems : techniques and applications* / edited by Cornelius T. Leondes. c2002.
SUBJECTS:
Distributed databases.
Computer networks.

Title: *Information and database quality* / edited by Mario G. Piattini, Coral Calero, Marcela Genero. 2002.
SUBJECTS:
Database management.
Databases–Quality control.

A work about databases relating to a specific field or subject is assigned headings of the type **[Topic]–Databases**, in addition to other appropriate headings:

Title: *Neuroscience databases : a practical guide* / edited by Rolf Kötter. c2003.
SUBJECTS:
Neuroinformatics.
Neurosciences–Databases.

Title: *Online ecological and environmental data* / Virginia Baldwin, editor. 2004.
SUBJECTS:
Environmental sciences–Computer network resources.
Environmental sciences–Databases.

A work about an individual database is assigned a subject heading in the form of the uniform title, in addition to other appropriate headings:

Title: *Experiences with Oracle for Linux on zSeries* / [Kathryn Arrell .... et al.]. 2003.
SUBJECTS:
Oracle (Computer file).
Linux.
Relational databases.

Title: *Oracle real application clusters* / Murali Vallath. c2004.
SUBJECTS:
Oracle (Computer file)
Relational databases.
Parallel processing (Electronic computers)
Electronic data processing–Distributed processing.
Beowulf clusters (Computer systems)

Title: *Sams teach yourself DB2 Universal Database in 21 days* / Susan M. Visser, Bill Wong. 2nd ed. c2004.
SUBJECTS:
IBM Database 2.
Relational databases.

Computer and Video Games

The heading **Computer games** or a heading indicating a specific type of computer game is assigned:

Title: *EA Sports NHL 2003* [electronic resource]. c2002.
SUBJECTS:
Hockey–Software.
Computer games–Software.

Title: *Stanley. Wild for sharks!* [electronic resource]. c2002.
SUBJECTS:
Sharks–Juvenile software.
Computer games–Juvenile software.
Sharks–Interactive multimedia.

Title: *Jeopardy! 2003* [electronic resource] : *the ultimate Jeopardy! experience!* c2002.
SUBJECTS:
Jeopardy (Television program)–Software.
Game shows–Software.
Computer games–Software.

Title: *Rise of nations* [electronic resource]. c2003.
SUBJECTS:
Computer war games–Software.
CD-ROMs.

Title: *Freelancer* [electronic resource] : [*the universe of possibility*]. c2003.
SUBJECTS:
Computer adventure games–Software.

Works about Computer and Video Games

In the past, works about specific computer and video games were assigned headings under the names of these games. Due to the high volume and ephemeral nature of these works, the Library of Congress changed its policy in 2001 to assigning only generic topical headings such as **Computer games** or **Video games**.[4] However, games that have become very well known and have many works written about them continue to be assigned specific headings under the names of the games.

Title: *Microsoft combat flight simulator 3 : battle for Europe* / Michael Rymaszewski. c2003.
SUBJECTS:
Computer war games.
Computer flight games.

Title: *Rules of play : game design fundamentals* / Katie Salen and Eric Zimmerman. 2003.
SUBJECTS:
Computer games–Design.
Computer games–Programming.

Title: *The gmax handbook* / Clayton E. Crooks II. c2003.
SUBJECTS:
Gmax.
Computer games–Programming.
Three-dimensional display systems.

Title: *NBA Street. Vol. 2 : Prima's official strategy guide* / Dan Leahy. c2003.
SUBJECTS:
Video games.

Internet or Web Resources

The subdivision **–Databases** is not used under subjects for electronic resources that are essentially textual in nature and do not fit the definition of a database. Such materials include articles, conference proceedings, literary works, reference-type works, etc. Many web resources are of such nature and, as a result, are assigned subject headings similar to those assigned to print materials. There are no special subdivisions designating Internet resources or web resources. Examples are shown below:

Title: *Reclaiming the Everglades* [electronic resource] *: South Florida's natural history, 1884-1934* / University of Miami Library, Florida International University Libraries, and Historical Museum of Southern Florida. 2002.
SUBJECTS:
Nature conservation–Florida–Everglades.
Everglades (Fla.)–History.

Title: *The Angry Kid series* [electronic resource]. 2002.
SUBJECTS:
Animated films–Catalogs.

Title: *Slaves and the courts, 1740-1860* [electronic resource] / Law Library of Congress, Rare Book and Special Collections Division, and General Collections of the Library of Congress. [2002]
SUBJECTS:
Trials–United States.
Slavery–Law and legislation–United States–History–Sources.
Slavery–Law and legislation–United States–Cases.
Slavery–United States–History–Sources.

Title: *American roots music* [electronic resource]. [no date]
SUBJECTS:
Folk music–United States–History and criticism.
Popular music–United States–History and criticism.

For serially issued electronic resources, see the discussion in the section "Serial Publications" below.

Works about Internet or Web Resources:

The subdivision **–Computer network resources** is not a form subdivision but a topical subdivision used for works *about* electronic resources.

Title: *Information professional's guide to career development online* / Sarah L. Nesbeitt and Rachel Singer Gordon. c2002.
SUBJECTS:
Library science–Vocational guidance.
Information science–Vocational guidance.
Library science–Computer network resources.
Information science–Computer network resources.
Career development–Computer network resources.

Title: *European history highway : a guide to Internet resources* / Dennis A. Trinkle and Scott A. Merriman, editors. c2002.
SUBJECTS:
Europe–History–Research.
History–Computer network resources.
Internet.

Title: *Internet resources for nurses* / Joyce J. Fitzpatrick, Kristen S. Montgomery, editors. 2nd ed. c2003.
SUBJECTS:
Nursing–Computer network resources.
Internet.
Nursing informatics.
Medical care–Computer network resources.
Internet–Resource Guides.

Medical Informatics–Resource Guides.
Nursing–Resource Guides.

Title: *Internet resources and services for international marketing and advertising : a global guide* / James R. Coyle. c2002.
SUBJECTS:
Export marketing–Computer network resources–Directories.
Advertising–Computer network resources–Directories.

SERIAL PUBLICATIONS

Subject headings for serial publications in general, and for periodicals and journals in particular (see also discussion later in this chapter), are based on the subject range of a publication over its expected life, not the topics in individual issues. Topical and/or geographical headings are assigned as appropriate, with a form subdivision used to show the material's bibliographical form. Most Library of Congress form subdivisions are free-floating; the following list shows those that are most frequently used for serial publications:

–Congresses
–Directories
–Indexes
–Periodicals
–Societies, etc.

Of these, as might be expected, the one in widest use is **–Periodicals**. It is used as a form subdivision under topical, personal name, corporate name, and geographic headings. The subdivision **–Periodicals** may be combined with other form headings or form subdivisions when appropriate:

(1) It may be used with form headings, for example:

French poetry–Periodicals

(2) It may be further subdivided by other form subdivisions, for example:

–Periodicals–Bibliography
–Periodicals–Indexes
–Periodicals–Juvenile literature

(3) It may be used as a further subdivision under most other free-floating form subdivisions, for example:

–Abstracts–Periodicals
–Biography–Periodicals
–Statistics–Periodicals

However, it is *not* used as a further subdivision under the following form subdivisions:[5]

–Amateurs' manuals
–Atlases
–Calendars
–Cases
–Congresses
–Dictionaries
–Digests
–Directories
–Encyclopedias
–Gazetteers
–Guidebooks
–Handbooks, manuals, etc.
–Juvenile films
–Juvenile literature
–Juvenile software
–Juvenile sound recordings
–Laboratory manuals
–Maps
{also **–Maps, Comparative**; **–Maps, Manuscript**; **Maps for children**, etc.}
–Observers' manuals
–Outlines, syllabi, etc.
–Photo maps
–Registers
–Telephone directories

As a result, headings such as *[Topic]–Congresses–Periodicals* or *[Place] –Guidebooks–Periodicals* are not authorized for use.

In choosing a form subdivision, the cataloger should be guided by both the nature of the publication in question (not just by what is suggested by the wording of the title) and the scope notes in *Subject Cataloging Manual: Subject Headings* that apply to form subdivisions.

The following examples reflect current LC subject cataloging practice for various types of serial publications. When discussion of a given publication type is better suited to a different section of this book, a cross reference to the relevant pages is given.

Abstracts

See the discussion and examples in the section "Lists of Publications" below.

Annual Reports

See the discussion and examples in the section "Reports" below.

Biographical Reference Works

Title: *Contemporary Hispanic biography : profiles from the international Hispanic community.* c2002-
SUBJECTS:
Latin America–Biography–Periodicals.
Hispanic Americans–Biography–Periodicals.
Spain–Biography–Periodicals.

Title: *1000 world leaders of scientific influence.* c2002-
SUBJECTS:
Scientists–Biography–Periodicals.

Title: *Current biography international yearbook.* c2002.
SUBJECTS:
Biography–20th century–Periodicals.

Book and Media Reviews

Title: *DVD & video guide.* 2002-
SUBJECTS:
Video recordings–Reviews–Periodicals.
Motion pictures–Reviews–Periodicals.

Title: *Bookmarks.* 2002-
SUBJECTS:
Books–Reviews–Periodicals.
Books and reading–Periodicals.

Title: *Political studies review* / Political Studies Association. c2003-
SUBJECTS:
Political science–Book reviews–Periodicals.
Political science–Periodicals.

Title: *The children's buyer's guide.* c2002-
SUBJECTS:
Children's literature, English–Reviews–Periodicals.
Children's literature, English–Publishing–Periodicals.
Booksellers and bookselling–Great Britain–Periodicals.

Conference (Congress, Symposium, Etc.) Publications

Publications emanating from conferences, congresses, symposia, etc., are assigned topical or name headings with the subdivision **–Congresses.**[6] Such headings are not further subdivided by other forms, except for the subdivisions **–Calendars, –Directories,** or **–Juvenile literature.** The subdivisions **–Abstracts** and **–Periodicals** are not used after the subdivision **–Congresses** even when the publication in question consists of collected papers issued in condensed form or is serial in nature; in other words, the form *[Topic]–Congresses–Abstracts* or *[Topic]–Congresses–Periodicals* is not authorized for use. Examples include:

Title: *Advances in information retrieval : 25th European Conference on IR Research, ECIR 2003, Pisa, Italy, April 14-16, 2003 : proceedings* / Fabrizio Sebastiani. 2003.
SUBJECTS:
Database management–Congresses.
Information storage and retrieval systems–Congresses.

Title: *Management of shared fish stocks* / edited by A.I.L. Payne, C.M. O'Brien, and S.I. Rogers. 2004.
SUBJECTS:
Fish populations–Congresses.
Fishery management–Congresses.

For works about one or more congresses, the subdivision **–Congresses** is used as a topical subdivision further subdivided by an appropriate subdivision, for example, **–Congresses–Attendance**; **–Congresses–Calendars**; or **–Congresses–Directories**.

Directories

See the discussion in the section "Reference Materials" below.

Electronic Serials

An electronic serial is defined as "a work in a machine-readable format, issued in successive designated parts for an indefinite period of time (that is, it meets the definition of a serial),"[7] including remote access serials available on the Internet and direct access serial issued on CD-ROM, floppy disk, etc. An electronic serial is assigned appropriate headings subdivided by **–Periodicals**.

Title: *Law and literature* [electronic resource]. c2002-
SUBJECTS:
Law and literature–Periodicals.

Title: *ACM queue* [electronic resource] : *tomorrow's computing today.* 2003-
SUBJECTS:
Software engineering–Periodicals.
Computer software–Development–Periodicals.

Title: *Online journal of space communication* [electronic resource]. 2002-
SUBJECTS:
Artificial satellites in telecommunication–Periodicals.
Russian periodicals.

The subdivision **–Databases** (not further subdivided by **–Periodicals**) is used for serially issued databases, except for electronic serials of reference-type works such as bibliographies, catalogs, collections of abstracts, directories, dictionaries, indexes, etc.

Title: *FreeBooks4Doctors* [electronic resource] : *promoting free access to medical books.* 2002-
SUBJECTS:
Medical literature–Databases.
Medicine–Databases.

Title: *Sailing directions (enroute)* [electronic resource] : *Japan.* 8th ed. 2003-
SUBJECTS:
Pilot guides–Japan–Databases.

Headings of the type **[Topic]–Periodicals–Databases** are assigned to databases of periodicals on a particular subject, or to works about databases of periodicals in a particular field. The heading **Periodicals–Databases** is assigned to a work about databases of periodicals.

Title: *JSTOR : a history* / Roger C. Schonfeld. 2003.
SUBJECTS:
JSTOR (Computer file)
Periodicals–Databases.
JSTOR (Organization)–History.

Government Publications Issued Serially

Serially issued government publications are assigned subject headings appropriate to their subject content and form. In other words, no special subdivision is used to bring out the fact that a publication is issued by a government.

Title: *International migration report* / Dept. of Economic and Social Affairs, Population Division, United Nations. 2002-
SUBJECTS:
Emigration and immigration–Statistics–Periodicals.
Emigration and immigration law–Periodicals.

Title: *Annual report and accounts* / Defence Science and Technology Laboratory. 2002-
SUBJECTS:
Defence Science and Technology Laboratory (Great Britain)–Periodicals.
Military research–Great Britain–Periodicals.

Indexes

See the discussion in the section "Lists of Publications" below.

Periodicals and Journals

A periodical is defined as "a publication other than a newspaper that is actually or purportedly issued according to a regular schedule (monthly, quarterly, biennially, etc.) in successive parts, each of which bears a numerical or chronological designation, and that is intended to be continued indefinitely."[8] The headings assigned to a periodical or journal are based on the overall content of the publication rather than on specific topics treated in individual issues. Appropriate headings subdivided by **–Periodicals** are assigned. Examples include:

Title: *Guinness world records.* c2000-
SUBJECTS:
World records–Periodicals.

Title: *The citizen.* 2002-
SUBJECTS:
Kenya–Periodicals.

Title: *Strategic investment.* 2002-
SUBJECTS:
Economic forecasting–Periodicals.
International economic relations–Periodicals.
World politics–1945--Periodicals.

Title: *Computer languages, systems & structures.* c2002-
SUBJECTS:
Programming languages (Electronic computers)–Periodicals.
Computer networks–Periodicals.
Computer architecture–Periodicals.

Title: *Advanced engineering informatics.* c2002-
SUBJECTS:
Engineering–Data processing–Periodicals.
Artificial intelligence–Periodicals.
Expert systems (Computer science)–Periodicals.

Title: *The journal of medieval military history.* 2002-
SUBJECTS:
Military history, Medieval–Periodicals.
Military art and science–History–Medieval, 500-1500–Periodicals.

Title: *Consumer price index* / Federated States of Micronesia. 2002-
SUBJECTS:
Prices–Micronesia (Federated States)–Periodicals.
Micronesia (Federated States)–Price indexes–Periodicals.

Title: *Science in dispute.* c2002-
SUBJECTS:
Sciences–Miscellanea–Periodicals.

Periodicals that cover very broad or general subjects are not assigned subject headings.[9] Headings such as **American periodicals** indicate topic, not form; in other words, the heading **American periodicals** is assigned to a work *about* American periodicals but is not used with periodicals such as *Saturday Evening Post* or *Atlantic Monthly*. Other examples:

Title: *Nonfiction bestsellers.* c2001-
{No subject headings}

Title: *People.* 2002-
{No subject headings}

Reports

For serially issued reports by government agencies or other corporate bodies that contain substantive subject information, one or more topical headings, with the subdivision **–Periodicals**, are assigned.

Title: *Annual short range transit report.* 2000-
SUBJECTS:
Local transit–Arizona–Phoenix Metropolitan Area–Periodicals.

Title: *The Arab world competitiveness report* / World Economic Forum. 2003-
SUBJECTS:
Competition, International–Statistics–Periodicals.
Arab countries–Economic conditions–21st century–Statistics–Periodicals.

Title: *Museum Store Association museum retail industry report.* 2002-
SUBJECTS:
Museum stores–United States–Finance–Statistics–Periodicals.

If the publication contains information about the corporate body as well as substantive information, an additional heading under the name of the corporate body is assigned:

Title: *Estimates. Part III, Report on plans and priorities* / Canadian Nuclear Safety Commission. 2001-
SUBJECTS:
Canadian Nuclear Safety Commission–Periodicals.
Canadian Nuclear Safety Commission–Appropriations and expenditures–Periodicals.
Nuclear industry–Canada–Periodicals.
Nuclear energy–Canada–Periodicals.

Title: *Annual report of Maine Legislative Youth Advisory Council.* [2003-]
SUBJECTS:
Maine. Legislature. Legislative Youth Advisory Council–Periodicals.
Minors–Maine–Periodicals.
Youth–Maine–Social conditions–Periodicals.

Title: *Annual report* / Water Research Commission. 2002-
SUBJECTS:
South Africa. Water Research Commission–Periodicals.
Water resources development–South Africa–Periodicals.
Water–Research–South Africa–Periodicals.

If the publication contains only information about the corporate body, only the heading under the name of the body is assigned.

Serial Publications Devoted to Individual Persons

For a serial publication devoted to one person, a heading in the form of **[Name of person]–Periodicals** is assigned.

Title: *The Shakespearean international yearbook.* c1999-
SUBJECTS:
Shakespeare, William, 1564-1616–Periodicals.

Society Publications

Publications issued serially by societies are assigned subject headings appropriate to their subject content and form.

Title: *Journal of the Medical Library Association : JMLA.* c2002-
SUBJECTS:
Medical libraries–Periodicals.
Medicine–Information services–Periodicals.
Medicine–Library resources–Periodicals.

Title: *Eukaryotic cell.* c2002- [issued by the American Society for Microbiology]
SUBJECTS:
Eukaryotic cells–Periodicals.
Molecular biology–Periodicals.
Cytology–Periodicals.

Title: *Molecular imaging : official journal of the Society for Molecular Imaging.* c2002-
SUBJECTS:
Diagnostic imaging–Periodicals.
Molecular biology–Periodicals.

For reports *of* societies, see examples in the section "Reports" above. For works *about* societies, see the discussion and examples in the section "Works about Corporate Bodies" below.

Statistics

Title: *Amber waves : the economics of food, farming, natural resources, and rural America* / United States Department of Agriculture, Economic Research Service. 2003-
SUBJECTS:
Environmental economics–United States–Statistics–Periodicals.
Rural development–United States–Statistics–Periodicals.

Title: *California grain and feed report* [electronic resource]. 2003-
SUBJECTS:
Grain trade–Prices–California–Statistics–Periodicals.
Feeds–Prices–California–Statistics–Periodicals.

Union Lists

See the discussion in the section "Lists of Publications" below.

Yearbooks

The subdivision *–Yearbooks* is no longer valid; the subdivision **–Periodicals** is now used for yearbooks.

Title: *The ... annual competition & convention yearbook.* 2003-
SUBJECTS:
Dance–Competitions–United States–Periodicals.
Dance schools–United States–Directories.

Title: *CountryWatch forecast yearbook.* 2002-
SUBJECTS:
Economic history–1990-–Statistics–Periodicals.
Economic forecasting–Statistics–Periodicals.
Economic indicators–Periodicals.

Title: *Taiwan yearbook.* 2003-
SUBJECTS:
Taiwan–Periodicals.

LISTS OF PUBLICATIONS

Lists of publications appear in various forms, such as abstracts, bibliographies, and catalogs. These are normally brought out by free-floating form subdivisions such as:

–Abstracts
–Bibliography
–Catalogs
–Imprints {under names of places}
–Indexes
–Union lists

The following discussion and examples illuminate LC practice in the treatment of various types of lists and the proper use of relevant form subdivisions.

Abstracts[10]

Both **–Abstracts** and **–Bibliography** are free-floating form subdivisions that may be used under topical, geographic, corporate, or personal headings to bring out the form of a publication. However, some publications, such as lists of publications with annotations, may not fall clearly under either one of the two categories. To assist the cataloger, the Library of Congress has provided the following guidelines: The subdivision **–Abstracts** is used when a work lists publications and provides full bibliographical information together with substantive summaries or condensations of the facts, ideas, or opinions for each publication listed. The nature of the annotations or summaries is the criterion. The following characteristics are considered to be typical of abstracts:

They present briefly the essential points made in the original publication, usually including the conclusion, if any, drawn by its author.

They provide enough detail to enable the user to decide whether or not to refer to the original publication.

They evaluate or criticize the publication.[11]

Examples of abstracts include:

Title: *African studies abstracts online* [electronic resource]. c2003-
SUBJECTS:
Africa–Abstracts–Periodicals.

Title: *International abstracts of human resources : a guide to the literature of management, human resources, and personnel.* 2003-
SUBJECTS:
Personnel management–Abstracts–Periodicals.
Labor supply–Abstracts–Periodicals.

Title: *Hungarian R&D articles. Science and technology.* 2002-
SUBJECTS:
Technology–Abstracts–Periodicals.
Engineering–Abstracts–Periodicals.
Technology–Periodicals–Indexes–Periodicals.

For summaries of the proceedings of a congress or conference, instead of **–Abstracts,** the subdivision **–Congresses,** without further subdivision, is used.

Bibliographies

The free-floating subdivision **–Bibliography** is used for unannotated or annotated lists of publications. Annotations are distinguished from abstracts in that they give only a general indication of the subject matter of each publication listed, rather than try to distill its content, and they are seldom critical in nature.

Two subdivisions that seem especially difficult to distinguish are **–Indexes** and **–Bibliography**. (Indexes, as a form of publication, are discussed directly below.) The Library of Congress offers the following usage criteria for **–Bibliography** and **–Indexes**:

> **–Indexes** is used as a form subdivision under subject headings for works that provide a comprehensive subject approach to printed materials published in a specific field of knowledge . . . .
>
> The subdivision **–Bibliography** is used for works that merely list publications. Many bibliographies, however, are themselves indexed by

subject. When a subject-indexed bibliography is judged to be sufficiently comprehensive in scope as to be usable as a general index to the publications in a field, the subdivision **–Indexes** is used instead of **–Bibliography**.[12]

Examples of bibliographies include:

Title: *Introduction to reference sources in the health sciences* / [compiled by] Jo Anne Boorkman, Jeffrey Huber, Fred Roper. 4th ed. 2004.
SUBJECTS:
Medicine–Reference books–Bibliography.
Medicine–Bibliography.
Medicine–Information services.

Title: *Bibliography of American literature* / compiled by Jacob Blanck for the Bibliographical Society of America. 2003.
SUBJECTS:
American literature–Bibliography.

The combination *–Bibliography–Indexes* is not authorized for use. On the other hand, the subdivision **–Bibliography** may be combined with other form subdivisions to indicate specific types of bibliography, for example:

–Bibliography–Catalogs
–Bibliography–Early
–Bibliography–Graded lists
–Bibliography–Exhibitions
–Bibliography–Methodology
–Bibliography–Microform catalogs
–Bibliography–Union lists

Title: *The Shakespeare first folio : the history of the book* / Anthony James West. 2001-
SUBJECTS:
Shakespeare, William, 1564-1616–Bibliography–Folios. 1623.
Shakespeare, William, 1564-1616–Bibliography–Folios. 1623–Union lists.
Early printed books–England–London–17th century–Bibliography–Union lists.
Early printed books–England–London–17th century–Bibliography.
Books–Prices–History.

The heading **Bibliography of bibliographies** is assigned to a work consisting of a list of bibliographies not limited to any specific topic. For a work consisting of a list of bibliographies on a specific topic, a heading in the form of **[Topic]–Bibliography of bibliographies** is used.[13] Examples include:

Title: *Twentieth-century bibliography and textual criticism : an annotated bibliography* / compiled by William Baker and Kenneth Womack ; foreword by T.H. Howard-Hill. 2000.

SUBJECTS:

Bibliography of bibliographies.
Bibliographical literature–Bibliography.
Bibliography, Critical–Bibliography.
English literature–Bibliography of bibliographies.

For a bibliography that lists works by or about an individual person or an individual work, a personal name heading or a name/title heading for the work being discussed with the free-floating subdivision **–Bibliography** is used.[14]

Title: *Annotated Chaucer bibliography, 1986-1996* / Bege K. Bowers & Mark Allen, editors. c2002.

SUBJECTS:

Chaucer, Geoffrey, d. 1400–Bibliography.

Title: *As you like it, Much ado about nothing, and Twelfth night, or, What you will : an annotated bibliography of Shakespeare studies* / edited by Marilyn L. Williamson. 2003.

SUBJECTS:

Shakespeare, William, 1564-1616. As you like it–Bibliography.
Shakespeare, William, 1564-1616. Much ado about nothing–Bibliography.
Shakespeare, William, 1564-1616. Twelfth night–Bibliography.

Title: *Hamlet : an annotated bibliography of Shakespeare studies, 1604-1998* / Michael E. Mooney, editor. 1999.

SUBJECTS:

Shakespeare, William, 1564-1616. Hamlet–Bibliography.
Hamlet (Legendary character)–Bibliography.

If the work has a topical orientation, additional headings in the form of **[Topic]–Bibliography** are also assigned:

Title: *Shakespeare : life, language, and linguistics, textual studies, and the canon : an annotated bibliography of Shakespeare studies, 1623-2000* / Michael Warren, editor. 2003.

SUBJECTS:

Shakespeare, William, 1564-1616–Bibliography.
Shakespeare, William, 1564-1616–Language–Bibliography.
Shakespeare, William, 1564-1616–Authorship–Bibliography.
Shakespeare, William, 1564-1616–Criticism, Textual–Bibliography.
Shakespeare, William, 1564-1616–Biography–Sources–Bibliography.
Dramatists, English–Early modern, 1500-1700–Biography–Bibliography.

English language–Early modern, 1500-1700–Bibliography.
Canon (Literature)–Bibliography.

Indexes

The free-floating form subdivision **–Indexes** is used under subject headings for "works that provide a comprehensive subject approach to printed materials published in a specific field of knowledge."[15] The treatment of various kinds of indexes is illustrated below.

(1) *General indexes and indexes limited to specific subjects*:

Title: *AGRICOLA* [electronic resource]. Updated monthly (viewed Mar. 18, 2004)
SUBJECTS:
Agriculture–Indexes.
Forests and forestry–Indexes.
Animal industry–Indexes.

Title: *An index of excerpts and an overview of published orchestral bassoon excerpt collections with a comparison of three collections* / Tama I. Kott. c2003.
SUBJECTS:
Bassoon–Orchestral excerpts–Indexes.
Bassoon music–Bibliography.

Title: *Newbery and Caldecott awards : a subject index* / Denise Goetting ... [et al.]. c2003.
SUBJECTS:
Newbery Medal–Indexes.
Caldecott Medal–Indexes.
Children's literature, American–Indexes.
Picture books for children–United States–Indexes.

Title: *Index to Franklin County, Tennessee loose court records, 1870-1879* / compiled by James H. Brewer. c2003.
SUBJECTS:
Court records–Tennessee–Franklin County–Indexes.
Franklin County (Tenn.)–Genealogy.

Title: *The laws of Texas 1822-1897* / compiled and arranged by H.P.N. Gammel with an introduction by C.W. Raines. *Analytical index to the laws of Texas 1823-1905* / by Cadwell Walton Raines. 2004.
SUBJECTS:
Law–Texas–History–19th century.
Law–Texas–History–19th century–Indexes.

Title: *The Columbia Granger's index to poetry in anthologies* / edited by Tessa Kale. 2002.
SUBJECTS:
Poetry–Indexes.
English poetry–Indexes.

(2) *Indexes limited to specific forms of materials other than books.* A subdivision representing the specific form of material (except for indexes to films on a topic, for which the subdivision **–Film catalogs** is used instead), interposed between the topical heading and the subdivision **–Indexes**, or a form subdivision combining the specific form and index is used:

Title: *Directory of genealogical and historical society periodicals in the US and Canada* / edited by Dina C. Carson. c2000.
SUBJECTS:
Genealogy–Periodicals–Indexes.
History–Periodicals–Indexes.

Title: *PCI* [electronic resource] : *Periodicals contents index.* c2001.
SUBJECTS:
Periodicals–Indexes.
Arts–Periodicals–Indexes.
Humanities–Periodicals–Indexes.
Social sciences–Periodicals–Indexes.

Title: *The Holocaust film sourcebook* / edited by Caroline Joan "Kay" Picart. 2004.
SUBJECTS:
Holocaust, Jewish (1939-1945), in motion pictures–Sources–Bibliography.
Holocaust, Jewish (1939-1945)–Film catalogs.

(3) *Indexes to works of an individual author.* A heading in the form of **[Name of author]–[Form of publication,** if appropriate**]–Indexes** is assigned:

Title: *The index to Jabberwocky, the journal of the Lewis Carroll Society : 1969-1997* / compiled by Clare Imholtz. 2002.
SUBJECTS:
Carroll, Lewis, 1832-1898–Periodicals–Indexes.

Title: *Melville's allusions to religion : a comprehensive index and glossary* / compiled by Gail H. Coffler. 2004.
SUBJECTS:
Melville, Herman, 1819-1891–Religion.
Melville, Herman, 1819-1891–Indexes.
Religion in literature–Indexes.

(4) *Indexes to individual monographic works or individual serials.* See the discussion in the section "Works Related to Individual Works" later in the chapter.

The subdivision **–Indexes** may be further subdivided by another form subdivision representing the form of the index.

Catalogs of Publications

Catalogs of Library Materials[16]

The following types of headings are assigned to catalogs of various types of information resources:

[Topic of the works listed]–[Form of works listed]–Catalogs
[Name of institution]–Catalogs
[Name of collection, if any]–Catalogs

The most commonly used subdivisions for catalogs are:

–Audio-visual aids–Catalogs
–Bibliography–Catalogs
–Bibliography–Microform catalogs
–Discography
–Film catalogs
–Manuscripts–Catalogs
–Manuscripts–Microform catalogs
–Video catalogs
–Periodicals–Bibliography–Catalogs

Examples include:

Title: *Catalogue of the Spanish Collection of the Texas General Land Office* / compiled and written by Galen D. Greaser. 2003.
SUBJECTS:
Texas. General Land Office–History–Bibliography.
Land grants–Texas–Bibliography–Catalogs.
Texas–History–To 1846–Bibliography–Catalogs.

Title: *Sporting books in the Huntington Library* / compiled by Lyle H. Wright. 2003.
SUBJECTS:
Sports–Bibliography–Catalogs.

Title: *Seventeenth-century British keyboard sources* / Candace Bailey. 2003.
SUBJECTS:
Keyboard instrument music–Great Britain–17th century–Manuscripts–Catalogs.

Title: *Billboard's hottest hot 100 hits* / Fred Bronson. Updated & expanded 3rd ed. c2003.
SUBJECTS:
Popular music–United States–Discography.

Title: *The World War II combat film : anatomy of a genre* / Jeanine Basinger ; updated filmography by Jeremy Arnold. 2003.
SUBJECTS:
World War, 1939-1945–Motion pictures and the war–Film catalogs.
Motion pictures–United States–History.
War films–United States–History and criticism.

Title: *The young Louis Armstrong on records : a critical survey of the early recordings, 1923-1928* / Edward Brooks. 2002.
SUBJECTS:
Armstrong, Louis, 1901-1971–Criticism and interpretation.
Armstrong, Louis, 1901-1971–Discography.
Jazz–1921-1930–Analysis, appreciation.

For catalogs of objects, see the discussion in the section "Reference Materials" below.

Union Lists

For union lists or union catalogs, a heading in the form of **Catalogs, Union–[Place]** (referring to the location of the union list or catalog) is assigned in addition to other appropriate headings subdivided by **–Union lists**:

Title: *Union list of serials in Pacific Island libraries* / a cooperative project of the Pacific Islands Association of Libraries and Archives (PIALA), the Guam Public Library System and the University of Guam Robert F. Kennedy Memorial Library. 2002-
SUBJECTS:
Pacific Island periodicals–Bibliography–Union lists.
Catalogs, Union–Pacific Islands.

Title: *IUA journal holdings in the Washington, D.C. metropolitan area.* c2001-
SUBJECTS:
Periodicals–Bibliography–Union lists.
Catalogs, Union–Washington Metropolitan Area.
Catalogs, Union–Maryland–Baltimore Metropolitan Area.

Publishers' Catalogs[17]

The following types of headings are assigned to catalogs of individual publishing houses:

[Name of publishing house]–Catalogs
Catalogs, Publishers'–[Country]

and, in addition, one of the following three:

[Country]–Imprints–Catalogs
Government publications–[Country]–Bibliography–Catalogs
[Topic]–Bibliography–Catalogs

If the publications listed are in a specific form, headings similar to the following are assigned in addition:

Microforms–Catalogs {only for general microform catalogs}
Pamphlets in microform–Catalogs
Books on microfilm–Catalogs
Periodicals on microfiche–Catalogs

Examples include:

Title: *Bibliotheca chemico-mathematica : catalogue of works in many tongues on exact and applied science, with a subject-index* / compiled and annotated by H.Z. and H.C.S. 2003.
SUBJECTS:
Science–Bibliography–Catalogs.
Technology–Bibliography–Catalogs.
Henry Sotheran Ltd.–Catalogs.
Catalogs, Publishers'–Great Britain.

Title: *UNSW Press : a bibliography 1962-2002* / Charlotte Jarabak. 2002.
SUBJECTS:
University of New South Wales Press–Catalogs.
Catalogs, Publishers'–New South Wales–Sydney.
Australia–Imprints–Catalogs.

Imprints[18]

The following types of headings are assigned to lists of works published in a particular place and/or language:

[Place of origin]–Imprints
[Language] imprints–[Place]
{not assigned if the language is predominant in the place of question}
[Name of library]–Catalogs
{for a listing of a library's special collection of imprints}
[Topic]–Bibliography

Examples include:

Title: *A catalogue of the Persian printed books in the British Museum* / compiled by Edward Edwards. 2003.
SUBJECTS:
Persian imprints–Catalogs.
British Museum. Dept. of Oriental Printed Books and Manuscripts–Catalogs.
British Library. Oriental Collections–Catalogs.

Title: *Catalogue of important Hebrew printed books from the library of the late Salman Schocken (1877-1959).* 2003.
SUBJECTS:
Schoken, Salman, 1877-1959–Library–Catalogs.
Hebrew imprints–Catalogs.

For catalogs listing imprints existing at a specific locality or available from a specified source, headings in the form of **[Place of origin]–Imprints–Catalogs** or **[Language] imprints–Catalogs** are used. These headings are not further subdivided by **–Bibliography**, since the term *imprints* already implies lists of publications. The headings may be further subdivided by other appropriate form subdivisions. Examples include:

Title: *Descriptive catalogue of Japanese and Chinese illustrated books in the Ryerson Library of the Art Institute of Chicago* / by Kenji Toda. 2004.
SUBJECTS:
Illustrated books–Japan–Bibliography–Catalogs.
Illustrated books–China–Bibliography–Catalogs.
Art Institute of Chicago. Ryerson Library–Catalogs.
Illustration of books–Japan.
Japan–Imprints–Catalogs.

Title: *The Library of William Andrews Clark, Jr. The Kelmscott and Doves presses* / collated and compiled by Robert Ernest Cowan ; assisted by Cora Edgerton Sanders and Harrison Post ; with an introduction by Alfred W. Pollard. 2003.
SUBJECTS:
Clark, William Andrews, 1877-1934–Library–Catalogs.
Kelmscott Press–Bibliography–Catalogs.
Doves Press–Bibliography–Catalogs.
Private press books–Bibliography–Catalogs.
Private libraries–England–Catalogs.
Hammersmith (London, England)–Imprints–Catalogs.

Lists and Abstracts of Dissertations and Theses[19]

The following types of headings are assigned to lists and abstracts of dissertations and theses:

> **[Topic or Name]–Bibliography** [or **–Abstracts]**
> **[Institution]–Dissertations–Bibliography** [or **–Abstracts]**
> **Dissertations, Academic–[Country]–Bibliography** [or **–Abstracts]**

Examples include:

Title: *Bibliography of female economic thought to 1940* / Kirsten K. Madden, Janet A. Sietz & Michele Pujol. 2004.
SUBJECTS:
Economics–Bibliography.
Women economists–Bibliography.
Social problems–Bibliography.
Feminist economics–Bibliography.
Economic history–Sources–Bibliography.
Dissertations, Academic–Bibliography.

Title: *Canadian art and architecture : an annotated bibliography of theses and dissertations* / Diane E. Peters. 2003.
SUBJECTS:
Art, Canadian–Bibliography.
Architecture–Canada–Bibliography.
Dissertations, Academic–Canada–Bibliography.

REFERENCE MATERIALS

Works about Reference Books

The following types of headings are used for works about reference books:[20]

> **[Topic]–Reference books**
> **[Topic]–Reference books–Bibliography**
> **Reference books–[Place]**

Works about reference books are assigned the heading **Reference books**. This is a topical heading; it is not used for reference books per se. The heading **Reference books** is used without subdivision when the work being cataloged is not limited by topic; it may, however, be qualified by a language other than English, for example, **Reference books, German**. Examples include:

Title: *Libraries and reference materials* / John Hamilton. c2004.
SUBJECTS:
Libraries–Juvenile literature.
Reference books–Juvenile literature.
China–Reference books–Bibliography.

Bibliographies of Reference Books

Non-Topical Bibliographies

The heading **Reference books–Bibliography** or **Reference books**, [language] **–Bibliography** is assigned to a non-topical bibliography of reference books:

Title: *Know it all, find it fast : an A-Z source guide for the enquiry desk* / Bob Duckett, Peter Walker, Christinea Donnelly. 2002.
SUBJECTS:
Information resources–Great Britain–Directories.
Reference services (Libraries)–Great Britain.
Internet in library reference services.
Reference books–Bibliography.

Title: *Introduction to reference work* / William A. Katz. 8th ed. c2002.
SUBJECTS:
Reference services (Libraries)
Reference books–Bibliography.

Topical Bibliographies

For a bibliography of the reference sources in a particular field, two headings in the form of **[Topic]–Bibliography** and **[Topic]–Reference books–Bibliography** are used. Examples include:

Title: *United States history : a multicultural, interdisciplinary guide to information sources* / Anna H. Perrault and Ron Blazek. 2003.
SUBJECTS:
United States–History–Bibliography.
United States–History–Reference books–Bibliography.
United States–History–Databases–Directories.

Title: *Introduction to reference sources in the health sciences* / [compiled by] Jo Anne Boorkman, Jeffrey Huber, Fred Roper. 4th ed. 2004.
SUBJECTS:
Medicine–Reference books–Bibliography.
Medicine–Bibliography.
Medicine–Information services.

Title: *Reference and research guide to mystery and detective fiction* / Richard J. Bleiler. 2nd ed. 2003.
SUBJECTS:
Detective and mystery stories–Bibliography.
Detective and mystery stories–Reference books–Bibliography.

If the reference sources listed in the bibliography are limited to a specific language other than English, an additional heading in the form of **Reference books, [Language]–Bibliography** is also assigned.

Title: *Twentieth-century China, an annotated bibliography of reference works in Chinese, Japanese, and western languages: subjects* / edited by James H. Cole. 2003.
SUBJECTS:
Reference books, Chinese–Bibliography.
Reference books, Japanese–Bibliography.
China–Reference books–Bibliography.

Reference Works

In LCSH, several categories of reference works are given special treatment or represented by special subdivisions. These include almanacs, catalogs of objects, dictionaries, directories, and handbooks and manuals.

Almanacs

Form headings such as **Almanacs, American** and **Almanacs, Children's** are used to bring out the form of publication.

Title: *Days to celebrate : an almanac of people, events, and poetry* / Lee Bennett Hopkins. 2004.
SUBJECTS:
Almanacs, Children's.

Title: *Encyclopaedia Britannica almanac.* c2002-
SUBJECTS:
Almanacs, American–Periodicals.

Topical headings are assigned to bring out the subject of the almanac.

Title: *Ben Franklin's almanac of wit, wisdom, and practical advice : useful tips and fascinating facts for every day of the year* / by the editors of the Old Farmer's Almanac. 2003.
SUBJECTS:
Home economics–Miscellanea.
Almanacs, American.

Title: *The original thoroughbred times racing almanac.* c2002-
SUBJECTS:
Horse racing–United States–Periodicals.
Horse industry–United States–Periodicals.
Almanacs, American–Periodicals.

Title: *New view almanac* / computer graphics by David C. Bell and Bob Italiano ; text by Jenny Tesar ; Bruce S. Glassman, editor. 2003.
SUBJECTS:
Almanacs, Children's.
United States–Statistics–Juvenile literature.

Catalogs of Objects

The free-floating subdivision **–Catalogs** is used under headings for listings of various types of objects, including merchandise, art objects, collectors' items, technical equipment, etc., that have been produced, are available or located at particular places, or are offered on a particular market, often systematically arranged with descriptive details, prices, etc.[21]

The following types of headings are assigned:

[Objects]–Catalogs
[Kind of institution]–Catalogs
[Name of artist, craftsperson, or seller]–Catalogs
[Name of producer, store, institution or collection]–Catalogs

Title: *British Empire stamps and postal history, Thursday 21 and Friday 22 March 2002.* 2002.
SUBJECTS:
Postage stamps–Great Britain–Colonies–Catalogs.
Postal service–Great Britain–Colonies–Catalogs.

Title: *Hot wheels : the recent years* / Bob Parker. c2003.
SUBJECTS:
Hot Wheels toys–Collectors and collecting–Catalogs.
Hot Wheels toys–Prices–Catalogs.
Automobiles–Models–Collectors and collecting–Catalogs.

For catalogs of natural objects and musical instruments, the subdivision **–Catalogs and collections**, instead of **–Catalogs**, is used:

Title: *Smithsonian plant collections, Guyana : 1989-1991*, Lynn J. Gillespie / by Tom Hollowell ... [et al.]. 2003.
SUBJECTS:
Botany–Catalogs and collections–Guyana.
Plants–Guyana–Classification.
Plant collecting–Guyana.

Dictionaries[22]

The subdivision **–Dictionaries** is the most frequently used form subdivision for both language and subject dictionaries. However, many different kinds of dictionaries and dictionary-like publications exist. There is, therefore, a considerable list of free-floating subdivisions that may be applied to particular dictionaries or dictionary-like publications. These are listed below; full information on their use may be found in *Subject Cataloging Manual: Subject Headings.*

–Concordances
–Dictionaries, Juvenile
–Directories
–Encyclopedias
–Encyclopedias, Juvenile
–Gazetteers
–Glossaries, vocabularies, etc.
–Language–Glossaries, etc.
–Nomenclature
–Registers
–Terminology
–Terms and phrases

LC guidelines for the major categories of dictionaries are briefly summarized below.

(1) *Language dictionaries*. For a comprehensive, alphabetical list of words in one language, usually with definitions, a heading of the type **[Name of language]–Dictionaries** is used:

Title: *Compact Oxford English dictionary of current English* / edited by Catherine Soanes. 2003.
SUBJECTS:
English language–Dictionaries.

For a bilingual dictionary that gives the terms of one language in terms of the other, a heading of the type **[Name of first language]–Dictionaries–[Name of second language** (adjective only)**]** is used:

Title: *ABC Chinese-English comprehensive dictionary : alphabetically based computerized* / editor John DeFrancis ; associate editors Tom Bishop ... [et. al]. 2003.
SUBJECTS:
Chinese language–Dictionaries–English.

If the second language is also given in terms of the first, a duplicate heading with the languages reversed is also assigned:

Title: *The new Routledge Dutch dictionary : Dutch-English/English-Dutch* / N. Osselton and R. Hempelman. 2003.
SUBJECTS:
Dutch language–Dictionaries–English.
English language–Dictionaries–Dutch.

For a polyglot dictionary, when each language in a polyglot dictionary is given in terms of the others, the general heading **Dictionaries, Polyglot** is assigned.

Title: *5 language visual dictionary.* c2003.
SUBJECTS:
Picture dictionaries, Polyglot.
Dictionaries, Polyglot.

If one language is given in terms of more than one other language, a heading of the type **[Name of language]–Dictionaries–Polyglot** is assigned.

The subdivision **–Glossaries, vocabularies, etc.** is used for incomplete lists of words of a language, with or without definitions, arranged alphabetically or otherwise:

Title: *Italian vocabulary* / Marcel Danesi. c2003.
SUBJECTS:
Italian language–Conversation and phrase books–English.
Italian language–Glossaries, vocabularies, etc.

The subdivision **–Terms and phrases** is used if the work contains a list of expressions, phrases, etc., found in a particular language:

Title: *Roget's super thesaurus* / Marc McCutcheon. 3rd ed. 2003.
SUBJECTS:
English language–Synonyms and antonyms.
English language–Terms and phrases.

(2) *Subject dictionaries.* If the dictionary is limited to a subject field, a heading of the type **[Topic]–[Place**, if appropriate**]–Dictionaries–[Name of language** (other than English)] is assigned. For a subject dictionary in the English language, the subdivision by language is omitted. Examples include:

Title: *From polis to empire, the ancient world, c. 800 B.C.-A.D. 500 : a biographical dictionary* / edited by Andrew G. Traver. 2002.
SUBJECTS:
History, Ancient–Dictionaries.

Title: *Elsevier's dictionary of nuclear engineering : English-Russian* / by M. Rosenberg and S. Bobryakov. 2003.
SUBJECTS:
Nuclear engineering–Dictionaries.
English language–Dictionaries–Russian.

The subdivision **–Terminology** instead of **–Dictionaries** is used if the work contains a non-comprehensive list of terms on the topic, or if the comprehensive list is not arranged alphabetically:

Title: *Fabric glossary* / Mary Humphries. c2004.
SUBJECTS:
Textile fabrics–Terminology.
Textile fibers–Terminology.

For a bilingual or polyglot subject dictionary, language headings or headings with the subdivision **–Dictionaries–Polyglot** are assigned in addition to the topical headings:

Title: *English & Spanish medical words & phrases.* c2004.
SUBJECTS:
Medicine–Dictionaries.
Spanish language–Dictionaries–English.
Spanish language–Conversation and phrase books (for medical personnel)

Title: *El llibre manuscrit* / M. Josepa Arnall i Juan. 2002.
SUBJECTS:
Codicology–Dictionaries–Spanish.
Manuscripts–Dictionaries–Spanish.
Spanish language–Dictionaries–Polyglot.

Title: Dictionary of Central Asian Islamic terms / Allen J. Frank, Jahangir Mamatov. 2002.
SUBJECTS:
Islam–Dictionaries–Polyglot.
Islamic law–Dictionaries–Polyglot.

Title: *Elsevier's dictionary of nature and hunting in English, French, Russian, German, and Latin* / compiled by C. Zykov. 2002.
SUBJECTS:
Natural history–Dictionaries–Polyglot.
Nature conservation–Dictionaries–Polyglot.
Hunting–Dictionaries–Polyglot.
Dictionaries, Polyglot.

(3) *Biographical dictionaries.* A heading in the form of **[Class of persons, organizations, place, etc.]–Biography–Dictionaries** is assigned to biographical dictionaries. Examples include:

Title: *Biographical dictionary of modern world leaders.* 1900-1991 / [compiled] by John C. Fredriksen. 2004.
SUBJECTS:
Statesmen–Biography–Dictionaries.

Heads of state–Biography–Dictionaries.
Biography–20th century–Dictionaries.

Title: *Australian writers, 1950-1975* / edited by Selina Samuels. 2004.
SUBJECTS:
Australian literature–20th century–Bio-bibliography–Dictionaries.
Authors, Australian–20th century–Biography–Dictionaries.
Australian literature–20th century–Dictionaries.
Australia–In literature–Dictionaries.

Directories

A directory is defined as "an alphabetical or classified list containing names, addresses, and identifying data of persons, organizations, etc., intended to enable the user to locate and/or contact the individuals or organizations listed."[23] Works *about* directories and directory-making are assigned the heading **Directories**, which is a topical heading rather than a form heading. For directories per se, the free-floating form subdivision **–Directories** may be used under the following categories of headings:

- names of countries, cities, etc., for alphabetical or classified lists of names and addresses of the inhabitants or organizations of a place
- classes of persons, ethnic groups, and names of individual families
- types of organizations
- individual corporate bodies
- individual Christian denominations
- topical headings, including headings for disciplines, industries and activities, and headings for particular kinds of newspapers and periodicals

Examples include:

Title: *ACME* [electronic resource]. (viewed on June 27, 2003).
SUBJECTS:
Internet industry–United States–Directories.
Brand name products–United States–Directories.
Internet software industry–United States–Directories.

Title: *America's top doctors*. 3rd ed. 2003.
SUBJECTS:
Physicians–United States–Directories.

Title: *Art of northern California : painting, sculpture, photography, drawing, printmaking, mixed media.* c2003.
SUBJECTS:
Art, American–California, Northern–20th century.
Artists–California, Northern–Directories.

Title: *Best of history Web sites* [electronic resource]. (Viewed on Aug. 20, 2003).
SUBJECTS:
World history–Computer network resources–Directories.
History–Study and teaching–Computer network resources–Directories.
Scholarly Web sites–Directories.

The subdivision **–Directories** may not be further subdivided by **–Periodicals.**

If a list contains names of persons with or without identifying data, intended primarily to provide a record of the names associated with a particular event or topic, the subdivision **–Registers** is used instead:

Title: *Painters of Nevada, 1845-1980 : NevadaArtist.com.* [2003?]
SUBJECTS:
Painters–Nevada–Registers.

Title: *Soldiers of the War of 1812 with a Missouri connection* / Betty Harvey Williams. c2002.
SUBJECTS:
United States–History–War of 1812–Registers.
Missouri–Genealogy.
Soldiers–United States–Registers.
Soldiers–Missouri–Registers.

Handbooks and Manuals[24]

The free-floating subdivision **–Handbooks, manuals, etc.** may be used under headings of all types for concise reference works in which facts and information pertaining to a topic are arranged for ready reference and consultation rather than for continuous reading and study. The presence of the word "handbook" or "manual" in the title does not necessarily require the use of the subdivision.

Title: *The 5-minute pediatric consult* / editor, M. William Schwartz. 3rd ed. c2003.
SUBJECTS:
Pediatrics–Handbooks, manuals, etc.

Title: *The ARRL handbook for radio communications.* c2002-
SUBJECTS:
Radio–Amateurs' manuals.
Radio–Handbooks, manuals, etc.

Title: *AirForce handbook* / Department of the Air Force. [2002]
SUBJECTS:
United States. Air Force–Handbooks, manuals, etc.

For specialized manuals, the following subdivisions are used where appropriate: **–Amateurs' manuals**; **–Guidebooks**; **–Laboratory manuals**; **–Observers' manuals**; **–Tables**. Examples include:

Title: *Building decks : pro tips and simple steps.* c2002.
SUBJECTS:
Decks (Architecture, Domestic)–Design and construction–Amateurs' manuals.

Title: *Popular mechanics complete car care manual* / illustrations by Russell J. Von Sauers, Ron Carbone, and Don Mannes. 2003.
SUBJECTS:
Automobiles–Maintenance and repair–Amateurs' manuals.

Title: *Buy the best of Ireland : a shopping and learning guide to Irish foods and crafts* / Mary Jean Jecklin and Kelley V. Rea. 2004.
SUBJECTS:
Handicraft–Ireland–Guidebooks.

Title: *Antibody engineering : methods and protocols* / edited by Benny K.C. Lo. c2004.
SUBJECTS:
Immunotechnology–Laboratory manuals.
Antibodies–therapeutic use–Laboratory Manuals.
Antibodies–genetics–Laboratory Manuals.
Protein Engineering–methods–Laboratory Manuals.

Title: *Exploring the starry sky* / Robert Burnham and Wil Tirion. 2003.
SUBJECTS:
Astronomy–Observers' manuals.

CHILDREN'S MATERIALS[25]

In 1965 the Library of Congress initiated the Annotated Card (AC) Program for children's materials. The purpose of the program was to provide more appropriate and extensive subject cataloging of juvenile titles through more liberal application of subject headings and through the use of headings better suited to juvenile users. In some cases, existing Library of Congress subject headings were reinterpreted or modified; in others, new headings were created. As a result, a list of headings that represent exceptions to the master Library of Congress list was compiled. This list was first issued as a separate publication entitled *Subject headings for Children's Literature*. With the eighth edition of *Library of Congress Subject Headings*, the list was included in the main publication and also published separately. After 1979 the children's list was no longer published separately.

The term *annotated card* comes from the practice of providing a summary of the content of the work in a note. In subject cataloging at the Library of Congress, two sets of headings are assigned to juvenile works: (1) regular LC headings with appropriate subdivisions, such as **–Juvenile literature**; and (2) headings from the list *Subject Headings for Children's Literature*, without the juvenile subdivisions.

In the regular LC subject headings, subdivisions used to indicate children's materials include:

–Dictionaries, Juvenile
–Encyclopedias, Juvenile
–Juvenile drama
–Juvenile fiction
–Juvenile films
–Juvenile humor
–Juvenile literature
–Juvenile poetry
–Juvenile software
–Juvenile sound recordings

Note that the subdivision **–Juvenile literature** is used under topical headings but not for juvenile *belles lettres*, for which juvenile headings such as **Children's stories**; **Nursery rhymes**; **Children's poetry**; or headings with the subdivisions **–Juvenile drama**; **Juvenile fiction**; **–Juvenile humor**; **–Juvenile poetry** are used.

Many juvenile works are designated as such by their publishers, through such phrases as K-3 (kindergarten through third grade), 10 up, 14+, and so on. At the Library of Congress, all materials intended primarily for children through the age of fifteen (or the ninth grade) are treated as juvenile material and are included in the AC Program. For works in which the intended age is not explicitly stated, determination of level is based on content, format, publisher, treatment of previous works in the same series, and so on.

Juvenile headings in LC MARC records are distinguished by the second indicator 1 in the subject (6XX) fields and the omission of juvenile subdivisions. In addition, records for juvenile works typically include a summary.

Topical Juvenile Materials

For topical juvenile materials, the appropriate form subdivisions **–Juvenile literature, –Juvenile films, –Juvenile software, –Juvenile sound recordings**, etc., are added as the last element to the subject headings assigned. Following are examples of nonfiction juvenile works. AC headings, when included, are enclosed in square brackets in the examples below:

Title: *Life in the Australian Outback* / by Jann Einfeld. 2003.
SUBJECTS:
Australia–Social life and customs–Juvenile literature.
Australia–Juvenile literature.
[Australia.]

Title: *Hondo & Fabian* / written and illustrated by Peter McCarty. c2002.
SUBJECTS:
Dogs–Juvenile literature.
Cats–Juvenile literature.
Pets–Juvenile literature.

Title: *First thing my mama told me* / Susan Marie Swanson ; illustrated by Christine 2002.
SUBJECTS:
Names, Personal–Juvenile literature.
Identity–Juvenile literature.

Title: *Anne Bailey : frontier scout* / Mary R. Furbee. c2002.
SUBJECTS:
Bailey, Anne Hennis, 1742-1825–Juvenile literature.
Women pioneers–West Virginia–Biography–Juvenile literature.
Pioneers–West Virginia–Biography–Juvenile literature.
Frontier and pioneer life–West Virginia–Kanawha River Valley –Juvenile literature.
Kanawha River Valley (W. Va.)–History–Juvenile literature.
Kanawha River Valley (W. Va.)–Biography–Juvenile literature.

Title: *Timetables of world literature* / George Thomas Kurian. 2003.
SUBJECTS:
Literature–Chronology–Juvenile literature.
[Literature–Chronology.]

Title: *Travel guide to Shakespeare's London* / James Barter. 2003.
SUBJECTS:
Shakespeare, William, 1564-1616–Homes and haunts–England–London–Juvenile literature.
London (England)–Social life and customs–16th century–Juvenile literature.

[London (England)–Social life and customs–16th century.
London (England)–Social life and customs–17th century.]

Title: *Catherine the Great* / by Christine Hatt. 2003.
SUBJECTS:
Catherine II, Empress of Russia, 1729-1796–Juvenile literature.
Russia–History–Catherine II, 1762-1796–Juvenile literature.
Empresses–Russia–Biography–Juvenile literature.
[Catherine II, Empress of Russia, 1729-1796.
Kings, queens, rulers, etc.
Russia–History–Catherine II, 1762-1796.
Women–Biography.]

Title: *Conservation and natural resources.* 2004.
SUBJECTS:
Conservation of natural resources–Juvenile literature.
[Conservation of natural resources.]

Title: *The history of the Green Bay Packers* / by John Nichols. 2004.
SUBJECTS:
Green Bay Packers (Football team)–History–Juvenile literature.

Title: *I shook up the world : the incredible life of Muhammad Ali* / written by Maryum "May May" Ali. 2004.
SUBJECTS:
Ali, Muhammad, 1942-–Juvenile literature.
Boxers (Sports)–United States–Biography–Juvenile literature.

Textbooks intended for children up through age fifteen or the ninth grade are assigned headings of the type **[Topic]–Textbooks** (not further subdivided by **–Juvenile literature**) in the same manner as adult textbooks, with the exception of religious education textbooks, for which headings of the type **[Religious topic]–Textbooks for children** are assigned.

Juvenile *Belles Lettres*

For drama, fiction, poetry, or other literary works written for children,[26] by one author or several authors, headings of the type **Children's plays** and **Children's poetry** or **Children's poetry, [Language/nationality]**, etc., are always assigned in addition to other required form and topical headings for literature (see the discussion in the section "Literature" in chapter 10). Headings in the form of **Children's stories** or **Children's stories, [Language/nationality]** are assigned to collections by one author or several authors but not to individual works of juvenile fiction or young adult fiction.

If juvenile literary form headings are not available for particular genres, regular literary form headings without juvenile subdivisions are used, for example, **Detective and mystery stories**; **Fairy tales**.

Topical headings assigned to literature for children are subdivided by **–Juvenile poetry**; **–Juvenile drama**; and **–Juvenile fiction**. The subdivision **–Juvenile literature** is used only under topical headings for topical juvenile works, not for juvenile *belles lettres*.

The following examples show regular LC subject headings and AC headings (enclosed in square brackets) assigned to juvenile literary works:

Title: *The fish is me : bathtime rhymes* / selected by Neil Philip ; illustrated by Claire Henley. c2002.
SUBJECTS:
Baths–Juvenile poetry.
Children's poetry, American.
[Baths–Poetry.
Poetry–Collections.]

Title: *Joseph and his brothers* / by Guy Williams. 2003.
SUBJECTS:
Joseph (Son of Jacob)–Juvenile drama.
Bible. O.T. Genesis–History of Biblical events–Juvenile drama.
Children's plays, English.
[Joseph (Son of Jacob)–Drama.
Bible plays.
Plays.]

Title: *Animal quack-ups : foolish and funny jokes about animals* / Michael Dahl ; illustrated by Jeff Yesh. 2003.
SUBJECTS:
Animals–Juvenile humor.
Wit and humor, Juvenile.
[Animals–Humor.
Riddles.
Jokes.]

Title: *You must be joking : lots of cool jokes* / compiled and illustrated by Paul Brewer with an introduction by Kathleen Krull. 2003.
SUBJECTS:
Wit and humor, Juvenile.
[Jokes.
Riddles.]

Title: *Christmas presents : holiday poetry* / selected by Lee Bennett Hopkins; pictures by Melanie Hall. c2004.

SUBJECTS:

Christmas–Juvenile poetry.
Children's poetry, American.
[Christmas–Poetry.
American poetry–Collections.]

For fiction in particular, the use of topical headings subdivided by **–Fiction** and headings representing the form of literature is often more liberal in the AC program for children's books than in regular subject cataloging practice:

Title: *Before we were free* / Julia Alvarez. c2002.

SUBJECTS:

Dominican Republic–History–1930-1961–Juvenile fiction.
[Dominican Republic–History–1930-1961–Fiction.
Family life–Dominican Republic–Fiction.
Revolutions–Fiction.
Trujillo Molina, Rafael Leónidas, 1891-1961–Fiction.
Dominican Republic–Fiction.]

Title: *Babe Ruth and the ice cream mess* / by Dan Gutman ; illustrated by Elaine Garvin. 2004.

SUBJECTS:

Ruth, Babe, 1895-1948–Childhood and youth–Juvenile fiction.
[Ruth, Babe, 1895-1948–Childhood and youth–Fiction.
Baseball players–Fiction.
Stealing–Fiction.]

Title: *The greatest skating race : a WWII Story from the Netherlands* / Louise Borden ; illustrated by Niki Daly. 2004.

SUBJECTS:

World War, 1939-1945–Netherlands–Juvenile fiction.
[World War, 1939-1945–Netherlands–Fiction.
Escapes–Fiction.
Ice skating–Fiction.
Netherlands–History–German occupation, 1940-1945–Fiction.]

Title: *Cast two shadows : the American Revolution in the South* / Ann Rinaldi. 2004.

SUBJECTS:

South Carolina–History–Revolution, 1775-1783–Juvenile fiction.
[South Carolina–History–Revolution, 1775-1783–Fiction.
Family problems–Fiction.
African Americans–Fiction.
Slavery–Fiction.
United States–History–Revolution, 1775-1783–Fiction.]

CARTOGRAPHIC MATERIALS

The subdivision **–Maps** is free-floating under names of places, corporate bodies, and topical headings for individual maps, collections of maps, or atlases. When used under names of places, this subdivision may be qualified by terms indicating the nature or kinds of maps:

–Maps, Comparative
–Maps, Manuscript
–Maps, Mental
–Maps, Outline and base
–Maps, Physical
–Maps, Pictorial
–Maps, Topographic
–Maps, Tourist
–Maps for children
–Maps for people with visual disabilities
–Maps for the blind

Examples include:

Title: *Hammond world map.* [2003?]
SUBJECTS:
World maps.

Title: *Hammond South America map.* [2003?]
SUBJECTS:
South America–Maps.

Title: *Eastern Turkey and vicinity.* 2002.
SUBJECTS:
Turkey–Maps.
Turkey–Maps, Outline and base.
Middle East–Maps.
Middle East–Maps, Outline and base.
Transcaucasia–Maps.

Title: *United States.* [2002]
SUBJECTS:
United States–Maps.

Title: *Street map of Washington DC* / informational content edited by Geneva Reynolds. c2003.
SUBJECTS:
Washington (D.C.)–Maps.
Washington (D.C.)–Maps, Tourist.

Central business districts–Washington (D.C.)–Maps.
Subways–Washington (D.C.)–Maps.
Subways–Washington Metropolitan Area–Maps.

Title: *Where San Francisco maps : areas and attractions : drive Bay Area, Fisherman's Wharf, Union Square, dining, shopping, museums, art & antiques* / Where San Francisco. [2003?]
SUBJECTS:
Central business districts–California–San Francisco–Maps.
San Francisco (Calif.)–Maps, Tourist.
San Francisco Metropolitan Area (Calif.)–Maps, Tourist.

Title: *United Kingdom : scale 1:250,000* / produced by DGIA, MOD, UK, [year]. c2002-
SUBJECTS:
Maps, Military.
Great Britain–Maps, Topographic.

Title: *Canyonlands National Park, Needles & Island in the Sky, Utah, USA* /National Geographic Maps, Trails Illustrated. Rev. 2002. [2002]
SUBJECTS:
Outdoor recreation–Utah–Canyonlands National Park–Maps.
Canyonlands National Park (Utah)–Maps, Topographic.
Hiking–Utah–Canyonlands National Park–Maps.
Trails–Utah–Canyonlands National Park–Maps.

Title: *Hidden treasures of McKean County, Pennsylvania* / commissioned by the Allegheny National Forest Vacation Bureau. [2003?]
SUBJECTS:
Historic buildings–Pennsylvania–McKean County–Maps.
Historic buildings–Pennsylvania–McKean County–Pictorial works.
McKean County (Pa.)–Maps, Tourist.
Allegheny Mountains–Tours–Maps.

Title: *Napa Valley tour map* / designer, J. Michael Orr. [2002?]
SUBJECTS:
Wineries–California–Napa Valley–Maps.
Napa Valley (Calif.)–Maps, Tourist.
Napa Valley (Calif.)–Tours–Maps.
Napa Valley (Calif.)–Maps, Pictorial.

Form headings are assigned to world atlases, for example:

Title: *The pocket world atlas* / [cartography by Philip's]. 2003.
SUBJECTS:
Atlases.

If the atlas pertains to a particular area, a geographic heading with the subdivision **–Maps** is assigned:

Title: *Hudson Valley street atlas* / Jimapco. c2002.
SUBJECTS:
Hudson River Valley (N.Y. and N.J.)–Maps.
New York (State)–Maps.

The subdivision **–Atlases** is used for scientific and technical atlases.[27] It is not used under geographic names.

Title: *Atlas of cosmetic surgery* / [edited by] Michael S. Kaminer, Jeffrey S. Dover, Kenneth A. Arndt. c2002.
SUBJECTS:
Surgery, Plastic–Atlases.

Title: *Anatomica's body atlas* / text editors, Denise Imwold, Janet Parker. c2003.
SUBJECTS:
Human anatomy–Atlases.
Human physiology.

NONPRINT MATERIALS

General

In LC practice, the same types and forms of headings are assigned to works on the same subject whether they are in print or nonprint format. With a few exceptions, the medium of publication of a work is not brought out in its subject headings. There are only a few free-floating form subdivisions for nonprint materials: **–Juvenile films**; **–Juvenile sound recordings**; and **–Interactive multimedia**. For electronic resources, see the discussion in the section "Electronic Resources" at the beginning of this chapter.

The sections below include a discussion and examples of Library of Congress practice with regard to subject cataloging of films, non-music sound recordings, and interactive media.

Films[28]

In addition to subject headings assigned from LCSH, the Moving Image Section of the Motion Picture, Broadcasting and Recorded Sound Division at the Library of Congress has been assigning terms from its *Moving Image Genre-Form Guide* (migfg)[29] since October 1997. The guide contains 150 genre and form terms, which have been applied to inventory and cataloging records created in the Division—all types of material, features, television, film, and video.[30] "Migfg" is the subject/index term source code used in the 655 field of the MARC 21 format.

Topical (Nonfiction) Films

At least one subject heading is assigned to each topical film, and in general the rules governing the assignment of subject headings to books also apply to topical films. The treatment of topical or nonfiction films is described below.

(1) Each important topic mentioned in the summary statement on the cataloging record receives a subject heading. In particular, if one specific topic is especially emphasized in the summary to illustrate a more general concept, both the specific topic and the general concept are assigned subject headings.

(2) If a topic is treated in conjunction with a place, subject headings for both the topic and the place are provided.

(3) If a film uses a particular person as illustrative of a particular profession or activity, headings are assigned for both the person and the profession or activity. (Such films will normally not be regarded as biographies.)

(4) Genre/form headings such as **Documentary films** and **Family–Television special** are often assigned in addition to the subject headings. The source of the genre/form headings is the *Moving Image Genre-Form Guide* (migfg).

Examples of subject cataloging for topical films include:

Title: *Beyond regret* [videorecording] : *entering into healing and wholeness after an abortion* / Paraclete Video Productions ; producer, Charity Spatzeck-Olsen ; director, Hans Spatzeck-Olsen. c2002.
SUBJECTS:
Bereavement–Religious aspects–Christianity.
Abortion–Psychological aspects.
Feature films.
Genre/Form:
Documentary films.

Title: *In memoriam: New York, 9/11/01* / Home Box Office. {a videocassette}. 2002.
SUBJECTS:
September 11 Terrorist Attacks, 2001.
World Trade Center (New York, N.Y.)
Terrorism–New York (State)–New York.
Genre/Form:
Documentary–Television special.

Title: *Keep on walking* [videorecording] / Green Room Productions ... [et al.] ; a film by Tana Ross ... [et al.]. c2001.
SUBJECTS:
Nelson, Joshua.
African American Jews–Biography.
Gospel musicians–United States–Biography.
Genre/Form:
Documentary films.

Fiction Films

Fiction films for adults are generally not assigned topical headings. Genre/form headings are assigned from the *Moving image genre-form guide* (migfg), for example:

Title: *American wedding* / Universal Pictures ; directed by Jesse Dylan ; writing by Adam Herz. 2003.
Genre/Form:
Comedy–Feature.
Romance–Feature.

Title: *Harry Potter and the Chamber of Secrets* / a Warner Bros. Pictures presentation ; a Heyday Films/1492 Pictures production ; directed by Chris Columbus ; screenplay by Steve Kloves ; produced by David Heyman. 2002.
Genre/Form:
Fantasy–Feature.

Title: *The matrix reloaded* / directed and written by the Wachowski Brothers. 2003.
Genre/Form:
Feature.

Title: *Johnny English* / Universal Pictures and Studio Canal present a Working Title production; directed by Peter Howitt ; producers, Tim Bevan, Eric Fellner, Mark Huffarn ; written by Neal Purvis, Robert Wade, William Davies. 2003.
Genre/Form:
Adventure (Nonfiction)
Comedy–Feature.
Family–Feature.

Juvenile Films[31]

A juvenile film is defined as a film intended for persons through the age of fifteen. The subdivision **–Juvenile films** instead of **–Drama** is used for juvenile fiction films on particular subjects:

Washington, George, 1732-1799–Drama {adult film}
Washington, George, 1732-1799–Juvenile films {juvenile film}

Examples include:

Title: *When I grow up–I want to be a teacher* / Black Water Productions, Inc. ; producer-writer, Paul Rosentreter. c2000.
SUBJECTS:
Teaching–Vocational guidance–Juvenile films.
Video recordings for the hearing impaired.
Genre/Form:
Documentary.

Title: *Living on the American frontier* / Chariot Productions ; written/produced and directed by Joseph Sitko. c2000.
SUBJECTS:
Frontier and pioneer life–United States–Juvenile films.
Genre/Form:
Documentary.

Non-Music Sound Recordings

Non-music sound recordings are assigned headings similar to those for book form materials. Except for **–Juvenile sound recordings**, there are no special form subdivisions for sound recordings. Examples of sound recordings include:

Title: *Another branch of life stories* [sound recording] / Robin Echols Cooper. [2002?]
SUBJECTS:
Grandparents–Family relationships.
Alabama–Social life and customs.
Ohio–Social life and customs.

Title: *Star Wars–episode II* [sound recording] *: attack of the clones* / [by R.A. Salvatore ; read by Jonathan Davis ; based upon the story by George Lucas and the screenplay by George Lucas and Jonathan Hales]. p2002.
SUBJECTS:
Space warfare–Fiction.
Star Wars fiction.
Science fiction.

Title: *Enough* [sound recording] : *staying human in an engineered age* / Bill McKibben. p2003.
SUBJECTS:
Human genetics–Social aspects.
Genetic engineering–Social aspects.

Title: *Teaching the other* [sound recording] : *Muslims, non-Muslims, and the stories they teach.* 2003.
SUBJECTS:
Muslims–Non-Muslim countries–Congresses.

Title: *Stone and anvil* [sound recording] / Peter David. 2003.
SUBJECTS:
Star Trek fiction.
Science fiction.

Title: *Wild & wacky totally true Bible stories* [sound recording] : *all about prayer.* [2002]
SUBJECTS:
Prayer–Biblical teaching–Juvenile sound recordings.
Lord's prayer.
Bible stories, English.

Title: *Wild & wacky totally true Bible stories* [sound recording] : *all about angels.* [2002]
SUBJECTS:
Angels–Biblical teaching–Juvenile sound recordings.
Bible stories, English.

Title: *The wavedancer benefit* [sound recording] / featuring stories read by Stephen King ... [et al.]. p2002.
SUBJECTS:
{No subject headings}

For music sound recordings, see the discussion in the section "Music" in chapter 10.

Interactive Multimedia

The free-floating subdivision **–Interactive multimedia** is used as a form subdivision under topics:

Title: *SORCE* [interactive multimedia] : *solar radiation and climate experiment.* [2003]
SUBJECTS:
Goddard Space Flight Center–Interactive multimedia.
Solar radiation–Measurement–Interactive multimedia.

Artificial satellites–Sun–Interactive multimedia.
Sun–Interactive multimedia.

Title: *Tiger Woods PGA tour 2003* [interactive multimedia]. 2003.
SUBJECTS:
Woods, Tiger–Interactive multimedia.
Golf–Interactive multimedia.

Works about interactive multimedia in general are assigned the main heading **Interactive multimedia**.

Title: *Interactive multimedia in education and training* / Sanjaya Mishra, Ramesh C. Sharma, Editors. 2004.
SUBJECTS:
Interactive multimedia.

Title: *Interactive multimedia systems* / [edited by] Syed M. Rahman. c2002.
SUBJECTS:
Interactive multimedia.

Title: *Communication and collaboration in the online classroom : examples and applications* / Patricia Comeaux, editor. c2002.
SUBJECTS:
Distance education.
Computer-assisted instruction.
Interactive media.
Teaching–Computer network resources.
Education–Computer network resources.
Educational technology.

Works about individual programs are assigned headings for the specific programs.

Title: *SMIL 2.0 : interactive multimedia for Web and mobile devices* / Dick C.A. Bulterman, Lloyd Rutledge. 2004.
SUBJECTS:
SMIL (Document markup language)

BIOGRAPHY[32]

Definition

For the purposes of cataloging, *biography* (including *autobiography*) has been defined as "a narrative work more than 50% of which recounts the personal aspects of the life of one or more individuals. . . . **Personal aspects** include such details as the individual's early years, education, marriage and other personal relationships, personal habits and personality, family life, travels, personal experiences and tragedies, last years and death, etc."[33]

A biography of two or more individuals is called a *collective biography*, and a biography of one person an *individual biography*. A work of which less than 50 percent is biographical material is referred to as a *partial biography*.

Types of Headings Assigned to Biography

The types of headings generally used with biography are listed below:

(1) Personal name heading for the biographee(s) (no more than four). For forms of personal name headings, see chapter 4.

(2) "Class of persons" heading (also called "biographical heading") with the subdivision **–Biography**;

(3) Headings representing the person's association with a place or organization, or involvement with a specific event

(4) Topical headings, as appropriate

Subdivisions That Designate Biography

The Library of Congress uses the free-floating subdivisions listed in Table 9.1 to designate biography. They are used with main headings denoting classes of persons, disciplines, organizations, ethnic groups, places, and events. Subdivisions used under names of individuals are listed in appendix C. For special meanings and uses of the listed subdivisions, consult *Subject Cataloging Manual: Subject Headings*.

The Subdivision –Biography

The subdivision **–Biography** is used as the generic subdivision for the concept of biography, designating not only individual and collective biography but also autobiography, personal reminiscences, and personal narratives. It is used under the heading for the pertinent class of persons rather than that for the corresponding field or discipline, if a choice is possible.

Artists–Biography
Musicians–Biography
Musicians–Bolivia–Biography

A **[Topic]–Biography** heading is used if a heading representing a class of persons does not exist and cannot be formulated, for example:

Art–Biography
{for a collective biography of persons associated with art, including artists, art dealers, collectors, museum personnel, etc.}

Table 9.1. Subdivisions Designating Biography

	Individual Persons	Families	Class of Persons	General	Corporate Bodies	Ethnic Groups	Places	Events, Wars
–Anecdotes	X	X	X	X	X	X	X	
–Bio-bibliography				X		X	X	
–Biography			X	X	X	X	X	X
–Biography–Dictionaries			X	X	X	X	X	
–Biography–Portraits					X		X	
–Correspondence	X	X	X			X		
–Diaries	X	X	X			X		
–Genealogy			X		X	X	X	
–Interviews	X		X		X	X		
–Personal narratives				X				X
–Portraits	X	X	X			X		X

The Subdivision –Correspondence[34]

The form subdivision **–Correspondence** is free-floating under headings representing classes of persons, ethnic groups, families, as well as individual persons, for example:

> **Soldiers–Mississippi–Correspondence**
> **Editors–United States–Correspondence**
> **Leibniz, Gottfried Wilhelm, Freiherr von, 1646-1716–Correspondence**
> **Roosevelt, Franklin D. (Franklin Delano), 1882-1945 –Correspondence**
> **Stetson family–Correspondence**

For correspondence carried on by types of industries, organizations, etc., or for the correspondence of individual organizations, the subdivision –**Records and correspondence** is used.

The Subdivision –Personal Narratives[35]

The subdivision **–Personal narratives** is used only under names of events and wars as a form subdivision for collective or individual eyewitness reports and/or autobiographical accounts of experiences in connection with these events or wars. This subdivision may be qualified by a national or ethnic qualifier where appropriate, for example, **–Personal narratives, Canadian**; **–Personal narratives, Spanish**; etc.

Collective Biography

A collective biography containing the life histories of up to four individuals is assigned a personal name heading for each individual. The following discussion concerns collective biography of more than four persons.

Collective Biography of a Group of Persons Not Associated with a Particular Field or Discipline

The form heading **Biography**, with or without form subdivisions, is assigned to a work containing biographies of persons not limited to a particular period, place, organization, ethnic group, gender, or specific field or discipline:

Title: *The Houghton Mifflin dictionary of biography.* c2003.
SUBJECTS:
Biography–Dictionaries.

Title: *Chambers biographical dictionary* / editor, Una McGovern. 7th ed. 2002.
SUBJECTS:
Biography–Dictionaries.

The main heading **Biography** is subdivided by period if the biographees belong to a specific period:

Title: *Icons : 200 men and women who have made a difference* / Barbara Cady ; photography editor, Jean-Jacques Naudet ; special editor, Raymond McGrath. c2003.
SUBJECTS:
Biography–20th century.

Title: *Current biography international yearbook.* c2002.
SUBJECTS:
Biography–20th century–Periodicals.

If a collective biography does not pertain to a special field or discipline but involves an organization, an ethnic or national group, a place, an event, or a war, the appropriate heading (indicating the special aspect) is followed by the subdivision **–Biography** (or a more specific subdivision such as **–Genealogy**; **–Interviews**):

Title: *The human tradition in America since 1945* / edited by David L. Anderson. 2003.
SUBJECTS:
United States–History–1945--Biography.

Title: *The face of Texas : portraits of Texans* / with stories by Elizabeth O'Brien ; photographer Michael O'Brien. 2003.
SUBJECTS:
Texas–Biography.
Texas–Biography–Portraits.

Title: *Portraits of African American life since 1865* / edited by Nina Mjagkij. 2003.
SUBJECTS:
African Americans–Biography.
African Americans–History–19th century.
African Americans–History–20th century.

Title: *Freedoms journey : African American voices of the Civil War* / edited by Donald Yacovone. c2004.
SUBJECTS:
United States–History–Civil War, 1861-1865–African Americans.
United States–History–Civil War, 1861-1865–Personal narratives.
African Americans–Biography.
Slaves–United States–Biography.
African American soldiers–Biography.
African American political activists–Biography.

Title: *Secretaries and chiefs of staff of the United States Air Force : biographical sketches and portraits* / George M. Watson, Jr. 2001.
SUBJECTS:
United States. Dept. of the Air Force–Biography.
United States. Dept. of the Air Force. Chief of Staff–Biography.

If a work focuses on a specific place during a particular historical period, two headings are assigned: the main heading **Biography** with a period subdivision, and another for the place with the subdivision **–Biography**.

Title: *Advocates and activists, 1919-1941 : men and women who shaped the period between the wars* / edited by David Garrett Izzo. c2003.
SUBJECTS:
United States–Biography.
Biography–20th century.

Title: *The Scribner encyclopedia of American lives. The 1960s* / William L. O'Neill, volume editor. c2003.
SUBJECTS:
United States–Biography–Dictionaries.
Biography–20th century.

For a collective biography of spouses who have no special careers of their own, headings denoting specific groups of spouses, for example, **Army spouses**; **Diplomats' spouses**; **Teachers' spouses**; **Wives**; etc., subdivided by **–Biography**, are used.

Title: *First ladies* / Betty Boyd Caroli. 2003.
SUBJECTS:
Presidents' spouses–United States–Biography.

There are also headings for various other classes of persons not limited to a field or discipline, such as **Men**; **Women**; **Children**; **Teenage boys**; **Teenage girls**; **Young men**.

Title: *More than petticoats : remarkable Texas women* / Greta Anderson. c2002.
SUBJECTS:
Women–Texas–Biography.
Women–Texas–History.
Texas–Biography.

Collective Biography of Persons Belonging to a Particular Field or Discipline

For collective biographies of persons belonging to a particular field or discipline, headings in the form of **[Class of persons]–Biography** are used. The geographic subdivision, if applicable, is interposed between the main heading representing the class of persons and the biographical subdivision.

Title: *Biographical index of artists in Canada* / Evelyn de R. McMann. c2003.
SUBJECTS:
Artists–Canada–Biography–Indexes.

Title: *Biographical dictionary of modern world leaders. 1900-1991* / [compiled] by John C. Fredriksen. 2004.
SUBJECTS:
Statesmen–Biography–Dictionaries.
Heads of state–Biography–Dictionaries.
Biography–20th century–Dictionaries.

Title: *Political leaders of modern China : a biographical dictionary* / edited by Edwin Pak-wah Leung. 2002.
SUBJECTS:
Politicians–China–Biography–Dictionaries.
China–Politics and government–19th century–Biography–Dictionaries.
China–Politics and government–20th century–Biography–Dictionaries.

If appropriate for the work being cataloged, a more specific form subdivision is used instead of **–Biography**, for example, **Entertainers–Interviews**; **Poets, English–Correspondence**; **African-American artists–Portraits**.

Title: *Are you trying to seduce me, Miss Turner? : Richard Ouzounian, talking to the stars*. 2003.
SUBJECTS:
Entertainers–Interviews.
Celebrities–Interviews.

If a biographical work on persons associated with a field or discipline also involves an organization, an ethnic group, a place, or an event, headings indicating the other aspects as well as those indicating the fields—or headings combining both—are assigned, as shown below:

Title: *An uncertain tradition : U.S. senators from Illinois, 1818-2003* / David Kenney and Robert E. Hartley. c2003.
SUBJECTS:
Legislators–United States–Biography.
United States. Congress. Senate–Biography.
Illinois–Biography.
United States–Politics and government.
Illinois–Politics and government.

Title: *African-American architects : a biographical dictionary*, 1865-1945 / edited by Dreck Spurlock Wilson. 2003.
SUBJECTS:
African American architects–Biography–Dictionaries.

Title: *Civil War journal : the leaders* / edited by William C. Davis, Brian C. Pohanka, and Don Troiani. c2003.
SUBJECTS:
Generals–United States–Biography.
Generals–Confederate States of America–Biography.
United States–History–Civil War, 1861-1865–Biography.

Title: *Blue & gray at sea : naval memoirs of the Civil War* / edited by Brian M. Thomsen. 2003.
SUBJECTS:
United States–History–Civil War, 1861-1865–Naval operations.
United States–History–Civil War, 1861-1865–Personal narratives.
United States. Navy–Biography.
Confederate States of America. Navy–Biography.

If the biographical work covers other topics not designated by the class-of-persons heading(s), additional topical headings, generally without biographical subdivision, are assigned:

Title: *Classic country : the golden age of country music : the '20s through the '70s* / edited by Charles McCardell. 2003.
SUBJECTS:
Singers–United States–Biography.
Country musicians–United States–Biography.
Country music–History and criticism.

Family Histories

For the history of an individual family, the following types of headings are assigned:

[Surname] family
[Place]–Genealogy

Examples:

Title: *The Mohawk Valley Ehles and allied families* / Mack Dawson Duett. c2003.
SUBJECTS:
Ehle family.
Mohawk River Valley (N.Y.)–Genealogy.
New York (State)–Genealogy.

Title: *The Callihans of Fannin County, Georgia, 1843 to 2003* / compiled by Dave Callahan. [2003]
SUBJECTS:
Callahan family.
Irish Americans–Georgia–Fannin County–Genealogy.
Fannin County (Ga.)–Genealogy.

Title: *The southern Fairchild lines in America* / compiled by Jean Fairchild Gilmore. 2003.
SUBJECTS:
Fairchild family.
Southern States–Genealogy.

The heading under place is omitted in the case of **United States–Genealogy**.

Title: *The Kennedys : an American drama* / Peter Collier, David Horowitz. 2002.
SUBJECTS:
Kennedy family.

If more than one family is named on the title page, each family is designated by a separate heading if there are no more than three families:

Title: *The McManigal & Tovar families* / B. Hugh Tovar. 2003.
SUBJECTS:
McMonagle family.
Tovar family.
Irish Americans–Genealogy.
Colombian Americans–Genealogy.
Ireland–Genealogy.
Colombia–Genealogy.

If more than three families are named, subject headings are assigned for them individually or collectively, based on the cataloger's judgment.

If one or more of the members of the family are given prominent treatment in the work, a heading or headings under the personal name(s) are also assigned:

Title: *The Colemans of California : a family history focusing on the lives of John Crisp Coleman, Edward Coleman & Persis Sibley Coleman* / by Diantha Lamb Barstow. 2003.
SUBJECTS:
Coleman family.
Coleman, John Crisp, 1823-1919–Family.
Coleman, Edward, 1830-1915–Family.
Coleman, Persis Sibley, 1841-1915–Family.
California–Biography.

Title: *Kennedys at war, 1937-1945* / Edward J. Renehan, Jr. c2002.
SUBJECTS:
Kennedy family.
Kennedy, Joseph P. (Joseph Patrick), 1888-1969.
Kennedy, Joseph P. (Joseph Patrick), 1915-1944.
Kennedy, John F. (John Fitzgerald), 1917-1963.
Kennedy, Kathleen, d. 1948.
Politicians–United States–Biography.
World War, 1939-1945–United States.
World War, 1939-1945–England–London.
London (England)–Biography.

For the history of a royal or noble family,[36] an additional heading under the name of the relevant place is always assigned:

Title: *Bosworth Field to Bloody Mary : an encyclopedia of the early Tudors* / John A. Wagner. 2003.
SUBJECTS:
Great Britain–History–Tudors, 1485-1603–Encyclopedias.
Great Britain–History–Henry VIII, 1509-1547–Encyclopedias.
Great Britain–History–Henry VII, 1485-1509–Encyclopedias.
Great Britain–History–Edward VI, 1547-1553–Encyclopedias.
Great Britain–History–Mary I, 1553-1558–Encyclopedias.
England–Civilization–16th century–Encyclopedias.
Tudor, House of–Encyclopedias.

Title: *Vienna and Versailles : the courts of Europe's major dynastic rivals, ca. 1550-1780* / Jeroen Duindam. 2003.
SUBJECTS:
Habsburg, House of–History.
Vienna (Austria)–Court and courtiers.
Vienna (Austria)–Intellectual life.
Bourbon, House of–History.
Versailles (France)–Court and coutriers.
Versailles (France)–Intellectual life.
Paris (France)–Intellectual life.

For treatment of genealogical materials in general, see the discussion in chapter 10.

Individual Biography

Personal Name Headings

The name of the biographee serves as the primary heading for an individual biography. The form of the heading is the same as that used for main or added entries (see chapter 4 on name headings). The personal name heading is assigned even when it duplicates the main entry or an added entry.

Title: *Live from Baghdad : making journalism history behind the lines* / Robert Wiener. 2002.
SUBJECTS:
Wiener, Robert.
Cable News Network.
Persian Gulf War, 1991–Personal narratives, American.
Television producers and directors–United States–Biography.
MAIN ENTRY:
Wiener, Robert.

In general, a work containing the lives of up to four[37] persons treated either collectively or separately is not treated as a collective biography but is assigned an individual heading for each person.

Subdivisions under Personal Names

Appropriate subdivisions are added to the personal name heading if the biography deals with specific aspect(s) of the person's life. A list of free-floating subdivisions[38] used under names of persons appears in appendix C. Note that the subdivision **–Biography** is free-floating under class-of-persons headings but not under headings for individual persons.

Additional Headings for Individual Biography

(1) *[Class of persons]–Biography headings.* In addition to the personal name heading of the biographee, the same class-of-persons heading(s) assigned to a collective biography on the same topic are assigned to an individual biography also. An exception is that additional class-of-persons headings are not assigned to lives of legendary or fictitious characters.

In effect, the **[Class of persons]–Biography** heading in these cases represents generic posting, that is, listing under a generic heading that encompasses the personal heading. Such treatment is a deliberate departure from the general policy of not assigning both a general and a specific heading to the same body of material. The policy was probably adopted in the interest of collocating biographies of persons who belong in the same field or who share the same characteristics. These class-of-persons headings are particularly useful in a generic search, since many users look for biographical materials of a particular class of persons rather than individual persons.

The types of headings assigned to individual biographies are discussed below:

(a) *Headings for persons associated with a field or discipline.* To a biography of a person associated with a field or discipline, headings of the following types are assigned in addition to the personal name heading:

[Class of persons]–[Place]–[Biographical subdivision]
[Discipline]–Biography
{if the class-of-persons heading is not available}

[Organization, ethnic group, place, event, or gender]–[Biographical subdivision]
{The heading designating an ethnic group is assigned only if the point of the work is personal identification with the group. The place heading is assigned only when the person has local significance or when the class-of-persons heading is not available.}

Examples include:

Title: *Eric Moon : the life and library times* / by Kenneth F. Kister ; with a foreword by John N. Berry III. c2002.
SUBJECTS:
Moon, Eric,1923-
Librarians–Biography.
Library journal–History–20th century.
American Library Association–History–20th century.

Title: *Fly swatter : how my grandfather made his way in the world* / Nicholas Dawidoff. c2002.
SUBJECTS:
Gerschenkron, Alexander.
Economists–United States–Biography.
Harvard University. Dept. of Economics.

Title: *Thoughts from a queen-sized bed* / Mimi Schwartz. c2002.
SUBJECTS:
Schwartz, Mimi.
English teachers–United States–Biography.
Married women–United States–Biography.
Jewish women–United States–Biography.
Jewish families–United States.
Marriage–United States.

Title: *Mother Theresa : religious humanitarian* / Anne Marie Sullivan. 2003.
SUBJECTS:
Teresa, Mother, 1910-–Juvenile literature.
Missionaries of Charity–Biography–Juvenile literature.

For a person who is active in several fields, a single heading that best encompasses his or her career or lifelong pursuits is assigned. If there is no heading that adequately encompasses the person's career, multiple class-of-persons headings may be assigned to bring out those career aspects described in the work in hand. Examples include:

Title: *John E. Owens : nineteenth century American actor and manager* / Thomas A. Bogar. c2002.
SUBJECTS:
Owens, John E. (John Edmond), 1823-1886.
Theatrical managers–United States–Biography.
Actors–United States–Biography.

Title: *Napoleon of New York : Mayor Fiorello La Guardia* / H. Paul Jeffers. c2002.
SUBJECTS:
La Guardia, Fiorello H. (Fiorello Henry), 1882-1947.
Legislators–United States–Biography.
United States. Congress. House–Biography.
Mayors–New York (State)–New York–Biography.
New York (N.Y.)–Politics and government–1898-1951.
New York (N.Y.)–Biography.

If the work being cataloged focuses only on one career aspect, only the heading for that one aspect is assigned.

In the selection of the class of persons to which the biographee belongs, headings that represent career, profession, or special pursuit of the biographee are preferred over headings that imply value judgments. For example, Saddam Hussein is described as a head of state, not as a war criminal, tyrant, or dictator.

Title: *Saddam Hussein* / Jill C. Wheeler. c2004.
SUBJECTS:
Hussein, Saddam, 1937--Juvenile literature.
Presidents–Iraq–Biography–Juvenile literature.

Title: *The rise of Adolf Hitler* / Annette Dufner, book editor. 2003.
SUBJECTS:
Hitler, Adolf, 1889-1945.
Heads of state–Germany–Biography.
Germany–Politics and government–1933-1945.
National socialism.

(b) *Headings for persons belonging to no particular field or discipline*. If the individual biography does not pertain to a special field or discipline, headings in the form of **[Organization, ethnic group, place, event, or war] –Biography** are assigned to bring out any and all important associations by which the person may be identified:

Title: *Jane Wilkinson Long : Texas pioneer* / by Neila Skinner Petrick ; illustrated by Joyce Haynes. c2004.
SUBJECTS:
Long, Jane Herbert Wilkinson, 1798-1880–Juvenile literature.
Women pioneers–Texas–Biography–Juvenile literature.
Pioneers–Texas–Biography–Juvenile literature.
Texas–Biography–Juvenile literature.
Frontier and pioneer life–Texas–Juvenile literature.

Title: *Michael Collins : a biography* / Tim Pat Coogan. 2002.
SUBJECTS:
Collins, Michael, 1890-1922.
Ireland–History–War of Independence, 1919-1921–Biography.
Ireland–History–Civil War, 1922-1923–Biography.
Revolutionaries–Ireland–Biography.

(2) *Topical headings*. If the biographical work also contains discussions on special topics not designated by the class-of-persons headings, they are brought out by regular topical headings without biographical subdivisions:

Title: *Daniel "Chappy" James : the first African American four star general* / Earnest N. Bracey. 2003.
SUBJECTS:
James, Daniel, 1920-1978.
Generals–United States–Biography.
African American generals–Biography.
United States–Armed Forces–Biography.
United States–History, Military–20th century.

Title: *Clara : an ex-slave in gold rush Colorado* / by Roger Baker. 2003.
SUBJECTS:
Brown, Clara, 1800-1885.
African American women pioneers–Colorado–Biography.
Women pioneers–Colorado–Biography.
Free African Americans–Colorado–Biography.
Frontier and pioneer life–Colorado.

Individual Biography of Specific Classes of Persons

Biographies of certain classes of persons are given special treatment, as delineated below.

(1) *Artists*. See the discussion in the section "Art" in chapter 10.

(2) *Founders of religion*. A personal name heading is assigned, without the accompanying class-of-persons heading. The subdivision **–Biography** is not used under the personal name unless established in LCSH.

Title: *The life of Buddha as legend and history : an introduction to the Buddha* / by Edward J. Thomas. 2003.
SUBJECTS:
Gautama Buddha.
Gautama Buddha–Legends.

Title: *The mission of Jesus the Messiah* / E. Keith Howick. c2003.
SUBJECTS:
Jesus Christ–Biography.
Jesus Christ–Messiahship.

(3) *Literary authors*. See the discussion in the section "Literature" in chapter 10.

(4) *Music composers and musicians*. See the discussion in the section "Music" in chapter 10.

(5) *Heads of state, rulers, or statesmen*. When the work being cataloged presents personal facts concerning the life of a head of state, ruler, statesman, or politician, two headings are assigned:

- the personal name heading with topical subdivision, if appropriate, for heads of state and rulers, the personal name heading (e.g., **Kennedy, John F. (John Fitzgerald), 1917-1963**) rather than the official name heading (e.g., **United States. President (1961-1963 : Kennedy)** is used.
- the class-of-persons heading with an appropriate subdivision, for example, **Great Britain–Kings and rulers–Biography**; **Presidents–United States–Biography**; **Emperors–Rome–Biography**.

Examples include:

Title: *Elizabeth : behind palace doors* / Nicholas Davies. 2000.
SUBJECTS:
Elizabeth II, Queen of Great Britain, 1926-
Queens–Great Britain–Biography.

Title: *An unfinished life : John F. Kennedy, 1917-1963* / Robert Dallek. c2003.
SUBJECTS:
Kennedy, John F. (John Fitzgerald), 1917-1963.
Presidents–United States–Biography.

Title: *Man of the people : the life of John McCain* / Paul Alexander. c2003.
SUBJECTS:
McCain, John, 1936-
Legislators–United States–Biography.
United States. Congress. Senate–Biography.

If, in addition to personal facts, the work also discusses political affairs or events in which the biographee participated during a period of the country's history, a heading for this special aspect is also assigned, for example, **[Place]–History–[Period subdivision]**; **[Place]–Politics and government–[Period subdivision]**. Examples include:

Title: *John Quincy Adams* / Robert V. Remini. 2002.
SUBJECTS:
Adams, John Quincy, 1767-1848.
Presidents–United States–Biography.
United States–Politics and government–1825-1829.
United States–Politics and government–1789-1815.

Title: *Alexander Hamilton : ambivalent Anglophile* / Lawrence S. Kaplan. 2002.
SUBJECTS:
Hamilton, Alexander, 1757-1804.
Statesmen–United States–Biography.
United States–Foreign relations–1775-1783.
United States–Foreign relations–1783-1815.
United States–Foreign relations–Great Britain.
Great Britain–Foreign relations–United States.

Title: *White crow : the life and times of the Grand Duke Nicholas Mikhailovich Romanov : 1859-1919* / Jamie H. Cockfield. 2002.
SUBJECTS:
Nikolafi Mikhafilovich, Grand Duke of Russia, 1859-1919.
Nobility–Russia–Biography.
Intellectuals–Russia–Biography.
Russia–History–Nicholas II, 1894-1917.

Title: *Catherine the Great* / Simon Dixon. 2001.
SUBJECTS:
Catherine II, Empress of Russia, 1729-1796.
Russia–Kings and rulers–Biography.
Russia–History–Catherine II, 1762-1796.

For a work that describes the times in which a politician, statesman, etc., lived and the person's relationship to those times, but that devotes less than 50 percent of its content to biographical details about the person, the class-of-persons heading is omitted:

Title: *War and ruin : William T. Sherman and the Savannah campaign* / Anne J. Bailey. 2003.
SUBJECTS:
Sherman, William T. (William Tecumseh), 1820-1891.
Savannah (Ga.)–History–Siege, 1864.

Title: *Putin's Russia : past imperfect, future uncertain* / [edited by] Dale R. Herspring. 2003.
SUBJECTS:
Putin, Vladimir Vladimirovich, 1952-
Russia (Federation)–Politics and government–1991-

(6) *Spouses and family members.* A biography or autobiography of the spouse or a family member of a famous person, who is active in a special field, is treated in the normal manner. However, if the spouse or family member has no special career of his or her own, a biographical work that relates personal experiences in association with the famous person is assigned the following types of headings: **[Name of person]**; **[Name of famous person]**; **[Class-of-persons heading]**. Examples include:

Title: *Abigail Adams : famous First Lady* / Maya Glass. 2004.
SUBJECTS:
Adams, Abigail, 1744-1818–Juvenile literature.
Adams, John, 1735-1826–Juvenile literature.
Presidents' spouses–United States–Biography–Juvenile literature.

Title: *Some memories of a long life, 1854-1911* / Malvina Shanklin Harlan ; foreword by Ruth Bader Ginsburg ; epilogue by Amelia Newcomb ; afterword and notes by Linda Przybyszewski. 2002.
SUBJECTS:
Harlan, John Marshall, 1833-1911.
Harlan, Malvina Shanklin, 1838-1916.
Judges' spouses–United States–Biography.

Title: *Sweet Caroline : last child of Camelot* / Christopher Andersen. 2003.
SUBJECTS:
Kennedy, Caroline, 1957-
Kennedy, John F. (John Fitzgerald), 1917-1963–Family.
Children of presidents–United States–Biography.

Special Types of Biographical Works

Autobiographies and Autobiographical Writings

The personal name heading is assigned to an autobiography even though it duplicates the main entry:

Title: *Living history* / Hillary Rodham Clinton. c2003.
SUBJECTS:
Clinton, Hillary Rodham.
Presidents' spouses–United States–Biography.
Women legislators–United States–Biography.

Legislators–United States–Biography.
United States. Congress. Senate–Biography.
Clinton, Bill, 1946-
United States–Politics and government–1993-2001.
United States–Politics and government–2001-

MAIN ENTRY:
Clinton, Hillary Rodham.

Title: *My passage from India : a filmmaker's journey from Bombay to Hollywood and beyond* / Ismail Merchant. 2002.

SUBJECTS:
Merchant, Ismail.
Motion picture producers and directors–India–Biography.
India–In motion pictures.

MAIN ENTRY:
Merchant, Ismail.

Title: *Life of Josephus* / translation and commentary by Steve Mason. 2003.

SUBJECTS:
Josephus, Flavius.
Josephus, Flavius. Vita.
Jewish historians–Biography.
Jews–History–Rebellion, 66-73.

MAIN ENTRY:
Josephus, Flavius.

Other autobiographical writings such as memoirs, journals, diaries, etc., are treated similarly:

Title: *A soldier in World War I : the diary of Elmer W. Sherwood* / edited by Robert H. Ferrell. 2004.

SUBJECTS:
Sherwood, Elmer W.–Diaries.
United States. Army. Field Artillery Regiment, 150th.
United States. Army–Officers–Diaries.
World War, 1914-1918–Personal narratives, American.
World War, 1914-1918–Campaigns–France.
World War, 1914-1918–Regimental histories–United States.

Title: *The letters and diaries of Kathleen Ferrier* / edited by Christopher Fifield. c2003.

SUBJECTS:
Ferrier, Kathleen, 1912-1953–Correspondence.
Ferrier, Kathleen, 1912-1953–Diaries.
Contraltos–England–Correspondence.
Contraltos–England–Diaries.

Title: *Memoirs of an unregulated economist* / George J. Stigler. 2003.
SUBJECTS:
Stigler, George Joseph, 1911-
Economists–United States–Biography.
Chicago school of economics.

Correspondence[39]

To a collection of personal correspondence, the following complex of headings is assigned:

[Name of the letter writer]–Correspondence {no more than three}
[Name of the addressee]–Correspondence {no more than two}
[Class of persons or **ethnic group]–Correspondence**
[Special topics discussed in the letters]

Examples include:

Title: *Family letters of Louis D. Brandeis* / edited by Melvin I. Urofsky and David W. Levy. c2002.
SUBJECTS:
Brandeis, Louis Dembitz, 1856-1941–Correspondence.
Statesmen–United States–Correspondence.
Judges–United States–Correspondence.

Title: *The letters of John and Abigail Adams* / edited with an introduction by Frank Shuffelton. 2004.
SUBJECTS:
Adams, John, 1735-1826–Correspondence.
Adams, Abigail, 1744-1818–Correspondence.
Presidents–United States–Correspondence.
Presidents' spouses–United States–Correspondence.
United States–History–Revolution, 1775-1783–Sources.

Partial Biography[40]

A partial biography, that is, a work about a person's life and work, with at least 50 percent of the content devoted to personal details (except for people from ancient times about whom few personal details are known), is treated like an individual biography by assigning a personal heading and additional class-of-persons headings as appropriate. Additional headings are assigned to bring out the topical aspects if they have not been represented by the class-of-persons headings. Examples include:

Title: *George Washington's war : the forging of a Revolutionary leader and the American presidency* / by Bruce Chadwick. c2004.
SUBJECTS:
Washington, George, 1732-1799–Military leadership.
Command of troops–History–18th century.
United States. Continental Army–History.
United States–History–Revolution, 1775-1783–Campaigns.
Generals–United States–Biography.
Presidents–United States–Biography.

Title: *Stephen Hawking : a life in science* / Michael White and John Gribbin. c2002.
SUBJECTS:
Hawking, S. W. (Stephen W.)
Astrophysics.
Physicists–Great Britain–Biography.

Title: *Oskar Schindler* / Bruce Thompson, book editor. c2002.
SUBJECTS:
Schindler, Oskar, 1908-1974.
Righteous Gentiles in the Holocaust–Biography.
World War, 1939-1945–Jews–Rescue.
Holocaust, Jewish (1939-1945)

Title: *Princess Isabel of Brazil : gender and power in the nineteenth century* / Roderick J. Barman. c2002.
SUBJECTS:
Isabel, Princess of Brazil, 1846-1921.
Brazil–History–Empire, 1822-1889.
Sex role–Political aspects–Brazil.
Equality–Brazil–History–19th century.
Power (Social sciences)
Princesses–Brazil–Biography.

If a work about a person contains few or no personal details, class-of-persons headings are not assigned. The personal heading is assigned in all cases:

Title: *Indictment at The Hague : the Milosovíc [sic] regime and crimes of the Balkan Wars* / Norman Cigar and Paul Williams. c2002.
SUBJECTS:
Serbia–Politics and government–1992-
Milosevíc, Slobodan, 1941-
Yugoslav War, 1991-1995–Atrocities.
Kosovo (Serbia)–History–Civil War, 1998--Atrocities.

Title: *Against us, but for us : Martin Luther King, Jr. and the state* / Michael G. Long. 2002.
SUBJECTS:
King, Martin Luther, Jr., 1929-1968–Political and social views.
Political science–United States–History–20th century.
State, The–Philosophy.

Title: *John F. Kennedy and the politics of arms sales to Israel* / Abraham Ben-Zvi. 2002.
SUBJECTS:
United States–Foreign relations–Israel.
Israel–Foreign relations–United States.
Kennedy, John F. (John Fitzgerald), 1917-1963.
United States–Politics and government–1961-1963.
United States--Foreign relations–1961-1963.
Defense industries–United States–History–20th century.
Arms transfers–United States–History–20th century.
Hawk (Missile)–History.

Title: *Eisenhower's atoms for peace* / Ira Chernus. c2002.
SUBJECTS:
Nuclear energy–Government policy–United States–History – Sources.
Nuclear energy–Government policy–United States–History.
Eisenhower, Dwight D. (Dwight David), 1890-1969–Oratory.
Speeches, addresses, etc., American.
United States–Foreign relations–1953-1961.
United States–Politics and government–1945-1953.

True Stories about Animals and Pets[41]

To a work containing a collection of true-life stories about animals, a heading in the form of **[Type of animal]–[Place** (if appropriate)**]–Biography** [or–**Anecdotes**] is assigned:

Title: *Old friends : visits with my favorite thoroughbreds* / photos and text by Eclipse Award-winning photographer Barbara D. Livingston. 2002.
SUBJECTS:
Race horses–United States–Biography.
Thoroughbred horse–United States–Biography.
Race horses–United States–Pictorial works.
Thoroughbred horse–United States–Pictorial works.

To a true-life story of an individual animal or pet, the same type-of-animal heading is used. If the animal or pet has an established name, the name heading is also assigned.

Title: *Seabiscuit : an American legend* / Laura Hillenbrand. c2003.
SUBJECTS:
Seabiscuit (Race horse)
Race horses–United States–Biography.
Horse racing–United States.

For fictional accounts of animals, see the discussion in the section "Literature" in chapter 10.

WORKS ABOUT CORPORATE BODIES

The treatment of works about corporate bodies is similar in many ways to that of biography.

Corporate Bodies Discussed Collectively

For a work about a specific type of corporate body, the generic term is assigned as the heading, for example, **Libraries**; **Trade and professional associations**; **Labor unions, Catholic**; etc. Many of the headings for corporate bodies are subdivided by place, for example, **Libraries–Finland**; **Libraries–Alaska**. Examples include:

Title: *Private secondary schools.* c2001-
SUBJECTS:
Private schools–Directories.
Private schools–United States–Directories.
Private schools–Canada–Directories.
High schools–Directories.
High schools–United States–Directories.
High schools–Canada–Directories.

Title: *Complete guide to colleges.* c2002-
SUBJECTS:
Universities and colleges–United States–Directories.
Community colleges–United States–Directories.
Junior colleges–United States–Directories.

Title: *Morningstar stocks 500 : annual sourcebook.* c2002-
SUBJECTS:
Stocks–Prices–United States–Statistics–Periodicals.
Stocks–United States–Directories.
Corporations–United States–Finance–Statistics–Periodicals.
Corporations–United States–Finance–Directories.
Corporations–United States–Rankings–Periodicals.

Works about Individual Corporate Bodies

The name of the corporate body, as established according to *Anglo-American Cataloguing Rules* (*AACR2R*) (see chapter 4), is assigned as the subject heading for a work about an individual corporate body, even if the subject entry duplicates the main entry or an added entry.[42] Unlike the treatment of individual biographies, headings representing types of corporate bodies are not assigned to works about individual corporate bodies. Examples include:

Title: *Protecting all animals : a fifty-year history of the Humane Society of the United States* / by Bernard Unti. 2004.
SUBJECTS:
Humane Society of the United States–History.

Title: *A university for the 21st century* / James J. Duderstadt. c2002.
SUBJECTS:
University of Michigan–History.
Educational leadership–Michigan–Ann Arbor.
Educational change–Michigan–Ann Arbor.

Title: *The complete idiot's guide to the FBI* / by John Simeone and David Jacobs. c2003.
SUBJECTS:
United States. Federal Bureau of Investigation.
United States. Federal Bureau of Investigation–History.
Criminal investigation–United States–History.

Title: *Annual report and accounts* / Defence Science and Technology Laboratory. 2002-
SUBJECTS:
Defence Science and Technology Laboratory (Great Britain) –Periodicals.
Military research–Great Britain–Periodicals.

For the proceedings of a meeting or meetings of a society or institution dealing with a specific topic, a heading in the form of **[Topic]–Congresses** is assigned in addition to other appropriate headings.

Title: *The Persisting Osler, III : selected transactions of the American Osler Society, 1991-2000* / edited by Jeremiah A. Barondess, Charles G. Roland. 2002.
SUBJECTS:
Osler, William, Sir, 1849-1919.
American Osler Society.
Physicians–Canada–Biography–Congresses.
Physicians–Biography.
Physicians–Congresses.

Title: *Syllabus : 22nd IAJGS International Conference on Jewish Genealogy August 4-9, 2002* / IAJGS International Conference on Jewish Genealogy. 2002.

SUBJECTS:

Jewish Genealogical Society of Canada (Toronto)–Congresses.
Jews–Genealogy–Congresses.
Jews–Genealogy–Handbooks, manuals, etc.

However, for the annual meeting or meetings that deal with the internal affairs of the corporate body, a heading in the form of **[Name of corporate body]–Congresses** is used.

Name Changes in Corporate Bodies

When a corporate body changes its name, the present policy in accordance with *AACR2R* is to provide headings for all the names and link them with *see also* references. In assigning subject headings to corporate bodies that have changed their names, two different policies are in effect: one for corporate bodies in general, and one specifically for political jurisdictions.

For a work about a non-jurisdictional corporate body that has had a linear name change, a merger, or a split, the name current during the latest period covered by the work is assigned:[43]

Title: *The production and diffusion of public choice political economy : reflections on the V.P.I. Center* / edited by Joseph C. Pitt, Djavad Salehi-Isfahani, and Douglas W. Eckel. 2004.

SUBJECTS:

Virginia Polytechnic Institute and State University. Center for Study of Public Choice.
Social choice–Study and teaching.

{Earlier heading for the V.P.I. Center: **Virginia Polytechnic Institute. Center for Study of Public Choice**}

Title: *Public enemies : America's greatest crime wave and the birth of the FBI, 1933-34* / Bryan Burrough. 2004.

SUBJECTS:

United States. Federal Bureau of Investigation–History.
Crime–United States–History–20th century.
Criminals–United States–History–20th century.

{Earlier headings for the Bureau: **United States Bureau of Investigation; United States. Dept. of Justice. Division of Investigation**}

In addition, a heading under an earlier name is also assigned if the body was well-known by the earlier name and that name is featured prominently in the work being cataloged.

For a work about a political jurisdiction that has changed its name without involving territorial changes, the latest name is used as the subject heading or subdivision regardless of the period treated in the work:[44]

Title: *Colonial lessons : Africans' education in Southern Rhodesia, 1918-1940* / Carol Summers. c2002.
SUBJECTS:
Education–Zimbabwe–History–20th century.
Blacks–Education–Zimbabwe–History–20th century.
Segregation in education–Zimbabwe–History–20th century.
Zimbabwe–Colonial influence.

If the change is a complicated one involving, for example, territorial boundaries, the latest name corresponding to the area covered by the work is assigned:[45]

Title: *The coming of the Third Reich : a history* / Richard J. Evans. 2004.
SUBJECTS:
National socialism–History.
Germany–History–1871-1918.
Germany–History–1918-1933.

Title: *Resistance with the people : repression and resistance in Eastern Germany, 1945-1955* / Gary Bruce. c2003.
SUBJECTS:
Opposition (Political science)–Germany (East)
Protest movements–Germany (East)
Germany (East)–History–Uprising, 1953.
Internal security–Germany (East)
Germany (East)–Politics and government.

Title: *Rebuilding Germany : the creation of the social market economy, 1945-1957* / James C. Van Hook. 2004.
SUBJECTS:
Germany (West)–Economic policy.
Germany (West)–Economic conditions.
Free enterprise.
Germany (West)–Social policy.
United States–Foreign relations–Germany (West)
Germany (West)–Foreign relations–United States.

Title: *Germany* / text by Sonja Schanz ; photographs by Bob Smith. c2003.
SUBJECTS:
Germany–History–Unification, 1990–Juvenile literature.
Germany–History–1990--Juvenile literature.

Germany–Social conditions–1990- –Juvenile literature.
Germany–Ethnic relations–Juvenile literature.

Title: *Russia engages the world, 1453-1825* / edited by Cynthia Hyla Whittaker ; with Edward Kasinec and Robert H. Davis, Jr. 2003.
SUBJECTS:
Russia–History.

Title: *Early exploration of Russia* / edited by Marshall Poe. 2003.
SUBJECTS:
Russia–Description and travel.
Russia–History.

Title: *Revolutionary Russia : new approaches* / [selected and edited by] Rex A. Wade. 2004.
SUBJECTS:
Soviet Union–History–Revolution, 1917-1921.

Title: *Modeling Russia's economy in transition* / Peter Wehrheim. c2003.
SUBJECTS:
Russia (Federation)–Economic conditions–1991--Mathematical models.

Title: *Politics in Russia* / Thomas F. Remington. c2002.
SUBJECTS:
Constitutional history–Russia (Federation)
Russia (Federation)–Politics and government–1991-
Soviet Union–Politics and government.

WORKS ABOUT BUILDINGS AND OTHER STRUCTURES[46]

Works about Specific Types of Buildings or Structures

To a work that discusses collectively a certain type of building or structure, topical headings, with appropriate geographic subdivisions if applicable, are assigned:

Title: *Castles and cathedrals : the great buildings of medieval times* / David Hilliam. c2004.
SUBJECTS:
Architecture, Medieval–Juvenile literature.
Castles–Juvenile literature.
Cathedrals–Juvenile literature.

Title: *The most beautiful libraries in the world* / photographs by Guillaume de Laubier ; text by Jacques Bosser ; foreword by James H. Billington ; translated from the French by Laurel Hirsch. 2003.

SUBJECTS:

Library buildings.
Library architecture.
Libraries.
Library buildings–Pictorial works.
Library architecture–Pictorial works.
Libraries–Pictorial works.

Title: *The Italian Renaissance palace facade : structures of authority, surfaces of sense* / Charles Burroughs. 2002.

SUBJECTS:

Facades–Italy.
Palaces–Italy.
Architecture, Renaissance–Italy.
Symbolism in architecture–Italy.

If the work discusses a type or class of building or structure within a city from an architectural point of view or describes members of the class as physical entities, an additional heading in the form of **[City]–Buildings, structures, etc.** is assigned:[47]

Title: *Chicago's famous buildings* / Franz Schulze and Kevin Harrington. c2003.

SUBJECTS:

Architecture–Illinois–Chicago–Guidebooks.
Public buildings–Illinois–Chicago–Guidebooks.
Chicago (Ill.)–Buildings, structures, etc.–Guidebooks.

Title: *Classic country estates of Lake Forest : architecture and landscape design, 1856-1940* / Kim Coventry, Daniel Meyer, Arthur H. Miller. c2003.

SUBJECTS:

Architecture, Domestic–Illinois–Lake Forest.
Landscape design–Illinois–Lake Forest.
Lake Forest (Ill.)–Buildings, structures, etc.

Title: *Housing in New Halos : a Hellenistic town in Thessaly, Greece* / [H. Reinder Reinders, Wietske Prummel]. 2003.

SUBJECTS:

New Halos (Extinct city)
New Halos (Extinct city)–Buildings, structures, etc.
Dwellings–Greece–New Halos (Extinct city)

Works about Individual Buildings or Structures[48]

For a work about an individual building, the following types of headings are used:

[Name of structure]
[Name of city]–Buildings, structures, etc.
{If the building or structure is located within a city and the work discusses it from an architectural point of view}
[Name of architect or Architectural firm]
[Name of owner, resident, etc.]–Homes and haunts–[Place]
[Name of person memorialized]–Monuments–[Place]
[Special feature or topic]

Examples include:

Title: *National parks : significant progress made in preserving the Presidio and attaining financial self-sufficiency : report to congressional requesters* / United States General Accounting Office. 2001.
SUBJECTS:
Presidio Trust (U.S.)
Presidio of San Francisco (Calif.)
San Francisco (Calif.)–Buildings, structures, etc.

Title: *Thomas Jefferson's Monticello.* c2002.
SUBJECTS:
Jefferson, Thomas, 1743-1826–Homes and haunts–Virginia–Albemarle County–Pictorial works.
Monticello (Va.)–Pictorial works.
Monticello (Va.)–History.

Title: *Frank Lloyd Wright's Martin House : architecture as portraiture* / Jack Quinan. 2004.
SUBJECTS:
Darwin D. Martin House (Buffalo, N.Y.)
Wright, Frank Lloyd, 1867-1959–Criticism and interpretation.
Prairie school (Architecture)–New York (State)–Buffalo.
Buffalo (N.Y.)–Buildings, structures, etc.

Title: *Mount Vernon* / by Andrew Santella. 2004.
SUBJECTS:
Mount Vernon (Va. : Estate)–Juvenile literature.
Washington, George, 1732-1799–Homes and haunts–Virginia–Fairfax County–Juvenile literature.

Title: *The White House & President's Park : comprehensive design plan.* 2000.

SUBJECTS:

White House (Washington, D.C.)
President's Park (Washington, D.C.)
Architecture–Environmental aspects–Washington (D.C.)
Washington (D.C.)–Buildings, structures, etc.

Title: *Das Brandenburger Tor : Weg in die Geschichte, Tor in die Zukunft* / herausgegeben von der Stiftung Denkmalschutz Berlin. c2003.

SUBJECTS:

Brandenburger Tor (Berlin, Germany)–History.
Architecture and state–Germany–Berlin.
Berlin (Germany)–Buildings, structures, etc.
Berlin (Germany)–History.

Title: *Taj Mahal* / Caroline Arnold and Madeleine Comora ; illustrated by Rahul Bhushan. 2004.

SUBJECTS:

Taj Mahal (Agra, India)–Juvenile literature.
Architecture, Mogul–India–Agra–Juvenile literature.
Agra (India)–Buildings, structures, etc.–Juvenile literature.

WORKS INVOLVING CITY DISTRICTS, SECTIONS, AND QUARTERS[49]

When a work deals with a topic in a city district, section, or quarter, the following types of headings are assigned:

[Topic]–[Larger geographic entity]–[City]
[Name of district, section, or quarter]–[Subdivision, if appropriate]
[City]–[Subdivision]

This approach is taken because the lowest level of geographic subdivision in the LC subject headings system is the city. In other words, subjects are not subdivided by city districts, sections, or quarters.

Title: *Crossing the blvd : strangers, neighbors, aliens in a new America* / Warren Lehrer & Judith Sloan ; photography and design by Warren Lehrer. 2003.

SUBJECTS:

Immigrants–New York (State)–New York.
Queens (New York, N.Y.)

Title: *The lower Manhattan plan : the 1966 vision for downtown New York* / essays by Ann Buttenwieser, Paul Willen, and James Rossant ; Carol Willis, editor. c2002.

SUBJECTS:

City planning–New York (State)–New York–History–20th century.
Manhattan (New York, N.Y.)

If the topic involved corresponds to one of the concepts represented by the free-floating subdivisions under names of places, the same subdivision is used under the heading for the district and under the heading for the city. Examples include:

Title: *New York streetscapes : tales of Manhattan's significant buildings and landmarks* / Christopher Gray ; research by Suzanne Braley. 2003.

SUBJECTS:

Architecture–New York (State)–New York.
Historic buildings–New York (State)–New York.
New York (N.Y.)–Buildings, structures, etc.
Manhattan (New York, N.Y.)–Buildings, structures, etc.

WORKS RELATED TO INDIVIDUAL WORKS

To a work related to another work—a commentary or criticism, an edition, an index, a concordance, or a supplement—a heading representing the work being discussed is generally assigned, in addition to other appropriate headings.

Commentary versus Edition

A commentary is defined as "a work that criticizes or comments on another work."[50] Commentaries are sometimes published separately as independent works and sometimes published along with the text of the work being discussed. In the latter case, the subject headings assigned vary, depending on whether the work as a whole is treated as a commentary or as an edition. The decision about treating such a work as a commentary or as an edition generally parallels the decision made in descriptive cataloging according to *AACR2R*. If main entry is under the author or the uniform title of the work being discussed, it is treated as an edition. On the other hand, if main entry is under the name of the commentator, it is treated as a commentary.

Commentaries on Individual Works

To a commentary on an individual work other than a literary work or a work about sacred scriptures or a liturgical work, two types of headings are assigned: (1) a name/title heading (or uniform title for a work entered under title) for the work being discussed and (2) the same topical headings that were assigned to the work being commented on. Examples of subject headings assigned to commentaries include:

Title: *Kants Critique of pure reason, 1959* / Theodor W. Adorno ; edited by Rolf Tiedemann ; translated by Rodney Livingstone. 2001.
SUBJECTS:
Kant, Immanuel, 1724-1804. Kritik der reinen Vernunft.
Knowledge, Theory of.
Causation.
Reason.

Original text:

Title: *Critique of pure reason* / translated and edited by Paul Guyer, Allen W. Wood. 1998.
SUBJECTS:
Knowledge, Theory of.
Causation.
Reason.

Title: *Dreaming by the book : Freud's Interpretation of dreams and the history of the psychoanalytic movement* / Lydia Marinelli, Andreas Mayer ; translated by Susan Fairfield. c2003.
SUBJECTS:
Freud, Sigmund, 1856-1939. Traumdeutung.
Dream interpretation–History.
Psychoanalysis–History.

Original text:

Title: *The interpretation of dreams* / Sigmund Freud ; translated by Joyce Crick ; with an introduction and notes by Ritchie Robertson. 1999.
SUBJECTS:
Dream interpretation.
Psychoanalysis.

The title in the subject heading is the uniform title, not necessarily the title as it appears in the commentary. The reason for using the uniform title is to group together all commentaries about a particular work regardless of variant titles or titles in the different languages under which the work has appeared. If the work being discussed is a commentary in itself (i.e., a commentary on a commentary), name/title headings for both the original work and the commentary being discussed are assigned.

The topical headings used are those that have been or would be assigned to the work being discussed. However, if the headings assigned to the text are only used as form headings, such as **Agriculture–Periodicals** or **Egypt–History–Fiction**, they are converted to their topical equivalents, for example, **Agriculture–Periodicals–History** or **Egypt–In literature**.

The topical headings are assigned even if the commentary does not contain the original text. If, however, the commentary consists purely of textual criticism (i.e., commentary on the text as text and not the substantive matter of the work being discussed), the topical headings assigned to the work being discussed are not assigned to the commentary.

Variant Editions of a Work[51]

It is the policy of the Library of Congress to assign to each variant edition of a work with an imprint date of 1981 or later the same subject headings as those assigned to the original edition, provided that the content of the variant edition does not vary significantly from that of the original.

Title: *Critique of pure reason* / Immanuel Kant ; translated by J.M.D. Meiklejohn. 2003.
SUBJECTS:
Knowledge, Theory of.
Causation.
Reason.

Different and/or additional headings are assigned if variations in content are significant.

If the edition of a work contains a substantial amount of commentary, that is, at least 20 percent of the work, a subject heading in the form of **[Name. Title]** or **[Uniform title]** is assigned, even though it may duplicate the main entry or an added entry of the work.

Supplementary Works

A supplementary work is defined as "a separately issued *subordinate* work which continues or complements a previously issued work."[52] Included in this definition are supplements, appendices, indexes, addenda, continuations of texts without volume numbering, etc.

For a work that supplements a monograph, the same subject headings assigned to the original work are used for its separately published supplementary works. If a supplement treats other topics as well, additional headings are assigned. Form subdivision such as **–Bibliography**; **–Pictorial works**; etc., may be added to the headings to bring out the form of the supplementary work. Examples include:

Title: *Comprehensive asymmetric catalysis. Supplement* / with contributions by numerous experts ; Eric N. Jacobsen, Andreas Pfaltz, Hisashi Yamamoto (eds.). c2004-

SUBJECTS:

Catalysis.
Asymmetric synthesis.

Title: *On the trail of the buffalo soldier : a supplement with all new and revised biographies of African Americans in the U.S. Army, 1866-1917* / compiled and edited by Irene Schubert, Frank N. Schubert. 2004.

SUBJECTS:

African American soldiers–Biography.
United States. Army–Biography.
African American soldiers–History–20th century.
African American soldiers–History–19th century.

Title: *British writers. Supplement IX* / Jay Parini, editor. 2003.

SUBJECTS:

English literature–20th century–Bio-bibliography.
English literature–20th century–History and criticism.
Commonwealth literature (English)–History and criticism.
Commonwealth literature (English)–Bio-bibliography.
Authors, Commonwealth–20th century–Biography.
Authors, English–20th century–Biography.

For a work that supplements a serial, headings appropriate to the topic of the supplement are assigned.

Title: *The Calcutta municipal gazette : Tagore memorial special supplement.* 2002.

SUBJECTS:

Tagore, Rabindranath, 1861-1941–Criticism and interpretation.

Indexes and Concordances to Individual Works

Two types of headings are assigned to an index of an individual work:[53]

[Name. Title or Uniform title]–Indexes [or **Concordances**]
[Same heading assigned to work being indexed]–Indexes

Examples include:

Title: *The Encyclopaedia of Islam, new edition. Index of subjects to volumes I-XI and to the Supplement, fascicules 1-6* / compiled by P.J. Bearman. [5th ed.] 2003.

SUBJECTS:

Encyclopaedia of Islam–Indexes.
Islam–Indexes.
Islamic countries–Indexes.

Title: *Index to Roster of California pioneers* / by Native Daughters of the Golden West. 2002.

SUBJECTS:

Roster of California pioneers–Indexes.
California–Genealogy–Indexes.
Pioneers–California–Genealogy–Indexes.
California–Registers.

Title: *The universal spectator (London 1728-1746) : an annotated record of the literary contents* / Edward William Pitcher. 2004.

SUBJECTS:

Universal spectator and weekly journal–Indexes.
English literature–18th century–Indexes.
English periodicals–Indexes.

Title: *La revue musicale, 1901-1912* / préparé par Doris Pyee-Cohen ; données traitées et revues au RIPM International Center, Baltimore, Maryland. c2002.

SUBJECTS:

Revue d'histoire et de critique musicales–Indexes.
Revue musicale (Paris, France : 1902)–Indexes.
Music–Periodicals–Indexes.
Music–France–Periodicals–Indexes.

Title: *The Dead Sea scrolls concordance* / by Martin G. Abegg, Jr. with James E. Bowley & Edward M. Cook ; & in consultation with Emanuel Tov. 2003-

SUBJECTS:

Dead Sea scrolls–Concordances.

NOTES

1. Library of Congress, Cataloging Policy and Support Office, *Subject Cataloging Manual: Subject Headings*, 5th ed., 2000 cumulation (Washington, D.C.: Library of Congress, 2000), H2070.

2. Library of Congress, *Subject Cataloging Manual*, H1520, p. 1.

3. Library of Congress, *Subject Cataloging Manual*, H1520.

4. "Subject Cataloging of Works about Specific Computer and Video Games," *Cataloging Service Bulletin*, 91 (Winter 2001): 24-25.

5. Library of Congress, *Subject Cataloging Manual*, H1927, p. 2.

6. Library of Congress, *Subject Cataloging Manual*, H1460.

7. Library of Congress, *Subject Cataloging Manual*, H1580.5, p. 1.

8. Library of Congress, *Subject Cataloging Manual*, H1927, p. 1.

9. Library of Congress, *Subject Cataloging Manual*, H180.

10. Library of Congress, *Subject Cataloging Manual*, H1205.

11. Library of Congress, *Subject Cataloging Manual*, H1205, p. 2.

12. Library of Congress, *Subject Cataloging Manual: Subject Headings*, H1670, p. 1.

13. Library of Congress, *Subject Cataloging Manual*, H1325.

14. Library of Congress, *Subject Cataloging Manual*, H1322.

15. Library of Congress, *Subject Cataloging Manual*, H1670, p. 1.

16. Library of Congress, *Subject Cataloging Manual*, H1361.

17. Library of Congress, *Subject Cataloging Manual*, H1965.

18. Library of Congress, *Subject Cataloging Manual*, H1660.

19. Library of Congress, *Subject Cataloging Manual*, H1570.

20. Library of Congress, *Subject Cataloging Manual*, H1980.

21. Library of Congress, *Subject Cataloging Manual*, H1360.

22. Library of Congress, *Subject Cataloging Manual*, H1540.

23. Library of Congress, *Subject Cataloging Manual*, H1558, p. 1.

24. Library of Congress, *Subject Cataloging Manual*, H1646.

25. Library of Congress, *Subject Cataloging Manual* H1690.

26. Library of Congress, *Subject Cataloging Manual*, H1690, H1780, H1790, H1800.

27. Library of Congress, *Subject Cataloging Manual*, H1095, H1935.

28. Library of Congress, *Subject Cataloging Manual*, H2230.

29. Library of Congress, Motion Picture/Broadcasting/Recorded Sound Division, *The Moving Image Genre-Form Guide,* comp. Brian Taves, Judi Hoffman, and Karen Lund (Washington, DC: Library of Congress. MBRS, 1998), http://lcweb.loc.gov/rr/mopic/migintro.html.

30. http://www.loc.gov/catdir/cpso/formgenr.html.

31. Library of Congress, *Subject Cataloging Manual*, H1690, p. 2.

32. Library of Congress, *Subject Cataloging Manual*, H1330.

33. Library of Congress, *Subject Cataloging Manual*, H1330, p. 1.

34. Library of Congress, *Subject Cataloging Manual*, H1480.

35. Library of Congress, *Subject Cataloging Manual*, H1928.

36. Library of Congress, *Subject Cataloging Manual*, H1574.

37. Library of Congress, *Subject Cataloging Manual*, H1330, p. 1.

38. Library of Congress, *Subject Cataloging Manual*, H1110.

39. Library of Congress, *Subject Cataloging Manual*, H1480.

40. Library of Congress, *Subject Cataloging Manual*, H1330.

41. Library of Congress, *Subject Cataloging Manual*, H1720.

42. Library of Congress, *Subject Cataloging Manual*, H184.

43. Library of Congress, *Subject Cataloging Manual*, H460.

44. Library of Congress, *Subject Cataloging Manual*, H708, p. 1.

45. Library of Congress, *Subject Cataloging Manual*, H710.

46. Library of Congress, *Subject Cataloging Manual*, H1334, H1334.5.

47. Library of Congress, *Subject Cataloging Manual*, H1334.5.

48. Library of Congress, *Subject Cataloging Manual*, H1334, p. 9.

49. Library of Congress, *Subject Cataloging Manual*, H720.

50. Library of Congress, *Subject Cataloging Manual*, H1435, p. 1.

51. Library of Congress, *Subject Cataloging Manual*, H175.

52. Library of Congress, *Subject Cataloging Manual*, H2145, p. 1.

53. Library of Congress, *Subject Cataloging Manual*, H1670, p. 2.

10 Subject Areas Requiring Special Treatment

LITERATURE

Types of Headings

Four types of Library of Congress (LC) subject headings are used for works in the field of literature (*belles lettres*): literary genre headings; topical headings representing themes, literary movements, characters, or features in literary works; headings combining form and topic; and other topical headings. In addition, genre/form headings from *Guidelines on Subject Access to Individual Works of Fiction, Drama, Etc.*[1] are assigned to selected items. These headings are discussed below.

Literary Genre Headings

(1) *Headings representing literary forms or genres*. Examples include:

Drama
Poetry
Fiction
Romances
Satire

(2) *Headings indicating language or nationality*. Examples include:

American literature
Japanese literature
French literature
Hindu literature

(3) *Headings that combine language/nationality and literary form/genre*. Examples include:

American poetry
English drama (Comedy)
Epic poetry, Italian

Prose poems, American
French drama
African drama (English)
Ghanaian poetry (English)

Time period and locality are generally expressed in subdivisions.

The heading **English literature** serves as the pattern heading for subdivisions that may be used under headings for individual literatures and under genres of those literatures, for example, **Swedish literature**; **French drama**; **German essays**; **Epic poetry, Finnish**; **Short stories, Chinese**; etc.[2] Chronological subdivisions listed under the pattern heading are not used under headings for minor genres (i.e., genres other than fiction, drama, poetry, essays, and prose literature) or under inverted headings, and they are not free-floating under headings with qualifiers, for example, **Nigerian fiction (English)**. Needless to say, chronological subdivisions that are unique to English literature (e.g., **–Old English, ca. 450-1100)** are not used under headings for other literatures. Chronological subdivisions that are unique to a particular literature are established separately and displayed under the appropriate heading in LCSH.

The chronological subdivision under a literary genre heading may be followed by a subdivision indicating the nature of the work or the bibliographic form of the item being cataloged, for example, **American poetry–20th century–History and criticism**; **American poetry–20th century–Periodicals.**

In applying free-floating subdivisions under literary genre headings, Library of Congress policy does not authorize the combination of a chronological subdivision with a geographic subdivision that brings out a specific place of origin (i.e., **American literature–Southern States** not further subdivided by period) or with topical subdivisions such as **–...authors** (e.g., **American poetry–Women authors** not further subdivided by period). Instead, to bring out the time aspect, the main heading is doubled by assigning an additional heading with chronological subdivision, for example:

American fiction–Southern States–History and criticism.
American fiction–20th century–History and criticism.

Topical Headings Representing Themes, Literary Movements, Characters, or Features in Literary Works

For literary works the following types of headings are used:

[Topic or **Name]–Drama**
[Topic or **Name]–Fiction**
[Topic or **Name]–Literary collections**
[Topic or **Name]–Poetry**

The subdivisions in these cases are free-floating. Examples include:

Columbus, Christopher–Fiction
Michelangelo Buonarroti, 1475-1564–Drama
America–Discovery and exploration–Poetry
Horses–Fiction
World War, 1939-1945–Literary collections

For works *about* literature the following types of headings are used:

[Topic] in literature {not free-floating}
[Personal name, family, place, corporate body, or **sacred books]–In literature** {free-floating}
[Name of event or **war]–Literature and the war, [revolution, etc.]** {free-floating}

Examples include:

Animals in literature
Antislavery movements in literature
Lincoln, Abraham, 1809-1865–In literature
Shakespeare, William, 1564-1616–In literature
Roosevelt family–In literature
West (U.S.)–In literature
Bible–In literature
Cuba–History–Revolution, 1959–Literature and the revolution
World War, 1914-1918–Literature and the war

Headings Combining Topic and Form/Genre

Examples include:

Christmas plays
Patriotic poetry
Detective and mystery stories, English
Western stories

Other Topical Headings

Examples include:

Criticism, Textual
Literary forgeries and mystifications
Literature–Research
Literature and medicine
Poetry and children
Religion and literature

Genre/Form Headings from *Guidelines on Subject Access to Individual Works of Fiction, Drama, Etc.*

Examples include:

Domestic fiction
Bildungsromans
Humorous fiction
Love stories
Musical fiction

Application[3]

Works in the field of literature fall into two broad categories: (1) literary texts and (2) works *about* literature in general or *about* individual authors or individual works. Their treatment is described in the following pages.

Literary Texts

Collections of Literary Texts by Several Authors

(1) *Literary genre headings.* Literary genre headings with appropriate subdivisions are assigned to collections of two or more independent works by different authors:

Title: *The Norton anthology of modern and contemporary poetry* / edited by Jahan Ramazani, Richard Ellmann, Robert O'Clair. 3rd ed. c2003.
SUBJECTS:
American poetry–20th century.
English poetry–20th century.
American poetry–19th century.
English poetry–19th century.

Title: *Great short stories of the masters* / edited by Charles Neider. 2003.
SUBJECTS:
Short stories–Translations into English.
Short stories, American.
Short stories, English.

Title: *The Victoria reader : a treasury of timeless stories* / edited by Michele Slung. c2003.
SUBJECTS:
Short stories, English.
Short stories, American.

When the works in a collection belong to a minor literary form and the genre heading has no provision for chronological subdivisions, a second, broader genre heading with the appropriate chronological subdivision is also assigned to represent the time aspect:

Title: *Victorian theatrical burlesques* / edited by Richard W. Schoch. c2003.
SUBJECTS:
Burlesques.
English drama–19th century.

Title: *Contes de campagne : dix-sept nouvelles de France* / [Patrick Besson ... et al.]. 2002.
SUBJECTS:
Short stories, French.
French fiction–20th century.

The subdivision **–Collections** is not free-floating. It is established under the following literary headings only: **Drama**; **Fiction**; **Literature**; **Poetry**.

Title: *The Norton introduction to literature* / [edited by] Jerome Beaty ... [et al.]. c2002.
SUBJECTS:
Literature–Collections.

Title: *Poetry : an introduction* / [edited by] Michael Meyer. 4th ed. c2004.
SUBJECTS:
Poetry–Collections.
College readers.

Title: *12 plays : a portable anthology* / edited by Janet E. Gardner. c2003.
SUBJECTS:
Drama–Collections.

Other headings that may be subdivided by **–Collections** are **Autographs**; **Charters**; **Manuscripts**; **Playbills**; **Treaties.**

(2) *Topical headings.* If the collection is centered on a theme, a person, a place, or an event, a topical heading subdivided by either the subdivision **–Literary collections** (when the works in the collection are written in two or more literary forms) or by one of the major literary form subdivisions (**–Drama**; **–Fiction**; **–Poetry**)[4] is assigned in addition to the appropriate literary genre headings. The form subdivisions **–Drama**; **–Fiction**; **–Poetry**; and **–Literary collections** are used under an identifiable topic for a collection of literary works on that topic. Examples include:

Title: *Love of quilts : a treasury of classic quilting stories* / Compiled by Cuesta Ray Benberry and Carol Pinney Crabb. c2004.
SUBJECTS:
Quilts–Fiction.
Women–United States–Fiction.
Short stories, American.
Quiltmakers–Fiction.
Quilting–Fiction.

Title: *Anthology of African American literature* / Keith Gilyard, Anissa Wardi. 2004.
SUBJECTS:
American literature–African American authors.
African Americans–Literary collections.

Title: *Literature and science in the nineteenth century : an anthology* / edited with an introduction and notes by Laura Otis. 2002.
SUBJECTS:
English literature–19th century.
Science–Literary collections.
American literature–19th century.
Science–History–19th century–Sources.

Some phrase headings combine topical and form aspects, for example, **Detective and mystery stories, American**; **Science fiction, American**; **Sea stories**; **Love stories**; **Christmas plays**; **Ghost plays**; **Political plays**. When such headings exist, they are used instead of separate topic and genre headings:

Title: *Zen poems* / edited by Manu Bazzano ; illustrations, André Sollier. 2002.
SUBJECTS:
Zen poetry.

Title: *Rendezvous with death: American poems of the Great War* / edited by Mark W. Van Wienen. c2002.
SUBJECTS:
American poetry–20th century.
World War, 1914-1918–Poetry.
War poetry, American.

If, however, a heading is assigned for a very specific topic, the topic/genre heading for a more general topic is not used. Instead, a literary genre heading is assigned. For example, the following headings are assigned to a collection of American drama on the theme of Trinity:[5]

American drama
Trinity–Drama
{Not *Christian drama, American*}

In the case of fiction about animals, the heading **Animals** [or **Kind of animals**]**–Fiction** or **Animals** [or **Kind of animals**]**–Juvenile fiction** is used. The subdivision *–Legends and stories,* previously used under types of animals is no longer valid. The subdivision **–Folklore** is now used under the heading **Animals** or type of animal (e.g., **Dogs**) for one or more legends about them. The subdivision **–Anecdotes** is used for anecdotal accounts, and the subdivision **–Biography** is used for true accounts about animals.

Works by Individual Authors[6]

Collected Works

(1) *Literary genre headings.* In general, literary genre headings are not assigned to collected works in a major form by an individual author. In other words, the heading **English drama–Early modern and Elizabethan, 1500-1600** is not used with the complete plays of Shakespeare.

Title: *Collected works* / Silo. 2003.
{No subject headings assigned}

Title: *Selected poems* / Walt Whitman ; Harold Bloom, editor. c2003.
{No subject headings assigned}

However, there are two exceptions to this general rule. The literary genre heading is assigned if it combines in one heading nationality or language and a highly specific genre, for example, **Sonnets, American**; **Love stories, French**; or a genre and theme, such as **Detective and mystery plays**; **Sea poetry, English**; **Love poetry**; **War poetry**; and **Western stories**:

Title: *The complete love poems of May Swenson.* 2003.
SUBJECTS:
Love poetry, American.

Title: *Shakespeare's sonnets ; and, A lover's complaint* / edited, with an introduction, by Stanley Wells. 2003.
SUBJECTS:
Sonnets, English.

The genre heading is also assigned if the form is highly specific, such as **Allegories**; **Fairy tales**; **Radio stories**; **Carnival plays**; **Children's plays**; **College and school drama**; **Concrete poetry, German**; **Didactic drama**; **Radio plays**; **Sonnets, American**:

Title: V*ery short fairy tales to read together* / by Mary Ann Hoberman ; illustrated by Michael Emberly. 2004.
SUBJECTS:
Readers (Primary)
Fairy tales.

Title: *Advice to a player : a collection of monologues from Shakespeare with explanatory notes* / by Donald MacKechnie ; foreword by Joan Plowright. 2002.
SUBJECTS:
Acting–Auditions.
Monologues.
Shakespeare, William, 1564-1616–Quotations.

Title: *American sonnets : poems* / Gerald Stern. c2002.
SUBJECTS:
Sonnets, American.

Headings of the following types are *not* considered "highly specific": **American fiction**; **Short stories**; **English drama**; **English drama (Comedy)**; **Comedy**; **Farces**; **Melodrama**; **One-act plays**; **Tragedy**; **Tragicomedy**.

(2) *Topical headings.* If the works in the collection are centered on an identifiable topic or based on an event or on the life of an individual, a topical heading with an appropriate literary form subdivision (**–Fiction**; **–Drama**; **–Poetry**; **–Literary collections**) is assigned.

Title: *Battle-pieces and aspects of the war : Civil War poems* / Herman Melville ; foreword by James M. McPherson ; introduction by Richard H. Cox and Paul M. Dowling ; interpretive essays by Helen Vendler ... [et al.]. 2001.
SUBJECTS:
War poetry, American.
United States–History–Civil War, 1861-1865–Poetry.

Title: *The resurrection of the animals : poems* / by Anita Skeen. c2002.
SUBJECTS:
Nature–Poetry.
Animals–Poetry.
Human-animal relationships–Poetry.

A phrase heading combining form and topic is used if it is available.

Title: *A whale at the port quarter : a treasure chest of sea stories* / Chuck Gnaegy ; editor, Phyllis Klucinec. c2001.
SUBJECTS:
Sea stories, American.

The subdivisions **–Juvenile fiction**; **–Juvenile drama**; **–Juvenile poetry** are used for juvenile *belles lettres*. The subdivision **–Juvenile literature**, on the other hand, is used with headings assigned to non-literary works for children. Note also specific juvenile headings such as **Children's stories**; **Nursery rhymes**; etc.

Title: *Extraordinary women from U.S. history : readers theatre for grades 4-8* / by Chari R. Smith. c2003.
SUBJECTS:
Women–United States–Juvenile drama.
Children's plays, American.

Title: *Unexpected magic : collected stories* / Diana Wynne Jones. 2003.
SUBJECTS:
Fantasy fiction, English.
Children's stories, English.

Title: *Father Fox's Christmas rhymes* / Clyde Watson ; pictures by Wendy Watson. 2003.
SUBJECTS:
Christmas–Juvenile poetry.
Children's poetry, American.

Individual Works

(1) *Literary genre headings.* Headings representing major literary genres or forms, such as **English drama** and **American fiction**, are *not* assigned to individual literary works, for example:

Title: *Pride and prejudice* / Jane Austen. 2003.
{No subject headings assigned}

Title: *The odd couple I and II : the original screen plays* / Neil Simon. c2000.
{No subject headings assigned}

However, genre headings of the types listed below are assigned:

(a) Genre headings for children's drama and poetry, for example, **Children's plays, American**; **Children's poetry, English**; etc., are assigned to individual plays and poems for children, but not to children's fiction or young adult fiction:

Title: *Five little ducks* / illustrated by Pamela Paparone. 2004.
SUBJECTS:
Nursery rhymes.
Children's poetry.

Title: *Bigfoot!* / by William Hezlep. 2004.
SUBJECTS:
Sasquatch–Drama.
Anthropologists–Drama.
Northwest, Pacific–Drama.
Children's plays, American.

(b) Genre headings that include a topical aspect, such as **Detective and mystery plays, American**; **War poetry, American**, are assigned to individual works of drama and poetry, but not to individual works of fiction:

Title: *Ramblings from a cockpit* / Michael S. Alexatos. c2003.
SUBJECTS:
War poetry, American.
Fighter pilots–Poetry.
World War, 1939-1945–Aerial operations, American–Poetry.
World War, 1939-1945–Campaigns–Pacific Ocean–Poetry.
Korean War, 1950-1953–Aerial operations–Poetry.

(c) Headings representing highly specific forms, such as **Carnival plays**; **Nonsense verses**; **Nursery rhymes, American,** are assigned to individual works of drama and poetry, but not to individual works of fiction:

Title: *Fiddle-i-fee* / Will Hillenbrand. 2002.
SUBJECTS:
Folk songs, English–United States–Texts.
Children's songs–Texts.
Nursery rhymes, American.
Children's poetry, American.

(d) In addition, genre/form terms are assigned to selected literary works according to the *Guidelines on Subject Access to Individual Works of Fiction, Drama, Etc.* (gsafd), developed by the Association of Library Collections and Technical Services (ALCTS). These genre/form terms provide additional access points for works of fiction, drama, etc., for example, ***Apprenticeship novels; Autobiographical fiction; War films; Mystery comic books, strips, etc.*** In LC MARC records, they are different from the established LC literary form headings discussed above. The LC literary form headings are placed in regular subject heading fields, while the genre/form terms are placed in a different field (655) from that (650) for an LC literary form heading in the MARC 21 record.

(2) *Topical headings.* An individual work of drama or poetry that focuses on an identifiable topic or is based on the life of a person is assigned a topical or name heading with the subdivision **–Poetry** or **–Drama**. Such headings are not assigned for very general or vague topics such as mankind, fate, belief, malaise, etc. Examples include:

Title: *Henry V* / edited by John Crowther. c2004.
SUBJECTS:
Henry V, King of England, 1387-1422–Drama.
Great Britain–History–Henry V, 1413-1422–Drama.
Genre/Form:
Historical drama.

Title: *Old money* / Wendy Wasserstein. c2002.
SUBJECTS:
Manhattan (New York, N.Y.)–Drama.
Social classes–Drama.
Rich people–Drama.

Title: *Raising the dead* / Ron Rash. c2002.
SUBJECTS:
Appalachian Region, Southern–Poetry.
Loss (Psychology)–Poetry.
North Carolina–Poetry.
Mountain life–Poetry.

Title: *Itch like crazy* / Wendy Rose. c2002.
SUBJECTS:
Family–Poetry.
Racially mixed people–Poetry.
Indians of North America–Poetry.

For individual works of fiction, topical headings are assigned, according to established policy, to biographical fiction, historical fiction, and animal stories only.[7]

(a) For biographical fiction, examples include:

Title: *Clara* / Janice Galloway. [2003]
SUBJECTS:
Schumann, Clara, 1819-1896–Fiction.
Schumann, Robert, 1810-1856–Fiction.
Composers' spouses–Fiction.
Women composers–Fiction.
Composers–Fiction.
Pianists–Fiction.
Germany–Fiction.
Genre/Form:
Biographical fiction.
Historical fiction.
Musical fiction.

Title: *Sequoyah* / Robert J. Conley. c2002.
SUBJECTS:
Sequoyah, 1770?-1843–Fiction.
Cherokee Indians–Fiction.
Kings and rulers–Fiction.
Genre/Form:
Biographical fiction.

Title: *The virtues of war : a novel of Alexander the Great* / Steven Pressfield. 2004.
SUBJECTS:
Alexander, the Great, 356-323 B.C.–Fiction.
Greece–History–Macedonian Expansion, 359-323 B.C.–Fiction.
Genre/Form:
Biographical fiction.
War stories.

Title: *Mr. Lincoln's wars : a novel in thirteen stories* / Adam Braver. c2003.
SUBJECTS:
Lincoln, Abraham, 1809-1865–Fiction.
United States–History–Civil War, 1861-1865–Fiction.
Historical fiction, American.
War stories, American.
Presidents–Fiction.

Title: *The impending storm : a novel* / by Ron Carter. c2003.
SUBJECTS:
United States–History–Revolution, 1775-1783–Fiction.
Washington, George, 1732-1799–Fiction.
Genre/form:
Historical fiction.
War stories.

(b) A heading representing the specific historical event or period with the subdivision **–Fiction** is assigned to a historical novel or story. The term "historical fiction" is defined "broadly to include works about entities such as movements, corporate bodies other than jurisdictions, camps, parks, structures, geographical features other than regions, ethnic groups, disasters, categories of events, etc."[8] Examples include:

Title: *Under fire* / W.E.B. Griffin. c2002.
SUBJECTS:
United States–History, Military–20th century–Fiction.
United States. Marine Corps–Fiction.
Korean War, 1950-1953–Fiction.

Genre/Form:
Historical fiction.
War stories.

Title: *Up country* / Nelson DeMille. 2002.
SUBJECTS:
Vietnamese Conflict, 1961-1975–Fiction.
Government investigators–Fiction.
Americans–Vietnam–Fiction.
Vietnam–Fiction.
Genre/Form:
Mystery fiction.
War stories.

According to LC policy, the topical heading is not assigned when the event or period is merely the backdrop to the actual story; it is assigned only when the event or period is the principal focus of the work. In practice, however, since 2001, in an attempt to provide assistance to the average public library user in selecting recreational reading, catalogers are encouraged to assign additional headings to individual fiction.[9] As a result, the following categories of headings are often added by catalogers for enhanced subject access to selected works of individual fiction:

Headings for individual character(s) and classes of persons
Setting
Topical access
Genre or form headings from LCSH or from the *Guidelines on Subject Access to Individual Works of Fiction, Drama, Etc.*

Title: *High water* / Lynn Hightower. 2002.
SUBJECTS:
Beaufort (S.C.)–Fiction.
Genre/Form:
Domestic fiction.
Mystery fiction.

Title: *Nanny diaries : a novel* / Emma McLaughlin and Nicola Kraus. 2002.
SUBJECTS:
Manhattan (New York, N.Y.)–Fiction.
Park Avenue (New York, N.Y.)–Fiction.
Rich people–Fiction.
Nannies–Fiction.
Genre/Form:
Humorous fiction.
Satire.

Title: *Remnant : on the brink of Armageddon* / Tim LaHaye, Jerry B. Jenkins. c2002.
SUBJECTS:
Steele, Rayford (Fictitious character)–Fiction.
Rapture (Christian eschatology)–Fiction.
Armageddon–Fiction.
Genre/Form:
Christian fiction.
Fantasy fiction.

Title: *Everything is illuminated : a novel* / Jonathan Safran Foer. 2002.
SUBJECTS:
Americans–Ukraine–Fiction.
World War, 1939-1945–Ukraine–Fiction.
Jewish families–Fiction.
Grandfathers–Fiction.
Novelists–Fiction.
Young men–Fiction.
Ukraine–Fiction.
Genre/Form:
Humorous fiction.
Domestic fiction.
Bildungsromans.
Jewish fiction.

(c) For a fictional work about animals in general or about a particular kind of animal,[10] a heading in the form of **Animals–Fiction** or **[Kind of animal]–Fiction** is assigned:

Title: *Unhappy Appy* / Dandi Daley Mackall. c2003.
SUBJECTS:
Horses–Fiction.
Teenage girls–Fiction.
Genre/Form:
Young adult fiction.
Religious fiction.

Medieval Legends and Romances[11]

To literary versions of legendary tales, including individual works and collections in prose, verse, or dramatic form, headings designating the dominant character or motif, with the form subdivision **–Legends** or **–Romances**, are assigned. Additional headings appropriate for folklore materials or for individual works of drama, fiction, or poetry may also be assigned.

The subdivision **–Legends** is used under names of individual persons, legendary characters, and uniform titles of sacred works, as well as under religious topics for collected or individual literary versions of legendary tales, including sagas, about them.[12]

Nicholas, Saint, Bp. of Myra–Legends
Grail–Legends

The subdivision **–Romances** is used under names of individual persons and legendary characters for texts of medieval (i.e. pre-1501) European tales based chiefly on legends of chivalric love and adventure in which these persons or characters are the dominant characters.

Charlemagne (Romances , etc.)
Arthurian romances
{an exception to the usual form, which would be *Arthur, King–Romances*}
Lancelot (Legendary character)–Romances

Examples of medieval legends and romances include:

Title: *The seven champions of Christendom : 1596-7* / Richard Johnson ; [edited by] Jennifer Fellows. 2004.
SUBJECTS:
Christian saints–Legends–Early works to 1800.

Title: *The Lancelot-Grail reader : selections from the medieval French Arthurian cycle* / Norris J. Lacy, editor. 2000.
SUBJECTS:
Lancelot (Legendary character)–Romances.
French prose literature–To 1500–Translations into English.
Arthurian romances.

Title: *German romance* / edited and translated by Michael Resler. 2003-
SUBJECTS:
German poetry–Middle High German, 1050-1500–Translations into English.
Romances, German–Translations into English.
Arthurian romances.

The same headings and subdivisions assigned to medieval legends and romances are also used for modern versions (after 1501) of legends and romances, provided that the characters and plots are essentially unaltered from their original.

Title: *Sir Gawain and the Green Knight* / retold in modern prose, with prefaces and notes, by Jessie L. Weston. 2003.
SUBJECTS:
Gawain (Legendary character)–Romances.
Arthurian romances.
{*not* Arthur, King–Poetry}

Title: *The song of Roland* / Anonymous ; [translated into English verse by Leonard Bacon]. 2002.
SUBJECTS:
Roland (Legendary character)–Romances.
Epic poetry, French–Translations into English.
Knights and knighthood–Poetry.

Modern versions of legends and romances that have been altered to the extent that they are no longer recognizable as a retelling of their medieval origins are treated as literary works. The subdivisions **–Fiction**, **–Drama**, and **–Poetry** are used as they normally would be for works of this kind written after 1501. Examples include:

Title: *Idylls of the king and a selection of poems* / Alfred, Lord Tennyson ; with a new introduction by Glenn Everett. [2003]
SUBJECTS:
Arthur, King–Poetry.
Arthurian romances–Adaptations.
Knights and knighthood–Poetry.

Title: *A kind of travelling : the Grail quest retold* / Philippa Craig. c2001.
SUBJECTS:
Grail–Fiction.
Arthurian romances–Adaptations.
Christian fiction, English.
Fantasy fiction, English.

Works about Literature

Works about literature in general, exclusive of those about individual authors and their works (see discussion below), are assigned headings that represent their subject content:

Title: *Reference guide to world literature* / editors, Sara Pendergast, Tom Pendergast. 2003.
SUBJECTS:
Literature–History and criticism.

Title: *Attributing authorship : an introduction* / Harold Love. 2002.
SUBJECTS:
Authorship, Disputed.
Style, Literary.
Language and languages–Style.

Title: *Essay on the tragic* / Peter Szondi ; translated by Paul Fleming. 2002.
SUBJECTS:
Tragic, The.
Tragedy–History and criticism.

Title: *Literary theory, an anthology* / edited by Julie Rivkin and Michael Ryan. 2nd ed. 2004.
SUBJECTS:
Literature–Philosophy.
Literature–History and criticism–Theory, etc.

If the work focuses on a particular literature or genre, one or more literary genre headings, with the subdivision **–History and criticism** or another appropriate subdivision to show that it is a work about literature rather than a collection of texts, are assigned:

Title: *Chinese literature : overview and bibliography* / James L. Claren (editor). c2002.
SUBJECTS:
Chinese literature–Bibliography.
Chinese literature–History and criticism.

Title: *Perspectives on Restoration drama* / Susan J. Owen. 2002.
SUBJECTS:
English drama–Restoration, 1660-1700–History and criticism.

Title: *African-American poets : Robert Hayden through Rita Dove* / edited and with an introduction by Harold Bloom. 2003.
SUBJECTS:
American poetry–African American authors–History and criticism.
American poetry–20th century–History and criticism.
African Americans–Intellectual life–20th century.
African Americans in literature.

Title: *Science fiction from Wells to Heinlein* / Leon Stover. c2002.
SUBJECTS:
Science fiction, English–History and criticism.
Science fiction, American–History and criticism.

The subdivision **–History and criticism** may be further subdivided:

Title: *American literary studies : a methodological reader* / edited by Michael A. Elliott and Claudia Stokes. c2003.
SUBJECTS:
American literature–History and criticism–Theory, etc.

Title: *Reference guide to science fiction, fantasy, and horror* / Michael Burgess, Lisa R. Bartle. 2002.
SUBJECTS:
Science fiction–Reference books–Bibliography.
Science fiction–History and criticism–Bibliography.
Fantasy fiction–Reference books–Bibliography.
Fantasy fiction–History and criticism–Bibliography.

Horror tales–Reference books–Bibliography.
Horror tales–History and criticism–Bibliography.

As noted earlier, the heading **English literature** serves as the pattern heading for subdivisions that may be used under headings for individual literatures and under genres of those literatures, for example, **Swedish literature**; **French drama**; **German essays**; **Epic poetry, Finnish**; **Short stories, Chinese**.

Frequently, when a work deals with a minor form of a particular period, but the relevant literary genre heading has no provision for chronological subdivisions, a second, broader heading with the appropriate chronological subdivision is also assigned:

Title: *Approaches to comedy in German drama* / Gillian Pye. c2002.
SUBJECTS:
German drama (Comedy)–History and criticism.
German drama–20th century–History and criticism.
Theater–Germany–History–20th century.

For discussions about particular themes with regard to a particular literature and/or form, paired headings are assigned:

[Literary genre heading]–History and criticism
[Topic] in literature {as established; no longer free-floating}

Title: *Shifting ground : reinventing landscape in modern American poetry* / Bonnie Costello. 2003.
SUBJECTS:
American poetry–20th century–History and criticism.
Landscape in literature.

Title: *Sleuthing ethnicity : the detective in multiethnic crime fiction* / edited by Dorothea Fischer-Hornung and Monika Mueller. 2003.
SUBJECTS:
Detective and mystery stories, American–History and criticism.
American fiction–Minority authors–History and criticism.
Detective and mystery stories–History and criticism.
Ethnic groups in literature.
Minorities in literature.
Crime in literature.

Title: *African-American literature* : *an overview and bibliography* / Paul Q. Tilden. 2003.
SUBJECTS:
American literature–African American authors–History and criticism.
American literature–African American authors–Bibliography.
African Americans–Intellectual life–Bibliography.
African Americans in literature–Bibliography.

African Americans–Intellectual life.
African Americans in literature.

For discussions of the theme of wars in literature, the headings assigned are in the form of **[Name of war or event]–Literature and the war, [revolution etc.]**:

Title: *The unwritten war : American writers and the Civil War* / by Daniel Aaron. 2003.
SUBJECTS:
American literature–19th century–History and criticism.
United States–History–Civil War, 1861-1865–Literature and the war.
American literature–20th century–History and criticism.
War and literature–United States.
War in literature.

A heading that combines form and topic may also be subdivided by **–History and criticism**, for example, **Detective and mystery stories, American–History and criticism**; **War stories–History and criticism**. An example is:

Title: *At home, at war : domesticity and World War I in American literature* / Jennifer Haytock. 2003.
SUBJECTS:
American fiction–20th century–History and criticism.
World War, 1914-1918–United States–Literature and the war.
Domestic fiction, American–History and criticism.
War stories, American–History and criticism.
War in literature.
Home in literature.

For a work that discusses the portrayal of a person (including literary authors) or place in literature, a heading in the form of **[Name of person** or **place]–In literature** is assigned in addition to one or more literary genre headings:

Title: *Plotting early modern London : new essays on Jacobean city comedy* / editors, Dieter Mehl, Angela Stock, Anne-Julia Zwierlein. c2004.
SUBJECTS:
English drama–17th century–History and criticism.
English drama (Comedy)–History and criticism.
City and town life in literature.
London (England)–In literature.

Title: *Representing Elizabeth in Stuart England : literature, history, sovereignty* / John Watkins. 2002.
SUBJECTS:
English literature–Early modern, 1500-1700–History and criticism.
Elizabeth I, Queen of England, 1533-1603–In literature.

Literature and history–Great Britain–History–17th century.
Great Britain–History–Elizabeth, 1558-1603–Historiography.
Monarchy–Great Britain–History–16th century–Historiography.
Elizabeth I, Queen of England, 1533-1603.
England–Intellectual life–17th century.
Monarchy in literature.
Queens in literature.

Works about Medieval Legends and Romances

The history and criticism of medieval legends and romances[13] in general, as well as the indexes, concordances, etc., to them, requires a heading representing legends or romances subdivided by **–History and criticism**; **–Concordances**; **–Indexes**, or whatever other subdivision is appropriate. In addition, appropriate literary genre headings with similar subdivisions are also assigned:

Title: *The Holy Grail : imagination and belief* / Richard Barber. 2004.
SUBJECTS:
Grail–Legends–History and criticism.

Title: *The misadventure of Francis of Assisi : toward a historical use of the Franciscan legends* / Jacques Dalarun ; translated from the Italian by Edward Hagman. 2002.
SUBJECTS:
Francis, of Assisi, Saint, 1182-1226–Legends–History and criticism.

Title: *Adapting the Arthurian legends for children : essays on Arthurian juvenalia* / edited by Barbara Tepa Lupack. 2004.
SUBJECTS:
Arthurian romances–Adaptations–History and criticism.
Children's literature, English–History and criticism.
Children's literature, American–History and criticism.
Children–Books and reading–English-speaking countries.

Title: *Arthurian romance : a short introduction* / Derek Pearsall. 2003.
SUBJECTS:
Arthurian romances–History and criticism.

If the work focuses on a specific character rather than on the legend or romance, the heading for the character without literary form subdivision is assigned.

Works about Individual Authors

Works about individual authors and/or their works are assigned headings in the form of the name of the author with the subdivision **–Criticism and interpretation** or another, more specific subdivision from the list of free-floating subdivisions for names of persons.[14] Topical headings are assigned to bring out themes, style, characters, and other aspects of the author's works. (For works about an individual literary work, see the discussion in the next section.) Examples include:

Title: *Walt Whitman* / edited and with an introduction by Harold Bloom. c2003.
SUBJECTS:
Whitman, Walt, 1819-1892–Criticism and interpretation.

Title: *Witness to the journey : James Baldwin's later fiction* / Lynn Orilla Scott. c2002.
SUBJECTS:
Baldwin, James, 1924-–Criticism and interpretation.
African Americans in literature.

Title: *The Cambridge companion to James Joyce* / [edited by] Derek Attridge. 2nd ed. 2004.
SUBJECTS:
Joyce, James, 1882-1941–Criticism and interpretation–Handbooks, manuals, etc.
Ireland–In literature–Handbooks, manuals, etc.

Title: *Grave concerns, trickster turns : the novels of Louis Owens* / Chris LaLonde. c2002.
SUBJECTS:
Owens, Louis–Criticism and interpretation.
Tricksters in literature.
Indians in literature.

Title: *Jane Austen* / edited and with an introduction by Harold Bloom. 2003.
SUBJECTS:
Austen, Jane, 1775-1817–Criticism and interpretation.
Women and literature–England–History–19th century.

Title: *Dickens dictionary : a key to the characters and places in the books of Charles Dickens* / by Alex J. Philip and the staff of Research & Education Association ; Carl Fuchs, chief editor. c2002.
SUBJECTS:
Dickens, Charles, 1812-1870–Dictionaries.
Dickens, Charles, 1812-1870–Characters–Dictionaries.
Dickens, Charles, 1812-1870–Settings–Dictionaries.

Title: *Poetry as prayer : Gerard Manley Hopkins* / by Maria Lichtmann ; artwork by Douglas Bertanzetti. c2002.
SUBJECTS:
Hopkins, Gerard Manley, 1844-1889–Criticism and interpretation.
Christian poetry, English–History and criticism.

Hopkins, Gerard Manley, 1844-1889–Religion.
Catholics–England–Intellectual life.
Sonnets, English–History and criticism.
Prayer in literature.

Title: *War and the works of J.R.R. Tolkien* / Janet Brennan Croft. 2004.
SUBJECTS:
Tolkien, J. R. R. (John Ronald Reuel), 1892-1973–Criticism and interpretation.
Literature and history–Great Britain–History–20th century.
Tolkien, J. R. R. (John Ronald Reuel), 1892-1973–Knowledge–History.
Fantasy literature, English–History and criticism.
Middle Earth (Imaginary place)
War in literature.

Title: *The language and craft of William Barnes, English poet and philologist, 1801-1886* / Frances Austin and Bernard Jones. c2002.
SUBJECTS:
Barnes, William, 1801-1886–Language.
Dialect poetry, English–England–Dorset–History and criticism.
Barnes, William, 1801-1886–Technique.
English language–Versification.
Dorset (England)–In literature.

Title: *Reading Shakespeare's poems in early modern England* / Sasha Roberts. 2002.
SUBJECTS:
Shakespeare, William, 1564-1616–Poetic works.
Shakespeare, William, 1564-1616–Criticism and interpretation–History–17th century.
Transmission of texts–England–History–17th century.
Authors and readers–England–History–17th century.
Shakespeare, William, 1564-1616–Criticism, Textual.
Narrative poetry, English–Criticism, Textual.
Sonnets, English–Criticism, Textual.

For an author who has more than one established heading because he or she writes under various names, the heading that serves as the "base heading," that is, the heading that has the complete set of references in the name authority record, is used as the subject headings for works about the author. In the following example, the heading for Mark Twain is used instead of the heading for Samuel Langhorne Clemens (Mark Twain's real name):

Title: *Searching for Jim : slavery in Sam Clemens's world* / Terrell Dempsey. c2003.
SUBJECTS:
Twain, Mark, 1835-1910–Political and social views.
Twain, Mark, 1835-1910–Homes and haunts–Missouri–Hannibal.
Twain, Mark, 1835-1910–Family.
Literature and society–United States–History–19th century.
Antislavery movements–United States–History–19th century.
Slavery–Missouri–Hannibal–History–19th century.
Slavery–United States–History–19th century.
Authors, American–19th century–Biography.
Slavery in literature.
Racism in literature.
Hannibal (Mo.)–Intellectual life–19th century.
Hannibal (Mo.)–Social conditions.

If, in addition to criticism of the author's literary efforts, at least 50 percent of the work contains biographical information, two headings are assigned: the name of the author without subdivision, and a class-of-persons heading:[15]

Title: *J.R.R. Tolkien : his life and works* / Stanley P. Baldwin. c2003.
SUBJECTS:
Tolkien, J. R. R. (John Ronald Reuel), 1892-1973.
Fantasy literature, English–History and criticism.
Authors, English–20th century–Biography.
Middle Earth (Imaginary place)

To a true biography of a literary author, two headings are assigned: the name of the author with an appropriate subdivision (excluding the subdivision **–Biography**, which is not used under headings for persons except for Shakespeare) and one or more class-of-persons headings:

Title: *Isak Dinesen : gothic storyteller* / Roger Leslie. c2004.
SUBJECTS:
Dinesen, Isak, 1885-1962–Juvenile literature.
Women authors, Danish–20th century–Biography–Juvenile literature.

Title: *Sylvia Plath : a literary life* / Linda Wagner-Martin. 2003.
SUBJECTS:
Plath, Sylvia.
Poets, American–20th century–Biography.

Title: *Hemingway : the grace and the pressure* / Aubrey Dillon-Malone. 2002.
SUBJECTS:
Hemingway, Ernest, 1899-1961.
Authors, American–20th century–Biography.
Journalists–United States–Biography.

In the case of a biography in a special form or on a special aspect or theme, the required headings specified above with appropriate subdivisions and any additional appropriate headings are assigned:

Title: *My wars are laid away in books : the life of Emily Dickinson* / Alfred Habegger. c2001.
SUBJECTS:
Dickinson, Emily, 1830-1886.
Poets, American–19th century–Biography.
Women and literature–United States–History–19th century.

Title: *Amy Lowell, American modern* / edited by Adrienne Munich and Melissa Bradshaw. c2004.
SUBJECTS:
Lowell, Amy, 1874-1925.
Women and literature–United States–History–20th century.
Poets, American–20th century–Biography.
Imagist poetry–History and criticism.
Modernism (Literature)–United States.

Works about Individual Literary Works

For a work about an individual literary work, a **[Name. Title]** or **[Uniform title]** heading is used. Except for special forms such as **Children's poetry,** literary genre headings such as **American poetry** or **German drama** are not assigned to works about individual works. In addition, the author's name with the subdivision **–Criticism and interpretation** is sometimes also assigned.

Title: *Thomas Mann's Death in Venice : a reference guide* / Ellis Shookman. 2004.
SUBJECTS:
Mann, Thomas, 1875-1955. Tod in Venedig.
Mann, Thomas, 1875-1955–Criticism and interpretation.

Title: *Gabriel García Márquez's One hundred years of solitude : [essays]* / edited and with an introduction by Harold Bloom. 2003.
SUBJECTS:
García Márquez, Gabriel, 1928- Cien años de soledad.
García Márquez, Gabriel, 1928--Criticism and interpretation.

For a work about an individual literary work with special themes, additional headings designating the themes are assigned:

Title: *Upton Sinclair's The jungle* / edited and with an introduction by Harold Bloom. c2002.
SUBJECTS:
Sinclair, Upton, 1878-1968. Jungle.

Political fiction, American–History and criticism.
Chicago (Ill.)–In literature.
Working class in literature.
Immigrants in literature.

Title: *Ernest Hemingway's A farewell to arms : a reference guide* / Linda Wagner-Martin. 2003.
SUBJECTS:
Hemingway, Ernest, 1899-1961. Farewell to arms.
World War, 1914-1918–United States–Literature and the war.
War stories, American–History and criticism.

Title: *Stephen King's The dark tower : a concordance* / Robin Furth ; introduction by Stephen King. c2003.
SUBJECTS:
King, Stephen, 1947- Dark tower–Concordances.
Fantasy fiction, American–Concordances.
Roland (Fictitious character)

Title: *Homeric variations on a lament by Briseis* / Casey Dube. c2002.
SUBJECTS:
Homer. Iliad.
Briseis (Legendary character)
Homer–Characters–Briseis.
Epic poetry, Greek–History and criticism.
Women and literature–Greece.
Women and literature–Rome.

If a work contains both a text and commentaries, subject headings appropriate for both are assigned.

Title: *Ajax* / Sophocles ; a new translation and commentary by Shomit Dutta ; introduction to the Greek theatre by P.E. Easterling. 2001.
SUBJECTS:
Sophocles. Ajax.
Ajax (Greek mythology)–Drama.

The **[Name. Title]** heading may be subdivided by those subdivisions authorized for use under subjects in general, for example, **–Bibliography**; **–Periodicals**, etc., and those authorized for use under individual works, for example, **–Concordances**; **–Sources**, etc., listed in H1095 of the *Subject Cataloging Manual: Subject Headings*.

Title: *Jane Austen's pride and prejudice* / text by William Blanchard ; illustrations by Richard Fortunato. c2002.
SUBJECTS:
Austen, Jane, 1775-1817. Pride and prejudice–Examinations–Study guides.

Title: *CliffNotes on Twain's The adventures of Huckleberry Finn* / by Robert Bruce. 2000.
SUBJECTS:
Twain, Mark, 1835-1910. Adventures of Huckleberry Finn–Examinations–Study guides.
Finn, Huckleberry (Fictitious character)

In addition, the following free-floating subdivisions may also be used with a **[Name. Title]** heading:[16]

–Criticism, Textual
–Illustrations
–Pictorial works

Examples include:

Title: *F. Scott Fitzgerald's Tender is the night : a documentary volume*/ edited by Matthew J. Bruccoli and George Parker Anderson. c2003.
SUBJECTS:
Fitzgerald, F. Scott (Francis Scott), 1896-1940. Tender is the night.
Fitzgerald, F. Scott (Francis Scott), 1896-1940. Tender is the night–Criticism, Textual.

Title: *Who reads Ulysses? : the rhetoric of the Joyce wars and the common reader* / Julie Sloan Brannon. 2003.
SUBJECTS:
Joyce, James, 1882-1941. Ulysses–Criticism, Textual.
Joyce, James, 1882-1941–Criticism and interpretation–History–20th century.
Authors and readers–History–20th century.
Criticism, Textual–History–20th century.
Books and reading–History–20th century.

If the original work is entered under title, as in the case of anonymous or multi-authored works, the subject entry consists of the uniform title:

Title: *The Arabian nights encyclopedia* / by Ulrich Marzolph and Richard van Leeuwen ; with the collaboration of Hassan Wassouf ; with fourteen introductory essays by internationally renowned specialists. 2004.
SUBJECTS:
Arabian nights.

The **[Uniform title]** heading may be subdivided by those subdivisions authorized for use under subjects in general, for example, **–Bibliography**; **–Periodicals**, etc., and those authorized for use under individual works, for example, **–Concordances**; **–Sources**, etc., listed in H1095 of the *Subject Cataloging Manual: Subject Headings*. In addition, the following free-floating subdivisions may also be used with a **[Uniform title]** heading:[17]

–Adaptations
–Appreciation
–Authorship
–Characters
–Criticism, Textual
–Dramatic production
–Illustrations
–Language
–Language–Glossaries, etc.
–Parodies, imitations, etc.
–Style
–Translations
–Translations–History and criticism
–Translations into French, [German, etc.]
–Translations into French, [German, etc.]–History and criticism
–Versification

Title: *The metre of Beowulf : a constraint-based approach* / by Michael Getty. 2002.
SUBJECTS:
Beowulf–Versification.
English language–Old English, ca. 450-1100–Versification.
English language–Old English, ca. 450-1100–Rhythm.

The subdivision **–Criticism and interpretation** is not used under name-title or uniform title heading for a literary work. For a work of general criticism and interpretation, or a discussion combining the approaches represented by several of these subdivisions, the name-title or uniform title heading for the literary work without subdivision is assigned. If another aspect of the work not represented in the lists is to be brought out, a separate heading is assigned in addition to the name-title or uniform title heading:

Title: *Paradise lost, 1668-1968 : three centuries of commentary* / Earl Miner, editor ; William Moeck, co-editor ; Steven Jablonski, corresponding editor. 2003.
SUBJECTS:
Milton, John, 1608-1674. Paradise lost.

Religious poetry, English–Early modern, 1500-1700–History and criticism.
Epic poetry, English–History and criticism.
Adam (Biblical figure)–In literature.
Eve (Biblical figure)–In literature.
Fall of man in literature.

For an index to a literary work, the following types of headings are used:

[Name. Title]–Indexes
[Uniform title]–Indexes

An example is:

Title: *Plutarch Moralia : index* / compiled by Edward N. O'Neil. 2004.
SUBJECTS:
Plutarch. Moralia–Indexes.
Ethics, Ancient–Indexes.

Works about Individual Medieval Legends and Romances[18]

To a work that discusses a single legend or romance, or a specific version of it, two headings are assigned: the heading for the specific legend or romance (i.e., the uniform title or the name-title entry) and the genre heading assigned to the texts subdivided by **–History and criticism** or another appropriate subdivision such as **–Concordances** or **–Indexes**:

Title: *A companion to Gottfried von Strassburg's Tristan* / edited by Will Hasty. c2003.
SUBJECTS:
Gottfried, von Strassburg, 13th cent. Tristan.
Tristan (Legendary character)–Romances–History and criticism.
Arthurian romances–History and criticism.

Title: *Le morte Darthur, or, The hoole book of Kyng Arthur and of his noble knyghtes of the Rounde Table : authoritative text, sources and backgrounds, criticism* / Sir Thomas Malory ; edited by Stephen H.A. Shepherd. 2004.
SUBJECTS:
Malory, Thomas, Sir, 15th cent. Morte d'Arthur.
Arthurian romances.
Arthurian romances–History and criticism.
Knights and knighthood in literature.
Kings and rulers in literature.

Title: *Wolfram's Parzival : on the genesis of its poetry* / Marianne Wynn. 2003.

SUBJECTS:

Wolfram, von Eschenbach, 12th cent. Parzival.
Perceval (Legendary character)–Romances–History and criticism.
Arthurian romances–History and criticism.
Knights and knighthood in literature.

Title: *The artistry & tradition of Tennyson's battle poetry* / by J. Timothy Lovelace. 2003.

SUBJECTS:

Tennyson, Alfred Tennyson, Baron, 1809-1892–Knowledge–Military art and science.
Tennyson, Alfred Tennyson, Baron, 1809-1892. Idylls of the king.
Tennyson, Alfred Tennyson, Baron, 1809-1892. Maud.
Classicism–England–History–19th century.
Military art and science in literature.
English poetry–Greek influences.
Battles in literature.
Homer–Influence.

Title: *The song of Roland, on absolutes and relative values* / Marianne J. Ailes. c2002.

SUBJECTS:

Chanson de Roland.
Christianity in literature.
Ethics in literature.
Roland (Legendary character)–Romances–History and criticism.
Roncesvalles, Battle of, Spain, 778, in literature.
Epic poetry, French–History and criticism.

MUSIC

Types of Headings

Various types of headings are used in the subject cataloging of music. Some represent music in general; others indicate various kinds or aspects of music such as musical forms and genres, types of compositions, medium of performance, style, function, music for special seasons or occasions, musical settings of special texts, etc.

Detailed instructions regarding music headings and their application are give in *Subject Cataloging Manual: Subject Headings.*[19] Following is a brief summary with examples illustrating current LC policies and practice regarding subject headings applied to music.

Music Headings

Previously, separate terms had been established for some forms and types of musical compositions to be used for works about those forms or types and for the compositions themselves, for example, **Sonata** (as a chamber music form) and **Sonatas** (for the compositions); **Church music** (for works about the compositions) and **Sacred music** (for the compositions). Many of these have been changed by canceling the separate topical form. However, separate headings that represent very large files (such as **Symphony** and **Symphonies**; **Opera** and **Operas;** and **Sonata** and **Sonatas)** are retained and continue to be used. As a result, the cataloger must check the subject authority records to determine the correct forms of the headings.[20]

In the past, almost all music headings were printed in *Library of Congress Subject Headings*. In the mid-1970s, the Library established standard citation patterns for headings for musical compositions that include medium of performance. With certain exceptions such as headings that require specific cross references or unique subdivisions, authority records are no longer made for music form/genre headings that include medium of performance. As a result, many valid LC headings for music are not enumerated in LCSH. By category, these are:

- Headings for compositions not in a specific form or of a specific type, qualified by instrumental medium, for example:

  Trios
  Brass trios
  Wind trios
  Woodwind trios
  Quartets
  String quartets
  Quintets
  Etc.

- Headings for musical forms that take qualifiers for instrumental medium, for example:

  Canons, fugues, etc.
  Chorale preludes
  Marches
  Overtures
  Overtures (String quartet), Arranged
  Passacaglias
  Sacred monologues with music
  Sonatas
  Symphonic poems
  Symphonies
  Etc.

- Certain headings for vocal music, for example:

Choruses
Choruses, Sacred } {qualified by number of vocal parts and accompanying medium}
Choruses, Secular

When the headings contain solo instruments, the specified order of instruments is:[21]

(1) keyboard instruments
(2) wind instruments
(3) plucked instruments
(4) percussion, electronic, and other instruments
(5) bowed stringed instruments
(6) unspecified instruments
(7) continuo

Instruments within each category are given in alphabetical order, with the exception of bowed string instruments, which are given in score order, high to low, for example, (**Violin**, **viola**, **violoncello**, **double bass**). The order is based on the range of each instrument as described in standard music reference sources. No more than nine instrumental soloists are listed in a heading. If the group contains more than nine soloists, the appropriate heading containing the term "**ensemble**" is used.

The number of each instrument, if more than one, is indicated by a number (written in Arabic numerals) enclosed in parentheses following the name of the instrument. However, the number of percussion players is not indicated.

Following are examples of headings formulated according to the established citation patterns:

Wind quintets (Bassoon, clarinet, flute, horn, oboe)
Concertos (Organs (2), violins (2) with string orchestra)
Suites (Instrumental ensemble)
Trios (Piano, flute, violoncello)
Trios (Bassoon, flute, harp)
Brass nonets (Trombones (4), trumpets (4), tuba)
Nonets (Bassoon, clarinet, horn, oboe, violins (2), viola, violoncello, double bass)
Octets (Harpsichord, flutes (2), theorbo, violins (2), viola da gamba, double bass)
Octets (Piano, clarinet, flute, horn, percussion, violin, viola, violoncello)
Octets (Piano, English horn, oboe, trombone, percussion, viola, violoncello, double bass)
Overtures (Horn, trombone, trumpets (2), tuba)
Quartets (Harpsichord, flute, oboe, violoncello)
Sonatas (Viola da gamba and harpsichord)
String quintets (Violins (2), violas (2), violoncello)

Suites (Brass band)
Suites (Chamber orchestra)
Suites (Violins (2), viola, violoncello, double bass)
Choruses, Sacred (Mixed voices, 8 parts) with continuo

Headings for duets do not always follow the same citation order. All headings for duets are enumerated in LCSH because USE references from the alternative form are required. Catalogers should consult LCSH for these headings.

Free-Floating Phrase Headings

The phrase heading **[Medium** or **form/genre for instrumental music], Arranged** is free-floating with instrumental music headings that indicate medium of performance, for example, **Guitar music, Arranged**; **Overtures (Band), Arranged**; **Wind ensembles, Arranged**; **Percussion and piano music, Arranged**. Its use is much more restricted with vocal music headings. For arranged excerpts, the free-floating subdivision **–Excerpts, Arranged** is used.

Free-Floating Subdivisions under Pattern Headings

Operas, **Piano**, and **Clarinet** have been designated as pattern headings for subdivisions in the field of music. The heading **Operas**[22] provides the pattern for musical compositions, including musical forms and types of compositions, medium of performance, style, function, music for special seasons or occasions, musical settings of special texts, etc., for example, **Concertos (Piano)**; **Trios (Piano, flute, violin)**; **Rock music**; **Easter music**; **Magnificat (Music)**. However, the free-floating subdivisions listed under **Operas** are not applicable to the general heading **Music**.

The headings **Piano** and **Clarinet**[23] together serve as the pattern for musical instruments, either specific instruments or families of instruments, for example, **Flute**; **Wind instruments**. The free-floating subdivisions listed under **Piano** are not applicable to the general heading **Musical instruments**.

Chronological Subdivisions[24]

The following chronological subdivisions are free-floating under headings for musical compositions:

–To 500
–500-1400
–15th century
–16th century
–17th century
–18th century
–19th century

–20th century
–21st century

Chronological subdivisions are used for collections of musical works and for topical materials when chronological focus is stated or implied in the title or series statement of the item being cataloged. They are not used for (1) jazz and popular music, (2) folk or non-Western music, (3) collections of compositions by only one composer, (3) individual musical works, or (4) following the subdivisions **–Hymns**; **–Music**; **–Musical settings**; and **–Songs and music**. Under headings for popular music, chronological subdivisions are individually established in LCSH, for example, **Jazz–1941-1950**.

The chronological subdivision is placed after the geographic subdivision and before other free-floating subdivisions:

Dramatic music–Italy–17th century–History and criticism
Instrumental music–England–17th century
Music–France–19th century–History and criticism
Songs, English–England–16th century
Songs, English–England–16th century–Texts–History and criticism
Songs, German–Germany–15th century

Non-Music Topical Headings with Subdivisions Indicating Music

In addition to the music headings discussed above, other topical headings with music subdivisions are also used in cataloging music. Examples of such headings are:

Civil rights movements–Songs and music
Dickinson, Emily, 1830-1886–Musical settings
Hanukkah–Songs and music
Mormon Church–United States–Hymns
Railroads–Songs and music
United States–History–Civil War, 1861-1865–Songs and music

Application

Works in the field of music may be divided into two broad categories: (1) music scores and texts and (2) works about music. As in the field of literature, specimens and works *about* the subject are treated differently in subject cataloging.

Music Scores and Texts

Works containing scores and texts, including instrumental and vocal music, are assigned genre headings (i.e., headings that describe what the works *are* rather than what the works are *about*) as appropriate.

Instrumental Music

For instrumental music, subject headings bring out the following aspects: musical form (e.g., **Canons, fugues, etc.**; **Overtures**; **Sonatas**; **Symphonies**), medium of performance (e.g., **Guitar music**; **Hu qin music**; **Piano music**), and performing group (e.g., **Trios**; **Octets**; **String quartets**; and **Woodwind septets**) are chamber music headings that indicate the number of solo instruments. **String quartets** and **Woodwind septets** also represent the medium of performance in terms of the family of instruments. Sometimes it is appropriate to specify the instruments in the family. **Band music** and **Orchestral music** are medium-of-performance headings for types of larger ensembles. Other topical headings with music subdivisions are also assigned as appropriate. Examples include:

Title: *The library of piano duets* / editor, Amy Appleby. c2001.
SUBJECTS:
Piano music (4 hands)
Piano music (4 hands), Arranged.

Title: *Fantasia : A dialogue with wind : for flute/piccolo, oboe, Bb bass clarinet/clarinet, violin, viola, cello, harp, and percussion* / Kui Dong. 2003.
SUBJECTS:
Nonets (Clarinet, flute, oboe, harp, percussion, violin, viola, violoncello, double bass)–Scores and parts.

Title: *Tours de force ; Nel cor più non mi sento ; Duo for violin solo* / Niccolo Paganini ; edited by Yair Kless. 2001.
SUBJECTS:
Variations (Violin)
Sonatas (Violin)
Violin–Studies and exercises.

Title: *LaUt De MiLa : Viola solo, 1992/93* / Mela Meierhans. c2002.
SUBJECTS:
Viola music.

Title: *Andalusia : bolero brillant, op. 159, per arpa* / Karl Oberthür ; a cura di Anna Pasetti. c2002.
SUBJECTS:
Harp music.

Boleros (Music)
Andalusia (Spain)–Songs and music.

Title: *Concertate il suono : pour orchestre* / Marc-André Dalbavie. c2002.
SUBJECTS:
Concerti grossi–Scores.

Title: *Konzert für Trompete und Orchester = Concerto for trumpet and orchestra* / Jürgen Buttkewitz ; Ausgabe für Trompete und Piano eingerichtet vom Komponisten. c2001.
SUBJECTS:
Concertos (Trumpet)–Solo with piano.

Title: *Marching to Carcassonne : serenade for piano and 12 instruments, op. 75 (2002)* / Alexander Goehr. c2003.
SUBJECTS:
Suites (Piano with instrumental ensemble)–Scores.

Title: *Mizar : für Ensemble, 1996/97, 2001* / Knut Müller. c2002.
SUBJECTS:
Octets (Piano, clarinet, flute, oboe, violins (2), viola, violoncello) –Scores.
Mizar–Songs and music.

Title: *Floctet : for 8-part flute choir* / by Matt Doran. c2002.
SUBJECTS:
Woodwind octets (Flutes (8))–Scores and parts.
Flute choir music–Scores and parts.

Title: *Cello counterpoint* / Steve Reich. 2003.
SUBJECTS:
String octets (Violoncellos (8))–Scores.

Title: *Light the first light of evening : [for chamber orchestra]* / Augusta Read Thomas. c2002.
SUBJECTS:
Chamber orchestra music–Scores.

Vocal Music

For vocal music, headings that bring out the form, voice range, number of vocal parts, and accompanying medium are used. The medium is not specified for larger works such as operas, oratorios, etc.

Following are terms for vocal range and the types of voices for each range:

High voice: soprano, counter tenor, tenor
Medium voice: mezzo-soprano, baritone
Low voice: alto, contralto, bass

Typical headings for vocal music are:

- Secular vocal music

  Ballads, English
  Cantatas, Secular (Unison)
  Choruses, Secular (Women's voices)
  Madrigals
  Operas
  Part songs, English
  Songs
  {also headings for various kinds of songs, e.g., **Children's songs**; **War songs**}
  Songs (High voice) with chamber orchestra
  Vocal duets with instrumental ensemble
  Vocal trios with piano

- Sacred vocal music

  Cantatas, Sacred (Women's voices)
  Carols
  Chants
  Chorales
  Choruses, Sacred (Mixed voices, 4 parts) with organ
  Choruses, Secular (Men's voices, 4 parts), Unaccompanied
  Hymns
  Masses
  Motets
  Oratorios
  Part songs, Sacred
  Psalms (Music)
  Requiems (Unison)–Vocal scores with organ
  Sacred songs (Medium voice) with harpsichord
  Solo cantatas
  Vespers (Music)

Following are examples of subject headings assigned to works containing vocal music:

Title: *Giuseppe Verdi : le prime : libretti della prima rappresentazione = premieres : librettos of the premieres.* c2002.
SUBJECTS:
Operas–Librettos.

Title: *All rise : for symphony orchestra, jazz orchestra, and chorus /* Wynton Marsalis. 2002.
SUBJECTS:
Choruses, Secular (Mixed voices) with orchestra–Scores.
Jazz.

Title: *The songs of Richard Rodgers : high voice /* edited by Richard Walters ; Bryan Stanley, assistant editor. [2002?]
SUBJECTS:
Musicals–Excerpts–Vocal scores with piano.
Songs (High voice) with piano.

Title: *The complete art songs of Franz Lehár = Sämtliche Kunstlieder.* 2002-
SUBJECTS:
Songs with piano.
Song cycles.
Vocal duets with piano.

Title: *Serenades and songs for voice and guitar /* Mozart and Schubert ; [transcribed and edited by] Allen Krantz. c2002.
SUBJECTS:
Songs (High voice) with guitar.

Title: *Let freedom ring : [14 patriotic favorites /* arranged by Phillip Keveren]. c2002.
SUBJECTS:
Piano music, Arranged.
Patriotic music–United States.

Whenever appropriate, topical headings with music subdivisions are assigned in addition to the music headings discussed above.

Title: *A Blake triptych : for upper voices and piano /* Andrew Carter. c2002.
SUBJECTS:
Blake, William, 1757-1827–Musical settings.
Choruses, Secular (Women's voices, 3 parts) with piano.

Title: *The new Oxford easy anthem book : a collection of 63 anthems for the church's year.* 2002.
SUBJECTS:
Anthems.
Choruses, Sacred (Mixed voices, 4 parts) with organ.
Choruses, Sacred (Mixed voices, 4 parts), Unaccompanied.
Church year–Songs and music.

Title: *Arachne : a dramatic song cycle for solo soprano with crotale /* words by Jordan Smith ; music by Hilary Tann. c2002.
SUBJECTS:
Song cycles.
Songs (High voice) with crotale.
Arachne (Greek mythology)–Songs and music.
Smith, Jordan, 1954--Musical settings.

Title: *The faith we sing* / [Hoyt L. Hickman, general editor]. c2000.
SUBJECTS:
United Methodist Church (U.S.)–Hymns.
Hymns, English–United States.
Methodist Church–Hymns.

Sound Recordings

Sound recordings of music are treated in the same manner as other musical works. No special subdivisions are used to bring out the format, except for recordings for children, for which the subdivision **–Juvenile sound recordings** is used:

Title: *Concertos and chamber music* [sound recording] / Graun. p2002.
SUBJECTS:
Concertos (Harpsichord with string orchestra)
Trio sonatas (Flute, oboe, continuo)
Sonatas (Flute and continuo)
Quartets (Oboe d'amore, violins (2), continuo)

Title: *Charlie Barnet and his orchestra, 1939* [sound recording]. [2002]
SUBJECTS:
Jazz–1931-1940.
Saxophone music (Jazz)

Title: *In concert* [sound recording]. [2001]
SUBJECTS:
Sonatas (Piano)
Waltzes.
Piano music, Arranged.
Piano music.

Title: *Romantic tenors* [sound recording] / José Carreras ; Plácido Domingo ; Luciano Pavarotti. p2002.
SUBJECTS:
Songs (High voice) with orchestra.
Operas–Excerpts.

Title: *Prelude* [sound recording] : *the best of Charlotte Church.* p2002.
SUBJECTS:
Songs (High voice) with orchestra.
Popular music–1991-2000.
Popular music–2001-2010.

Title: *2002 New Year's concert* [sound recording] = *Neujahrskonzert.* p2002.
SUBJECTS:
Overtures.
Waltzes.
Marches (Orchestra)
Polkas.
Orchestral music.

Title: *Kidtunes* [sound recording]. p2002.
SUBJECTS:
Children's songs–Juvenile sound recordings.
Popular music.

Title: *Wild & wacky totally true Bible stories* [sound recording] : *all about angels.* 2002.
SUBJECTS:
Angels–Biblical teaching–Juvenile sound recordings.
Bible stories, English.

If the recording contains works in more than one form, separate headings are assigned to represent the forms of individual works:

Title: *Five* [sound recording] / Michael Dellaira. [2002]
SUBJECTS:
Dickinson, Emily, 1830-1886–Musical settings.
Howard, Richard, 1929--Musical settings.
Operas–Excerpts.
Choruses, Secular (Mixed voices), Unaccompanied.
Orchestral music.
Choruses, Secular (Mixed voices) with orchestra.
Song cycles.
Songs (Medium voice) with piano.

Dance Music

A work containing music for a specific dance form is assigned a heading for the name of the dance form. Previously, headings for dance forms were qualified with names of instruments when appropriate. Currently, headings for dance forms are no longer qualified by names of instruments. Additional headings may be assigned for the medium and other aspects or topics.

Title: *Polonaise brillante : opus 3, for string bass and piano* / Chopin ; [transcribed and edited by] Mark Bernat. c2002.
SUBJECTS:
Double bass and piano music, Arranged–Scores and parts.
Polonaises.

Title: *Lullaby waltz* / composed by Bob Curnow. c2002.
SUBJECTS:
Waltzes.
Piano with band–Scores.

Title: *Collection de différentes danses : op. 6, für Klavier, Flöte und Violine* / Friedrich Wieck ; bearbeitet und herausgegeben von Eckart Haupt. c2002.
SUBJECTS:
Trios (Piano, flute, violin)–Scores and parts.
Dance music.

Music of Ethnic and National Groups[25]

The following types of headings are assigned to works that consist of or discuss the music of ethnic groups, music that has a national emphasis, religious music of certain groups, and non-Western art music:

[Ethnic or national group]–[Place]–Music [or **Songs and music]**
[Heading(s) for music of individual religious group(s)–[Place]
[Heading(s) for musical genre, type, or style, for ballads and songs, or for songs with national emphasis]
[Heading(s) qualified by language of text]
Musical instruments–[Place]
[Other topical headings, as applicable]

Headings in the first three categories are assigned to musical works; the others are assigned as appropriate. Examples include:

Title: *Midnight in Madrid* [sound recording] *: the pulse of new flamenco* / Chuscales. p2001.
SUBJECTS:
Flamenco music.
Guitar music (Flamenco)
Popular instrumental music–Spain–2001-2010.

Title: *The Huron carol* / by Father Jean de Brebeuf ; illustrated by Frances Tyrrell. 2003.
SUBJECTS:
Jesus Christ–Nativity–Songs and music.
Wyandot Indians–Songs and music.

Carols.
Christmas music.

For works consisting of ballads, folk songs, children's songs, or songs of ethnic groups, headings for the particular musical form qualified by the original language of the text are assigned.

Title: *Fairytale* [sound recording] / Donovan. 2002.
SUBJECTS:
Folk songs, English.
Popular music–1961-1970.

Title: *Folk song lullabies* [sound recording] / by Phil Rosenthal & family. p2001.
SUBJECTS:
Lullabies.
Folk songs, English.

Title: *The Petrie collection of the ancient music of Ireland* / edited by David Cooper ; Irish modernized and edited by Lillis Ó Laoire. c2002.
SUBJECTS:
Folk music–Ireland.
Folk dance music–Ireland.
Folk songs, Irish–Ireland.
Folk music–Ireland–History and criticism.

Jazz and Popular Music[26]

The following types of headings are assigned to jazz music:

Jazz–[Place]–[Chronological subdivision]
[Instrument] music (Jazz)
(Headings of the type **Trumpet with jazz ensemble** or **Concertos (Piano and saxophone with jazz ensemble)**
[Specific genre or **style of jazz] music**
Jazz vocals

The following types of headings are assigned to popular music:

Popular music {for works consisting of vocal popular music only or of both vocal and instrumental popular music}
Popular instrumental music {for works consisting of instrumental popular music only}

Under headings where special chronological subdivisions have been established in LCSH, these subdivisions are used instead of the free-floating chronological subdivisions under music headings in general.

Title: *In full swing* [sound recording] / Mark O'Connor's Hot Swing Trio. p2003.
SUBJECTS:
Swing (Music)
Jazz–2001-2010.
Jazz vocals.

Title: *Charlie Barnet and his orchestra, 1939* [sound recording]. [2002]
SUBJECTS:
Jazz–1931-1940.
Saxophone music (Jazz)

Title: *100 years of popular music. 30s : piano/vocal/chords.* c2003.
SUBJECTS:
Popular music–1931-1940.

Title: *The original guitar hero* [sound recording] / Charlie Christian. p2002.
SUBJECTS:
Jazz–1931-1940.
Jazz–1941-1950.

Title: *Disney's Superstar hits* [sound recording]. p2002.
SUBJECTS:
Motion picture music–Excerpts.
Rock music–1991-2000.
Rock music–2001-2010.
Popular music–1991-2000.
Popular music–2001-2010.

Works about Music

Works about music are assigned topical headings that reflect the subject content of the works. The subdivision **–Instruction and study** is used with headings for musical compositions and instruments instead of **–Study and teaching**, and **–History and criticism** is used instead of **–History** for musical compositions except under the heading **Operas**.[27] Following are examples of works about music:

Title: *Analyzing popular music* / edited by Allan F. Moore 2003.
SUBJECTS:
Popular music–Analysis, appreciation.
Popular music–History and criticism.
Musical analysis.

Title: *A history of music in Western culture* / Mark Evan Bonds. c2003.
SUBJECTS:
Music–History and criticism.

Title: *Russian folk songs : musical genres and history* / Vadim Prokhorov. 2002.
SUBJECTS:
Folk songs, Russian–Russia (Federation)–History and criticism.
Folk music–Russia (Federation)–History and criticism.

Title: *The symphonic repertoire* / A. Peter Brown.
SUBJECTS:
Symphony.
Symphonies–Analysis, appreciation.

Title: *Guide to chamber music* / Melvin Berger. 3rd, corr. ed. c2001.
SUBJECTS:
Chamber music–History and criticism.
Chamber music–Analysis, appreciation.

Title: *Motives for allusion : context and content in nineteenth-century music* / Christopher Alan Reynolds. 2003.
SUBJECTS:
Quotation in music.
Music–19th century–History and criticism.

Title: *"With one heart and one voice" : a core repertory of hymn tunes published for use in the Methodist Episcopal Church in the United States, 1808-1878* / Fred Kimball Graham. c2004.
SUBJECTS:
Methodist Church–United States–Hymns–History and criticism.
Hymn tunes–History and criticism.
Hymns, English–United States–19th century–History and criticism.

Title: *A guide to piano music by women composers* / Pamela Youngdahl Dees. 2002.
SUBJECTS:
Piano music–Bibliography.
Music by women composers–Bio-bibliography.

Title: *Woodwinds : fundamental performance techniques* / Gene A. Saucier. c2002.
SUBJECTS:
Woodwind instruments–Instruction and study.

Title: *The Cambridge companion to blues and gospel music* / edited by Allan Moore. 2002.
SUBJECTS:
Blues (Music)
Gospel music.
Blues (Music)–Analysis, appreciation.
Gospel music–Analysis, appreciation.

Title: *Opera for libraries : a guide to core works, audio and video recordings, books and serials* / Clyde T. McCants. c2003.
SUBJECTS:
Operas–Bibliography.
Operas–Discography.
Music libraries–Collection development.

Title: *An orchestra conductor's guide to repertoire and programming* / Richard Eldon Yaklich. c2003.
SUBJECTS:
Orchestral music–Bibliography.

Title: *The Broadway musical : a critical and musical survey* / Joseph P. Swain. 2nd ed., rev. and expanded. 2002.
SUBJECTS:
Musicals–United States–History and criticism.

Works about the Music of Ethnic, National, and Religious Groups

Works about the music of ethnic and national groups, and about their musical instruments, are assigned the same headings that are used for the music itself, with the addition of subdivisions such as **–Bibliography**; **–Discography**; **–History and criticism**. However, the subdivision **–History** is used under the heading **Musical instruments** and headings for specific musical instruments. Examples of works about the music of ethnic, national, and religious groups are:

Title: *The trouble I've seen : the big book of Negro spirituals* / Bruno Cheny ; translated from the French by Eugene V. LaPlante. 2003.
SUBJECTS:
Spirituals (Songs)–History and criticism.
African-Americans–Music–History and criticism.

Title: *Music of El Dorado : the ethnomusicology of ancient South American cultures* / Dale A. Olsen. c2002.
SUBJECTS:
Indians of South America–Music–History and criticism.
Musical instruments, Ancient–South America.
Ethnomusicology–South America.

Title: *Anthology of Bulgarian folk musicians* / Todor Bakalov. 2002.
SUBJECTS:
Folk musicians–Bulgaria–Biography.
Folk music–Bulgaria–History and criticism.

Title: *The British folk revival, 1944-2002* / Michael Brocken. 2003.
SUBJECTS:
Folk music–Great Britain–History and criticism.
Popular music–Great Britain–History and criticism.

Title: *Holy brotherhood : Romani music in a Hungarian Pentecostal church* / Barbara Rose Lange. 2003.
SUBJECTS:
Isten Gyülekezet (Pécs, Hungary)
Romanies–Hungary–Pécs–Music–History and criticism.
Pentecostals–Hungary–Pécs–Hymns–History and criticism.
Pentecostals–Hungary–History.
Pentecostals–United States–History.
Romanies–Hungary–Religion.
Hungary–Ethnic relations.

Works about Individual Composers and Musicians

Personal name headings and class-of-persons headings are assigned to works about the lives, or lives and works, of individual composers or musicians, in accordance with the general guidelines for biography (see the discussion of biography in chapter 9):

Title: *George Gershwin : a new biography* / by William G. Hyland. 2003.
SUBJECTS:
Gershwin, George, 1898-1937.
Composers–United States–Biography.

Title: *John Lennon imagined : cultural history of a rock star* / Janne Mäkelä. 2003.
SUBJECTS:
Lennon, John, 1940-1980.
Rock musicians–England–Biography.
Beatles.
Fame–Social aspects.

Title: *The sound of their music : the story of Rodgers & Hammerstein* / by Frederick Nolan. c2002.
SUBJECTS:
Rodgers, Richard, 1902-
Hammerstein, Oscar, 1895-1960.
Composers–United States–Biography.
Librettists–United States–Biography.

Title: *Loretta Lynn : still woman enough : a memoir* / Loretta Lynn ; with Patsi Bale Cox. c2002.
SUBJECTS:
Lynn, Loretta.
Country musicians–United States–Biography.

Headings for names of musicians and composers may be subdivided by the free-floating subdivisions used under names of persons. (A list of these free-floating subdivisions is given in appendix C.)

Title: *Beethoven : the music and the life* / Lewis Lockwood. c2003.
SUBJECTS:
Beethoven, Ludwig van, 1770-1827.
Beethoven, Ludwig van, 1770-1827–Criticism and interpretation.
Composers–Austria–Biography.

Title: *Mozart : il genio giovane* / Alberto Conforti. 2001.
SUBJECTS:
Mozart, Wolfgang Amadeus, 1756-1791.
Mozart, Wolfgang Amadeus, 1756-1791–Pictorial works.
Composers–Austria–Biography.

Title: *Elvis, America the beautiful* / [compiled by] Joseph A. Tunzi. c2002.
SUBJECTS:
Presley, Elvis, 1935-1977–Portraits.
Rock musicians–United States–Portraits.

Title: *Letters to Melanie Köchert* / Hugo Wolf. 2003.
SUBJECTS:
Wolf, Hugo, 1860-1903–Correspondence.
Köchert, Melanie.
Composers–Austria–Correspondence.

The personal name heading subdivided by **–Criticism and interpretation** is assigned to comprehensive discussions or criticism of a composer's works.[28]

Title: *Bach performance practice, 1945-1975 : a comprehensive review of sound recordings and literature* / Dorottya Fabian. 2002.
SUBJECTS:
Bach, Johann Sebastian, 1685-1750–Criticism and interpretation.
Performance practice (Music)–20th century.

Title: *Something to live for : the music of Billy Strayhorn* / Walter van de Leur. 2002.
SUBJECTS:
Strayhorn, Billy–Criticism and interpretation.

Other free-floating subdivisions used under headings for composers include:

–Appreciation
–Discography
–Dramaturgy
–Harmony
–Influence
–Performances
–Sources
–Stories, plots, etc.
–Symbolism
–Thematic catalogs
{used under composers for listings of the themes of their musical compositions}
–Written works

Examples are:

Title: *Peter Schickele : a bio-bibliography* / by Tammy Ravas. 2004.
SUBJECTS:
Schickele, Peter–Bibliography.
Schickele, Peter–Discography.

Title: *The Tchaikovsky handbook : a guide to the man and his music* / compiled by Alexander Poznansky and Brett Langston. c2002.
SUBJECTS:
Tchaikovsky, Peter Ilich, 1840-1893–Bibliography.
Tchaikovsky, Peter Ilich, 1840-1893–Thematic catalogs.

If the work does not pertain to the personal life of the composer or musician, the heading **[Class of persons]–Biography** is not assigned:

Title: *The Cambridge companion to Mozart* / edited by Simon P. Keefe. 2003.
SUBJECTS:
Mozart, Wolfgang Amadeus, 1756-1791–Criticism and interpretation.

Title: *The Richard Strauss companion* / edited by Mark-Daniel Schmid. 2003.
SUBJECTS:
Strauss, Richard, 1864-1949–Criticism and interpretation.

Title: *Giuseppe Verdi und seine Zeit* / Markus Engelhardt (Hg.). c2001.
SUBJECTS:
Verdi, Giuseppe, 1813-1901–Criticism and interpretation.

Works about Individual Musical Works[29]

Name-title headings are assigned to works about individual musical compositions. Other music or topical headings are assigned as appropriate:

Title: *Shostakovich: String quartet no. 8* / David Fanning. 2004.
SUBJECTS:
Shostakovich, Dmitrii Dmitrievich, 1906-1975. Quartets, strings, no. 8, op. 110, C minor.
String quartets–Analysis, appreciation.

Title: *The magic flute = Die Zauberflöte : an alchemical allegory* / by M.F.M. van den Berk. 2003.
SUBJECTS:
Mozart, Wolfgang Amadeus, 1756-1791. Zauberflöte.
Mozart, Wolfgang Amadeus, 1756-1791–Symbolism.
Music and magic.
Alchemy in literature.

Title: *Tempo in the soprano arias of Puccini's La Boheme, Tosca, and Madame Butterfly* / Mei Zhong. c2002.
SUBJECTS:
Puccini, Giacomo, 1858-1924. Boheme.
Puccini, Giacomo, 1858-1924. Tosca.
Puccini, Giacomo, 1858-1924. Madama Butterfly.
Tempo (Music)
Operas–Interpretation (Phrasing, dynamics, etc.)

Title: *A simple twist of fate : Bob Dylan and the making of Blood on the tracks* / Andy Gill & Kevin Odegard. 2004.
SUBJECTS:
Dylan, Bob, 1941- Blood on the tracks.
Dylan, Bob, 1941-

For a work about the compositions by one composer in a specific form or medium, a heading in the form of **[Name of composer. Subheading]** is used:

Title: *Mozart's piano concertos* / John Irving. c2003.
SUBJECTS:
Mozart, Wolfgang Amadeus, 1756-1791. Concertos, piano, orchestra.
Concertos (Piano)–History and criticism.

Title: *Symphonic metamorphoses : subjectivity and alienation in Mahler's re-cycled songs* / Raymond Knapp. c2003.
SUBJECTS:
Mahler, Gustav, 1860-1911. Symphonies.
Mahler, Gustav, 1860-1911. Songs.

Subjectivity in music.
Alienation (Philosophy)
Quotation in music.

Title: *Playing the Beethoven piano sonatas* / Robert Taub. 2002.
SUBJECTS:
Beethoven, Ludwig van, 1770-1827. Sonatas, piano.
Sonatas (Piano)–Analysis, appreciation.

Title: *Schubert's Goethe settings* / Lorraine Byrne. c2003.
SUBJECTS:
Schubert, Franz, 1797-1828. Songs.
Goethe, Johann Wolfgang von, 1749-1832.
Songs, German–19th century–History and criticism.
Songs with piano–19th century–History and criticism.
Music and literature.

Title: *Schubert's late Lieder : beyond the song-cycles* / Susan Youens. 2002.
SUBJECTS:
Schubert, Franz, 1797-1828. Songs.
Songs, German–19th century–History and criticism.

The subheading used after the name of the composer corresponds to the uniform title used in cataloging the music of individual composers according to *Anglo-American Cataloguing Rules*, second edition, 2002 revision (*AACR2R*).[30] Examples of authorized subheadings used in subject cataloging include:

- Subheadings for general and specific mediums of performance

Brass music
Chamber music
Choral music
Instrumental music
Keyboard music
Orchestra music
Piano music, 4 hands
Piano music, pianos (2)
String quartet music
Violin, piano music
Vocal music

- Subheadings for types of compositions with qualifiers for medium, as appropriate

Concertos
Operas
Overtures

Polonaises, piano
Quartets, strings
Sonatas
Sonatas, violin, piano
Songs
Symphonies

FINE ART[31]

The heading **Art** represents fine art (i.e., "those art forms whose primary characteristic is beauty rather than practical use") collectively as well as visual arts (a collective term for fine art, architecture, and the decorative arts). On the other hand, the heading **Arts** represents a broader concept encompassing visual arts, literature, and the performing arts.

The following discussion focuses on the treatment of fine art.

Types of Headings

The following types of subject headings are assigned to represent various topics or aspects of art:

[Name of artist or **Group of artists]**
[Art form with national, regional, ethnic, or **religious qualifier]–[Place of origin]–[Period subdivision]**
[Art form with period qualifier]–[Place of origin]
[Style, movement, etc.]–[Place of origin]
[Theme]
[Art form]–[Present location]
[Owner]
[Other headings, as appropriate]

Form subdivisions are not used to bring out the fact that the work consists of photographic reproductions or illustrations of works of art.

Free-Floating Subdivisions

Art, Italian serves as the pattern for free-floating subdivisions, except under **Art, Chinese**; **Art, Japanese**; and **Art, Korean**. The following list shows the free-floating subdivisions used under art headings:[32]

–Appreciation *(May Subd Geog)*
–Attribution
–Catalogs

{For exhibition catalogs, the subdivision **–Exhibitions** rather than **–Catalogs** is used}

–Chronology
–Conservation and restoration *(May Subd Geog)*
–Copying
–Expertising *(May Subd Geog)*
–Foreign influences
{Not valid under period subdivisions}
–Forgeries *(May Subd Geog)*
–Influence
–Reproduction
–Technique
–Themes, motives

The general free-floating subdivisions (see the discussion in chapter 5) may be used with art headings with the exceptions noted in *Subject Cataloging Manual: Subject Headings*. Some of the most commonly used subdivisions under headings for art or artists are:

–Biography
{Free-floating only when used under headings for classes of persons, e.g., **Painters**}
–Collectors and collecting *(May Subd Geog)*
–Exhibitions

Subdivisions under **Art, Chinese**; **Art, Japanese**; and **Art, Korean** are established separately.

Geographic Subdivisions

In art headings, the concept of the place where the art originates is normally expressed by geographic subdivision except when the place is implied in the qualifier for the nationality or the ethnic background of the artists, for example, **Painting, Italian**; **Painting, Japanese**, not *Painting, Italian–Italy; Painting, Japanese–Japan.*

The concept of the location of the art is also represented by geographic subdivisions, for example, **Painting, Italian–Italy–Florence**; **Painting, Japanese–Japan–Tokyo**.

Chronological Subdivisions

The concept of time is often implied in the period qualifier in the main heading, for example, **Art, Ancient**; **Marble sculpture, Medieval**; etc. For other headings, the period is brought out by means of chronological subdivisions, for example:

Art, Modern–20th century
Drawing–18th century
Painting, Modern–19th century
Engraving–14th century

The previous practice of further subdividing the period by place has been discontinued. Since 2001, the facets in art headings conform to the general citation order of **[Topic]–[Place]–[Period]**, for example, **Sculpture, French–France–Burgundy–12th century**.

Chronological subdivisions under **Art, Chinese**; **Art, Japanese**; and **Art, Korean** are editorially established. Catalogers are advised to consult LCSH when considering chronological subdivisions under these headings. Examples include:

Art, Chinese–Tang-Five dynasties, 618-960
Painting, Japanese–Meiji period, 1868-1912

The following chronological subdivisions are free-floating under headings for art and art forms of other nations, regions, and ethnic groups:

–10th century
–11th century
–12th century
–13th century
–14th century
–15th century
–16th century
–17th century
–18th century
–19th century
–20th century
–21st century

Application

Subject headings assigned to works of art, that is, works containing examples of art, and those assigned to works about art (appreciation, history, and criticism) are in the same form. The free-floating subdivision **–History** is used only for art headings assigned to general, all-inclusive items, for example, **Painting– History**. However, it is not used for materials limited to one country nor under form subdivisions such as **–Art**; **–Illustrations**; **–Portraits**; etc. The subdivision **–History and criticism** does not apply to art headings either.[33]

Works of Art and about Art by More Than One Artist Treated Collectively

Works of art by more than one artist and works about such art are assigned headings of the following types:[34]

[Art form], [National, regional, ethnic, or **religious qualifier]–[Place of origin]–[Period subdivision]**
[Art form with period qualifier]–[Place of origin]
[Style, movement, etc.]–[Place of origin]
[Theme]
[Art form]–[Present location]
[Owner]
[Other headings, as appropriate**]**

Examples include:

Title: *Italian Gothic sculpture : c. 1250-c. 1400* / Anita Fiderer Moskowitz. 2001.
SUBJECTS:
Sculpture, Italian.
Sculpture, Gothic–Italy.

Title: *Impressionist cats and dogs : pets in the painting of modern life* / James H. Rubin. c2003.
SUBJECTS:
Cats in art.
Dogs in art.
Painting, French.
Impressionism (Art)–France.

Title: *Monet and the Impressionists for kids : their lives and ideas, 21 activities* / Carol Sabbeth. c2002.
SUBJECTS:
Impressionism (Art)–Juvenile literature.
Art, French–19th century–Juvenile literature.
Impressionist artists–France–Biography–Juvenile literature.

Place in Art[35]

A heading in the form of **[Place]–In art** is assigned to art works with a specific place as a theme and to works discussing the treatment of specific places in art.

Title: *The impressionists' Paris : walking tours of the painters' studios, homes, and the sites they painted* / by Ellen Williams. 2002.
SUBJECTS:
Impressionist artists–Homes and haunts–France–Paris–Guidebooks.

Artists' studios–France–Paris–Guidebooks.
Paris (France)–In art.
Paris (France)–Guidebooks.

Title: *Envisioning New England : treasures from community art museums* / edited by Pamela J. Belanger. 2004.
SUBJECTS:
New England–In art–Exhibitions.
Painting, American–New England–19th century–Exhibitions.
Painting, American–New England–20th century–Exhibitions.
Art museums–New England–Exhibitions.

A heading in the form of **[Place]–Pictorial works** is assigned to works consisting of photographs of a place, or of paintings made before the invention of photography presenting views of a place.

Title: *Wings over the Alaska highway : a photographic history of aviation on the Alaska highway* / Bruce McAllister, Peter Corley-Smith. c2001.
SUBJECTS:
Aeronautics–Alaska–History.
Alaska–Pictorial works.
Alaska Highway–Pictorial works.

Catalogs of Art Museums, Collections, and Exhibitions

For catalogs of art that is permanently housed in or owned by a particular institution the following types of headings are assigned:

[Type of object]–Catalogs
[Type of object]–[Chronological subdivision]–Catalogs
[Type of object]–[Place]–Catalogs
[Name of institution]–Catalogs
[Name of collection]–Catalogs

Examples include:

Title: *Painting and sculpture in the collection of the National Academy of Design* / edited by David B. Dearinger. 2004.
SUBJECTS:
Art, American–19th century–Catalogs.
Art, American–20th century–Catalogs.
Art–New York (State)–New York–Catalogs.
National Academy of Design (U.S.)–Catalogs.
Artists–United States–Biography.

Title: *European sculpture of the nineteenth century* / Ruth Butler, Suzanne G. Lindsay with Alison Luchs ... [et al.]. c2000.

SUBJECTS:

Sculpture, European–19th century–Catalogs.
Sculpture–Washington (D.C.)–Catalogs.
National Gallery of Art (U.S.)–Catalogs.

Title: *The Chinese collection : selected works from the Norton Museum of Art* / John R. Finlay, with essays by Colin Mackenzie and Jenny F. So. c2003.

SUBJECTS:

Art, Chinese–Catalogs.
Art–Florida–West Palm Beach–Catalogs.
Norton Museum of Art–Catalogs.

Title: *Scandinavian glass : creative energies* / by William Geary. c2003.

SUBJECTS:

Glassware–Scandinavia–History–20th century–Catalogs.
Art glass–Scandinavia–History–20th century–Catalogs.

The subdivision **–Exhibitions** is used instead of **–Catalogs** for the catalog of an exhibition. The combination *–Exhibitions–Catalogs* is not valid.

Title: *Envisioning architecture : drawings from the Museum of Modern Art* / Matilda McQuaid ; with an introduction by Terence Riley. c2002.

SUBJECTS:

Architectural drawing–20th century–Exhibitions.
Architectural drawing–New York (State)–New York–Exhibitions.
Museum of Modern Art (New York, N.Y.)–Exhibitions.

Title: *Eye contact : modern American portrait drawings from the National Portrait Gallery* / Wendy Wick Reaves ; with an essay by Bernard F. Reilly Jr. ; and contributions by Ann Prentice Wagner ... [et al.]. c2002.

SUBJECTS:

Portrait drawing, American–20th century–Exhibitions.
United States–Biography–Portraits–Exhibitions.
Portrait drawing–Washington (D.C.)–Exhibitions.
National Portrait Gallery (Smithsonian Institution)–Exhibitions.

Title: *Inverted utopias : the avant-garde in Latin America* / Mari Carmen Ramirez, Hector Olea. 2004.

SUBJECTS:

Art, Latin American–20th century–Exhibitions.
Avant-garde (Aesthetics)–Latin America–History–20th century–Exhibitions.

Title: *The moon has no home : Japanese color woodblock prints from the collection of Virginia Art Museum* / essays by Sandy Kita and Stephen Margulies. 2003.

SUBJECTS:

Ukiyo-e–Exhibitions.
Color prints, Japanese–19th century–Exhibitions.
Prints–Virginia–Charlottesville–Exhibitions.
University of Virginia. Art Museum–Exhibitions.

Title: *Transmitting the forms of divinity : early Buddhist art from Korea and Japan* / Washizuka Hiromitsu, Park Youngbok and Kang Woo-bang. c2003.

SUBJECTS:

Art, Japanese–To 1600–Exhibitions.
Art, Buddhist–Japan–Exhibitions.
Art, Korean–To 935–Exhibitions.
Art, Buddhist–Korea–Exhibitions.

Private Art Collections

For catalogs of private art collections, including those that have been donated or sold to public institutions but are still known by their original names, the following types of headings are used in addition to the headings discussed above.

[Name of owner]–Art collections–Catalogs [or **–Exhibitions]**
[Topical or **genre heading]–Private collections** [or **another appropriate subdivision]–[Place]–Catalogs** [or **–Exhibitions]**

Examples include:

Title: *Coming home : American paintings, 1930/1950, from the Schoen collection* / with an essay by Erika Doss. c2003.

SUBJECTS:

Painting, American–20th century–Exhibitions.
Realism in art–United States–Exhibitions.
National characteristics in art–Exhibitions.
Schoen, Jason, 1958--Art collections–Exhibitions.
Painting–Private collections–California–Exhibitions.

Title: *The changing of the avant-garde : visionary architectural drawings from the Howard Gilman collection* / contributions by Terence Riley ... [et al.]. 2002.

SUBJECTS:

Architectural drawing–20th century–Exhibitions.
Gilman, Howard, 1924-1998–Art collections–Exhibitions.

Architectural drawing–Private collections–New York (State)–New York–Exhibitions.
Visionary architecture.
Museum of Modern Art (New York, N.Y.)–Exhibitions.

Title: *Something all our own : the Grant Hill collection of African American art* / Grant Hill. 2004.
SUBJECTS:
African American art–20th century–Catalogs.
Hill, Grant–Art collections–Catalogs.
Art–Private collections–United States–Catalogs.

Title: *Art and aesthetics in Chinese popular prints : selections from the Muban Foundation collection* / Ellen Johnston Laing. c2002.
SUBJECTS:
Wood-engraving, Chinese–Ming-Qing dynasties, 1368-1912–Catalogs.
Wood-engraving, Chinese–20th century–Catalogs.
Gods in art–Catalogs.
Folk art–China–Catalogs.
Prints–Private collections–England–London–Catalogs.
Muban Foundation–Catalogs.

Works by and about Individual Artists[36]

An individual artist's works (with main entry or added entry under the artist's name) and works about an individual artist's work (with main entry other than the artist) are assigned a heading under the name of the artist regardless of whether it duplicates the main or added entry. The artist's name may be subdivided by the free-floating subdivisions used under names of persons (see appendix C) in order to bring out other aspects of the work. Additional headings are assigned to bring out form, style, period (for discussions of an architect's work), theme, type of art objects, and name of institution or collection where the art works are permanently housed. Examples include:

Title: *William Eggleston* / [curator of the exhibition, Hervbe Chandaes]. 2002.
SUBJECTS:
Eggleston, William, 1939-–Exhibitions.
Photography, Artistic–Exhibitions.

Title: *Rodin's art : the Rodin collection of the Iris & B. Gerald Cantor Center for Visual Arts at Stanford University* / Albert E. Elsen with Rosalyn Frankel Jamison ; edited by Bernard Barryte ; with photography by Frank Wing. 2003.

SUBJECTS:
Rodin, Auguste, 1840-1917–Catalogs.
Sculpture–California–Palo Alto–Catalogs.
Sculpture–Private collections–California–Palo Alto–Catalogs.
Cantor, B. Gerald, 1916-–Art collections–Catalogs.
Cantor, Iris–Art collections–Catalogs.
Iris & B. Gerald Cantor Center for Visual Arts at Stanford University –Catalogs.

Title: *Salvador Dalí* / by Robert Descharnes ; translated by Eleanor R. Morse. c2003.
SUBJECTS:
Dalí, Salvador, 1904-–Criticism and interpretation.
Surrealism in art–Spain.

Title: *Gwen Raverat, wood engraver* / Joanna Selborne and Lindsay Newman. 2003.
SUBJECTS:
Raverat, Gwen, 1885-1957–Criticism and interpretation.
Wood-engraving–England–20th century.

Title: *The visual grammar of Pablo Picasso* / Enrique Mallen. c2004.
SUBJECTS:
Picasso, Pablo, 1881-1973–Criticism and interpretation.
Semiotics and art–France.
Cubism–France.
Visual perception.

Title: *Picasso : the cubist portraits of Fernande Olivier* / Jeffrey Weiss, Valerie J. Fletcher, Kathryn A. Tuma. 2003.
SUBJECTS:
Picasso, Pablo, 1881-1973–Exhibitions.
Picasso, Pablo, 1881-1973–Criticism and interpretation.
Olivier, Fernande–Portraits–Exhibitions.
Cubism–France–Exhibitions.

A biography of an individual artist is assigned a personal name heading without the subdivision **–Biography** and one or more class-of-persons headings:

Title: *Leonardo* / Enrica Crispino. 2002.
SUBJECTS:
Leonardo, da Vinci, 1452-1519.
Artists–Italy–Biography.

Title: *Dalí* / Fiorella Nicosia. 2002.
SUBJECTS:
Dalí, Salvador, 1904-

Artists–Spain–Biography.
Surrealism–Spain.

The class-of-persons heading is not assigned to a work about an artist's works unless the work being cataloged also contains substantial information (at least 20 percent of the text) about the artist's personal life:

Title: *Leonardo da Vinci* / by Jack Wasserman. c2003.
SUBJECTS:
Leonardo, da Vinci, 1452-1519–Criticism and interpretation.

Title: *Auguste Rodin* / Rainer Maria Rilke ; translated from the German by Daniel Slager. 2004.
SUBJECTS:
Rodin, Auguste, 1840-1917–Criticism and interpretation.

Title: *Francisco Goya* / Evan S. Connell. 2004.
SUBJECTS:
Goya, Francisco, 1746-1828.
Goya, Francisco, 1746-1828–Criticism and interpretation.
Artists–Spain–Biography.

Title: *Monet : in the time of the water lilies : the Musée Marmottan Monet collections* / Marianne Delafond and Caroline Genet-Bondeville ; [translation, Judith Hayward]. c2002.
SUBJECTS:
Monet, Claude, 1840-1926–Catalogs.
Painting–France–Paris–Catalogs.
Musée Marmottan–Catalogs.
Monet, Claude, 1840-1926.
Artists–France–Biography.

Works about Individual Works of Art

The following types of headings are assigned to works discussing individual works of art:

[Name of artist. Uniform title of work]
[Uniform title of work]
{for a work by an unknown artist}
[Heading for style, type of art, movement, theme, etc.]

Examples of works about individual works of art include:

Title: *The work of His hands : the agony and the ecstasy of being conformed to the image of Christ* / Ken Gire. c2002.
SUBJECTS:
Spiritual formation.
Michelangelo Buonarroti, 1475-1564. Pietà.

Title: *Mona Lisa : the history of the world's most famous painting* / Donald Sassoon. 2001.
SUBJECTS:
Leonardo, da Vinci, 1452-1519. Mona Lisa.
Leonardo, da Vinci, 1452-1519–Influence.

Title: *Picasso's brothel : les demoiselles d'Avignon* / Wayne Andersen. c2002.
SUBJECTS:
Picasso, Pablo, 1881-1973. Demoiselles d'Avignon.
Picasso, Pablo, 1881-1973–Criticism and interpretation.
Prostitution in art.
Cubism–France.

Title: *Salvador Dalí's Dream of Venus : the surrealist funhouse from the 1939 World's Fair* / Ingrid Schaffner ; photographs by Eric Schaal. c2002.
SUBJECTS:
Dalí, Salvador, 1904- Dream of Venus.
Dalí, Salvador, 1904-–Criticism and interpretation.
Installations (Art)–New York (State)–New York.
Surrealism–Exhibitions.
New York World's Fair (1939-1940)
Schaal, Eric.

Title: *Disarmed : the story of the Venus de Milo* / Greg Curtis. 2003.
SUBJECTS:
Venus de Milo.
Aphrodite (Greek deity)–Art.
Marble sculpture, Greek.
Marble sculpture, Ancient–Greece.
Sculpture–France–Paris.
Musée du Louvre.

RELIGION

Types of Headings

Headings Representing Religions or Religious Concepts[37]

A large number of Library of Congress subject headings represent religions or religious concepts. Some examples are:

Buddhism
Catholic Church
Christianity
Church and state
Church history
Hinduism
Meditation
Muslims
Mysticism
Ordination
Salvation

Many of these headings may be subdivided according to the pattern headings listed below:

Category	*Pattern heading*
Religions	**Buddhism**
Sacred works (including parts)	**Bible**
Christian denominations	**Catholic Church**
Religious and monastic orders	**Jesuits**

There are also a number of headings that may be subdivided by religion and/or denomination. These are established in LCSH by means of "multiple" subdivisions:

Baptism–Anglican Communion, [Catholic Church, etc.]
{may be subdivided by any Christian denomination}
Lord's Supper–Catholic Church, [Presbyterian Church, etc.]
{may be subdivided by any Christian denomination}
Mysticism–Catholic Church, [Orthodox Eastern Church, etc.]
{may be subdivided by any Christian denomination}
Mysticism–Brahmanism, [Judaism, Nestorian Church, etc.]
{may be subdivided by any religion}

Headings for Non-Religious Topics with Religious Aspects[38]

Many non-religious topics are subdivided by the subdivision **–Religious aspects** or **–Mythology** to represent a religious or mythological point of view. These subdivisions are free-floating under specific categories of headings, such as animals, organs of the body, and plants and crops. They may also appear under other types of headings as established. Examples include:

Marriage–Religious aspects
Stars–Mythology

The subdivision **–Religious aspects** may be further subdivided by **–[Religion** or **denomination]** for example:

> **Birth control–Religious aspects–Baptists, [Catholic Church, etc.]**
> **Marriage–Religious aspects–Buddhism, [Christianity, etc.]**

The multiple subdivisions shown above authorize the following headings:

> **Birth control–Religious aspects–Catholic Church**
> **Marriage–Religious aspects–Judaism**

The subdivision **–Religious aspects** is not used under headings for classes of persons or ethnic groups; the subdivision **–Religious life** is used instead.

Application

Works on Religious Topics

Appropriate topical headings are assigned according to the normal procedures for subject cataloging:

Title: *Buddhism : introducing the Buddhist experience* / Donald W. Mitchell. 2002.
SUBJECTS:
Buddhism–History.

Title: *Zen contemplation for Christians* / Elaine MacInnes. c2003.
SUBJECTS:
Zen meditations.
Christianity and other religions–Buddhism.
Buddhism–Relations–Christianity.

Title: *Restoring the ties that bind : the grassroots transformation of the Episcopal Church* / William Sachs and Thomas Holland. 2003.
SUBJECTS:
Episcopal Church.
Episcopalians.

Title: *Catholic theology facing the future : historical perspectives* / edited by Dermot A. Lane. c2003.
SUBJECTS:
Catholic Church–Doctrines–Congresses.
Theology–Congresses.

Title: *Mysticism, Christian and Buddhist* / D.T. Suzuki. 2002.
SUBJECTS:
Mysticism–Comparative studies.
Mysticism–Catholic Church.
Mysticism–Buddhism.

Title: *Encyclopedia of Islam and the Muslim world* / edited by Richard C. Martin. 2003.
SUBJECTS:
Islam–Encyclopedias.

Title: *Islam in Europe* / Jack Goody. 2004.
SUBJECTS:
Islam–Europe.
Muslims–Europe.
East and West.
Terrorism–Religious aspects–Islam.

When a heading of the type **[Topic]–[Church** or **denomination]** is assigned to a work, an additional heading under **[Religion** or **denomination]–[Topical subdivision]** is assigned:

Title: *A practical guide for starting an adult faith formation program* / Richard C. Brown. 2003.
SUBJECTS:
Catholic Church–Adult education.
Catechetics–Catholic Church.
Christian education of adults.

Title: *Signs of freedom : theology of the Christian sacraments* / German Martinez. 2004.
SUBJECTS:
Sacraments–Catholic Church.
Catholic Church–Doctrines.

Geographic subdivisions are not interposed between the topic and the subdivision **–Religious aspects**. An additional heading in the form of **[Topic]–[Place]** is assigned to bring out the geographical aspect.

Works on Non-Religious Topics Treated from a Religious Point of View

When assigning a non-religious topical heading with the subdivision **–Religious aspects**, **–Moral and ethical aspects**, or **–Mythology**, the following guidelines should be observed.

The subdivision **–Religious aspects** is used under headings for non-religious topics for works that discuss the topic from a religious standpoint, that is, how it occurs as a theme in religious beliefs and practices, its importance in religious doctrines, the relationship in general between the topic and religion, etc.:

Title: *Specter of speciesism : Buddhist and Christian views of animals /* Paul Waldau. 2002.
SUBJECTS:
Speciesism–Religious aspects–Buddhism.
Speciesism–Religious aspects.
Animal rights–Environmental aspects.
Animal welfare–Moral and ethical aspects.

Title: *Women's rights : the Quran and Islam /* Lisa Spray. 2002.
SUBJECTS:
Muslim women.
Women's rights–Religious aspects–Islam.
Muslim women–Conduct of life.

Title: *Love the sin : sexual regulation and the limits of religious tolerance /* Janet R. Jakobsen and Ann Pellegrini. c2003.
SUBJECTS:
Homosexuality–Religious aspects–Christianity.
Gay rights–Religious aspects–Christianity.
Homosexuality–Government policy–United States.
Gay rights–United States.

When a heading of the type **[Topic]–Religious aspects–[Name of religion** or **Denomination]** is assigned to a work, an additional heading in the form of **[Religion** or **Denomination]–[Topical subdivision]** is often assigned. The topical subdivisions that may be used under the heading for the religion or denomination, however, are restricted to those under the relevant pattern headings. For this reason, the topic expressed in the **[Religion** or **Denomination]–[Topical subdivision]** headings is often more general than the one expressed in the **[Topic]–Religious aspects** heading:

Title: *A Christian theology of marriage and family /* Julie Hanlon Rubio. c2003.
SUBJECTS:
Marriage–Religious aspects–Catholic Church.
Family–Religious aspects–Catholic Church.
Catholic Church–Doctrines.

Title: *The passionate Buddha : wisdom on intimacy and enduring love /* Robert Sachs. c2002.
SUBJECTS:
Love–Religious aspects–Buddhism.
Interpersonal relations–Religious aspects–Buddhism.
Buddhism–Social aspects.

If the work being cataloged discusses the topic from a moral or ethical standpoint as well as a religious point of view, an additional heading with the subdivision **–Moral and ethical aspects** is assigned:

Title: *At the beginning of life : dilemmas in theological bioethics* / Edwin C. Hui. c2002.
SUBJECTS:
Human reproductive technology–Moral and ethical aspects.
Human reproductive technology–Religious aspects–Christianity.
Abortion–Moral and ethical aspects.
Abortion–Religious aspects–Christianity.
Bioethics.
Christian ethics.

Title: *Birth control for Christians : making wise choices* / Jenell Williams Paris. c2003.
SUBJECTS:
Contraception–Religious aspects–Christianity.
Contraception–Popular works.
Birth control–Moral and ethical aspects.

The subdivision **–Mythology** is used under non-religious or non-ethical topics to represent the topics as themes in mythology. Additional headings may be assigned to bring out types of mythology, for example, **Indian mythology**; **Mythology, Greek**; **Mythology, Japanese**; etc. Example:

Title: *Animales y plantas en la cosmovisión mesoamericana* / Yolotl González Torres, coordinadora. 2001.
SUBJECTS:
Indians of Mexico–Religion.
Mayas–Religion.
Indian mythology–Mexico.
Indian mythology–Central America.
Animals–Mythology.
Plants–Mythology.

If the work discusses the religious implications of the theme in mythology from the standpoint of a particular religion or denomination, an additional heading of the type **[Topic]–Religious aspects–[Religion** or **Denomination]** is assigned. This heading is not necessary unless a particular religion or denomination is involved.

Sacred Scriptures

The Bible

Biblical Texts

Subject headings are not assigned to biblical texts except in the cases listed below. Examples include:

Title: *The English majority text version of the Holy Bible* / translated by Paul W. Esposito. c2003.
{No subject headings}

Title: *The Holy Bible : English Standard Version : the Psalms.* c2003.
{No subject headings}

Title: *The parallel Bible : Hebrew-English Old Testament.* 2003.
{No subject headings}

Exceptions:

(1) *Paraphrases of biblical texts.* Because paraphrases of biblical texts are entered under the name of the paraphraser according to *AACR2R*, subject headings are assigned as follows:

Bible–Paraphrases
{used for texts of paraphrases in two or more languages}
Bible–Paraphrases, English, [French, German, etc.]
{used for texts of paraphrases in a particular language}

Paraphrases of parts of the Bible follow the same pattern, for example, **Bible. O.T. Psalms–Paraphrases, English**. Examples include:

Title: *Essential writings* / Clarence Jordan ; selected with an introduction by Joyce Hollyday. 2003.
SUBJECTS:
Bible. N.T.–Paraphrases, English.
Sermons, American–20th century.
Baptists–Sermons.

(2) *Harmonies.* The pattern for paraphrases of biblical texts is followed for harmonies:

Title: *A simplified harmony of the Gospels* / George Knight. c2001.
SUBJECTS:
Bible. N.T. Gospels–Harmonies, English.

(3) *Translations of early versions.*[39] Because in descriptive cataloging the main entry for the translation of a version of a biblical text is under the uniform title for the Bible containing the name of the modern version but ignoring the

version from which the translation is made, a subject heading of the type **[Uniform title for the early version]–Translations into [name of language]**, for example, **Bible. O.T. Pentateuch. Aramaic. Targum Pseudo-Jonathan–Translations into English**, is assigned to bring out the earlier version. For example:

Title: *The Targum of Psalms* / [introduction, translation, and notes by] David M. Stec. c2004.
SUBJECTS:
Bible. O.T. Psalms. Aramaic. Targum–Translations into English.
Bible. O.T. Psalms. Aramaic–Versions–Targum.
MAIN ENTRY [uniform title]:
[Bible. O.T. Psalms. English. Stec. 2004.]

Works About the Bible[40]

Works about the Bible or its parts receive subject headings in the form of the uniform title used in descriptive cataloging, except that designations for the language, version, and date are omitted. Appropriate subdivisions are added:

Title: *The Bible : a history : the making and impact of the Bible* / Stephen M. Miller & Robert V. Huber. North American ed. 2004.
SUBJECTS:
Bible–History.

Title: *The Bible through metaphor and translation : a cognitive semantic perspective* / Kurt Feyaerts (ed.). c2003.
SUBJECTS:
Bible–Language, style–Congresses.
Metaphor in the Bible–Congresses.
Bible–Translating–Congresses.

Title: *The Bible knowledge key word study : Genesis-Deuteronomy* / editor, Eugene H. Merrill. c2003.
SUBJECTS:
Bible. O.T. Pentateuch–Language, style.
Bible. O.T. Pentateuch–Commentaries.

Title: *Kohelet : a modern commentary* / by Leonard S. Kravitz and Kerry M. Olitzky. 2003.
SUBJECTS:
Bible. O.T. Ecclesiastes–Commentaries.

Title: *1 & 2 Chronicles : from biblical text—to contemporary life* / Andrew E. Hill. c2003.
SUBJECTS:
Bible. O.T. Chronicles–Criticism, interpretation, etc.

Title: *The Epistles of John : an expositional commentary* / James Montgomery Boice. 2004.
SUBJECTS:
Bible. N.T. Epistles of John–Commentaries.

However, if the work is about a particular version or translation of the Bible, it is specifically designated.[41] The following types of headings with appropriate subdivisions are used:

[Uniform title]–Versions [e.g., **Bible–Versions**; **Bible. N.T.–Versions]**
{For general works discussing collectively versions of the Bible}

[Uniform title]–Versions, [Name of language group] [e.g., **Bible–Versions, Slavic]**
{For works discussing collectively the translations of the Bible or its individual parts into a particular language group}

[Uniform title]. [Language of translation]–Versions [e.g., **Bible. English–Versions–Authorized**; **Bible. N.T. Latin–Versions–Vulgate]**
{For works on the translations of the Bible or its individual parts into a particular language}

[Uniform title]–Versions, [Name of denomination] [e.g., **Bible. English–Versions, Baptist]**
{For works about denominational versions}

[Uniform title]. [Language]–Versions–[Name of version]
{For works about particular translations of the Bible}

For example:

Title: *The facts on the King James only debate* / John Ankerberg & John Weldon. [2003?]
SUBJECTS:
Bible. English–Versions–Authorized.

Title: *Truth in translation : accuracy and bias in English translations of the New Testament* / Jason David BeDuhn. 2003.
SUBJECTS:
Bible. N.T.–Criticism, Textual.
Bible. N.T. English–Versions.
Bible. N.T.–Translating.

Title: *The use of the Septuagint in New Testament* / R. Timothy McLay. 2003.
SUBJECTS:
Bible. O.T. Greek–Versions–Septuagint.
Bible. N.T.–Criticism, Textual.
Bible. N.T.–Relation to the Old Testament.

Title: *Consistency of translation techniques in the tabernacle accounts of Exodus in the Old Greek* / Martha Lynn Wade. c2003.
SUBJECTS:
Bible. O.T. Exodus. Greek–Versions–Septuagint.
Bible. O.T. Exodus–Translating.
Tabernacle.

Works about paraphrases of the Bible or its parts are assigned headings such as

Bible–Paraphrases–History and criticism
Bible–Paraphrases, English–History and criticism
Bible. O.T. Psalms–Paraphrases, English–History and criticism

For example:

Title: *The literal sense and the Gospel of John in late-medieval commentary and literature* / Mark Hazard. 2002.
SUBJECTS:
Nicholas, of Lyra, ca. 1270-1349. Postillae perpetuae.
Bible. N.T. John–Commentaries–History and criticism.
Cursor mundi.
Bible–Paraphrases, English (Middle)–History and criticism.
Christian poetry, English (Middle)–History and criticism.

Special themes in the Bible are brought out by headings of the type **[Topic] in the Bible** (not free-floating).

Apocryphal Books

The headings **Apocryphal books**; **Apocryphal books (New Testament)**; **Apocryphal books (Old Testament)**, with appropriate subdivisions, are assigned to works dealing collectively with apocryphal books. Subdivisions follow the patterns established under the Bible:

Apocryphal books–Introductions
Apocryphal books (New Testament)–Commentaries
Apocryphal books (New Testament)–Theology
Apocryphal books (Old Testament)–Criticism, interpretation, etc.

Examples include:

Title: *Lost scriptures : books that did not make it into the New Testament* / [edited by] Bart D. Ehrman. 2003.
SUBJECTS:
Apocryphal books (New Testament)

Title: *Pseudepigrapha of the Old Testament as part of Christian literature : the case of the testaments of the twelve patriarchs and the Greek Life of Adam and Eve* / by M. De Jonge. 2003.
SUBJECTS:
Apocryphal books (Old Testament)–Criticism, interpretation, etc.
Testaments of the Twelve Patriarchs–Criticism, interpretation, etc.
Life of Adam and Eve–Criticism, interpretation, etc.

Other Sacred Scriptures

The heading **Bible** serves as the pattern for subdivisions for other sacred scriptures, for example, **Vedas. Atharvaveda–Criticism, interpretation, etc**.; **Koran–Commentaries**. Examples include:

Title: *Atharaveda-paippalada, kanda five : text, translation, commentary* / Alexander Lubotsky. 2002.
{No subject headings}

Title: *An interpretation of the Qur'an : English translation of the meanings : a bilingual edition* / translated by Majid Fakhry. 2002.
{No subject headings}

Title: *The Babylonian Talmud : a topical guide* / Judith Z. Abrams. 2002.
SUBJECTS:
Talmud–Commentaries.

Title: *Explaining the Qur'an : a socio-scientific inquiry* / Masadul Alam Choudhury. 2003.
SUBJECTS:
Koran–Criticism, interpretation, etc.
Koran–Commentaries.
Koran–Hermeneutics.

Title: *God, goddess the astrologer : soul, karma, and reincarnation : how we continually create our own destiny* / Jeffrey Armstrong. 2001.
SUBJECTS:
Vedas–Criticism, interpretation, etc.
Hindu astrology.

Title: *New dimensions in the Atharvaveda : Prof. K.C. Acharya commemoration volume* / edited by Prafulla K. Mishra. 2003.
SUBJECTS:
Vedas. Atharvaveda–Criticism, interpretation, etc.

Liturgy

The term liturgy refers to services such as prayers, rituals, and ceremonies used in public worship in accordance with the authorized or standard forms of a religion or denomination. Liturgical texts and works about liturgy or about liturgical books are assigned similar headings with different form subdivisions. Examples are given below.

Texts of Liturgy

To a collection of liturgies, an individual liturgy, or a selection from one or more liturgies, one or more headings of the following types are assigned:

[Name of religion, sect, or **Christian denomination]–Liturgy–Texts**
[Name of religion or **sect]–Rituals–Texts**
Judaism–Liturgy–Texts
[Type of liturgical book]–Texts

Examples include:

Title: *The common worship lectionary : New Revised Standard version : common worship Psalter.* 2001.
SUBJECTS:
Church of England–Liturgy–Texts.
Bible–Liturgical lessons, English.
Lectionaries.
Psalters.

Title: *The Sherborne missal* [electronic resource]. c2002.
SUBJECTS:
Sherborne missal.
Illumination of books and manuscripts, Medieval–Facsimiles.
Illumination of books and manuscripts, English–Facsimiles.
Manuscripts, Latin (Medieval and modern)–Facsimiles.
Catholic Church–Liturgy–Texts.

If the work is limited to a particular ceremony, ritual, holiday, etc., an additional heading in the form of **[Type of ceremony,** etc.**]–Liturgy–Texts** is also assigned:

Title: *The Rav Shach Haggadah* / adapted by Yaakov Blinder from the Hebrew Haggadah Kinyan Torah ; compiled by Asher Bergman in association with Shalom Meir Wallach. c2003.
SUBJECTS:
Haggadot–Texts.
Seder–Liturgy–Texts.
Judaism–Liturgy–Texts.
Haggadah.

Title: *The open door : a Passover Haggadah* / edited by Sue Levi Elwell ; art by Ruth Weisberg. 2001.

SUBJECTS:

Haggadot–Texts.
Seder–Liturgy–Texts.
Reform Judaism–Liturgy–Texts.

Works about Liturgy

A heading of the type **Judaism–Liturgy** or **[Name of Christian denomination]–Liturgy** is assigned to a general work about Judaistic liturgy or the liturgy of a particular Christian denomination. The subdivision **–Liturgy** may be further subdivided by other free-floating form subdivisions.

Title: *The Orthodox Jewish woman and ritual : options and opportunities* / [edited by Jennifer Breger and Lisa Schlaff]. [2000?-]

SUBJECTS:

Jewish women–Religious life.
Orthodox Judaism–Customs and practices.
Women–Legal status, laws, etc. (Jewish law)
Women in Judaism.
Judaism–Liturgy.

Title: *Welcome to Sunday : an introduction to worship in the Episcopal Church* / Christopher L. Webber. c2003.

SUBJECTS:

Public worship–Episcopal Church.
Episcopal Church–Liturgy.

Title: *Acolyte leader's resource guide* / Donna H. Barthle. c2003.

SUBJECTS:

Acolytes–Episcopal Church.
Episcopal Church–Liturgy.

For a work discussing the liturgy of a particular ceremony, ritual, holiday, etc., headings of the following types are assigned:

[Name of religion or **denomination]–Liturgy**
[Type of ceremony, etc.**]–[Name of religion** or **denomination]**

Examples include:

Title: *The psalms of the Tamid service : a liturgical text from the Second Temple* / by Peter Trudinger. 2003.

SUBJECTS:

Tamid psalms–Commentaries.
Tamid.
Judaism–Liturgy.

Temple of Jerusalem (Jerusalem)
Judaism–History–Post-exilic period, 586 B.C.-210 A.D.

Title: *The reform of baptism and confirmation in American Lutheranism /* Jeffrey A. Truscott. 2003.
SUBJECTS:
Lutheran Church–United States–Liturgy.
Baptism–Lutheran Church.
Confirmation–Lutheran Church.

Works about Liturgical Books

For a work about a type of liturgy or individual liturgical texts, one or more headings of the following types are used:

Judaism–Liturgy–Texts–History and criticism
[Name of Christian denomination]–Liturgy–Texts–History and criticism
[Type of liturgy]
[Type of ceremony, ritual, holiday, etc.]
[Uniform title of the individual liturgy]

Examples include:

Title: *The structure of the High Holiday services /* Stephen R. Schach. c2002.
SUBJECTS:
Mahzor. High Holidays.
High Holidays–Liturgy–Outlines, syllabi, etc.
Judaism–Liturgy–Outlines, syllabi, etc.

Title: *What think you of Christ? : meditations on the daily mass scriptures /* by John A. Marshall. 2003.
SUBJECTS:
Church year meditations.
Catholic Church–Liturgy–Meditatons.

Title: *Celebration! : reflections on the Divine and Holy liturgy /* by Archbishop Joseph Raya. c2003.
SUBJECTS:
Catholic Church. Liturgy of Saint John Chrysostom.
Catholic Church–Byzantine rite–Liturgy–Texts–History and criticism.

Title: *Words in threes : discovering meaning, discerning direction, deepening faith through exploration of the Liturgy /* Nancy Dering Martin. 2003.
SUBJECTS:
Episcopal Church. Book of common prayer.
Bible–Devotional use.

Title: *Focus on the prayer book facilitator guide : discovering meaning, discerning direction, deepening faith through exploration of the liturgy* / Nancy Dering Martin. c2003.
SUBJECTS:
Episcopal Church. Book of common prayer (1979)–Study and teaching.
Episcopal Church–Liturgy–Texts–History and criticism.

Title: *Crossing : reclaiming the landscape of our lives* / Mark Barrett foreword by Phyllis Tickle. 2002.
SUBJECTS:
Spiritual life–Catholic Church.
Catholic Church. Liturgy of the hours.

Sermons[42]

The following types of headings are assigned to sermons:

Sermons
Sermons, [Language]
Sermons, [Language]–[Class of authors, e.g.,**–Women authors]**
[Denomination]–Sermons
[Religion] sermons
[Religion] sermons, [Language]
[Name of sect]–Sermons
[Uniform title of sacred scripture]–Sermons
[Topic]–Sermons
[Phrase headings such as **Christmas sermons]**

Examples of Collections of Sermons by Two or More Authors

Title: *The world's greatest preachers* / Ray Comfort and Kirk Cameron. 2003.
SUBJECTS:
Sermons, English.

Title: *The sixth Times book of best sermons* / edited and introduced by Ruth Gledhill ; foreword by Canon Michael Saward. 2001.
SUBJECTS:
Sermons, English.
Jewish sermons.

Examples of Collections of Sermons by an Individual Author

Title: *The wisdom of Meister Eckhart* / Selected and edited by Jan Stryz ; with an introduction by Arthur Versluis. c2003.

SUBJECTS:

Mysticism–Sermons.
Catholic Church–Sermons.
Sermons, English.

Title: *My soul finds rest : reflections on the Psalms* / by Dietrich Bonhoeffer ; editor & translator, Edwin Robertson. c2002.

SUBJECTS:

Bible. O.T. Psalms–Meditations.
Bible. O.T. Psalms–Sermons.
Lutheran Church–Sermons.
Sermons, German–Tranlsations into English.

Title: *Practical godliness : the ornament of all religion : being the subject of several sermons upon Titus 2:10* / by Vincent Alsop ; edited by Don Kistler. c2004.

SUBJECTS:

Bible. N.T. Titus II, 10–Sermons.
Christian life–Early works to 1800.
Christian life–Biblical teaching.
Sermons, English–17th century.
Presbyterian Church–Sermons.

Title: *The unsearchable riches of Christ* / James Durham ; edited by Don Kistler. c2002.

SUBJECTS:

Puritans–Doctrines.
Puritans–Sermons.
Sermons, English–17th century.

Title: *The standard sermons [of John Wesley] in modern English* / [edited by] Kenneth Cain Kinghorn. 2002-2003.

SUBJECTS:

Methodist Church–Sermons.
Sermons, English.

Individual Sermons

Title: *With God in solitary confinement* / Richard Wurmbrand. Rev. ed. 2001.

SUBJECTS:

Persecution–Romania–Sermons.
Lutheran Church–Sermons.
Sermons, English.

Title: *The praise of a Godly woman (1627)* / by Hannibal Gamon ; a facsimile reproduction with an introduction by Bettie Anne Doebler and Retha M. Warnicke. 2001.
SUBJECTS:
Robartes of Truro, Frances Robartes, Baroness, d. 1626–Sermons.
Funeral sermons–England.
Church of England–Sermons.
Sermons, English–17th century.

Canon Law

General works on canon law and works on the canon law of the Catholic Church are assigned the heading **Canon law**. Special topics of canon law are represented by headings in the form of **[Topic] (Canon law)** such as:

Adoption (Canon law)
Census (Canon law)
Church architecture (Canon law)
Domestic relations (Canon law)
Parent and child (Canon law)

Following is an example of a work containing canon law:

Title: *Code of canon law annotated : prepared under the responsibility of the Instituto Martín de Azpilcueta* / edited by Ernest Caparros, Michel Thériault, Jean Thorn. 2nd ed., rev. and updated of the 6th Spanish language ed. 2003.
SUBJECTS:
Canon law.

Examples of works *about* canon law include:

Title: *The early development of Canon law and the Council of Serdica* / Hamilton Hess. 2002.
SUBJECTS:
Canon law–History.
Canon law–Sources.
Council of Serdica (343)

Title: *The canon law collection of the Library of Congress : a general bibliography with selective annotations* / compiled by Darío C. Ferreira-Ibarra. 2003.
SUBJECTS:
Canon law–Bibliography–Catalogs.
Library of Congress–Catalogs.

Title: *Spiritual dimensions of the holy canons* / Lewis J. Patsavos. 2003.
SUBJECTS:
Canon law, Orthodox Eastern–Sources.

Title: *Guide to the implementation of the U.S. bishops' essential norms for diocesan/eparchial policies dealing with allegations of sexual abuse of minors by priests or deacons*. c2003.
SUBJECTS:
Child sexual abuse by clergy (Canon law)
Child sexual abuse by clergy–United States.
Catholic Church–United States–Clergy–Sexual behavior.

Title: *The obligations and rights of the pastor of a parish : according to the Code of Canon Law* / Edward A. Sweeny. 2002.
SUBJECTS:
Clergy (Canon law)
Parishes (Canon law)

Title: *Exegetical commentary on the Code of canon law* / Martin de Azpilcueta Institute, Faculty of Canon Law, University of Navarre ; edited by Angel Marzoa, Jorge Miras, and Rafael Rodriguez-Ocaña. 2004.
SUBJECTS:
Catholic Church. Codex Juris Canonici (1983)
Canon law.

LAW[43]

Types of Headings

Legal Headings

Law headings represent different forms of legal texts, systems and branches of law, and specific legal topics:

Charters
Commercial law
Common law
Constitutional amendments
Constitutional law
Deeds
Habeas corpus
Insurance law
Law

Law, Medieval
Law, Slavic
Liens
Maya law
Ordinances, Municipal
Roman law
Treaties

The heading **Labor laws and legislation** serves as the pattern heading for subdivisions.[44]

For canon law, see discussion in the section "Religion" above.

Topical Headings with Legal Subdivisions

Legal texts and works about law are often assigned topical headings with legal subdivisions such as the following:

–Law and legislation (*May Subd Geog*)
{free-floating under specific categories covered by pattern headings}
–Legal status, laws, etc. (*May Subd Geog*)
{free-floating under classes of persons and ethnic groups}
–Safety regulations (*May Subd Geog*)
{free-floating under general topics and industries}

These subdivisions may be further divided by the subdivisions listed under the pattern heading **Labor laws and legislation**.

The subdivision **–Law and legislation** is used under topical headings, for example:

Firearms–Law and legislation–United States
Income tax–Law and legislation–United States–Popular works
Smoking–Law and legislation

This subdivision is not used if (1) the topical heading itself is inherently legal, for example, **Torts**; (2) there is a phrase heading for the topic, for example, **Trade regulation**; or (3) the topical heading represents a group of people, in which case, the subdivision **–Legal status, laws, etc.** (*May Subd Geog*) is used, for example, **Children–Legal status, laws, etc.–United States.**

The free-floating subdivision **–Safety regulations** (*May Subd Geog*) is used under headings for types of objects, chemicals, materials, machines, installations, industries, or activities, or under names of disciplines for safety rules or orders that have the force of law, for example:

Coal mines and mining–Safety regulations–United States
Ships–Safety regulations
Food industry and trade–Safety regulations–United States–Periodicals

Legal headings and headings of the type **[Topic]–Law and legislation** may be subdivided by special form subdivisions such as:

–Digests[45]

{for monographic or serial works consisting of systematically arranged compilations of brief summaries of individual statues, regulations, court decisions, or regulatory agency decisions on particular topics, e.g., **Constitutional law–United States–Digests**}

–Legal research[46]

{for works discussing the use of legal research tools such as court reports, codes, digests, citators, etc., in determining the status of statutory, regulatory, or case law on a legal topic, e.g., **Taxation–Law and legislation–United States–Legal research**}

–Research[47]

{for descriptions of proposed research, including details such as management, personnel, methodology, etc.}

Application

Legal Texts

General Laws (Nontopical Compilations)

A subject heading in the form of **Law–[Place]** is assigned to a nontopical compilation of laws when main entry has been made under the name of a jurisdiction:[48]

Title: *Zhonghua Renmin Gongheguo xian xing fa lü ji li fa wen jian* / zhu bian Yu Youmin, Qiao Xiaoyang ; fu zhu bian Lei Ying, Wu Gaosheng. 2002.
SUBJECTS:
Law–China.

Title: *West's Oregon revised statutes annotated.* 2003-
SUBJECTS:
Law–Oregon.

General Laws (Topical Compilations)

If the laws pertain to a particular topic, a law heading subdivided by the jurisdiction is assigned, for example:

Title: *Compilation of federal ethics laws* / prepared by the United States Office of Government Ethics. [2003]
SUBJECTS:
Civil service ethics–United States.
Conflict of interests–United States.
Financial disclosure–Law and legislation–United States.

Title: *Wyoming library laws, 2002 : extracted from Wyoming statutes of 2002 as amended* / compiled by Jerry Krois and Lyndsay Griffin, designed by Lyndsay Griffin. [2002]
SUBJECTS:
Library legislation–Wyoming.

Title: *Compilation of railroad laws relating to railroad regulation, as amended through December 31, 2002* / prepared for the use of the Committee on Transportation and Infrastructure, U.S. House of Representatives. 2003.
SUBJECTS:
Railroads–Employees–Legal status, laws, etc.–United States.
Labor laws and legislation–United States.
Railroads–Employees–Pensions–Law and legislation–United States.

Individual Acts

Same types of heading assigned to topical collections are used for works containing individual acts:

Title: *The Merchant Marine Act, 1936, the Maritime Security Act of 2003, the Shipping Act of 1984, and related acts : as amended through the first session of the 108th Congress* / prepared by the Office of Chief Counsel, Maritime Administration. 2004.
SUBJECTS:
Maritime law–United States.

Title: *The Public Land Act, Revised Forestry Code, and related laws : with Urban Development and Housing Act of 1992, law on illegal squatting and their pertinent issuances and related special laws* / compiled & edited by CBSI editorial staff. 12th ed. c2004.
SUBJECTS:
Public lands–Philippines.
Forestry law and legislation–Philippines.

Title: *Income Tax Act 1967 (Act 53) with selected regulations & rules : as at 25th March 2003* / compiled by Legal Research Board. 2003.
SUBJECTS:
Income tax–Law and legislation–Malaysia.

Constitutions[49]

The heading **Constitutions** is used for a general collection of texts of constitutions. The heading is subdivided by place if the work contains the texts of constitutions of a particular region or an individual constitution.

Title: *Modern constitutions : a collection of the fundamental laws of twenty-two of the most important countries of the world : with historical and bibliographical notes* / by Walter Fairleigh Dodd, [editor]. 2003.
SUBJECTS:
Constitutions.
Constitutional law.

Title: *Constitution, State of Missouri ; Constitution of the United States. Rev. January 2003.* [2003]
SUBJECTS:
Constitutions–Missouri.
Constitutions–United States.

For collections of the constitutions of the political divisions of a particular place, headings in the form of **Constitutions–[Place]–[States** or **Provinces]** are used:

Title: *The federal and state constitutions, colonial charters, and other organic laws of the United States* / compiled under an order of the United States Senate by Ben. Perley Poore. 2001.
SUBJECTS:
Constitutions–United States–States.
Constitutional history–United States–States–Sources.
Constitutional history–United States–Sources.

A heading in the form of **Constitutional amendments–[Place]** is assigned to a work containing the text of one or more particular amendments to a constitution, in addition to the appropriate topical headings.

Title: *Proposed amendments to the U.S. Constitution, 1787-2001* / John R. Vile, editor. 2003.
SUBJECTS:
Constitutional amendments–United States.

Title: *Balanced budget amendment : hearing before the Subcommittee on the Constitution of the Committee on the Judiciary, House of Representatives, One Hundred Eighth Congress, first session, on H.J. Res. 22, March 6, 2003.* 2003.
SUBJECTS:
Budget–Law and legislation–United States.
Debts, Public–Law and legislation–United States.
Constitutional amendments–United States.

Ordinances

The heading **Ordinances, Municipal** is used for nontopical collections of texts of ordinances passed by municipal corporations and works about these ordinances. A heading of the type **Ordinances, Municipal–[Place]** is assigned to the text of a nontopical compilation of ordinances of a particular place:

Title: *Kommentariĭk Ustavu goroda Moskvy* / [redakt͡sionnai͡a kollegii͡a, Petrov A.V. ... et al.]. 2002.
SUBJECTS:
Law–Russia (Federation)–Moscow.
Ordinances, Municipal–Russia (Federation)–Moscow.
Moscow (Russia)–Charters, grants, privileges.

For municipal law, the heading **Municipal corporations**, subdivided by the appropriate place, is used.

Title: *Leyes de los municipios* / Oficina del Contralor, Estado Libre Asociado de Puerto Rico. Ed. De 2002. 2002.
SUBJECTS:
Municipal corporations–Puerto Rico.

Title: *Massachusetts municipal law* / editors, James B. Lampke, Joseph P.J. Vrabel ; authors, William M. Appel ... [et al.]. 2002-
SUBJECTS:
Municipal corporations–Massachusetts.
Local government–Law and legislation–Massachusetts.

Charters

One or more of the following types of headings are assigned to the text of a compilation of published charters: **Charters**; **County charters**; **Municipal charters**. Examples include:

Title: *Model government charters : a city, county, regional, state, and federal handbook* / edited by Roger L. Kemp. c2003.
SUBJECTS:
Federal government–United States.
Local government–United States.
Municipal government–United States.
Charters.

For the text or a work about charters in specific places, the following types of headings are used:

[Name of state, county, city of the United States]–Charters
{for places in the United States}
[Name of foreign country, city, etc.**]–Charters, grants, privileges**
{for places in other countries}

Examples include:

Title: *The city at stake : secession, reform, and battle for Los Angeles* / Raphael J. Sonenshein. c2004.
SUBJECTS:
Los Angeles (Calif.)–Politics and government.
Los Angeles County (Calif.)–Politics and government.
Los Angeles (Calif.)–Charters.
Secession–California–Los Angeles County.
Secession–California–Los Angeles.
Los Angeles (Calif.)–Race relations.

Title: *Charters of the New Minster, Winchester* / edited by Sean Miller. c2001.
SUBJECTS:
Winchester (England)–Charters, grants, privileges.
Hyde Abbey (Winchester, England)–Charters, grants, privileges.
Anglo-Saxons–England–Winchester–Sources.
Winchester (England)–History–Sources.

Title: *La Carta municipal de Barcelona y el ordenamiento local : el régimen especial del Municipio de Barcelona* / Alfredo Galán Galán. 2001.
SUBJECTS:
Municipal corporations–Spain–Barcelona.
Barcelona (Spain)–Charters, grants, privileges.
Barcelona (Spain)–Politics and government.

Court Rules

Title: *Rules of evidence.* c2003.
SUBJECTS:
Evidence (Law)–Texas.
Court rules–Texas.

Title: *Appellate rules annotated.* 4th ed. 2003.
SUBJECTS:
Appellate procedure–Minnesota.
Court rules–Minnesota.

Title: *Rules of court annotated* / by Miriam Defensor Santiago. 2nd rev. ed. 2002. c2002.
SUBJECTS:
Court rules–Philippines.
Procedure (Law)–Philippines.

Works about Law

Works about law in general are assigned the heading **Law** with appropriate subdivisions:

Title: *A legal primer for the digital age* / TyAnna K. Herrington. 2003.
SUBJECTS:
Law–United States–Popular works.

Title: *Understanding China's legal system : essays in honor of Jerome A. Cohen* / edited by C. Stephen Hsu. c2003.
SUBJECTS:
Law–China.
Law–China–History.

Title: *Florida statutes tables, 1919 to 1990.* 2001.
SUBJECTS:
Law–Florida–Indexes.

Title: *Nolo's guide to California law.* 2001-
SUBJECTS:
Law–California–Popular works.

For works on specific branches or topics of law, the same types of headings assigned to the texts of such laws are used. Geographic and form subdivisions are added as appropriate:

Title: *Ark of the broken covenant : protecting the world's biodiversity hotspots* / John Charles Kunich. 2003.
SUBJECTS:
Environmental law.
Biological diversity.

Title: *Manual de operaciones bancarias y financieras* / Robert A. Muguillo, director. [2002]
SUBJECTS:
Banking law–Argentina.
Financial institutions–Law and legislation–Argentina.

Title: *Right to home school : a guide to the law on parents' rights in education* / Christopher J. Klicka. c2002.
SUBJECTS:
Home schooling–Law and legislation–United States.
Parent and child (Law)–United States.

Title: *New IRAs and how to make them work for you* / Neil Downing. c2002.
SUBJECTS:
Individual retirement accounts–Law and legislation–United States–Popular works.
Tax planning–United States–Popular works.

Title: *Children, parents, and the law : public and private authority in the home, schools, and juvenile courts* / Leslie J. Harris, Lee E. Teitelbaum. c2002.
SUBJECTS:
Parent and child (Law)–United States–Cases.
Juvenile courts–United States–Cases.
Child abuse–Law and legislation–United States–Cases.

Title: *Health care law* / Jonathan Montgomery. 2nd ed. 2002.
SUBJECTS:
Medical laws and legislation–Great Britain.
Medical care–Law and legislation–Great Britain.

Title: *A treatise on the law of assessments* / D.W. Welty. 2003.
SUBJECTS:
Tax assessment–Law and legislation–New York (State)

Title: *Massachusetts basic practice manual* / authors, Dana E. Casher ... [et al.]. 2000 rev. ed. 2000-
SUBJECTS:
Law–Massachusetts.
Procedure (Law)–Massachusetts.
Practice of law–Massachusetts.
Forms (Law)–Massachusetts.

For a periodical or journal of law that also contains information about a particular jurisdiction, a heading in the form of **Law–[Place]–Periodicals** is assigned in addition to other headings:

Title: *New York law journal magazine.* 2002-
SUBJECTS:
Practice of law–New York (State)–New York–Periodicals.
Law–New York (State)–Periodicals.

A work about a particular act is assigned a heading under the name of the act, that is, the uniform title of the law, in addition to other appropriate topical headings assigned to the original text:

Title: *Governance by decree : the impact of the Voting Rights Act in Dallas* / Ruth P. Morgan. c2004.
SUBJECTS:
Dallas (Tex.)–Politics and government.
Dallas (Tex.)–Race relations.
Dallas (Tex.)–Social conditions.
Election law–United States.
United States. Voting Rights Act of 1965.

Title: *Clean Water Act : law and regulation : October 23-25, 2002, Washington, D.C. : ALI-ABA course of study materials* / cosponsored by the ABA Section of Environment, Energy, and Resources and the Environmental Law Institute. c2002.
SUBJECTS:
Water–Pollution–Law and legislation–United States.
United States. Federal Water Pollution Control Act.

Title: *Library Services and Technology Act : five-year plan for Michigan, October 1, 2002-September 30, 2007.* [2002]
SUBJECTS:
Federal aid to libraries–Michigan.
United States. Library Services and Technology Act.
Libraries–Aims and objectives–Michigan.

Legislative Histories

A legislative history is "a collection of texts of committee hearings, reports, floor debates, etc., leading up to the enactment of a law." [50] A nontopical collection of legislative histories is assigned the heading **Legislative histories–[Place**, if appropriate]:

Title: *Legislative histories* / Charlene Bangs Bickford and Helen E. Veit, editors. 1986.
SUBJECTS:
Bills, Legislative–United States.
Legislative histories–United States.

Collections of legislative histories on a particular topic are assigned headings of the type **[Legal topic]–[Place]–Legislative history,** for example:

Title: *Seidman's legislative history of federal income tax laws, 1938-1861* / by J.S. Seidman. 2003.
SUBJECTS:
Income tax–Law and legislation–United States–Legislative history.

A legislative history of an individual enactment is assigned the heading containing the uniform title of the act with the subdivision **–Legislative history** and appropriate topical headings with the subdivision **–Legislative history**, for example:

Title: *Victory on the Potomac : the Goldwater-Nichols Act unifies the Pentagon* / James R. Locher, III ; foreword by Sam Nunn. c2002.
SUBJECTS:
United States. Goldwater-Nichols Department of Defense Reorganization Act of 1986–Legislative history.
United States. Dept. of Defense–Reorganization–Legislative history.
United States–Armed Forces–Reorganization–Legislative history.

Works on the techniques for compiling or using legislative histories are assigned the heading **Legislative histories–[Place**, if appropriate], for example:

Title: *Using legislative history in American statutory interpretation* / Christian E. Mammen. 2002.
SUBJECTS:
Legislative histories–United States.
Law–United States–Interpretation and construction.
United States. Supreme Court.

Works about Constitutions and Constitutional Law

To a work that discusses constitutions or constitutional law in general, the heading **Constitutional law** is assigned. Works that discuss the constitutions or constitutional law of particular regions, countries, states, provinces, etc., are assigned headings in the form of **Constitutional law–[Jurisdiction]–[States** or **Provinces** if appropriate]. Examples include:

Title: *Asia-Pacific constitutional systems* / Graham Hassall, Cheryl Saunders. 2002.
SUBJECTS:
Constitutional law–East Asia.
Constitutional law–Asia, Southeastern.
Constitutional law–Pacific Area.
East Asia–Politics and government.
Asia, Southeastern–Politics and government.
Pacific Area–Politics and government.

Title: *We the kids : the preamble to the Constitution of the United States* / illustrations and foreword by David Catrow. c2002.
SUBJECTS:
Constitutional law–United States–Juvenile literature.

Title: *The words we live by : your annotated guide to the constitution* / Linda R. Monk. c2003.
SUBJECTS:
Constitutional law–United States–Popular works.
Constitutional history–United States–Popular works.

If the work discusses a specific constitution as a document or includes a significant amount of material about its construction and formulation, a name-title heading for the constitution is assigned in addition to other appropriate headings.

Title: *A view of the Constitution of the United States of America* / by William Rawle. 2003.
SUBJECTS:
United States. Constitution.
Constitutional law–United States.
Constitutions–United States.

A work discussing constitutional amendments and the amending process in general is assigned the heading **Constitutional amendments**. Works discussing constitutional amendments or state constitutional amendments of a particular country, state, province, etc., are assigned headings in the form of **Constitutional amendments–[Jurisdiction]–[States** or **–Provinces** if appropriate].

Title: *Encyclopedia of constitutional amendments, proposed amendments, and amending issues, 1789-2002* / John R. Vile. 2nd ed. 2003.
SUBJECTS:
Constitutional amendments–United States.

Title: *The revision and amendment of state constitutions* / by Walter Fairleigh Dodd. 1999.
SUBJECTS:
Constitutional law–United States–States.
Constitutional amendments–United States–States.

Title: *Emendas constitucionais e limites flexíveis* / José Carlos Francisco. 2003.
SUBJECTS:
Constitutional amendments.
Constitutional amendments–Brazil.

A work discussing a specific constitutional amendment is assigned a heading in the form of name-title for the amendment, in addition to other topical headings representing the subject of the amendment.

Title: *The adoption of the Fourteenth Amendment* / by Horace Edgar Flack. c2003.
SUBJECTS:
United States. Constitution. 14th Amendment.
African Americans–Civil rights.
Equality before the law–United States.
Privileges and immunities–United States.
Due process of law–United States.

Title: *Property rights : from Magna Carta to the Fourteenth Amendment* / Bernard H. Siegan. 2001.
SUBJECTS:
United States. Constitution. 14th Amendment.
Right of property–United States–History.
Right of property–Great Britain–History.

Title: *Ratification of the Twenty-first Amendment to the Constitution of the United States : state convention records and laws* / compiled by Everett Somerville Brown. 2002.
SUBJECTS:
United States. Constitution. 21st amendment.
United States. Constitution. 18th amendment.
Liquor laws–United States.

Treaties[51]

Texts of Treaties

(1) For general (nontopical) collections of treaties, general genre headings are used as appropriate, for example, **Peace treaties**; **Treaties–Collections**; **[Place]–Foreign relations–Treaties**. The subdivision **–Treaties** is used only with the names of ethnic groups and names of wars, and with headings of the type **[Place]–Foreign relations** and the heading **[Catholic Church]–Foreign relations**. Examples include:

Title: *The major international treaties of the twentieth century* / edited by John Grenville and Bernard Wasserstein. 2000.
SUBJECTS:
Treaties–Collections.

Title: *Major peace treaties of modern history* / introductory essays by Arnold B. Toynbee, Hans J. Morgenthau, George J. Mitchell ; editor, Fred L. Israel ; associate editor, Michael P. Kelly ; commentaries, Emanuel Chill. c2002.
SUBJECTS:
Peace treaties.

Title: *International legislation : a collection of the texts of multipartite international instruments of general interest, beginning with the Covenant of The League of Nations* / edited by Manley O. Hudson. 2000.
SUBJECTS:
International law–Sources.
Treaties–Collections.

(2) For topical collections of treaties, appropriate topical headings are assigned, for example, **Environmental law, International**; **Chemical warfare (International law)**; **Postal conventions**; **Commercial treaties**; **Sex discrimination against women–Law and legislation**; **World War, 1939-1945–Treaties**. Examples include:

Title: *International environmental conventions and treaties* / [compiled by] Mohd. Afandi Salleh. 2002.
SUBJECTS:
Environmental law, International.
Pollution–Law and legislation.
Wildlife conservation–Law and legislation.
Treaties.

Title: *European treaties bearing on the history of the United States and its dependencies* / edited by Frances Gardiner Davenport. 2004.
SUBJECTS:
United States–International status–History–Sources.
United States–History–Sources.
Europe–Foreign relations–Treaties.

(3) For individual treaties, the same types of headings used for topical collections of treaties are assigned:

Title: *WIPO Performances and Phonograms Treaty (WPPT) (1996) : with the agreed statements of the Diplomatic Conference that adopted the Treaty, and the provisions of the Berne Convention (1971) and of the Rome Convention (1961) referred to in the Treaty.* 2002.
SUBJECTS:
World Intellectual Property Organization Performances and Phonograms Treaty (1996)

Berne Convention for the Protection of Literary and Artistic Works (1971)
International Convention for the Protection of Performers, Producers of Phonograms and Broadcasting Organizations (1961)
Copyright, International.
Copyright–Artistic performance.
Copyright–Sound recordings.

The heading for the name of the treaty is not assigned as a subject heading to a work that contains only the text of the treaty.

Works about Treaties

For works about treaties treated collectively, headings in the form of **[Place]–Foreign relations–Treaties** or **[Place]–Commercial treaties** are assigned in addition to other appropriate topical headings:

Title: *Treaties, their making and enforcement* / by Samuel B. Crandall. 2002.
SUBJECTS:
Treaties.
Treaty-making power–United States.
United States–Foreign relations–Treaties.

Title: *Peace treaties and international law in European history : from the late Middle Ages to World War One* / edited by Randall Lesaffer. 2004.
SUBJECTS:
Peace treaties–History.
Europe–Foreign relations–Treaties.
International law–Europe–History.

Title: *Treaty interpretation, the constitution, and the rule of law* / by John Norton Moore. c2001.
SUBJECTS:
Treaties–Interpretation and construction.
Constitutional law.
Rule of law.
United States–Foreign relations–Treaties.

A work about a particular treaty is assigned the uniform-title heading for the treaty or the international convention, established according to *AACR2R*, in addition to any topical headings:

Title: *NAFTA's second decade : assessing opportunities in the Mexican and Canadian markets* / Louis E.V. Nevaer. c2004.
SUBJECTS:
Free trade–North America.
Foreign trade regulation–North America.
Canada. Treaties, etc. 1992 Oct. 7.
Free trade–Canada.
Free trade–United States.
Free trade–Mexico.
North America–Economic integration.

Title: *Peace at last? : the impact of the Good Friday agreement on Northern Ireland* / with a foreword by Lord Alderdice ; edited by Jörg Neuheiser and Stefan Wolff. c2002.
SUBJECTS:
Northern Ireland–Politics and government–1998-
Great Britain. Treaties, etc. Ireland, 1998 Apr. 10.
Great Britain–Relations–Ireland.
Ireland–Relations–Great Britain.
Peace movements–Northern Ireland.

Title: *U.S.-Mexican economic integration : NAFTA at the grassroots* / edited by John Bailey. 2001.
SUBJECTS:
United States–Foreign economic relations–Mexico.
Mexico–Foreign economic relations–United States.
North America–Economic integration.
Canada. Treaties, etc. 1992 Oct. 7.

Title: *Beyond Nunn-Lugar : curbing the next wave of weapons proliferation threats from Russia* / edited by Henry D. Sokolski and Thomas Riisager. [2002]
SUBJECTS:
Nuclear nonproliferation.
United States–Foreign relations–Russia (Federation)
Russia (Federation)–Foreign relations–United States.
Soviet Union. Treaties, etc. United States. 1972 May 26 (ABM)

Trials[52]

The same types of headings are assigned to the proceedings of a trial or trials as are assigned to works discussing them.

General Works

The heading **Trials–[Place]** is assigned to a nontopical collection of proceedings of trials and to a work describing various trials:

Title: *Great American trials* / Edward W. Knappman, editor ; Stephen G. Christianson and Lisa Paddock, consulting legal editors. 2nd ed. c2002.
SUBJECTS:
Trials–United States.

Title: *Reverse your verdict* / Vincent Brome. 2001.
SUBJECTS:
Trials–Great Britain.

Title: *A complete collection of state trials and proceedings for high treason and other crimes and misdemeanors, from the earliest period to the year 1783 : with notes and other illustrations ...* / compiled by T.B. Howell. 2000.
SUBJECTS:
Trials–Great Britain.

Particular Types of Trials

A heading of the type **Trials ([Topic])–[Place]** is assigned to a collection of proceedings of a particular type of civil or criminal trial or to a work describing several trials of a specific type:

Title: *English witchcraft, 1560-1736* / edited by James Sharpe and Richard M. Golden. 2003-
SUBJECTS:
Witchcraft–England–History–Sources.
Trials (Witchcraft)–England–History–Sources.

Title: *Great murder trials of the Old West* / Johnny D. Boggs. c2002.
SUBJECTS:
Trials (Murder)–West (U.S.)

Individual Criminal Trials

The following types of headings are assigned in the order listed below for works containing the proceedings of a criminal trial and for works about a particular trial:

[Name of the trial] {if it has been established as a heading}
or, **[Name of defendant]–Trials, litigation, etc.**
Trials ([Topic])–[Place]
[Topical headings, as appropriate]

Examples are:

Title: *Dr. Sam Sheppard on trial : the prosecutors and the Marilyn Sheppard murder* / by Jack P. DeSario and William D. Mason. c2003.

SUBJECTS:

Sheppard, Sam–Trials, litigation, etc.
Trials (Murder)–Ohio–Cleveland.
Prosecution–Ohio–Cleveland.

Title: *The trial of Julius and Ethel Rosenberg : a primary source account* / by Betty Burnett. 2003.

SUBJECTS:

Rosenberg, Julius, 1918-1953–Trials, litigation, etc.
Rosenberg, Ethel, 1916-1953–Trials, litigation, etc.
Trials (Espionage)–New York (State)–New York.
Trials (Conspiracy)–New York (State)–New York.

Title: *One man's castle : Clarence Darrow in defense of the American dream* / Phyllis Vine. 2004.

SUBJECTS:

Sweet, Ossian, 1895-1960–Trials, litigation, etc.
Darrow, Clarence, 1857-1938.
Trials (Murder)–Michigan–Detroit.
African Americans–Civil rights–History–20th century.

Title: *The Lindbergh baby kidnapping trial : a primary source account* / By Greg Roensch. 2003.

SUBJECTS:

Hauptmann, Bruno Richard, 1899-1936–Trials, litigation, etc.
Lindbergh, Charles Augustus, 1930-1932–Kidnapping, 1932.
Trials (Kidnapping)–New Jersey.
Trials (Murder)–New Jersey.

Title: *The terrorist trial of the 1993 bombing of the World Trade Center : a headline court case* / Michael J. Pellowski. c2003.

SUBJECTS:

Trials (Terrorism)–United States–New York (State)–New York–Juvenile literature.
World Trade Center Bombing, New York, N.Y., 1993–Juvenile literature.
Terrorism–New York (State)–New York–Juvenile literature.

For a work about the trial of Jesus, the heading **Jesus Christ–Trial** is used, for example:

Title: *Christ on trial : how the Gospel unsettles our judgment* / Rowan Williams. 2003.
SUBJECTS:
Jesus Christ–Trial.

Individual Civil Trials

The following types of headings are assigned to works containing the proceedings of a civil trial and for works about a particular trial:

[Name of party initiating civil action]–Trials, litigation, etc.
[Name(s) of major party or parties, against whom the action was brought]–Trials, litigation, etc.
Trials ([Topic])–[Place]
[Topical headings, as appropriate]

Examples are:

Title: *Brown v. Board of Education : the case against school segregation* / by Wayne Anderson. c2003.
SUBJECTS:
Brown, Oliver, 1918--Trials, litigation, etc.
Topeka (Kans.). Board of Education–Trials, litigation, etc.
Discrimination in education–Law and legislation–United States.

Title: *Leaving reality behind : Etoy vs. EToys.com & other battles to control cyberspace* / Adam Wishart and Regula Bochsler. 2003.
SUBJECTS:
EToys.com (Firm)–Trials, litigation, etc.
Etoy.Corporation–Trials, litigation, etc.
Internet domain names–Law and legislation.
Internet–History.

War Crime Trials

To proceedings of and works about a war crime trial, the following types of headings are assigned in addition to other topical headings: **[Name of defendant or trial]**; **War crime trials–[Place]**. Examples include:

Title: *The state of Israel vs. Adolf Eichmann* / Hanna Yablonka ; translated from the Hebrew by Ora Cummings with David Herman. 2004.
SUBJECTS:
Eichmann, Adolf, 1906-1962–Trials, litigation, etc.
Trials (Genocide)–Jerusalem.
War crime trials–Social aspects–Israel.

Title: *Justice in the Balkans : prosecuting war crimes in the Hague Tribunal* / John Hagan. c2003.
SUBJECTS:
International Tribunal for the Prosecution of Persons Responsible for Serious Violations of International Humanitarian Law Committed in the Territory of the Former Yugoslavia since 1991.
War crime trials–Netherlands–The Hague.
Yugoslav War, 1991-1995–Atrocities.

Title: *The Tokyo trial : a bibliographic guide to English-language sources* / Jeanie M. Welch. 2002.
SUBJECTS:
Tokyo Trial, Tokyo, Japan, 1946-1948–Bibliography.
War crime trials–Japan–Bibliography.

SOURCE MATERIALS IN THE FIELDS OF HISTORY AND GENEALOGY[53]

Many publications of interest to genealogists and historians, especially local historians, are assigned headings of the type **[Topic]–[Place]**. An additional heading of the type **[Place]–[Topic]** is also assigned. The topical subdivision in this case is chosen from the following list:

–Antiquities
–Biography
–Church history
–Description and travel
–Economic conditions
–Ethnic relations
–Genealogy
–History
{including the various modifications of the subdivision, e.g., **–History, Local**, **–History, Military**}
–Race relations
–Religion
–Religious life and customs
–Social conditions
–Social life and customs

All these are free-floating subdivisions. The subdivision **–Genealogy** or **–History** is used when none of the other more specific subdivisions listed above is appropriate to the work in hand.

The Subdivision –History[54]

The subdivision **–History** is a free-floating subdivision that is widely used under a variety of topics to designate historical treatment. However, certain restrictions to its use have developed over the years, as explained in the following discussion.

General Use

The subdivision **–History** is free-floating under topical headings, classes of persons, ethnic groups, uniform titles of sacred works, and names of places and corporate bodies for descriptions and explanations of past events concerning the topic, group, sacred work, place, or organization, for example, **Aeronautics–History**; **Indians of North America–History**; **Washington (D.C.)–History**; **Catholic Church–History**; **General Motors Corporation–History**.

Exceptions

However, the subdivision **–History** is *not* used:

(1) under historical headings or headings with an obvious historical connotation, such as a historical time period or a historical event, for example, **Church history**; **Social history**; **Renaissance**; **Paris Peace Conference (1919-1920)**

(2) under literary, music, or film genre headings; in these cases, the subdivision **–History and criticism** is used instead, for example, **English poetry–History and criticism**; **Music–19th century–History and criticism**; **Western films–History and criticism**

(3) under art genre headings qualified by names of national, ethnic, or religious groups, for example, **Painting–History** but not *Painting, French–History*

(4) under name-title headings or uniform titles other than sacred works

(5) under names of individual persons or families, including dynasties and royal houses

(6) under the free-floating topical subdivisions listed below:[55]

–Annexation to [...]
–Anniversaries, etc.
–Antiquities
–Art
–Centennial celebrations, etc.
–Chronology
–Church history

–Civilization
–Description and travel
–Discovery and exploration
–Economic conditions
–Economic policy
–Foreign economic relations
–Foreign relations
–Genealogy
–Geography
–Gold discoveries
–Historical geography
–Historiography
–History
–History, Local
–History, Military
–History, Naval
–History of doctrines
–Illustrations
–Intellectual life
–Kings and rulers
–Military policy
–Military relations
–Origin
–Politics and government
–Portraits
–Queens
–Relations
–Religion
–Religious life and customs
–Rural conditions
–Social conditions
–Social life and customs
–Social policy

Chronological Subdivisions

Under certain headings, especially names of places, the subdivision **–History** is further subdivided by period when there is sufficient material to warrant it. If one of the exceptional headings or subdivisions noted above is to be further subdivided by period, the chronological subdivision follows immediately after the heading or the topical subdivision without the interposition of **–History**, for example, **Social history–20th century**; **Great Britain–Economic conditions–20th century**; **Chicago (Ill.)–Politics and government–To 1950**.

Historical Source Materials

The combination **–History–Sources** is used under headings where the free-floating subdivision is applicable. However, the subdivision **–Sources** follows directly after the exceptional headings and subdivisions noted above without the interposition of the subdivision **–History**, for example, **Beowulf–Sources**; **World War, 1914-1918–Sources**; **China–Foreign relations–Sources**; **United States–Politics and government–1783-1789–Sources**. Examples include:

Title: *1960* / Loreta M. Medina, book editor. 2004.
SUBJECTS:
United States–History–1953-1961–Sources.
Nineteen sixty, A.D.–Sources.

Title: *America at war : the Philippines, 1898-1913* / [edited by] A.B. Feuer ; forewords by Dominic J. Caraccilo and Michael G. Price. 2002.
SUBJECTS:
Philippines–History, Military–19th century–Sources.
Philippines–History, Military–20th century–Sources.
Spanish-American War, 1898–Campaigns–Philippines–Sources.
Philippines–History–Philippine American War, 1899-1902–Personal narratives.
Philippines–History–1898-1946–Sources.

Archives and Archival Resources[56]

The free-floating subdivision **–Archives** is used for collections or discussions of documentary material, such as manuscripts, household records, diaries, correspondence, photographs, or memorabilia. It can be used as either a form or topical subdivision under headings for types of corporate bodies and educational institutions, for classes of persons, and for ethnic groups, as well as under names of individual corporate bodies, educational institutions, persons, and families. Topical headings are assigned in addition, to bring out any subject content of the documents. Examples include:

Title: *John C. Calhoun : selected writings and speeches* / edited with headnotes and an introduction by H. Lee Cheek, Jr. c2003.
SUBJECTS:
Calhoun, John C. (John Caldwell), 1782-1850–Archives.
Statesmen–United States–Archives.
Legislators–United States–Archives.
United States–Politics and government–1815-1861–Sources.

Title: *Guide to the Winterthur Library : the Joseph Downs Collection and the Winterthur Archives* / compiled by E. Richard McKinstry. 2003.
SUBJECTS:
Joseph Downs Collection of Manuscripts & Printed Ephemera–Catalogs.
Winterthur Archives–Catalogs.
Winterthur Library–Catalogs.
Manuscripts, American–Catalogs.
American diaries–Bibliography–Catalogs.
United States–History–Sources–Bibliography–Catalogs.
Decorative arts–United States–History–Sources–Bibliography–Catalogs.
Du Pont family–Archives–Catalogs.

Title: *Black family research : records of post-Civil War federal agencies at the National Archives* / compiled by Reginald Washington. [2003]
SUBJECTS:
United States. Bureau of Refugees, Freedmen, and Abandoned Lands–Archives–Catalogs.
United States. Commissioners of Claims–Archives–Catalogs.
Freedman's Savings and Trust Company–Archives–Catalogs.
United States. National Archives and Records Administration–Catalogs.
Freedmen–United States–History–Sources–Bibliography–Catalogs.
African American families–History–Sources–Bibliography–Catalogs.
African Americans–Genealogy–Bibliography–Catalogs.

Title: *Washington on Washington* / edited by Paul M. Zall. c2003.
SUBJECTS:
Washington, George, 1732-1799.
Presidents–United States–Biography.
United States–Politics and government–1775-1783–Sources.
United States–Politics and government–1783-1809–Sources.
Washington, George, 1732-1799–Archives.
Washington, George, 1732-1799–Quotations.

The free-floating subdivision **–Archival resources** is used under topical headings and names of places for brief descriptions of available types of documents and historical records that pertain to the topic or place in question. For example:

Title: *Judaica in the Slavic realm, Slavica in the Judaic realm : repositories, collections, projects, publications* / Zachary M. Baker, editor. 2004.
SUBJECTS:
Jews–Slavic countries–Archival resources.
Jews–Europe, Eastern–Archival resources.

Jews–Slavic countries–Library resources.
Jews–Europe, Eastern–Library resources.
Jewish literature–Bibliography.

The subdivision **–Archival resources** may be further subdivided by **–Directories** for works containing the names, addresses, and brief descriptions of institutions housing archival materials on a particular topic, for example:

Title: *Exploring Civil War Wisconsin : a survival guide for researchers /* Brett Barker ; foreword by Alan T. Nolan. c2003.
SUBJECTS:
Wisconsin–History–Civil War, 1861-1865–Archival resources–Directories.
United States–History–Civil War, 1861-1865–Archival resources–Directories.
Wisconsin–History–Civil War, 1861-1865–Registers–Handbooks, manuals, etc.
United States–History–Civil War, 1861-1865–Registers–Handbooks, manuals, etc.
Wisconsin–Genealogy–Handbooks, manuals, etc.
Wisconsin Historical Society–Archives–Directories.
Wisconsin Historical Society–Library–Directories.

Title: *Civil War research guide : a guide for researching your Civil War ancestor /* Stephen McManus, Thomas Churchill, Donald Thompson. c2003.
SUBJECTS:
United States–History–Civil War, 1861-1865–Registers–Handbooks, manuals, etc.
United States–Genealogy–Handbooks, manuals, etc.
United States–History–Civil War, 1861-1865–Archival resources–Directories.

Form Subdivisions

To bring out the bibliographic or physical form of a work, the subdivision **–History** may be subdivided by an appropriate free-floating form subdivision:

Science–History–Miscellanea
Science–History–Outlines, syllabi, etc.
Science–History–Popular works

Title: *50 years of DNA* / edited by Julie Clayton and Carina Dennis ; foreword by Philip Campbell. 2003.
SUBJECTS:
DNA–History–Popular works.

Title: *More unsolved mysteries of American history* / Paul Aron. c2004.
SUBJECTS:
United States–History–Miscellanea.

Title: *Student almanac of African American history* / Media Project, Inc. 2003.
SUBJECTS:
African Americans–History–Miscellanea–Juvenile literature.
African Americans–History–Sources–Juvenile literature.
Almanacs, American–Juvenile literature.
[African Americans–History.]

Genealogical Materials[57]

For works of interest to genealogists and local historians, topical headings are assigned according to general guidelines. The following types of headings are commonly assigned:

[Topic]–[Place]
[Place]–[Topic]
[Place]–Genealogy
[Genre headings]

Topical headings with appropriate subdivisions are assigned according to general guidelines. If the work pertains to a particular place and the topical heading is in the form of **[Topic]–[Place]**, an additional heading under the name of the place with one of the following topical subdivisions is assigned:

–Antiquities
–Biography
–Church history
–Description and travel
–Economic conditions
–Ethnic relations
–Genealogy
–History {or one of its variations, e.g., **–History, Military**}
–Race relations
–Religion
–Religious life and customs
–Social conditions
–Social life and customs

The subdivision **–History** or **–Genealogy** is used if none of the more specific subdivisions applies.

For works of value in the study of the origin, descent, and relationship of named families, especially those works that assemble such information from family papers, deeds, wills, public records, parish registers, cemetery inscriptions, ship lists, etc., a heading in the form of **[Place]–Genealogy** is always assigned even if the place is a country or a larger region.

When appropriate, a genre heading is also assigned. Typical headings of this nature are:

Archives
Business records
Church records and registers
Court records
Criminal registers
Deeds
Epitaphs
Families of royal descent
Heraldry
Inscriptions
Inventories of decedents' estates
Land grants
Marriage records
Mining claims
Names
Obituaries
Probate records
Public land records
Public records
Registers of births, etc.
Slave records
Taxation–Lists
Titles of honor and nobility
Trials
Voting registers
Wills

Examples include:

Title: *Vermont religious certificates* / compiled by Alden M. Rollins. c2003.
SUBJECTS:
Vermont–Genealogy.
Church records and registers–Vermont.
Vermont–Religion.

Title: *Georgia, Heard County marriages.* 2003-
SUBJECTS:
Heard County (Ga.)–Genealogy.
Marriage records–Georgia–Heard County.

Title: *People of Ness : records 1718-1830* / [compilation and introductory material by Michael Robson]. 2003.
SUBJECTS:
Registers of births, etc.–Scotland–Port of Ness (Lewis with Harris Island)
Port of Ness (Lewis with Harris Island, Scotland)–Genealogy.

Title: *The family tree guide book to Europe : your passport to tracing your genealogy across Europe* / the editors of Family Tree Magazine. c2003.
SUBJECTS:
Europe–Genealogy–Handbooks, manuals, etc.
European Americans–Genealogy–Handbooks, manuals, etc.

Title: *Index to wills, estates, guardianships, and partitions, Fairfield County, Ohio, 1803-1900.* c2003.
SUBJECTS:
Fairfield County (Ohio)–Genealogy.
Wills–Ohio–Fairfield County–Indexes.
Decedents' estates–Ohio–Fairfield County–Indexes.
Guardian and ward–Ohio–Fairfield County–Indexes.
Partition of decedents' estates–Ohio–Fairfield County–Indexes.
Fairfield County (Ohio)–Registers.

Title: *The vital record.* [2003-]
SUBJECTS:
Genealogy–Periodicals.
United States–Genealogy–Periodicals.
Registers of births, etc.–United States–Periodicals.

Title: *Ohio Genealogical Society quarterly.* c2002-
SUBJECTS:
Ohio–Genealogy–Periodicals.
Registers of births, etc.–Ohio–Periodicals.
Ohio Genealogical Society–Periodicals.

For a discussion and examples of works about individual families, see the section "Biography" in chapter 9.

Other Works of Interest to Historians[58]

The following types of materials are also considered of interest to historians.

(1) *Activities*. Typical headings include:

Cattle trade
Country life
Frontier and pioneer life
Fur trade
Mountain life
Plantation life
Printing–History
Ranch life

(2) *Archaeological evidence*. Typical headings include:

Christian antiquities
Earthworks (Archaeology)
Excavations (Archaeology)
Industrial archaeology
Kitchen-middens
Mounds

For works on the archaeology of particular places, see the section "Archaeological Works" below.

(3) *Classes of persons*. Typical headings include:

Cowboys
Lawyers
Minorities
Physicians
Pirates
Politicians

(4) *Monuments and memorials*. Typical headings include:

Cemeteries
Epitaphs
Historical markers
Inscriptions
Memorials
Monuments
Sepulchral monuments
Soldiers' monuments
Statues

Tombs
War memorials

(5) *Particular uses of land; historic structures.* Typical headings include:

Bridges
Churches
Farms
Fountains
Historic sites
Hotels
Taverns (Inns)
Mines and mineral resources
Parks
Roads

(6) *Historic events.* Typical headings include:

Battles
Earthquakes
Epidemics
Fires
Storms

If the work is historical in nature and requires one of the headings of the types listed above, the additional heading **[Place]–[Topic]** is usually also assigned.

Title: *The ancient Maya of the Belize Valley : half a century of archaeological research* / edited by James F. Garber. 2004.
SUBJECTS:
Mayas–Belize River Valley (Guatemala and Belize)–Antiquities.
Excavations (Archaeology)–Belize River Valley (Guatemala and Belize) –History.
Belize River Valley (Guatemala and Belize)–Antiquities.

Title: *Under the canopy : the archaeology of tropical rain forests* / edited by Julio Mercader. c2003.
SUBJECTS:
Prehistoric peoples–Tropics.
Hunting and gathering societies–Tropics.
Excavations (Archaeology)–Tropics.
Rain forests.
Tropics–Antiquities.

Title: *Sacred sites : Christian perspectives on the Holy Land* / Webster T. Patterson. c2004.

SUBJECTS:

Christian antiquities–Palestine.
Christian shrines–Palestine.
Sacred space–Palestine.
Palestine–Antiquities.
Palestine–Church history.

Title: *Myths of the plantation society : slavery in the American South and the West Indies* / Nathalie Dessens. 2004.

SUBJECTS:

Slavery–Southern States–History.
Slaves–Southern States–Social conditions.
African Americans–Southern States–Social conditions.
Plantation life–Southern States–History.
Southern States–Race relations.
Slavery–West Indies–History.
Slaves–West Indies–Social conditions.
Blacks–West Indies–Social conditions.
Plantation life–West Indies–History.
West Indies–Race relations.

ARCHAEOLOGICAL WORKS[59]

Types of Headings

For works on the archaeology of particular places, one or more of the following types of headings are used:

[Name of site] {if the work is about a specific site}
[Place]–Antiquities or **[Place]–Antiquities, Roman,** [or **Byzantine**; **Celtic**; **Germanic**; **Phoenician**; **Roman**; **Slavic**; **Turkish]**
Antiquities, Prehistoric–[Place]
[Name of people, prehistoric culture or **period,** etc.]
{This heading is subdivided by **–Antiquities** if the people are still extant in modern times, e.g., **Mayas–Antiquities**}
Excavations (Archaeology)–[Place]
[Other special topics, as needed]

Application

Works Not Limited to a Single Site

The heading for the place and the heading for the people are assigned to an archaeological work if both a single area (but not a single site) and a single people are under discussion. If two peoples are involved, a separate heading for each is assigned. If more than two peoples are involved or if the names of the peoples cannot be identified from the work being cataloged, people headings may be omitted. If the name of the relevant jurisdiction corresponds closely to that of the people (e.g., **Egypt** and **Egyptians**), only the heading for the place is assigned. The heading **Romans** is not used if the work is assigned one of the following headings: **Rome–Antiquities**; **Italy–Antiquities**; or **[Place within Italy]–Antiquities, Roman**.

Examples of works *not* limited to a single site include:

Title: *First Americans : in pursuit of archaeology's greatest mystery* / J. M. Adovasio with Jake Page. c2002.
SUBJECTS:
Indians–Origin.
Paleo-Indians.
America–Antiquities.

Title: *Landmarks of American women's history* / Page Putnam Miller. c2003.
SUBJECTS:
Historic sites–United States.
Historic buildings–United States.
Women–United States–History.
Women–Monuments–United States.
United States–History, Local.
United States–Antiquities.

Title: *Landscape archaeology in southern Epirus, Greece* / edited by James Wiseman and Konstantinos Zachos. 2003.
SUBJECTS:
Preveza (Greece)–Antiquities.
Excavations (Archaeology)–Greece–Preveza.
Landscape archaeology–Greece–Preveza.
Arta (Greece : Nome)–Antiquities.
Excavations (Archaeology)–Greece–Arta (Nome)
Landscape archaeology–Greece–Arta (Nome)

Title: *Indian mounds of the middle Ohio Valley : a guide to mounds and earthworks of the Adena, Hopewell, Cole, and Fort Ancient people* / Susan L. Woodward and Jerry N. McDonald. 2002.

SUBJECTS:

Indians of North America–Ohio–Antiquities.
Mounds–Ohio.
Adena culture–Ohio.
Hopewell culture–Ohio.
Fort Ancient culture–Ohio.
Ohio–Antiquities.

Title: *African historical archaeologies* / edited by Andrew M. Reid and Paul J. Lane c2004.

SUBJECTS:

Archaeology and history–Africa.
Excavations (Archaeology)–Africa.
Africa–Antiquities
Africa–History, Local.

Title: *Ancient Rome* /,Fiona Macdonald. 2004.

SUBJECTS:

Rome–Civilization–Juvenile literature.
Rome–Antiquities–Juvenile literature.

Title: *Buddhist sites and shrines in India : history, art, and architecture* / D.C. Ahir. 2003.

SUBJECTS:

Buddhist shrines–India.
Buddhist antiquities–India.
Historic sites–India.

Works on Individual Sites

A work about an individual archaeological site is assigned one or more of the following types of headings:

[Name of site]
[Place]–Antiquities
{the place in this case is below the level of a country or below the level of a political division in the United States, Great Britain, and Canada}
[Special topics]

Examples include:

Title: *Cobble circles and standing stones : archaeology at the Rivas Site, Costa Rica* / by Jeffrey Quilter. c2004.

SUBJECTS:

Rivas Site (Costa Rica)

Panteón de la Reina Site (Costa Rica)
Indians of Central America–Costa Rica–San Isidro de El General Region–Antiquities.
Excavations (Archaeology)–Costa Rica–San Isidro de El General Region.
San Isidro de El General Region (Costa Rica)–Antiquities.

Title: *Debating Qumran : collected essays on its archaeology* / Jodi Magness. 2003.
SUBJECTS:
Qumran community.
Excavations (Archaeology)–West Bank.
Qumran Site (West Bank)

Title: *Dragon Bone Hill : an Ice-Age saga of Homo erectus* / Noel T. Boaz, Russell L. Ciochon. 2004.
SUBJECTS:
Peking man.
Excavations (Archaeology)–China–Zhoukoudian.
Zhoukoudian (China)–Antiquities.

Title: *The tomb of Tutankhamen* / Howard Carter. 2003.
SUBJECTS:
Tutankhamen, King of Egypt–Tomb.
Excavations (Archaeology)–Egypt–Valley of the Kings.

Title: *In search of King David's lost tomb & treasure* / by Gary Arvidson. c2002.
SUBJECTS:
David, King of Israel–Death and burial.
Jews–Kings and rulers–Death and burial.
Tomb of David (Jerusalem)
Excavations (Archaeology)–Jerusalem.
`Ir David (Jerusalem)–Antiquities.
Jerusalem–Antiquities.

Title: *Copán : the history of an ancient Maya kingdom* / edited by E. Wyllys Andrews and William L. Fash. 2004.
SUBJECTS:
Mayas–Honduras–Copán (Dept.)–Antiquities.
Maya architecture–Honduras–Copán (Dept.)
Maya sculpture–Honduras–Copán (Dept.)
Inscriptions, Mayan–Honduras–Copán (Dept.)
Copán Site (Honduras)
Copán (Honduras : Dept.)–Antiquities.

NOTES

1. Association for Library Collections & Technical Services, Cataloging and Classification Section, Subject Analysis Committee, Subcommittee on the Revision of the Guidelines on Subject Access to Individual Works of Fiction, *Guidelines on Subject Access to Individual Works of Fiction, Drama, Etc.*, 2nd ed. (Chicago: American Library Association, 2000).

2. Library of Congress, Cataloging Policy and Support Office, *Subject Cataloging Manual: Subject Headings*, 5th ed., 2000 cumulation (Washington, D.C.: Library of Congress, 2000), H1156.

3. Library of Congress, *Subject Cataloging Manual*, H1775, H1780, H1790, H1795, H1800.

4. The subdivision *–Stories* used under topical headings has been discontinued. However, there still exist a few phrase headings that are used for certain kinds of stories, for example, **Sea stories**; **Detective and mystery stories**.

5. Library of Congress, *Subject Cataloging Manual*, H1780, p. 1.

6. Works by joint authors, such as *The Maid's Tragedy* by Beaumont and Fletcher, are treated in the same manner as works by individual authors.

7. Library of Congress, *Subject Cataloging Manual*, H1790.

8. Library of Congress, *Subject Cataloging Manual*, H1790, p. 3.

9. Library of Congress, *Subject Cataloging Manual*, H1790, pp. 5-8.

10. Library of Congress, *Subject Cataloging Manual*, H1720.

11. Library of Congress, *Subject Cataloging Manual*, H1795.

12. Library of Congress, *Subject Cataloging Manual*, H1095.

13. Library of Congress, *Subject Cataloging Manual*, H1795.

14. Library of Congress, *Subject Cataloging Manual*, H1110.

15. Library of Congress, *Subject Cataloging Manual*, H1330.

16. Library of Congress, *Subject Cataloging Manual*, H1155.6.

17. Library of Congress, *Subject Cataloging Manual*, H1155.8.

18. Library of Congress, *Subject Cataloging Manual*, H1795, pp. 3-4.

19. Library of Congress, *Subject Cataloging Manual*, H250, H1160, H1161, H1438, H1916.3, H1916.5, H1917, H1917.5, H1918.

20. Library of Congress, *Subject Cataloging Manual*, H1160.

21. Library of Congress, *Subject Cataloging Manual*, H1917.5, p. 9.

22. Library of Congress, *Subject Cataloging Manual*, H1160.

23. Library of Congress, *Subject Cataloging Manual*, H1161.

24. Library of Congress, *Subject Cataloging Manual*, H1160, p. 2.

25. Library of Congress, *Subject Cataloging Manual*, H1917.

26. Library of Congress, *Subject Cataloging Manual*, H1916.5.

27. Library of Congress, *Subject Cataloging Manual*, H1160.

28. Library of Congress, *Subject Cataloging Manual*, H1438.

29. Library of Congress, *Subject Cataloging Manual*, H1438, p. 2.

30. *Anglo-American Cataloguing Rules*, 2nd ed., 2002 rev., prepared under the direction of the Joint Steering Committee for Revision of AACR, a committee of: the American Library Association, the Australian Committee on Cataloguing, the British Library, the Canadian Committee on Cataloguing, Chartered Institute of Library and Information Professionals, the Library of Congress (Chicago: American Library Association, 2002), rules 25.34C1-25.34C2.

31. Library of Congress, *Subject Cataloging Manual*, H1250.

32. Library of Congress, *Subject Cataloging Manual*, H1148.

33. Library of Congress, *Subject Cataloging Manual*, H1250.

34. Library of Congress, *Subject Cataloging Manual*, H1250, p. 2.

35. Library of Congress, *Subject Cataloging Manual*, H910.

36. Library of Congress, *Subject Cataloging Manual*, H1250.

37. Library of Congress, *Subject Cataloging Manual*, H1997, H2015.

38. Library of Congress, *Subject Cataloging Manual: Subject Headings*, H1998.

39. Library of Congress, *Subject Cataloging Manual: Subject Headings*, H1300, p. 2.

40. Library of Congress, *Subject Cataloging Manual: Subject Headings*, H1295, H1300, H1435, p. 3-4.

41. Library of Congress, *Subject Cataloging Manual*, H1300.

42. Library of Congress, *Subject Cataloging Manual*, H2032.

43. Library of Congress, *Subject Cataloging Manual*, H1154.5, H1550, H1705, H1710, H1715.

44. Library of Congress, *Subject Cataloging Manual*, H1154.5.

45. Library of Congress, *Subject Cataloging Manual*, H1550.

46. Library of Congress, *Subject Cataloging Manual*, H1710.

47. Library of Congress, *Subject Cataloging Manual*, H1710.

48. Library of Congress, *Subject Cataloging Manual*, H1715.

49. Library of Congress, *Subject Cataloging Manual*, H1465.

50. Library of Congress, *Subject Cataloging Manual*, H1715, p. 3.

51. Library of Congress, *Subject Cataloging Manual*, H2227.

52. Library of Congress, *Subject Cataloging Manual*, H2228.

53. Library of Congress, *Subject Cataloging Manual*, H1845.

54. Library of Congress, *Subject Cataloging Manual*, H1647.

55. Library of Congress, *Subject Cataloging Manual*, H1647, p. 6.

56. Library of Congress, *Subject Cataloging Manual*, H1230.

57. Library of Congress, *Subject Cataloging Manual*, H1845.

58. Library of Congress, *Subject Cataloging Manual*, H1845, p. 3.

59. Library of Congress, *Subject Cataloging Manual*, H1225.

PART 3

CURRENT AND FUTURE PROSPECTS

11 Library of Congress Subject Headings in the Electronic Environment

INTRODUCTION

Since the early 1990s, there have been major advances in the retrieval options available to information seekers. This chapter discusses the likely future prospects of the Library of Congress subject headings system in the context of a retrieval environment in which a very large segment of the information-seeking community has access to the World Wide Web, and many have access to quite sophisticated online retrieval systems.

The first thing to take into consideration is that the store of electronic information, particularly what is available on the Web, is huge, in fact, overwhelmingly so. Much of it is also highly volatile, changing from moment to moment. There are many systems already in operation that provide subject access to materials in this information store, and in many cases users appear to be satisfied with their performance. Others are frustrated by these systems' lack of precision and by the possibility that, in a particular search, the best resources on the topic sought may not have been retrieved. Thus, weighed against the long-established measures of precision and recall, the search results that these systems produce are often disappointing when compared to those attained through more highly structured systems. A number of questions come to mind. What measures—within the realm of what is possible to implement—will do the most good? Is greater use of controlled vocabulary the answer? Does LCSH, as one of the, if not the, largest, richest, and most widely used controlled-vocabulary systems in the world, have a role to play in a much wider area than it has occupied in the past?

SUBJECT ACCESS IN THE ELECTRONIC ENVIRONMENT

During the past few decades, the introduction and increasing popularity of (and in some cases total reliance on) natural language or keyword searching has made many people ask, "Is there still a need for controlled vocabulary?" Information professionals with a background in bibliographical control, and who have long appreciated the power of controlled vocabulary, have always responded with a confident "yes." From those in the larger information community, the affirmative answer began emerging only when searching became bogged down by the sheer number of retrieved results. Controlled vocabulary increases precision and recall through synonym and homograph control and term relationships, which are rarely available in the free-text approach. This is because in keyword searching a given input term delivers only those postings in which that term occurs, even though there may be many documents in the system in which the desired concept is discussed under a synonym. A controlled-vocabulary system, on the other hand, is designed to deliver all items that match either the input term or any of its synonyms. Thus, even in the age of automatic indexing and easy keyword searching, controlled vocabulary has much to offer in improving retrieval results, in part because such a vocabulary relieves the user of the burden of trying to control for both synonyms and homographs. For many years, Elaine Svenonius[1] has been arguing that using controlled vocabulary retrieves more relevant records for this very reason: Using controlled vocabulary places the burden on the indexing system and the indexer rather than on the user. David Batty makes a similar observation: "There is a burden of effort in information storage and retrieval that may be shifted from shoulder to shoulder, from author, to indexer, to index language designer, to searcher, to user. It may even be shared in different proportions. But it will not go away."[2]

Controlled vocabulary systems offer significant advantages in retrieval. At the same time, it is also important to note that they are much more expensive to implement and to maintain. The discussion that follows should help both decision-makers and those new to retrieval theory to understand the issues that must be faced as the information world struggles to improve retrieval of web-based resources.

VOCABULARY CONTROL IN THE ELECTRONIC ENVIRONMENT[3]

Vocabulary control and structured organization of information have been major factors in providing subject access to library materials, as well as to sources in other relatively structured retrieval environments. This is in spite of the fact that, in many online systems, the potential of controlled vocabularies has not always been fully optimized because of an inadequate mechanism for displaying synonyms and related terms. In sophisticated online retrieval systems, including many online public access catalogs (OPACs) and commercial databases, controlled vocabulary has been used effectively to provide subject access to various types of resources. The salient new question is whether vocabulary control and structured organization can also be effective in dealing with networked digital resources, given the economic and other conditions (size and lack of structure, particularly) that prevail in the web environment. In other words, can established information models provide the power to navigate networked resources with the same, or nearly the same, levels of efficiency in terms of precision and recall that have been achieved with information resources organized according to more structured methods, such as those used for library catalogs or online databases?

There is a source of evidence that bears on this question. OPACs have been in use for decades and have grown increasingly sophisticated during that time. They have also been studied intensively and extensively. It is true that most operational conditions on the Web are less structured than those in the OPAC environment, but the two venues have many points in common. In the effort to identify information-resource description needs and future directions, therefore, it seems that what has been learned from our experience with OPACs should be helpful in solving problems now facing the Web. It also seems appropriate that OPACs should be viewed as a part of the overall information storage and retrieval apparatus on the Web rather than as something apart from it. At the same time, it is important not to carry the Web/OPAC parallel too far. Deliberations on bibliographic control for the Web (and the tools used for its implementation) must take into consideration the nature of the Web, the characteristics of web resources, and the variety of information retrieval approaches and mechanisms now available and used in that environment. All of these factors are quite different from those affecting OPACs.

While traditional subject access tools such as subject headings and classification schemes have served library users well and for a long time, there are certain limitations to their extended applicability to networked resources. These include the cost of maintaining most subject headings systems, their incompatibility with most tools now used on the Web, and, finally—and perhaps most telling—the need for trained catalogers who know how to apply them according to current policies and procedures. Because of the sheer volume of web resources, it is economically and functionally impossible to employ people with formal training in bibliographic control for the preparation and provision of metadata for all web resources. For a retrieval vocabulary to be useful for indexing web resources, therefore, it must first of all fulfill the criterion of simplicity, that is, it must be able to be applied effectively by persons without extensive prior training. It should also be amenable to computer manipulation, thereby capitalizing on the processing power of technology. An additional advantage here is that a system that is easy for indexers to apply is also easy for searchers to use in drafting effective queries.

Several other operational requirements must be met for a retrieval system to cope with the challenges of web resources. A basic one is the ability to deal efficiently with a very large volume of resources. Unlike OPACs, the networked environment is diverse in its user communities, and web resources are multifarious in their content, format, and language. Other especially important requirements for effective subject access tools are interoperability and scalability. By interoperability we mean the ability of a system to function across different information environments and within a variety of retrieval models. By scalability we mean the ability of a system to function in systems of varying levels of sophistication. Schemes that are scalable in semantics and flexible in syntax, structure, and application are more likely able to meet the requirements of a diverse set of information retrieval environments and of diverse user communities.

Controlled vocabulary most likely will not replace keyword searching, but it can be used to supplement and complement keyword searching in enhancing retrieval results. The basic functions of controlled vocabulary, that is, better recall through synonym control and term relationships and greater precision through homograph control, have not been completely supplanted by keyword searching, even with all the power a totally machine-driven system can bring to bear.

Subject heading lists and thesauri began as catalogers' and indexers' tools, as a source of, and an aid in choosing, appropriate index terms. Later, they were also made available to users as searching aids, particularly in online systems. Traditionally, controlled vocabulary terms embedded in bibliographic records have been used as a means of matching the user's information needs against the document collection. Subject headings and descriptors, with their attendant equivalent and related terms, facilitate the matching of the searchers' terms against assigned index terms. Manual mapping of users' input terms to controlled vocabulary terms—for example, consulting a thesaurus to identify appropriate search terms—is a tedious process and has never been widely embraced by end-users. With the availability of online thesaurus-display, the mapping is greatly facilitated by allowing the user to browse and select controlled vocabulary terms while searching. Controlled vocabulary thus serves as the bridge between the searcher's language and the author's language.

Recent years have witnessed the emergence of numerous metadata schemas for describing web resources. Most of these schemas include a "subject" element, and the use of controlled vocabulary is recommended for it. However, the decision about implementation and the selection of controlled vocabularies and organizational schemes are left to the individual applying agencies. The Subcommittee on Metadata and Subject Analysis of the Subject Analysis Committee of the Association of Library Collections and Technical Services (ALCTS), in an effort to provide guidance and suggestions, recommended that metadata for subject analysis of web resources include a mixture of keywords and controlled vocabulary.[4] The Subcommittee identified the following approaches to choosing a source of controlled vocabulary: using an existing schema, adapting or modifying an existing schema, or developing a new schema.

Each of these options offers clear advantages. The use of an existing schema is certainly the simplest approach if a suitable one can be found. Of the schemas already in existence, LCSH would seem the obvious choice, but as it stands its complex syntax is a drawback because of the extent to which its use by non-librarians is limited. There are many excellent subject-specific schemas available but, since the Web has become increasingly interdisciplinary and heterogeneous, combining diverse schemas is likely to create significant interoperability problems. Obtaining rights to the required schemas could also pose a serious challenge.

At first glance, developing an entirely new schema appears very tempting. Such a system could rest on a sound theoretical basis, one that incorporates decades of work on user needs and behavior, and one that is no longer burdened by mechanisms designed to meet problems that no longer exist. However, developing a new subject indexing system appears considerably less attractive upon further examination. It quickly becomes clear that developing a new comprehensive controlled vocabulary is a highly difficult task, and by implication, would take a very long time to complete and would require enormous financial resources. Also, there would be no guarantee that the new schema would be significantly superior to one that already exists—in other words, it is quite possible that a new system could trade a set of known problems with its own set of new problems. Probably for these reasons, the ALCTS Subcommittee concluded that the option of modifying an existing schema appeared the most practical; and for a general vocabulary covering all subject areas, the Subcommittee recommended adapting either LCSH or the *Sears List of Subject Headings*.

THE POTENTIAL ROLE OF LIBRARY OF CONGRESS SUBJECT HEADINGS

We now turn to LCSH itself, looking at its strengths and weaknesses as a candidate for serving as the base vocabulary for a web subject access tool. The central issue is: Can a system originally designed for the manual catalog continue to be a viable tool in the new environment? Many factors will determine what sort of system will be favored for subject access in the coming decades, and not the least among these is economics. Maximum possible effectiveness is, of course, essential, and logical, philosophical, and theoretical considerations also apply. It cannot be denied that systems that are theoretically more satisfying than

LCSH have been devised in the past. However, the question of whether to work with the present system or adopt another is not purely academic.

As was noted in chapter 1, LCSH, which now contains more than a quarter million terms, is the most comprehensive general-coverage controlled vocabulary in the English language. As the bibliographic universe has become increasingly global, cataloging records carrying LCSH are being used around the world. The subject heading language that began quietly in the summer of 1898 has not only been serving library communities worldwide[5] for many decades but now also offers subject access to a wide range of audiences in many different media and environments—from libraries to other venues of information storage and retrieval. Its particular advantages are:

- LCSH is a rich vocabulary covering all subject areas, easily the largest general indexing vocabulary in the English language;
- it offers both synonym and homograph control;
- it contains rich links (cross references indicating relationships) among terms;
- it is a precoordinate system that enhances precision in retrieval;
- it facilitates browsing of multiple-concept or multifaceted subjects; and
- it has been translated or adapted as a model for developing subject headings systems by so many countries around the world that it has become a de facto universal controlled vocabulary.

It is generally acknowledged by information professionals, however, that LCSH is far from an ideal system. It still shows considerable internal inconsistency and retains some characteristics that cater more to manual than to online systems. Furthermore, because of both its complicated syntax and the Library's intricate rules for heading formation and application, LCSH requires highly trained personnel to construct and to assign appropriate headings to documents. Still, it has grown remarkably over the years, and even now is not only holding its own but growing in popularity.

Such growth is impressive in a system that was conceived in the late 1800s. Several factors can be seen as central to its continued health. First, those responsible for it have kept it a dynamic system from the beginning, keeping it up to date and moving, albeit slowly, in the direction of increased ease of application. Second, the Library of Congress cataloging staff members have been diligent not only in informing the user public of additions and changes but also in seeking its recommendations. And third, from the very beginning the Library of Congress staff has accepted the whole library world as its client base. Overall, throughout the twentieth century, LCSH has clearly demonstrated its versatility in a wide range of conditions with respect to both user base and medium of retrieval. Thus, its history supports the prediction that LCSH can continue to evolve as needed to accommodate changing information environments and changing demands on and for information resources. The ultimate question now becomes: What would be the best direction for LCSH to take to optimize the likelihood of its being a major player in web retrieval without compromising its usefulness for its traditional clientele?

ADAPTING TO THE ELECTRONIC ENVIRONMENT

LCSH has long been one of the main staples for providing subject access not only for libraries but for other bibliographic information services. However, deliberations of the ALCTS Subcommittee suggest that if it and other traditional schemes are to be useful in the web environment, they must undergo rigorous scrutiny and rethinking, particularly in terms of their structure and the way they are applied. Sophisticated technology can be used to extend the usefulness and power of traditional tools, but it cannot do all that is needed. Appropriately redesigned, however, older approaches to content retrieval can complement the simple keyword approach and may offer improved, or perhaps highly superior, retrieval results than are possible through the methods currently used in full-text document analysis and retrieval on the Web.

As noted earlier, the ALCTS Subcommittee recommended modifying and adapting an existing vocabulary—citing LCSH or Sears as the most viable options as bases for an effective subject access tool in the networked environment. However, while the vocabulary, or semantics, of LCSH has much to contribute to the management of, and retrieval from, the enormous store of electronic resources, there are serious disadvantages in the way LCSH is currently applied. These disadvantages are:

- LC subject headings must be assigned by trained personnel because of the system's complex syntax and application rules.
- Subject heading strings in bibliographic or metadata records are costly to maintain.
- LCSH, in its present form and application, is not compatible in syntax with most other controlled vocabularies.
- LCSH is not amenable to search engines outside of the OPAC environment, particularly current web search engines.

These limitations mean that applying LCSH properly, in compliance with current policy and procedures, entails the following requirements: trained catalogers and indexers; systems with index browsing capability; systems with online thesaurus display; and sophisticated users.[6] In the current web environment such conditions rarely prevail. Thus, given LCSH as it stands—rules of application included—its acceptance as a major tool for web retrieval would seem doubtful. As suggested by the ALCTS Subcommittee, to gain wide acceptance in the networked environment, a subject access tool should possess the following characteristics:

- be simple and easy to apply and to comprehend;
- be intuitive so that sophisticated training in subject indexing and classification, while highly desirable, is not required to implement;
- be logical so that it requires the least effort to understand and implement; and
- be scalable for implementation from the simplest to the most sophisticated.

The question then becomes whether steps can be taken for LCSH to overcome its limitations and still remain useful in its traditional roles. In the face of these limitations, the ALCTS Subcommittee recommended separating LCSH application syntax from matters relating to semantics and syndetics, in other words, distinguishing between the vocabulary (the LCSH list) and the indexing system (the way LCSH is applied in particular implementations).

This recommendation involves several important concepts that warrant close scrutiny. Semantics and syntax are two distinct aspects of a controlled vocabulary. *Semantics* relates to the source vocabulary, that is, what appears in the term list (e.g., a thesaurus or a subject headings list) that contains the building blocks for constructing indexing terms or search statements. It covers scope and depth, the selection of terms to be included, the forms of valid terms, synonym and homograph control, and the syndetic (cross-referencing) devices. The semantics of a good thesaurus are governed by well-defined principles of vocabulary structure.

At the heart of the *syntax* concept is the representation of complex subjects through the combination of terms that represent different subjects and different facets, or aspects, of a subject.[7] There are two aspects of syntax: multiword term construction and application syntax. Term construction—that is, how words are chosen and put together to form basic units of indexing terms in the thesaurus or subject headings list—is an aspect of semantics and thus a matter of principle. On the other hand, application syntax—that is, how thesaurus terms are assigned to documents to reflect their contents—is a matter of policy, determined by practical factors such as user needs, available resources, and search engines and their capabilities.

Enumeration (i.e., the listing of preestablished, multiple-concept index terms in the thesaurus) and *faceting* (i.e., the separate listing of single-concept or single-facet terms defined in distinctive categories based on common, shared characteristics) are aspects of thesaurus construction. On the other hand, *precoordination* and *postcoordination*, referring to how and when single-concept terms are combined to represent compound and complex subjects, are aspects of application syntax. Term combination can occur at any of three stages in the process of information storage and retrieval: (1) during vocabulary construction, (2) at the stage of cataloging or indexing, or (3) at the point of query submission. When words or phrases representing different subjects or different facets of a subject are precombined at the point of thesaurus construction, we refer to the process as enumeration. The practice of combining terms at the stage of indexing or cataloging is called precoordination. In contrast, postcoordination refers to combining terms for searching. A totally enumerative vocabulary is by definition precoordinated. On the other hand, a faceted controlled vocabulary—that is, a system that provides individual terms in clearly defined categories, or facets—may be used either precoordinately or postcoordinately and is thus highly flexible.

Except when an enumerative thesaurus is the base of an indexing operation, it is an agency-specific matter of policy whether a precoordinate or postcoordinate approach is used in a particular implementation. In other words, for a particular implementing agency, a central issue with respect to indexing policy is the choice between precoordination or postcoordination or both. All of these approaches have precedence in cataloging and indexing practices. As Thomas Mann[8] convincingly argues, there are many advantages to a precoordinated approach, particularly in online catalogs or online databases, where browsing is a regular feature. Precoordination provides meaningful context and contributes to precision in retrieval. However, few indexing and retrieval services outside of the library community take the precoordinated approach; those that employ controlled vocabularies typically rely on postcoordination. For example, controlled vocabularies used in online databases consist primarily of single-concept descriptors, with users relying on postcoordination to retrieve complex subjects. For the sake of simplicity and semantic interoperability, the postcoordinate approach is more in line with the basic premises and characteristics of the networked environment.

Another relevant point in this context is the question of where LCSH currently stands with respect to enumeration and precoordination. Although LCSH began in the late nineteenth century as an enumerative scheme, it gradually took on some of the features of a faceted system, particularly in the adoption of commonly used form subdivisions and the increasing use of geographic subdivisions. In the latter part of the twentieth century LCSH took further steps, ever so cautiously, in the direction of more rigorous faceting. In 1974, the Library of Congress took a giant leap forward when it designated a large number of frequently used topical and form subdivisions as "free-floating," thus allowing great flexibility in application. Furthermore, the adoption of BT, NT, RT in the eleventh (1988) edition brought LCSH even more in line with thesaurus practice. After the 1991 Subject Subdivisions Conference,[9] the Library embarked on a program to convert many of its topical subdivisions into topical main headings.

Finally, in 1999, it implemented subfield $v for form subdivisions in the 6XX (subject-related) fields in the MARC format, moving LCSH yet another step closer to becoming a faceted system. Considering the gradual steps the Library of Congress has taken over the years, even a person not familiar with the history of LCSH must conclude that LCSH is heading in the direction of becoming a fully faceted vocabulary. It is not there yet but, with further effort, it can become a versatile system that is capable of functioning in heterogeneous environments and can indeed serve as the unified basis for supporting diversified uses.

There is probably no question that the Library of Congress will continue to serve its traditional client population, that is, OPACs and other carefully structured retrieval services. There is also probably no question that LCSH vocabulary can be adapted to make it practical and effective for web retrieval, or that this can be done without impinging on its usefulness to its traditional clients. At least one project is underway that attempts to answer this question. The FAST (Faceted Application of Subject Terminology) schema is being developed by OCLC Online Computer Library Center for use with the Dublin Core and other metadata schemas. The following chapter describes the development and the features of FAST.

NOTES

1. Elaine Svenonius, *The Intellectual Foundation of Information Organization*, (Cambridge, Mass.: MIT Press, 2000); Elaine Svenonius, "Unanswered Questions in the Design of Controlled Vocabularies," *Journal of the American Society for Information Science* 37 (1986): 31-40.

2. David Batty, "WWW—Wealth, Weariness or Waste: Controlled Vocabulary and Thesauri in Support of Online Information Access," *D-Lib Magazine* (November 1998), available: http://www.dlib.org/dlib/november98/11batty.html.

3. Lois Mai Chan, "Exploiting LCSH, LCC, and DDC to Retrieve Networked Resources: Issues and Challenges," in *Proceedings of the Bicentennial Conference on Bibliographic Control for the New Millennium: Confronting the Challenges of Networked Resources and the Web, Washington, D.C., November 15-17, 2000*, sponsored by the Library of Congress Cataloging Directorate, ed. Ann M. Sandberg-Fox (Washington, D.C.: Library of Congress, Cataloging Distribution Service, 2001), 159-178.

4. Association for Library Collections & Technical Services, Cataloging and Classification Section, Subject Analysis Committee, *Subject Data in the Metadata Record: Recommendations and Rationale: A Report from the ALCTS/CCS/SAC/Subcommittee on Metadata and Subject Analysis*, 1999, available: http://www.ala.org/alcts/organization/ccs/sac/metarept2.html.

5. Lois Mai Chan, "Still Robust at 100: A Century of LC Subject Headings," *The Library of Congress Information Bulletin* 57(8) (August 1998): 200-201.

6. Karen M. Drabenstott, Schelle Simcox, and Marie Williams, "Do Librarians Understand the Subject Headings in Library Catalogs?" *Reference & User Services Quarterly* 38(4) (Summer 1999): 369-387.

7. Batty, "WWW—Wealth, Weariness or Waste," *D-Lib Magazine,* available: http://www.dlib.org/dlib/november98/11batty.html.

8. Thomas Mann, "Why LC Subject Headings Are More Important Than Ever: The Solution to Some of Researchers' Biggest Problems Is Staring Us Right in Our Faces," *American Libraries* 34(9) (October 2003): 52-54.

9. Subject Subdivisions Conference (1991: Airlie, Va.), *The Future of Subdivisions in the Library of Congress Subject Headings System: Report from the Subject Subdivisions Conference*, ed. Martha O'Hara Conway (Washington, D.C.: Library of Congress. Cataloging Distribution Service, 1992).

12 FAST: Faceted Application of Subject Terminology

INTRODUCTION

Since the implementation of the Dublin Core Metadata schema in the late 1990s, OCLC has been exploring ways of providing subject access to metadata records in ways that would be amenable to machine manipulation in order to capitalize on the computer's capability and efficiency in handling enormous amounts of data. Encouraged by the arguments presented by the ALCTS/SAC/Subcommittee on Metadata and Subject Analysis[1] mentioned in the previous chapter, a group of research scientists from OCLC began investigating the development of a subject vocabulary suitable for use with newly emerging metadata schemas, particularly the Dublin Core Metadata Element Set.[2] From the outset, the FAST project team concluded that the most viable option for a general-purpose metadata subject schema was to adapt Library of Congress Subject Headings (LCSH).

The new schema, known as FAST (Faceted Application of Subject Terminology), is derived from LCSH but applied with a simpler syntax. The objective of the FAST project is to develop a subject heading schema based on LCSH that is suitable for metadata and is easy to use, understand, and maintain. To achieve this objective, FAST is designed to minimize the need to construct complex subject heading strings. The ultimate goal is to simplify the syntax while retaining the richness of the LCSH vocabulary.

REASONS FOR ADAPTING LIBRARY OF CONGRESS SUBJECT HEADINGS

LCSH is the most widely used indexing vocabulary in the world and offers many significant advantages:

- It is a well-established controlled vocabulary.
- It has a long and well-documented history.
- Its rich vocabulary covers all subject areas.
- It has the strong institutional support of the Library of Congress.
- It has been extensively used by libraries.
- It has been used to provide subject access points in millions of bibliographic records.

Retaining LCSH as subject access data in metadata records would ensure semantic interoperability between the enormous store of MARC records and records based on various metadata standards.

It was pointed out in the last chapter that, although LCSH has served libraries and their patrons well for over a century, its complexity greatly restricts its use beyond the traditional cataloging environment. Some of this complexity reflects its origin as a system designed for card catalogs, where the number of headings per item that could be assigned to a given item was severely restricted. Furthermore, since the card catalog was incompatible with postcoordination, the use of precoordinated headings was the only option available.

In the new information environment, because of the varied approaches to retrieval in different search environments and the different needs of diverse user communities, a vocabulary that is flexible enough to be used either precoordinately or postcoordinately would seem the most viable. A faceted schema can accommodate different application syntaxes, from the most complex (e.g., full-string approach typically found in OPACs) to the simplest (descriptor-like terms used in most indexes) and would also allow different degrees of sophistication. The advantages of a faceted controlled vocabulary can be summarized as follows:

- simplicity in structure,
- flexibility in application (i.e., able to accommodate a tiered approach to allow different levels of subject representation),
- amenability to software applications,[3]
- amenability to computer-assisted indexing and validation,

- interoperability with the majority of modern indexing vocabularies, and
- greater ease and economy in maintenance relative to an enumerated vocabulary.

On the last point regarding efficient thesaurus maintenance, Batty remarks: "Facet procedure has many advantages. By organizing the terms into smaller, related groups, each group of terms can be examined more easily and efficiently for consistency, order, hierarchical relationships, relationships to other groups, and the acceptability of the language used in the terms. The faceted approach is also useful for its flexibility in dealing with the addition of new terms and new relationships. Because each facet can stand alone, changes can usually be made easily in a facet at any time without disturbing the rest of the thesaurus."[4] Thus, a faceted LCSH would be easier to maintain. With the current LCSH, updating terminology sometimes can be a tedious operation. For example, when the heading "Moving-pictures" was replaced in 1987 by "Motion pictures," approximately 400 authority records were affected[5] because the phrase "moving picture" formed a part of many compound and complex headings in LCSH.

LCSH is not a true thesaurus in the sense of a comprehensive list of all usable subject headings. Rather, in order to apply LCSH, the cataloger or indexer must consult both the list itself (now five volumes in their printed form) and a four-volume manual of rules detailing the requirements for creating headings that are not established in the authority file and for the further subdivision of the established headings. Only about 3 percent of all the topical and geographic headings in OCLC's WorldCat are fully established in LCSH. The remaining 97 percent of the headings have been created, correctly or incorrectly, based on these rules. Assigning LCSH headings following LC policies is thus a highly complex matter.

The rules for using free-floating subdivisions controlled by pattern headings illustrate this complexity. Under specified conditions, these free-floating subdivisions can be added to established headings. The scope of patterns is limited to particular types (patterns) of headings. For example, **Autism–Patients–Family relationships** is a valid heading string formed by adding two pattern subdivisions to the established heading **Autism. Patients** is one of several hundred subdivisions that can be used with headings for diseases and other medical conditions. Therefore, it can be used to subdivide **Autism.** However, the addition of **Patients** changes the meaning of the heading from a medical condition to a class of persons. Now, since the subdivision **Family relationships** is authorized under the pattern for classes of persons, it can also be added to complete the heading.

While the rich vocabulary and semantic relationships in LCSH provide subject access far beyond the capabilities of keywords, its complex syntax presents a stumbling block that limits its application beyond the traditional cataloging environment. Not only are the rules for pattern headings complex, their application requires extensive domain knowledge since there is no explicit coding that identifies which pattern subdivisions are appropriate for particular headings.

The traditional practice of LCSH has resulted in a complex system requiring skilled professionals for its successful application and has prompted several simplification attempts in recent years. Among these, the Subject Subdivisions Conference[6] attempted to simplify the application of LCSH subdivisions. Recently, the ALCTS/SAC/Subcommittee on Metadata and Subject Analysis[7] recommended that LCSH strings be broken up—in other words faceted—into topic, place, period, language, etc., particularly in situations where non-catalogers are assigning the headings. The Library of Congress has also embarked on a series of efforts to simplify LCSH.

To facilitate the indexing of the enormous amount of electronic resources, OCLC decided to adopt a faceted approach with greater reliance on postcoordination in implementing FAST. A faceted LCSH is by no means a new idea. Earlier advocates of such an approach include Pauline A. Cochrane[8] and Mary Dykstra.[9] To remain viable in the networked environment, a controlled vocabulary such as LCSH must be able to accommodate different application policies. Except in OPACs, most search engines, including many used in library portals for web resources, lack the ability to accommodate full-string browsing and searching. Capabilities and degrees of sophistication also vary even among systems that can handle full strings. With a faceted vocabulary, it is not an either/or proposition between the precoordinate full-string application and the postcoordinate approach. Rather, the question is whether LCSH can be made to accommodate both, as well as any variations in between—a capability that is necessary to ensure maximum flexibility and scalability in application. Mechanisms for full-string implementation of LCSH are already in place; for example, in the OPAC environment, with highly trained personnel and the searching and browsing capabilities of integrated systems, the full-string syntax has long been employed in creating subject headings in MARC records. In the heterogeneous environment outside of the OPAC, however, there is a need for a more flexible system. With a simpler application syntax, a vocabulary based on LCSH can become such a tool, and its use can be extended to various metadata standards and with different encoding schemes. The FAST schema has been developed with these considerations in mind. An important consideration is the need to ensure that the FAST schema maintains upward compatibility with LCSH, and that any valid set of LC subject headings can be converted to FAST headings.

DEVELOPING THE FAST SCHEMA

While FAST is derived from LCSH, it has been redesigned as a postcoordinated faceted vocabulary for an online environment. The goals of FAST are to design a system that will:

- be usable by people with minimal training and experience,
- enable a broad range of users to assign subject terminology to Web resources,
- be amenable to computer-assisted authority control,
- be compatible with use as embedded metadata,
- focus on making use of LCSH as a postcoordinate system in an online environment,
- be efficient and have the capacity for handling large quantities of resources,
- be scalable and extensible,
- be interoperable with other systems,
- be easy to maintain,
- be amenable to computer-assisted indexing,
- be able to accommodate different retrieval models, and,
- facilitate the mapping of subject data and cross-domain searching.

The first phase of the FAST project included the development of facets based on the vocabulary found in LCSH topical and geographic headings; it was focused on four facets: topical, geographic, form, and period. In later phases, additional facets have been added for personal names, corporate names, conference/meetings, uniform titles, and name-title entries. With the exception of the period facet, all FAST headings will be fully established in a FAST authority file.

SEMANTICS

FAST consists of eight distinct facets: Topical, Geographic (Place) Name, Personal Name, Corporate Name, Form (Type, Genre), Chronological (Time, Period), Title as Subject, and Meeting Name. The name and title facets are limited to their use as subjects.

Literary warrant is the basis for determining which headings will be established. In theory, an infinite number of valid LCSH headings can be created. For example, 175 distinct musical instruments have been identified. Therefore, by taking all the different combinations of three instruments, in theory almost a million unique headings for trios could be formed. For nonets, over a billion billion (10^{18}) combinations of nine instruments are possible. Obviously, most of these combinations will never be needed—may not even be logical. Therefore, it is neither necessary nor feasible to create headings for every possible combination. The establishment of a particular FAST heading is determined by its usage in OCLC's WorldCat, which also includes all of the headings assigned by the Library of Congress. Headings that have never been assigned in WorldCat are not established in FAST even though they may be valid.

FAST continues the use of subdivisions but differs from LCSH in that, in a particular FAST heading, subdivisions must belong to the same facet as the main heading. Topical headings can be subdivided by other topical elements, geographic headings by other geographics, etc. That is, a particular main heading may not be subdivided by subdivisions from a different facet. Therefore, FAST precoordinates elements in the same facet, but elements from different facets are to be postcoordinated in retrieval.

Another difference between LCSH and FAST practices is that all free-floating topical subdivisions will be part of the established form of the FAST headings. Elements in the same facet are precombined to the extent allowed by Library of Congress application policies. However, only those that have actually been used will be established.

Furthermore, in FAST, all LC headings with multiple subdivisions will be expanded to applicable strings. Each of the common "multiples" will be individually established. For example, based on the multiple heading **Love–Religious aspects–Buddhism, [Christianity, etc.]**, each combination of **Love–Religious aspects** and a religion that has been used in WorldCat will be individually established as a FAST heading:

Love–Religious aspects–Buddhism
Love–Religious aspects–Christianity
Love–Religious aspects–Islam
Love–Religious aspects–Hinduism
etc.

However, headings will not be established for every known religion—only those combinations that have actually been assigned.

Topical Facet

The topical facet consists of topical main headings and their corresponding general subdivisions. FAST topical headings look very similar to the established form of LCSH topical headings with the exception that established headings will include all commonly used (i.e., free-floating) topical subdivisions.

FAST topical headings are created from:

- LCSH main headings from topical headings (650) assigned to MARC records
- All associated general topical ($x) subdivisions from any type of LCSH heading
- Period subdivisions containing topical aspects from any type of LCSH heading

Examples of typical FAST topical headings are shown below:

Blacksmithing–History
Burns and scalds–Patients–Family relationships
Colombian poetry
Education
Epic literature–History and criticism
Hospitals–Staff–Labor unions–Organizing
Industrial project management–Data processing
Loudspeakers–Design and construction
Natural gas pipelines–Economic aspects
Pets and travel
Photoconductivity–Measurement
Quartets (Pianos (2), percussion)
Revolution (United States, 1775-1783)
School psychologists
Travel–Safety measures
Urbanization

Geographic Facet

The geographic facet includes all geographic names, both jurisdictional and non-jurisdictional. In LCSH, place names used as main headings are entered in direct order, for example, **San Francisco (Calif.)**, according to *AACR2R*, but when they are used as subdivisions, those representing localities appear in indirect order, that is, **California–San Francisco**. In FAST, only one form, **California–San Francisco** is used; the direct form, *San Francisco (Calif.)*, is not used. Also, first level geographic names in FAST will be far more limited than in LCSH. They will be restricted to names from the *Geographic Area Codes* table.[10] Lower-level geographic names are entered as subdivisions under the name of the smallest first level geographic area in which it is fully contained. For example, the Maya forest, which spans Belize, Guatemala, and Mexico, would be established as **North America–Maya Forest** instead of simply as *Maya Forest*.

Qualifiers are only used to identify the type of geographic name (**Kingdom**, **Satellite**, **Duchy**, **Princely State**, etc.). As with topical headings, all geographic headings will be established in an authority file. Some examples of FAST geographic headings and their corresponding Geographic Area Codes are:

Bolivia–Cochabamba (Dept.) [s-bo]
Califorina–San Francisco–Chinatown [n-us-ca]
England–Chilton (Oxfordshire) [e-uk-en]
England–Coventry [e-uk-en]
France–Loir River Valley [e-fr]
Germany [e-gx]
Great Lakes [nl]
Great Lakes–Lake Erie [nl]
India–Limbdi (Princely State) [a-ii]
Italy [e-it]
Mars [zma]
Maryland–Worcester County [n-us-md]
Ohio–Columbus [n-us-oh]
Ohio–Columbus–Clintonville [n-us-oh]
Slovenia–Maribor [e-xv]

The reason for adopting the indirect form based on the Geographic Area Codes is to provide a hierarchical structure to geographic headings. This hierarchical structure allows collocation of geographic names at various levels of generality.

Furthermore, the Geographic Area Codes can be used to limit a search to a defined geographic area such as the United States or California. In LCSH, a comprehensive search for Washington, North Carolina, for example, requires searching for both **Washington (N.C.)** and **–North Carolina–Washington**. On the other hand, in FAST, comprehensive searches are simpler since only one form of the geographic name is required to retrieve all material.

Another advantage of the hierarchical structure is its scalability. Users of FAST who do not need the granularity of the geographic subdivisions may easily adopt a higher level of geographic headings, for example, at the country or state/province level without further subdivisions down to the county or city level.

Form Facet

Form or genre data are treated as a distinct facet. The form facet includes headings converted from a variety of sources. Many of the FAST form headings are extracted form subdivisions from LCSH authority records and from assigned headings found in cataloging records, including all form subdivisions used under LC topical and geographic headings.[11]

As with the topical and geographic facets, all form headings will be established in the FAST authority file. Some examples of FAST form headings are:

Abstracts
Bibliography–Union lists
Case studies
Census
Controversial literature–Early works to 1800
Correspondence
Dictionaries
Directories
Folklore
Periodicals
Records
Rules
Slides
Statistics–Databases
Textbooks for foreign speakers
Translations into Russian

Chronological Facet

The chronological or period facet follows the practice recommended by the ALCTS/SAC Subcommittee,[12] and the recommendations discussed at the Airlie Conference:[13] Chronological headings in FAST reflect the actual time period of coverage for the resource and may not represent specific periods associated with particular events. A period heading is expressed as either a single numeric date or as a date range. In cases where the date is expressed in LCSH as a century, such as **20th century**, the heading is converted to the date range: 1900-1999. Similarly, periods related to geological eras would be expressed as dates in addition to the name of the period. For example, the Jurassic period would be expressed both as **Jurassic** and as **From 140 to 190 million years ago**.

Period subdivisions in LCSH frequently contain valuable information beyond the date information. For example, if the subdivision **Sung dynasty, 960-1279**, was simply replaced by **960-1279**, useful information would be lost. In cases where the period heading contains information that cannot be captured in a numeric date range, the subdivision may also be retained as a FAST topical heading.

The only general restriction on FAST chronological headings is that when a date range is used, the second date must be greater than the first. Therefore, there is no need to routinely create authority records for chronological headings. For example, no authority record is needed for chronological period **1900-1999** corresponding to the 20th century. Authority records for chronological headings are only created when necessary for cross references.

Personal Names

Personal names (including family names) and corporate names are both derived from the Name Authority File.[14] The requirements for either a personal or a corporate name to be included in FAST are that (1) the name is used as a subject in at least one WorldCat record and (2) the name is established in the Name Authority File and is valid for subject use. For personal names, in addition to the name, the numeration, titles, dates, and the fuller form of the name are also included in the heading. Some examples of FAST personal name headings are:

Woodward, Bob
Dewey, Melvil, 1851-1931
Kennedy family
Edward II, King of England, 1284-1327
Bush, George W. (George Walker), 1946-

Corporate Names

For a corporate body, the name and all subordinate units are included in the heading. These corporate names include those of jurisdictions, in most cases identical to geographic names, as well as corporate bodies. The origins of the names and the requirements of their inclusion in FAST are the same as those for personal names.

Examples of FAST corporate name headings include:

OCLC
Bayerische Motoren Werke
United States. Coast Guard
Bodleian Library

Meeting Names and Titles

At the time of the writing of this book, headings for meeting names, titles, and name-titles, for example, **Smollett, Tobias George, 1721-1771. Expedition of Humphry Clinker**, that are used as subjects are still under development in FAST.

CREATION AND VALIDATION OF FAST HEADINGS

As mentioned earlier, FAST headings are being derived from headings enumerated in LCSH and from the set of LCSH headings assigned to the records in WorldCat by separating them into the appropriate facets. There are approximately eight million unique topical and geographic headings in OCLC's WorldCat. Each of these headings has been extracted and parsed into the appropriate facet. For example, the topical heading **Slavery–United States–Fiction** would be faceted into the following three FAST headings:

Slavery (Topical)
United States (Geographic)
Fiction (Form)

The geographic heading **United State–History–Civil War, 1861-1865–Sources** would be faceted into:

Civil War, 1861-1865 (United States) (Topical)
United States (Geographic)
1861-1865 (Period)
Sources (Form)

Each heading that has been created undergoes a validation process. For this validation process, first a file containing all unique LCSH topical and geographic subject headings extracted from OCLC's WorldCat was created. In early 2005, this file contained a total of 1,343,439 FAST headings, representing over 50 million individual subject heading assignments in MARC records. These headings and heading strings were then faceted to create the initial versions of the FAST topical, geographic, chronological, and form facets. A variety of algorithms have been developed for validating the headings automatically. This initial set of headings underwent extensive validation to minimize the number of erroneous entries. The entries remaining after this validation step were then established as FAST headings.

AUTHORITY RECORDS

The final step in developing FAST has been the creation of an authority record for each established and validated heading. Because of its wide acceptance, the MARC 21 format for authority data[15] was selected; the format is very comprehensive and meets most, if not all, of the FAST requirements. However, neither the authorities nor the bibliographic formats accommodated chronological headings—only chronological subdivisions. A proposal[16] was submitted to the MARBI (Machine-Readable Bibliographic Information) Committee, the interdivisional committee of the American Library Association charged with maintaining standards for the representation in machine-readable form of bibliographic information. That proposal was accepted with some minor enhancements in June 2002. As a result, additional fields have been added to the MARC 21 formats to accommodate the unique requirements of FAST. Examples of FAST authority records are shown in figures 12.1 and 12.2.

```
LDR     nz n
001     fast 611370
003     OCoLC
005     20021209141434.0
008     021209nneanz||babn n ana d
040     OCoLC $b eng $c OCoLC $f fast
050     RC684.D5
150     Heart $x Diseases $x Diet therapy
550     Heart $x Diseases $x Nutritional aspects
550     Heart $x Diseases $x Treatment
688     LC usage 64 (1999)
688     OCLC usage 394 (1999)
750   0 Heart $x Diseases $x Diet therapy $0 (DLC)sh 85059656
```

Figure 12.1. MARC 21 FAST Topical Authority Record for **Heart–Diseases–Diet therapy**

```
LDR    00661nz    2200181n   4500
001 fast 522597
003 OCoLC
005 20030321133146.0
008 030321nneanz||babn            n ana     d
040   $a OCoLC $b eng $c OCoLC $f fast
043   $a n-us-ga
151   $a Georgia $z Saint Simons Island
451   $a Georgia $z Saint Simons
451   $a Georgia $z St. Simons Island
451   $a Georgia $z Saint Simon Island
451   $a Georgia $z Saint Simons Village
670   $a GNIS, Feb. 12, 2002 $b (Saint Simons Island, PPL,
      31° 09′ 01" N, 81° 22′11" W, Glynn County, variants:
      Saint Simon Island, Saint Simons, Saint Simons Village)
751 0 $a Saint Simons Island (Ga.) $0 (DLC)n 82023244
```

Figure 12.2. MARC 21 FAST Geographic Authority Record for **Georgia–Saint Simon Island**

In FAST, authority records for topical and geographic headings and cross references from the original LC authority records are retained where appropriate.

APPLICATION SYNTAX

A main reason for developing FAST has been to create a rich controlled vocabulary based on LCSH but with a simpler syntax. Instead of complex heading strings containing multiple facets, FAST established separate headings for individual facets to be used in indexing. These facets are to be combined as appropriate in retrieval. While each heading represents basically only one facet, it may contain multiple elements from the same facet. In other words, concepts belonging to the same facet are precoordinated, while concepts from different facets are to be postcoordinated. The combination of elements in the same facet is built into the vocabulary and stored in authority records, and catalogers and indexers are not required to construct complex headings based on intricate rules and policies.

On the other hand, the disadvantages of a postcoordinate approach are well recognized. A precoordinated heading containing all facets provides a context for the individual terms within the string. In the postcoordinate approach, such context is often lost. Another drawback of postcoordination is the possibility of mismatched facets in retrieval, a form of cross-coordination. For example, a search for works on "gold mining in Colorado" will retrieve a work on "gold mining in California and silver mining in Colorado" because **Gold mining**, **Silver mining**, **California**, and **Colorado** have been assigned as separate headings to be freely combined for retrieval.

CONCLUSION

At the time of the writing of this book, much work remains to be done before the FAST authority files are complete and ready for use. Nonetheless, the project has demonstrated that it is possible to derive a new subject schema based on the terminology of LCSH but with simpler syntax and application rules. Upon completion, the FAST authority records will be extensively tested and evaluated. The evaluation will determine if the FAST team has achieved its goal of creating a new subject schema for metadata that retains the rich vocabulary of LCSH while being easy to maintain, apply, and use.

NOTES

1. Association for Library Collections & Technical Services, Cataloging and Classification Section, Subject Analysis Committee, Subcommittee on Metadata and Subject Analysis, *Subject Data in the Metadata Record Recommendations and Rationale: A Report from the ALCTS/SAC/Subcommittee on Metadata and Subject Analysis,* 1999, available: http://www.govst.edu/users/gddcasey/sac/MetadataReport.html.

2. Edward T. O'Neill and Lois Mai Chan, "FAST (Faceted Application of Subject Terminology): A Simplified Vocabulary Based on The Library Of Congress Subject Headings," *IFLA Journal* 29(4) (December 2003): 336-342.

3. David Batty, "WWW—Wealth, Weariness or Waste: Controlled Vocabulary and Thesauri in Support of Online Information Access," *D-Lib Magazine* (November 1998), available: http://www.dlib.org/dlib/november98/11batty.html.

4. Batty, "WWW—Wealth, Weariness or Waste."

5. Lynn M. El-Hoshy, "Charting a Changing Language with LCSH," *Library of Congress Information Bulletin* 57(8) (August 1998): 201.

6. Subject Subdivisions Conference (1991: Airlie, Va.)., *The Future of Subdivisions in the Library of Congress Subject Headings System: Report from the Subject Subdivisions Conference*, sponsored by the Library of Congress, May 9-12, 1991, ed. Martha O'Hara Conway (Washington, D.C.: Library of Congress, Cataloging Distribution Service, 1992).

7. Association for Library Collections & Technical Services, *Subject Data in the Metadata Record.*

8. Pauline A. Cochrane, *Improving LCSH for Use in Online Catalogs: Exercises for Self-Help with a Selection of Background Readings* (Littleton, CO: Libraries Unlimited, 1986).

9. Mary Dykstra, "LC Subject Headings Disguised as a Thesaurus," *Library Journal* 113 (March 1, 1988): 42-46.

10. Library of Congress, Network Development and MARC Standards Office. *MARC Code List for Geographic Areas,* Web version, last updated on March 11, 2003, available: http://www.loc.gov/marc/geoareas/gacshome.html.

11. Edward T. O'Neill, Lois Mai Chan, Eric Childress, Rebecca Dean, Lynn El-Hoshy, Kerre Kammerer, and Diane Vizine-Goetz. "Form Subdivisions: Their Identification and Use in LCSH," *Library Resources & Technical Services* 45(4) (2001): 187-197.

12. Association for Library Collections & Technical Services, *Subject Data in the Metadata Record.*

13. Subject Subdivisions Conference, *The Future of Subdivisions in the Library of Congress Subject Headings System.*

14. *Library of Congress Authorities,* available: http://authorities.loc.gov.

15. Library of Congress, Network Development and MARC Standards Office, *MARC 21 Format for Authority Data: Including Guidelines for Content Designation* (Washington, D.C.: Cataloging Distribution Service, Library of Congress, 1999).

16. *Changes for Faceted Application of Subject Terminology (FAST) Subject Headings, Proposal 202-13*, May 8, 2002, available: http://lcweb.loc.gov/marc/marbi/2002/2002-13.html (accessed March 10, 2003).

Appendix A:
Library of Congress Bibliographic Records with MARC 21 Coding

Examples taken from Library of Congress Online Catalog: http://catalog.loc.gov/.

LC Control Number: 2003058703

000 01353cam 2200301 a 450

001 13313490

005 20040506131420.0

008 030814s2004 nyuab b 001 0deng

010 __ |**a** 2003058703

020 __ |**a** 0375507388 (acid-free paper)

040 __ |**a** DLC |**c** DLC |**d** DLC

043 __ |**a** n-us---

050 00 |**a** E457.2 |**b** .P47 2004

082 00 |**a** 973.7/092 |**a** B |**2** 22

100 1_ |**a** Perret, Geoffrey.

245 10 |**a** Lincoln's war : |**b** the untold story of America's greatest president as commander in chief / |**c** Geoffrey Perret.

250 __ |**a** 1st ed.

260 __ |**a** New York : |**b** Random House, |**c** c2004.

300 __ |**a** xv, 470 p. : |**b** ill., maps ; |**c** 25 cm.

504 __ |**a** Includes bibliographical references (p. [407]-452) and index.

600 10 |**a** Lincoln, Abraham, |**d** 1809-1865 |**x** Military leadership.

651 _0 |**a** United States |**x** Politics and government |**y** 1861-1865.

650 _0 |**a** Executive power |**z** United States |**x** History |**y** 19th century.

651 _0 |**a** United States |**x** History |**y** Civil War, 1861-1865.

651 _0 |**a** United States |**x** History |**y** Civil War, 1861-1865 |**v** Biography.

LC Control Number: 2004045122

000 01273cam 2200325 a 450
001 13491734
005 20040528111731.0
008 040217s2004 nyua b 001 0ceng
010 __ |**a** 2004045122
020 __ |**a** 0385498632
040 __ |**a** DLC |**c** DLC |**d** DLC
043 __ |**a** n-us---
050 00 |**a** E904.B87 |**b** S39 2004
082 00 |**a** 929/.2/0973 |**2** 22
100 1_ |**a** Schweizer, Peter, |**d** 1964-
245 14 |**a** The Bushes : |**b** portrait of a dynasty / |**c** Peter Schweizer and Rochelle Schweizer.
250 __ |**a** 1st ed.
260 __ |**a** New York : |**b** Doubleday, |**c** c2004.
300 __ |**a** xvii, 574 p. : |**b** ill. ; |**c** 25 cm.
504 __ |**a** Includes bibliographical references and index.
600 30 |**a** Bush family.
600 10 |**a** Bush, George W. |**q** (George Walker), |**d** 1946- |**x** Family.
650 _0 |**a** Politicians |**z** United States |**v** Biography.
650 _0 |**a** Presidents |**z** United States |**v** Biography.
650 _0 |**a** Businessmen |**z** United States |**v** Biography.
651 _0 |**a** United States |**v** Biography.
700 1_ |**a** Schweizer, Rochelle, |**d** 1961-

LC Control Number: 2002005274

000 01339cam 22003134a 450
001 12730035
005 20021005110708.0
008 020404s2002 wauab b 001 0 eng
010 __ |**a** 2002005274
020 __ |**a** 0898868718 (pbk.)
040 __ |**a** DLC |**c** DLC |**d** DLC
042 __ |**a** pcc
043 __ |**a** a-cc--- |**a** a-np---
050 00 |**a** GV199.44.E85 |**b** H45 2002
082 00 |**a** 915.49/6 |**2** 21
100 1_ |**a** Hemmleb, Jochen, |**d** 1971-
245 10 |**a** Detectives on Everest : |**b** the 2001 Mallory & Irvine research expedition / |**c** Jochen Hemmleb with Eric Simonson ; contributions from Dave Hahn ... [et al.].
260 __ |**a** Seattle, WA : |**b** Mountaineers Books, |**c** c2002.
300 __ |**a** 205 p., [8] p. of plates : |**b** ill. (some col.), maps ; |**c** 24 cm.
504 __ |**a** Includes bibliographical references (p. 200-202) and index.
650 _0 |**a** Mountaineering expeditions |**z** Everest, Mount (China and Nepal)
600 10 |**a** Leigh-Mallory, George Herbert, |**d** 1886-1924.
600 10 |**a** Irvine, Andrew, |**d** 1902-1924.
611 20 |**a** Mount Everest Expedition |**d** (1924)
700 1_ |**a** Simonson, Eric R.
700 1_ |**a** Hahn, Dave.

LC Control Number: 2001046945

000 01322cam 22003014a 450
001 12561638
005 20020911085959.0
008 011011s2001 ctua bc 000 0 eng
010 __ |**a** 2001046945
020 __ |**a** 0894679511
040 __ |**a** DLC |**c** DLC |**d** DLC
042 __ |**a** pcc
043 __ |**a** e-fr--- |**a** n-us-ct
050 00 |**a** ND547.5.I4 |**b** Y35 2001
082 00 |**a** 759.4/09/0340747468 |**2** 21
110 2_ |**a** Yale University. |**b** Art Gallery.
245 12 |**a** A selection of French impressionist paintings from the Yale University Art Gallery / |**c** Susan D. Greenberg ; foreword by Robert L. Herbert.
260 __ |**a** New Haven, CT : |**b** Yale University Press, |**c** [2001]
300 __ |**a** 47 p. : |**b** ill. (some col.), maps ; |**c** 23 cm.
504 __ |**a** Includes bibliographical references.
650 _0 |**a** Impressionism (Art) |**z** France |**v** Catalogs.
650 _0 |**a** Painting, French |**y** 19th century |**v** Catalogs.
650 _0 |**a** Painting |**z** Connecticut |**z** New Haven |**v** Catalogs.
610 20 |**a** Yale University. |**b** Art Gallery |**v** Catalogs.
700 1_ |**a** Greenberg, Susan D., |**d** 1971-

LC Control Number: 2001019429

000 01305cam 2200289 a 450
001 12331047
005 20020926201556.0
008 010301s2001 nyuao b 001 0beng
010 __ **|a** 2001019429
020 __ **|a** 0679449868
040 __ **|a** DLC **|c** DLC **|d** DLC
043 __ **|a** n-us---
050 00 **|a** PS1541.Z5 **|b** H32 2001
082 00 **|a** 811/.4 **|a** B **|2** 21
100 1_ **|a** Habegger, Alfred.
245 00 **|a** My wars are laid away in books : **|b** the life of Emily Dickinson / **|c** Alfred Habegger.
250 __ **|a** 1st ed.
260 __ **|a** New York : **|b** Random House, **|c** c2001.
300 __ **|a** xvii, 764 p. : **|b** ill. ; **|c** 24 cm.
504 __ **|a** Includes bibliographical references (p. [660]-739) and indexes.
600 10 **|a** Dickinson, Emily, **|d** 1830-1886.
650 _0 **|a** Poets, American **|y** 19th century **|x** Biography.
650 _0 **|a** Women and literature **|z** United States **|x** History **|y** 19th century.
856 41 **|3** Table of contents **|u** http://www.loc.gov/catdir/toc/fy022/2001019429.html

LC Control Number: 2002017537

000 01369cam 22003254a 450
001 12651248
005 20030313125720.0
008 020122s2002 miu b 001 0 eng
010 __ |**a** 2002017537 |**z** 2002019704
020 __ |**a** 0892641525 (alk. paper)
020 __ |**a** 0892641533 (pbk. : alk. paper)
040 __ |**a** DLC |**c** DLC |**d** DLC
042 __ |**a** pcc
043 __ |**a** a-cc---
050 00 |**a** Z3106 |**b** .B76 2002 |**a** DS705
082 00 |**a** 016.9151 |**2** 21
100 1_ |**a** Brook, Timothy, |**d** 1951-
245 10 |**a** Geographical sources of Ming-Qing history / |**c** Timothy Brook.
250 __ |**a** 2nd ed.
260 __ |**a** Ann Arbor : |**b** Center for Chinese Studies, University of Michigan, |**c** c2002.
300 __ |**a** xx, 267 p. ; |**c** 24 cm.
490 1_ |**a** Michigan monographs in Chinese studies ; |**x** 1081-9053 |**v** v. 58
504 __ |**a** Includes bibliographical references and indexes.
651 _0 |**a** China |**v** Gazetteers |**v** Bibliography.
651 _0 |**a** China |**x** History |**y** Ming dynasty, 1368-1644.
651 _0 |**a** China |**x** History |**y** Qing dynasty, 1644-1912.
830 _0 |**a** Michigan monographs in Chinese studies ; |**v** no. 58.

LC Control Number: 2001017061

000 01836cam 22003854a 450

001 12273191

005 20030814180905.0

008 010106r20011944nyua b 000 0 eng

010 __ |**a** 2001017061

020 __ |**a** 0486417182 (pbk.)

040 __ |**a** DLC |**c** DLC |**d** DLC

042 __ |**a** pcc

043 __ |**a** n-us-dc

050 00 |**a** NA735.W3 |**b** D38 2001

082 00 |**a** 728/.0973 |**2** 21

100 1_ |**a** Davis, Deering.

245 10 |**a** Georgetown houses of the Federal period / |**c** Deering Davis, Stephen P. Dorsey, and Ralph Cole Hall ; foreword by Nancy McClelland.

260 __ |**a** Mineola, N.Y. : |**b** Dover Publications, |**c** 2001.

300 __ |**a** 130 p. : |**b** ill. ; |**c** 29 cm.

500 __ |**a** "Unabridged republication of the work originally published in 1944 by the Architectural Book Publishing Co., New York"—T.p. verso.

504 __ |**a** Includes bibliographical references (p. 129-130).

650 _0 |**a** Architecture, Domestic |**z** Washington (D.C.)

650 _0 |**a** Architecture |**z** Washington (D.C.) |**y** 18th century.

650 _0 |**a** Architecture |**z** Washington (D.C.) |**y** 19th century.

650 _0 |**a** Neoclassicism (Architecture) |**z** Washington (D.C.)

650 _0 |**a** Decoration and ornament |**z** Washington (D.C.) |**x** Federal style.

651 _0 |**a** Georgetown (Washington, D.C.)

651 _0 |**a** Washington (D.C.) |**x** Buildings, structures, etc.

651 _0 |**a** Georgetown (Washington, D.C.) |**x** Buildings, structures, etc.

700 1_ |**a** Dorsey, Stephen P. |**q** (Stephen Palmer), |**d** 1913-

700 1_ |**a** Hall, Ralph Cole, |**d** 1897-

856 42 |**3** Publisher description |**u** http://www.loc.gov/catdir/description/dover031/2001017061.html

LC Control Number: 2002040918

000 01132cam 2200277 a 450
001 12981204
005 20040123211015.0
008 021025s2003 nyu 000 1 eng
010 __ |**a** 2002040918
020 __ |**a** 0385504209 (alk. paper)
040 __ |**a** DLC |**c** DLC |**d** DLC
050 00 |**a** PS3552.R685434 |**b** D3 2003
082 00 |**a** 813/.54 |**2** 21
100 1_ |**a** Brown, Dan, |**d** 1964-
245 14 |**a** The Da Vinci code : |**b** a novel / |**c** Dan Brown.
250 __ |**a** 1st ed.
260 __ |**a** New York : |**b** Doubleday, |**c** 2003.
300 __ |**a** 454 p. ; |**c** 25 cm.
600 00 |**a** Leonardo, |**c** da Vinci, |**d** 1452-1519 |**v** Fiction.
650 _0 |**a** Grail |**v** Fiction.
650 _0 |**a** Cryptographers |**v** Fiction.
655 _7 |**a** Mystery fiction. |**2** gsafd
856 42 |**3** Publisher description |**u** http://www.loc.gov/catdir/description/random044/2002040918.html

LC Control Number: 2003045006

000 01814cam 2200361 a 450
001 13106226
005 20040121113241.0
008 030227s2004 wiuab c b 001 0beng
010 __ |**a** 2003045006
020 __ |**a** 0836855353 (lib. bdg.)
040 __ |**a** DLC |**c** DLC |**d** DLC
042 __ |**a** lcac
043 __ |**a** e-ur---
050 00 |**a** DK170 |**b** .H375 2004
082 00 |**a** 947/.063/092 |**a** B |**2** 21
100 1_ |**a** Hatt, Christine.
245 10 |**a** Catherine the Great / |**c** Christine Hatt.
260 __ |**a** Milwaukee, Wis. : |**b** World Almanac Library, |**c** 2004.
300 __ |**a** 64 p. : |**b** col. ill., col. maps ; |**c** 26 cm.
440 _0 |**a** Judge for yourself
520 __ |**a** A biography of the German princess who became the absolute ruler of the Russian empire and won for herself the reputation of being a great enlightened monarch.
504 __ |**a** Includes bibliographical references and index.
505 0_ |**a** Early years -- The Romanov dynasty -- A married woman -- The new empress -- Russian society -- War, rebellion, and reform -- Home and abroad -- The final years.
600 00 |**a** Catherine |**b** II, |**c** Empress of Russia, |**d** 1729-1796 |**v** Juvenile literature.
651 _0 |**a** Russia |**x** History |**y** Catherine II, 1762-1796 |**v** Juvenile literature.
650 _0 |**a** Empresses |**z** Russia |**v** Biography |**v** Juvenile literature.
600 01 |**a** Catherine |**b** II, |**c** Empress of Russia, |**d** 1729-1796.
650 _1 |**a** Kings, queens, rulers, etc.
651 _1 |**a** Russia |**x** History |**y** Catherine II, 1762-1796.
650 _1 |**a** Women |**v** Biography.

LC Control Number: 2003586718

000 01096cam 22003133a 45
001 13298626
005 20030801110139.0
008 030422s2003 ilua j 000 1 eng d
010 __ |**a** 2003586718
042 __ |**a** lccopycat
035 __ |**a** (OCoLC)ocm52102768
040 __ |**a** IMF |**c** IMF |**d** DLC
020 __ |**a** 0842355464 (pbk.) : |**c** $5.99
050 00 |**a** CPB Box no. 2036 vol. 17
100 1_ |**a** Mackall, Dandi Daley.
245 10 |**a** Unhappy Appy / |**c** Dandi Daley Mackall.
246 1_ |**i** At head of title: |**a** Winnie the horse gentler
260 __ |**a** Wheaton, Ill. : |**b** Tyndale House Publishers, |**c** c2003.
300 __ |**a** 183 p. : |**b** ill. ; |**c** 18 cm.
490 1_ |**a** Winnie, the horse gentler ; |**v** 5
500 __ |**a** "Tyndale kids."
650 _0 |**a** Horses |**v** Fiction.
650 _0 |**a** Teenage girls |**v** Fiction.
655 _7 |**a** Young adult fiction. |**2** lcsh
655 _7 |**a** Religious fiction. |**2** lcsh
710 2_ |**a** Copyright Paperback Collection (Library of Congress) |**5** DLC
800 1_ |**a** Mackall, Dandi Daley. |**t** Winnie the horse gentler ; |**v** 5.

Appendix B

Free-Floating Subdivisions: Form and Topical

Library of Congress, *Subject Cataloging Manual: Subject Headings*, H1095.

–Abbreviations
–Abbreviations–Dictionaries
–Abbreviations of titles
–Ability testing *(May Subd Geog)*
–Abstracting and indexing *(May Subd Geog)*
–Abstracts
–Access control *(May Subd Geog)*
–Accidents *(May Subd Geog)*
–Accidents–Investigation *(May Subd Geog)*
–Accounting
–Accreditation *(May Subd Geog)*
–Acronyms
–Acronyms–Dictionaries
–Administration
–Aerial photographs
–Air conditioning *(May Subd Geog)*
–Air conditioning–Control *(May Subd Geog)*
–Amateurs' manuals
–Analysis
–Anecdotes
–Anniversaries, etc.
–Archival resources
–Archives
–Archives–Microform catalogs
–Art
–Atlases
–Audio-visual aids
–Audio-visual aids–Catalogs
–Audiotape catalogs
–Auditing
–Authorship
–Automatic control
–Automation
–Autonomous communities
–Autonomous regions
–Awards *(May Subd Geog)*
–Barrier-free design *(May Subd Geog)*
–Biblical teaching
–Bibliography
–Bibliography–Catalogs
–Bibliography–Dictionaries
–Bibliography–Early
–Bibliography–Exhibitions
–Bibliography–Methodology
–Bibliography–Microform catalogs
–Bibliography–Union lists
–Bibliography of bibliographies
–Bio-bibliography
–Bio-bibliography–Dictionaries
–Biography
–Biography–Dictionaries
–Biography–Dictionaries–French, [Italian, etc.]
–Biography–History and criticism
–Book reviews
–Buildings
–By-laws
–By-products
–Calendars
–Calibration *(May Subd Geog)*
–Cantons
–Caricatures and cartoons
–Case studies
–Catalogs
–Catalogs and collections *(May Subd Geog)*
–CD-ROM catalogs
–Censorship *(May Subd Geog)*
–Centennial celebrations, etc.
–Certification *(May Subd Geog)*
–Charitable contributions *(May Subd Geog)*
–Charts, diagrams, etc.
–Chronology
–Citizen participation
–Classification
–Cleaning *(May Subd Geog)*
–Code numbers

–Code words
–Cold weather conditions
–Collectibles *(May Subd Geog)*
–Collection and preservation *(May Subd Geog)*
–Collectors and collecting *(May Subd Geog)*
–Colonies
–Comic books, strips, etc.
–Communication systems
–Compact disc catalogs
–Comparative method
–Comparative studies
–Competitions *(May Subd Geog)*
–Composition
–Computer-aided design *(May Subd Geog)*
–Computer-assisted instruction
–Computer games
–Computer network resources
–Computer networks *(May Subd Geog)*
–Computer networks–Security measures *(May Subd Geog)*
–Computer programs
–Computer simulation
–Concordances
–Congresses
–Congresses–Attendance
–Conservation and restoration *(May Subd Geog)*
–Control *(May Subd Geog)*
–Cooling *(May Subd Geog)*
–Corrosion *(May Subd Geog)*
–Corrupt practices *(May Subd Geog)*
–Cost control
–Cost effectiveness
–Cost of operation
–Costs
–Cross-cultural studies
–Cult *(May Subd Geog)*
–Curricula *(May Subd Geog)*
–Customer services *(May Subd Geog)*
–Data processing
–Data tape catalogs
–Databases
–Dating
–Decision making
–Defects *(May Subd Geog)*
–Defects–Reporting *(May Subd Geog)*
–Defense measures *(May Subd Geog)*
–Departments
–Design
–Design and construction
–Designs and plans
–Deterioration
–Dictionaries
–Dictionaries–French, [Italian, etc.]
–Dictionaries–Polyglot
–Dictionaries, Juvenile
–Digitization *(May Subd Geog)*
–Directories
–Discipline
–Discography
–Documentation *(May Subd Geog)*
–Drama
–Drawings
–Drying *(May Subd Geog)*
–Dust control *(May Subd Geog)*
–Early works to 1800
–Earthquake effects *(May Subd Geog)*
–Econometric models
–Economic aspects *(May Subd Geog)*
–Electromechanical analogies
–Electronic discussion groups
–Electronic information resources
–Employees
–Encyclopedias
–Encyclopedias, Juvenile
–Endowments
–Energy conservation *(May Subd Geog)*
–Energy consumption *(May Subd Geog)*
–Environmental aspects *(May Subd Geog)*
–Equipment and supplies
–Estimates *(May Subd Geog)*
–Evaluation
–Examinations
–Examinations–Study guides
–Examinations, questions, etc.
–Exhibitions
–Experiments
–Expertising *(May Subd Geog)*
–Facsimiles
–Fiction
–Field work
–Film catalogs
–Finance
–Fires and fire prevention *(May Subd Geog)*

–Folklore
–Food service *(May Subd Geog)*
–Forecasting
–Foreign countries
–Foreign influences
–Forgeries *(May Subd Geog)*
–Forms
–Fume control *(May Subd Geog)*
–Geographic information systems *(May Subd Geog)*
–Government policy *(May Subd Geog)*
–Grading *(May Subd Geog)*
–Graphic methods
–Guidebooks
–Handbooks, manuals, etc.
–Health aspects *(May Subd Geog)*
–Heating and ventilation *(May Subd Geog)*
–Heating and ventilation–Control *(May Subd Geog)*
–Heraldry
–Historiography
–History
–History–To 1500
–History–16th century
–History–17th century
–History–18th century
–History–19th century
–History–20th century
–History–21st century
–History–Chronology
–History–Philosophy
–History–Sources
–History and criticism
–History of doctrines
–History of doctrines–Early church, ca 30-600
–History of doctrines–Middle Ages, 600-1500
–History of doctrines–16th century
–History of doctrines–17th century
–History of doctrines–18th century
–History of doctrines–19th century
–History of doctrines–20th century
–History of doctrines–21st century
–Hot weather conditions *(May Subd Geog)*
–Humor
–Identification
–Illustrations
–In art
–Indexes
–Industrial applications *(May Subd Geog)*
–Influence
–Information resources
–Information resources management *(May Subd Geog)*
–Information services
–Information technology *(May Subd Geog)*
–Insignia
–Inspection *(May Subd Geog)*
–Installation *(May Subd Geog)*
–Instruments
–Interactive multimedia
–International cooperation
–Interpretation
–Inventories
–Inventory control *(May Subd Geog)*
–Job descriptions *(May Subd Geog)*
–Juvenile drama
–Juvenile fiction
–Juvenile films
–Juvenile humor
–Juvenile literature
–Juvenile poetry
–Juvenile software
–Juvenile sound recordings
–Labeling *(May Subd Geog)*
–Labor productivity *(May Subd Geog)*
–Laboratory manuals
–Landscape architecture *(May Subd Geog)*
–Language
–Legends
–Library resources
–Licenses *(May Subd Geog)*
–Licenses–Fees *(May Subd Geog)*
–Lighting *(May Subd Geog)*
–Linear programming
–Literary collections
–Liturgy
–Liturgy–Texts
–Location *(May Subd Geog)*
–Longitudinal studies
–Maintenance and repair
–Management

–Manuscripts
–Manuscripts–Catalogs
–Manuscripts–Facsimiles
–Manuscripts–Indexes
–Manuscripts–Microform catalogs
–Maps
–Maps–Bibliography
–Maps–Early works to 1800
–Maps–Facsimiles
–Maps–Symbols
–Maps, Comparative
–Maps, Manuscript
–Maps, Mental
–Maps, Outline and base
–Maps, Physical
–Maps, Pictorial
–Maps, Topographic
–Maps, Tourist
–Maps for children
–Maps for people with visual disabilities
–Maps for the blind
–Marketing
–Materials *(May Subd Geog)*
–Mathematical models
–Mathematics
–Measurement
–Medals *(May Subd Geog)*
–Medical examinations *(May Subd Geog)*
–Meditations
–Membership
–Methodology
–Microform catalogs
–Miscellanea
–Models *(May Subd Geog)*
–Moisture *(May Subd Geog)*
–Moral and ethical aspects *(May Subd Geog)*
–Museums *(May Subd Geog)*
–Mythology *(May Subd Geog)*
–Name
–Names
–Newspapers
–Noise
–Nomenclature
–Nomograms
–Notation
–Observations
–Observers' manuals
–Officials and employees
–On postage stamps
–Orbit
–Outlines, syllabi, etc.
–Packaging *(May Subd Geog)*
–Packing *(May Subd Geog)*
–Pamphlets
–Papal documents
–Parodies, imitations, etc.
–Passenger lists
–Patents
–Periodicals
–Periodicals–Abbreviations of titles
–Periodicals–Bibliography
–Periodicals–Bibliography–Catalogs
–Periodicals–Bibliography–Union lists
–Periodicals–Indexes
–Personal narratives
–Personal narratives–History and criticism
–Personnel management
–Philosophy
–Photographs
–Photographs from space
–Physiological aspects
–Physiological effect *(May Subd Geog)*
–Pictorial works
–Planning
–Poetry
–Political activity
–Political aspects *(May Subd Geog)*
–Popular works
–Posters
–Power supply *(May Subd Geog)*
–Practice *(May Subd Geog)*
–Prayer-books and devotions
–Prayer-books and devotions–English, [French, German, etc.]
–Prayer-books and devotions–History and criticism
–Preservation *(May Subd Geog)*
–Press coverage *(May Subd Geog)*
–Prevention
–Prices *(May Subd Geog)*
–Prices–Government policy *(May Subd Geog)*
–Private collections *(May Subd Geog)*
–Privileges and immunities

–Problems, exercises, etc.
–Production and direction *(May Subd Geog)*
–Production control *(May Subd Geog)*
–Production standards *(May Subd Geog)*
–Programmed instruction
–Programming *(May Subd Geog)*
–Prophecies
–Protection *(May Subd Geog)*
–Provinces
–Psychological aspects
–Psychology
–Public opinion
–Public relations *(May Subd Geog)*
–Publishing *(May Subd Geog)*
–Purchasing *(May Subd Geog)*
–Quality control
–Quotations, maxims, etc.
–Rates *(May Subd Geog)*
–Records and correspondence
–Recreational use *(May Subd Geog)*
–Reference books
–Regional disparities
–Regions
–Registers
–Reliability
–Religion
–Remodeling *(May Subd Geog)*
–Remote sensing
–Remote-sensing maps
–Repairing *(May Subd Geog)*
–Republics
–Research *(May Subd Geog)*
–Research grants *(May Subd Geog)*
–Reviews
–Risk assessment *(May Subd Geog)*
–Romances
–Rules
–Rules and practice
–Safety appliances *(May Subd Geog)*
–Safety measures
–Safety regulations *(May Subd Geog)*
–Sanitation *(May Subd Geog)*
–Scholarships, fellowships, etc *(May Subd Geog)*
–Scientific applications *(May Subd Geog)*
–Security measures *(May Subd Geog)*
–Sermons
–Sermons–History and criticism
–Sex differences
–Simulation methods
–Slang
–Slides
–Social aspects *(May Subd Geog)*
–Societies, etc.
–Sociological aspects
–Software
–Songs and music
–Songs and music–Discography
–Songs and music–History and criticism
–Songs and music–Texts
–Soundproofing *(May Subd Geog)*
–Sources
–Specifications *(May Subd Geog)*
–Specimens
–Spectra
–Speeches in Congress
–Stability
–Standards *(May Subd Geog)*
–State supervision
–States
–Statistical methods
–Statistical services
–Statistics
–Storage *(May Subd Geog)*
–Study and teaching *(May Subd Geog)*
–Study and teaching–Activity programs *(May Subd Geog)*
–Study and teaching–Audio-visual aids
–Study and teaching–Simulation methods
–Study and teaching–Supervision *(May Subd Geog)*
–Study and teaching (Continuing education) *(May Subd Geog)*
–Study and teaching (Continuing education)–Audio-visual aids
–Study and teaching (Early childhood) *(May Subd Geog)*
–Study and teaching (Early childhood)–Activity programs *(May Subd Geog)*
–Study and teaching (Early childhood)–Audio-visual aids
–Study and teaching (Elementary) *(May Subd Geog)*

–Study and teaching (Elementary)–Activity programs *(May Subd Geog)*
–Study and teaching (Elementary)–Audio-visual aids
–Study and teaching (Elementary)–Simulation methods
–Study and teaching (Graduate) *(May Subd Geog)*
–Study and teaching (Higher) *(May Subd Geog)*
–Study and teaching (Higher)–Activity programs *(May Subd Geog)*
–Study and teaching (Higher)–Audio-visual aids
–Study and teaching (Higher)–Simulation methods
–Study and teaching (Internship) *(May Subd Geog)*
–Study and teaching (Middle school) *(May Subd Geog)*
–Study and teaching (Middle school)–Activity programs *(May Subd Geog)*
–Study and teaching (Middle school)–Audio-visual aids
–Study and teaching (Preschool) *(May Subd Geog)*
–Study and teaching (Preschool)–Activity programs *(May Subd Geog)*
–Study and teaching (Preschool)–Audio-visual aids
–Study and teaching (Primary) *(May Subd Geog)*
–Study and teaching (Primary)–Activity programs *(May Subd Geog)*
–Study and teaching (Primary)–Audio-visual aids
–Study and teaching (Residency) *(May Subd Geog)*
–Study and teaching (Secondary) *(May Subd Geog)*
–Study and teaching (Secondary)–Activity programs *(May Subd Geog)*
–Study and teaching (Secondary)–Audio-visual aids
–Study and teaching (Secondary)–Simulation methods
–Study guides
–Tables
–Tables of contents
–Taxation *(May Subd Geog)*
–Taxation–Law and legislation *(May Subd Geog)*
–Technique
–Technological innovations *(May Subd Geog)*
–Telephone directories
–Terminology
–Terminology–Pronunciation
–Territories and possessions
–Testing
–Textbooks
–Texts
–Themes, motives
–Therapeutic use *(May Subd Geog)*
–Tombs *(May Subd Geog)*
–Toxicology *(May Subd Geog)*
–Trademarks
–Translating *(May Subd Geog)*
–Translations
–Translations into [*name of language*]
–Transportation *(May Subd Geog)*
–Tropical conditions
–Union lists
–Union territories
–Use studies
–Validity *(May Subd Geog)*
–Valuation *(May Subd Geog)*
–Vibration *(May Subd Geog)*
–Video catalogs
–Vocational guidance *(May Subd Geog)*
–Waste disposal *(May Subd Geog)*
–Waste minimization *(May Subd Geog)*
–Water-supply
–Weblogs
–Weight
–Weights and measures

Appendix C

Free-Floating Subdivisions: Names of Persons

Library of Congress, *Subject Cataloging Manual: Subject Headings*, H1110.

–Abdication, [date]
–Abstracts
–Adaptations
–Adversaries
–Aesthetics
–Alcohol use
–Allusions
–Anecdotes
–Anniversaries, etc.
–Anonyms and pseudonyms
–Appreciation *(May Subd Geog)*
–Archaeological collections
–Archives
–Art
–Art collections
–Art patronage
–Assassination
–Assassination attempt, [*date*]
–Assassination attempts
–Audio adaptations
–Audiotape catalogs
–Authorship
–Authorship–Collaboration
–Autographs
–Awards
–Bibliography
–Bibliography–First editions
–Birth
–Birthplace
–Bonsai collections
–Books and reading
–Calendars
–Captivity, [*dates*]
–Career in [*specific field or discipline*]
–Caricatures and cartoons
–Catalogs
–Catalogues raisonnés
–Censorship *(May Subd Geog)*
–Characters
–Characters–Children, [Jews, Physicians, etc.]
–Characters–[*name of individual character*]
–Childhood and youth
–Chronology
–Cipher
–Claims vs. ...
–Clothing
–Coin collections
–Collectibles *(May Subd Geog)*
–Comedies
–Comic books, strips, etc.
–Compact disc catalogs
–Concordances
–Contemporaries
–Contributions in [specific field or topic]
–Coronation
–Correspondence
–Correspondence–Microform catalogs
–Criticism and interpretation
–Criticism and interpretation–History
–Criticism and interpretation–History–To 1500
–Criticism and interpretation–History–16th century
–Criticism and interpretation–History–17th century
–Criticism and interpretation–History–18th century
–Criticism and interpretation–History–19th century
–Criticism and interpretation–History–20th century
–Criticism and interpretation–History–21st century
–Cult *(May Subd Geog)*

–Death and burial
–Death mask
–Diaries
–Disciples
–Discography
–Divorce
–Drama
–Dramatic production
–Dramatic works
–Dramaturgy
–Drug use
–Employees
–Estate
–Ethics
–Ethnological collections
–Ethnomusicological collections
–Examinations
–Examinations, questions, etc.
–Exile *(May Subd Geog)*
–Family
–Fiction
–Fictional works
–Film and video adaptations
–Finance, Personal
–First editions
–First editions–Bibliography
–Forgeries *(May Subd Geog)*
–Freemasonry
–Friends and associates
–Hadith
–Harmony
–Health
–Herbarium
–Homes and haunts *(May Subd Geog)*
–Humor
–Illustrations
–Impeachment
–Imprisonment
–In bookplates
–In literature
–In mass media
–In motion pictures
–Inauguration, [*date*]
–Influence
–Information services
–Interviews
–Juvenile drama
–Juvenile fiction
–Juvenile humor
–Juvenile poetry
–Kidnapping, [*date*]
–Knowledge–Agriculture, [America, etc.]
–Knowledge and learning
–Language
–Language–Glossaries, etc.
–Last years
–Legends
–Library
–Library–Marginal notes
–Library–Microform catalogs
–Library resources
–Literary art
–Literary collections
–Literary style
–Manuscripts
–Manuscripts–Facsimiles
–Map collections
–Marriage
–Medals
–Meditations
–Mental health
–Military leadership
–Miscellanea
–Monuments *(May Subd Geog)*
–Motion picture plays
–Museums *(May Subd Geog)*
–Musical instrument collections
–Musical settings
–Musical settings–History and criticism
–Name
–Natural history collections
–Notebooks, sketchbooks, etc.
–Numismatic collections
–Numismatics
–On postage stamps
–Oratory
–Outlines, syllabi, etc.
–Palaces *(May Subd Geog)*
–Pardon
–Parodies, imitations, etc.
–Performances *(May Subd Geog)*
–Philosophy
–Photograph collections
–Pictorial works
–Poetic works

–Poetry
–Political activity
–Political and social views
–Portraits
–Poster collections
–Posters
–Prayer-books and devotions
–Prayer-books and devotions–English, [French, German, etc.]
–Prayer-books and devotions–History and criticism
–Pre-existence
–Prophesies
–Prose
–Psychology
–Public opinion
–Quotations
–Radio and television plays
–Relations with [*specific class of persons or ethnic group*]
–Relations with men
–Relations with women
–Relics *(May Subd Geog)*
–Religion
–Resignation from office
–Romances
–Scholia
–Scientific apparatus collections
–Seal
–Self-portraits
–Sermons
–Settings
–Sexual behavior
–Shrines *(May Subd Geog)*
–Slide collections
–Slides
–Societies, etc.
–Songs and music
–Songs and music–History and criticism
–Songs and music–Texts
–Sources
–Spiritualistic interpretations
–Spurious and doubtful works
–Stage history *(May Subd Geog)*
–Stamp collections
–Statues *(May Subd Geog)*
–Stories, plots, etc.
–Symbolism
–Teachings
–Technique
–Thematic catalogs
–Themes, motives
–Titles
–Tomb
–Tragedies
–Tragicomedies
–Translations
–Translations–History and criticism
–Translations into French, [German, etc.]
–Translations into French, [German, etc.]–History and criticism
–Travel *(May Subd Geog)*
–Trials, litigation, etc.
–Versification
–Views on [*specific topic*]
–Weblogs
–Will
–Written works

Appendix D

Free-Floating Topical Subdivisions: Names of Places

Library of Congress, *Subject Cataloging Manual: Subject Headings*, H1140.

–Abstracting and indexing *(May Subd Geog)*
–Abstracts
–Administrative and political divisions
–Aerial exploration
–Aerial photographs
–Aerial views
–Altitudes
–Anecdotes
–Annexation to [...]
–Anniversaries, etc.
–Antiquities
–Antiquities–Collection and preservation *(May Subd Geog)*
–Antiquities–Collection and collecting *(May Subd Geog)*
–Antiquities, Byzantine
–Antiquities, Celtic
–Antiquities, Germanic
–Antiquities, Phoenician
–Antiquities, Roman
–Antiquities, Slavic
–Antiquities, Turkish
–Appropriations and expenditures
–Appropriations and expenditures–Effect of inflation on
–Archival resources
–Area
–Armed Forces *(May Subd Geog)*
–Audiotape catalogs
–Bathymetric maps
–Bio-bibliography
–Biography
–Biography–Anecdotes
–Biography–Caricatures and cartoons
–Biography–Dictionaries
–Biography–Dictionaries–French, [Italian, etc.]
–Biography–History and criticism
–Biography–Humor
–Biography–Pictorial works
–Biography–Portraits
–Biography–Sources
–Book reviews
–Boundaries *(May Subd Geog)*
–Buildings, structures, etc.
–Calendars
–Capital and capitol
–Census
–Census–Law and legislation
–Census, [*date*]
–Centennial celebrations, etc.
–Charters
–Charters, grants, privileges
–Church history
–Church history–16th century
–Church history–17th century
–Church history–18th century
–Church history–19th century
–Church history–20th century
–Church history–21st century
–Civilization
–Civilization–16th century
–Civilization–17th century
–Civilization–18th century
–Civilization–19th century
–Civilization–20th century
–Civilization–21st century
–Civilization–Foreign influences
–Civilization–Philosophy
–Claims
–Claims vs. ...

–Climate
–Climate–Observations
–Colonial influence
–Colonies
–Colonization
–Commerce *(May Subd Geog)*
–Commercial policy
–Commercial treaties
–Compact disc catalogs
–Court and courtiers
–Court and courtiers–Clothing
–Court and courtiers–Food
–Court and courtiers–Language
–Cultural policy
–Defenses
–Defenses–Economic aspects
–Defenses–Law and legislation
–Dependency on [*place*]
–Dependency on foreign countries
–Description and travel
–Directories
–Discovery and exploration
–Discovery and exploration–French, [Spanish, etc.]
–Distances, etc.
–Drama
–Early works to 1800
–Economic conditions
–Economic conditions–16th century
–Economic conditions–17th century
–Economic conditions–18th century
–Economic conditions–19th century
–Economic conditions–20th century
–Economic conditions–21st century
–Economic conditions–[*period subdivision*]–Regional disparities
–Economic conditions–Regional disparities
–Economic integration
–Economic policy
–Emigration and immigration
–Emigration and immigration–Economic aspects
–Emigration and immigration–Government policy
–Emigration and immigration–Religious aspects
–Emigration and immigration–Religious aspects–Baptists, [Catholic Church, etc.]
–Emigration and immigration–Religious aspects–Buddhism, [Christianity, etc.]
–Emigration and immigration–Social aspects
–Environmental conditions
–Eruption, [*date*]
–Eruptions
–Ethnic relations
–Ethnic relations–Economic aspects
–Ethnic relations–Political aspects
–Fiction
–Folklore
–Forecasting
–Foreign economic relations *(May Subd Geog)*
–Foreign public opinion
–Foreign public opinion, Austrian, [British, etc.]
–Foreign relations *(May Subd Geog)*
–Foreign relations–Catholic Church
–Foreign relations–Executive agreements
–Foreign relations–Law and legislation
–Foreign relations–Philosophy
–Foreign relations–Treaties
–Foreign relations administration
–Gazetteers
–Genealogy
–Genealogy–Religious aspects
–Geography
–Gold discoveries
–Guidebooks
–Historical geography
–Historical geography–Maps
–Historiography
–History
–History–16th century
–History–17th century
–History–18th century
–History–19th century
–History–20th century
–History–21st century
–History–[*period subdivision*]–Biography

–History–[period *subdivision*]–Biography–Anecdotes
–History–[*period subdivision*]–Biography–Portraits
–History–[*period subdivision*]–Biography–Sources
–History–[*period subdivision*]–Chronology
–History–[*period subdivision*]–Historiography
–History–[*period subdivision*]–Philosophy
–History–[*period subdivision*]–Sources
–History–Anecdotes
–History–Autonomy and independence movements
–History–Chronology
–History–Comic books, strips, etc.
–History–Errors, inventions, etc.
–History–Humor
–History–Periodization
–History–Philosophy
–History–Pictorial works
–History–Prophecies
–History–Religious aspects
–History–Religious aspects–Baptists, [Catholic Church, etc.]
–History–Religious aspects–Buddhism, [Christianity, etc.]
–History–Sources
–History, Local
–History, Local–Collectibles
–History, Military
–History, Military–16th century
–History, Military–17th century
–History, Military–18th century
–History, Military–19th century
–History, Military–20th century
–History, Military–21st century
–History, Military–Religious aspects
–History, Naval
–History, Naval–16th century
–History, Naval–17th century
–History, Naval–18th century
–History, Naval–19th century
–History, Naval–20th century
–History, Naval–21st century
–Humor
–Imprints
–In art
–In bookplates
–In literature
–In mass media
–In motion pictures
–Index maps
–Information services
–Intellectual life
–Intellectual life–16th century
–Intellectual life–17th century
–Intellectual life–18th century
–Intellectual life–19th century
–Intellectual life–20th century
–Intellectual life–21st century
–International status
–Juvenile drama
–Juvenile fiction
–Juvenile humor
–Juvenile poetry
–Kings and rulers
–Kings and rulers–Abdication
–Kings and rulers–Art patronage
–Kings and rulers–Brothers
–Kings and rulers–Children
–Kings and rulers–Death and burial
–Kings and rulers–Dwellings
–Kings and rulers–Education
–Kings and rulers–Folklore
–Kings and rulers–Genealogy
–Kings and rulers–Heraldry
–Kings and rulers–Mistresses
–Kings and rulers–Mythology
–Kings and rulers–Religious aspects
–Kings and rulers–Sisters
–Kings and rulers–Succession
–Kings and rulers–Tombs
–Kings and rulers–Travel
–Languages
–Languages–Law and legislation
–Languages–Political aspects
–Languages–Texts
–Library resources
–Literary collections
–Literatures
–Maps
–Maps–Bibliography
–Maps–Early works to 1800

–Maps–Facsimiles
–Maps, Comparative
–Maps, Manuscript
–Maps, Mental
–Maps, Outline and base
–Maps, Physical
–Maps, Pictorial
–Maps, Topographic
–Maps, Tourist
–Maps for children
–Maps for people with visual disabilities
–Maps for the blind
–Military policy
–Military policy–Religious aspects
–Military relations *(May Subd Geog)*
–Military relations–Foreign countries
–Militia
–Miscellanea
–Moral conditions
–Name
–National Guard
–Naval militia
–Newspapers
–Officials and employees *(May Subd Geog)*
–Officials and employees–Accidents *(May Subd Geog)*
–Officials and employees–Foreign countries
–Officials and employees–Foreign countries–Foreign language competency
–Officials and employees–Furloughs
–Officials and employees–Leave regulations
–Officials and employees–Payroll deductions
–Officials and employees–Salaries, etc. *(May Subd Geog)*
–Officials and employees–Salaries, etc.–Regional disparities
–Officials and employees–Turnover
–Officials and employees, Alien
–Officials and employees, Honorary
–Officials and employees, Retired
–On postage stamps
–On television
–Photographs from space
–Pictorial works
–Poetry
–Politics and government
–Politics and government–16th century
–Politics and government–17th century
–Politics and government–18th century
–Politics and government–19th century
–Politics and government–20th century
–Politics and government–21st century
–Politics and government–[*period subdivision*]–Philosophy
–Politics and government–Philosophy
–Population
–Population–Economic aspects
–Population–Environmental aspects
–Population policy
–Posters
–Press coverage *(May Subd Geog)*
–Quotations, maxims, etc.
–Race relations
–Race relations–Economic aspects
–Race relations–Political aspects
–Registers
–Relations *(May Subd Geog)*
–Relations–Foreign countries
–Relief models
–Religion
–Religion–16th century
–Religion–17th century
–Religion–18th century
–Religion–19th century
–Religion–20th century
–Religion–21st century
–Religion–Economic aspects
–Religious life and customs
–Remote-sensing images
–Remote-sensing maps
–Research *(May Subd Geog)*
–Rural conditions
–Scheduled tribes
–Seal
–Slides
–Social conditions
–Social conditions–16th century
–Social conditions–17th century
–Social conditions–18th century
–Social conditions–19th century
–Social conditions–20th century

–Social conditions–21st century
–Social life and customs
–Social life and customs–16th century
–Social life and customs–17th century
–Social life and customs–18th century
–Social life and customs–19th century
–Social life and customs–20th century
–Social life and customs–21st century
–Social policy
–Songs and music
–Songs and music–History and criticism
–Songs and music–Texts
–Statistical services
–Statistical services–Law and legislation
–Statistics
–Statistics, Medical
–Statistics, Vital
–Strategic aspects
–Study and teaching *(May Subd Geog)*
–Study and teaching–Law and legislation *(May Subd Geog)*
–Surveys
–Telephone directories
–Telephone directories–Yellow pages
–Territorial expansion
–Territories and possessions
–Tours
–Trials, litigation, etc.

Also free-froating:
... Metropolitan Area ([*geographic qualifier*])
... Suburban area ([*geographic qualifier*])
... Region ([*geographic qualifier*])

Appendix E

General Reference Sources Used in Establishing Headings

Library of Congress, *Subject Cataloging Manual: Subject Headings*, H203.

GENERAL (AND CHILDREN'S LIT) REFERENCE SOURCES

Title	*Citation form*
Academic American encyclopedia	Acad. Am. encyc.
The bookfinder / Dreyer	Bookfinder
Canada gazetteer atlas	Can gaz. atlas
Children's books in print	Child. BIP
Children's catalog	Child. cat.
Collier's encyclopedia	Collier's
The Columbia Lippincott gazetteer of the world	Lippincott
Compton's encyclopedia and fact-index	Compton's
Decisions on geographic names in the United States	Dec. geog. names
Dictionary of American slang / Wentworth	Dict. Am. slang
The Elementary school library collection	ESLC
The Encyclopedia Americana	Americana
Encyclopedia Britannica. [14th ed.]	Britannica 14
Encyclopedia Britannica. 15th ed. Micropaedia	Britannica Micro.
Encyclopedia Britannica. 15th ed. Macropaedia	Britannica Macro.
Encyclopedia international	Encyc. intl.
Hennepin County Library cumulative authority list	Hennepin
Information Access Company Resource File	IAC
Merit students encyclopedia	Merit
The national gazetteer	Nat. gaz.
National Geographic atlas of North America	Nat. Geog. atlas N. Am.
National Geographic atlas of the world	Nat. Geog. atlas
The New York times index	NYT index
9,000 words : a supplement to Webster's third new international dictionary	9000 words
The Oxford English dictionary	OED

Rand McNally commercial atlas and marketing guide	Rand McNally
The Random House dictionary of the English language	Random House
Readers' guide to periodical literature	Readers' guide
Scott, Foresman advanced dictionary / Thorndike, Barnhart	TB adv. dict.
Scott, Foresman beginning dictionary / Thorndike, Barnhart	TB beg. dict.
Scott, Foresman intermediate dictionary / Thorndike, Barnhart	TB inter. dict.
Sears list of subject headings	Sears
The Standard encyclopedia of the world's mountains	Encyc. world mts.
The Statesman's year-book	Statesman's yrbk.
The Times atlas of the world	Times atlas
The Third Barnhart dictionary of new English	BDNE
Websters' new geographical dictionary	Web. geog.
Webster's third new international dictionary of the English language, unabridged	Web. 3
The World Book encyclopedia	World Book

Appendix F

First-Order Political Divisions of the Exceptional Countries

Library of Congress, *Subject Cataloging Manual: Subject Headings*, H810.

First Order Division	***Form in Qualifier***
Australia	
Australian Capital Territory	(A.C.T.)
New South Wales	(N.S.W.)
Northern Territory	(N.T.)
Queensland	(Qld.)
South Australia	(S. Aust.)
Tasmania	(Tas.)
Victoria	(Vic.)
Western Australia	(W.A.)
Canada	
Alberta	(Alta.)
British Columbia	(B.C.)
Manitoba	(Man.)
New Brunswick	(N.B.)
Newfoundland and Labrador	(N.L.)
Northwest Territories	(N.W.T.)
Nova Scotia	(N.S.)
Nunavut	(Nunavut)
Ontario	(Ont.)
Prince Edward Island	(P.E.I.)
Québec (Province)	(Québec)
Saskatchewan	(Sask.)
Yukon Territory	(Yukon)
Great Britain	
England	(England)
Northern Ireland	(Northern Ireland)
Scotland	(Scotland)
Wales	(Wales)

Malaysia

Johor	(Johor)
Kedah	(Kedah)
Kelantan	(Kelantan)
Kuala Lumpur (Malaysia)	(Kuala Lumpur, Malaysia)
Malacca (State)	(Malacca)
Negeri Sembilan	(Negeri Sembilan)
Pahang	(Pahang)
Pinang	(Pinang)
Perak	(Perak)
Perlis	(Perlis)
Sabah	(Sabah)
Sarawak	(Sarawak)
Selangor	(Selangor)
Terengganu	(Terengganu)

Serbia and Montenegro

Montenegro	(Montenegro)
Serbia	(Serbia)

United States

Alabama	(Ala.)
Alaska	(Alaska)
Arizona	(Ariz.)
Arkansas	(Ark.)
California	(Calif.)
Colorado	(Colo.)
Connecticut	(Conn.)
Delaware	(Del.)
Florida	(Fla.)
Georgia	(Ga.)
Hawaii	(Hawaii)
Idaho	(Idaho)
Illinois	(Ill.)
Indiana	(Ind.)
Iowa	(Iowa)
Kansas	(Kan.)
Kentucky	(Ky.)
Louisiana	(La.)
Maine	(Me.)

Maryland	(Md.)
Massachusetts	(Mass.)
Michigan	(Mich.)
Minnesota	(Minn.)
Mississippi	(Miss.)
Missouri	(Mo.)
Montana	(Mont.)
Nebraska	(Neb.)
Nevada	(Nev.)
New Hampshire	(N.H.)
New Jersey	(N.J.)
New Mexico	(N.M.)
New York (State)	(N.Y.)
North Carolina	(N.C.)
North Dakota	(N.D.)
Ohio	(Ohio)
Oklahoma	(Okla.)
Oregon	(Or.)
Pennsylvania	(Pa.)
Rhode Island	(R.I.)
South Carolina	(S.C.)
South Dakota	(S.D.)
Tennessee	(Tenn.)
Texas	(Tex.)
Utah	(Utah)
Vermont	(Vt.)
Virginia	(Va.)
Washington (State)	(Wash.)
West Virginia	(W. Va.)
Wisconsin	(Wis.)
Wyoming	(Wyo.)

Yugoslavia. *See* **Serbia and Montenegro**

OTHER JURISDICTIONS THAT ARE ABBREVIATED WHEN USED AS QUALIFIERS

Jurisdiction	***Form in Qualifier***
British Virgin Islands	(V.I)
New Zealand	(N.Z.)
Puerto Rico	(P.R.)
United States	(U.S.)
Virgin Islands of the United States	(V.I.)

Appendix G

MARC 21 Coding for Subject Information

Library of Congress, Network Development and MARC Standards Office, *MARC 21 Concise Format for Authority Data* (http://www.loc.gov/marc/authority/).

AUTHORITY DATA

The *MARC 21 Format for Authority Data* is designed to be a carrier for information concerning the authorized forms of names and subjects to be used as access points in MARC records, the forms of these names, subjects and subdivisions to be used as references to the authorized forms, and the interrelationships among these forms. A **name** may be used as a main, added, subject added, or series added access entry. The term **name** refers to:

- Personal names (X00)
- Corporate names (X10)
- Meeting names (X11)
- Names of jurisdictions (X51)
- Uniform titles (X30)
- Name/title combinations

A **subject** may be used only as a subject access entry. The term **subject** refers to:

- Chronological terms (X48)
- Topical terms (X50)
- Geographic names (X51)
- Names with subject subdivisions
- Terms and names used as subject subdivisions

Kinds of Authority Records

MARC authority records are distinguished from all other types of MARC records by code z (Authority data) in Leader/06 (Type of record). The *MARC 21 Format for Authority Data* further identifies seven kinds of authority records in 008/09, Kind of record:

Established heading (Code a)

A record in which the 100-155 fields contain established headings. An established heading record may also contain tracing fields for variant and related headings and notes recording such information as the sources used to establish the heading and series treatment.

Reference (Code b or c)

A record in which the 100-155 fields contain unestablished headings. The record also contains either a 260 (Complex See Reference Subject), a 664 (Complex See Reference Name), or a 666 (General Explanatory Reference Name) field to guide the user to an established heading. Separate codes are defined in 008/09 for **traced** and **untraced** reference records. The distinction depends upon whether the 1XX heading in the record is also traced as a 4XX see-from tracing in an established heading record.

Subdivision (Code d)

A record in which the 18X field contains an unestablished partial heading that is meant to be used as a subject subdivision part of an established heading.

Established heading and subdivision (Code f)

A record in which the 15X field contains an established heading that may also be used as a subject subdivision with another established heading. (An organization may choose to create instead separate established heading and subdivision records.)

Reference and subdivision (Code g)

A record in which the 15X field contains an unestablished heading that may be used as a reference term and as a subject subdivision with an established heading. (An organization may choose to create instead separate reference and subdivision records.)

Node label (Code e)

A record in which the 150 field contains a term that is meant to be used in the systematic section of a thesaurus to indicate the logical basis on which a category has been divided. The term is not an established heading and is not assigned to documents as an indexing term.

Typographical Conventions

Throughout this document, the following typographical conventions are used:

0 - The graphic 0 represents the digit zero in tags, fixed-position character position citations, and indicator positions. This character is distinct from an uppercase letter O used in examples or text.

- The graphic symbol # is used for a blank (hex 20) in coded fields and in other special situations where the existence of the character blank might be ambiguous.

$ - The graphic symbol $ is used for the delimiter (hex 1F) portion of a subfield code. Within the text, subfield codes are referred to as subfield ǂa, for example:

/ - Specific character positions of fixed-length data elements, such as those in the Leader, Directory, and field 008, are expressed using a slash and the number of the character position, for example, Leader/06.

1 - The graphic 1 (hex 31) represents the digit one. This character must be distinguished from a lowercase roman alphabet letter l (el) and the uppercase alphabetic letter I (eye) in examples or text.

| - The graphic | represents a fill character (hex 7C).

100 - HEADING—PERSONAL NAME (NR)

An established personal name used in name, name/title, or extended subject heading established heading records or an unestablished personal name used in these types of headings in reference records.

Indicators

- First - Type of personal name entry element
  - 0 - Forename
    The name is a forename or is a name consisting of words, initials, letters, etc., that are formatted in direct order.
  - 1 - Surname
    The name is a surname formatted in inverted order or a name without forenames that is known to be a surname.
  - 3 - Family name
    The name represents a family, clan, dynasty, house, or other such group and may be formatted in direct or inverted order.

- Second - Undefined

  # - Undefined

Subfield Codes

- $a - Personal name (NR)
  A surname and/or forename; letters, initials, abbreviations, phrases, or numbers used in place of a name; or a family name.
- $b - Numeration (NR)
  A roman numeral or a roman numeral and a subsequent part of a forename when the first indicator value is 0.
- $c - Titles and other words associated with a name (R)
- $d - Dates associated with a name (NR)
  Dates of birth, death, or flourishing, or any other date associated with a name.
- $e - Relator term (R)
  Describes the relationship between a name and a work.
- $f - Date of a work (NR)
  A date of publication used with a title of a work in a name/title heading.
- $g - Miscellaneous information (NR)
  A data element not more appropriately contained in another defined subfield.
- $h - Medium (NR)
  A media qualifier used with a title of a work in a name/title heading.
- $j - Attribution qualifier (R)
  Attribution information for names when the responsibility is unknown, uncertain, fictitious, or pseudonymous.
- $k - Form subheading (R)
- $l - Language of a work (NR)
  The name of a language(s) used with a title of a work in a name/title heading.
- $m - Medium of performance for music (R)
- $n - Number of part/section of a work (R)
  A number designation for a part or section of a work used with a title in a name/title heading.

- $o - Arranged statement for music (NR)
  The abbreviation *arr.* used in a uniform title for a work in a name/title heading.
- $p - Name of part/section of a work (R)
  A name designation of a part or section of a work used with a title in a name/title heading.
- $q - Fuller form of name (NR)
  A more complete form of the name contained in subfield $a.
- $r - Key for music (NR)
  The statement of key used in a uniform title for a work in a name/title heading.
- $s - Version (NR)
  Version, edition, etc., information used with a title of a work in a name/title heading.
- $t - Title of a work (NR)
  A uniform title, a title page title of a work, or a series title used in a name/title heading.
- $v - Form subdivision (R)
- $x - General subdivision (R)
- $y - Chronological subdivision (R)
- $z - Geographic subdivision (R)
- $6 - Linkage (NR)
- $8 - Field link and sequence number (R)

110 - HEADING—CORPORATE NAME (NR)

An established corporate name used in a name, name/title, or extended subject heading in established heading records or an unestablished corporate name used in these types of headings in reference records.

Indicators

- First - Type of corporate name entry element
  - 0 - Inverted name
    The corporate name begins with a personal name in inverted order.
  - 1 - Jurisdiction name
    The entry element is a name of a jurisdiction that is also an ecclesi-

astical entity or is a jurisdiction name under which a corporate name, a city section, or a title of a work is entered.

2 - Name in direct order

- Second - Undefined

- Undefined

Subfield Codes

- $a - Corporate name or jurisdiction name as entry element (NR)
A name of a corporate body, or the first entity when subordinate units are present; a jurisdiction name under which a corporate body, city section, or a title of a work is entered; or a jurisdictional name that is also an ecclesiastical entity.

- $b - Subordinate unit (R)
A name of a subordinate corporate unit, a name of a city section, or a name of a meeting entered under a corporate or jurisdiction name.

- $c - Location of meeting (NR)
A place name or a name of an institution where a meeting was held.

- $d - Date of meeting or treaty signing (R)
The date a meeting was held or, in a name/title field, the date a treaty was signed.

- $e - Relator term (R)
Describes the relationship between a name and a work.

- $f - Date of a work (NR)
A date of publication used with a title of a work in a name/title heading.

- $g - Miscellaneous information (NR)
The name of the *other party* to a treaty in a name/title heading; a subelement that is not more appropriately contained in subfield $c, $d, or $n in a heading for a meeting entered under a corporate name; or a data element that is not more appropriately contained in another defined subfield in any other type of corporate name heading.

- $h - Medium (NR)

- $k - Form subheading (R)

- $l - Language of a work (NR)
The name of a language(s) used with a title of a work in a name/title heading

- $m - Medium of performance for music (R)

- $n - Number of part/section/meeting (R)
  A number designation for a meeting entered under a corporate name or for a part or section of a work used with a title in a name/title heading.
- $o - Arranged statement for music (NR)
  The abbreviation *arr.* used in a uniform title for a work in a name/title heading.
- $p - Name of part/section of a work (R)
  A name designation of a part or section of a work used with a title in a name/title heading.
- $r - Key for music (NR)
  The statement of key used in a uniform title for a work in a name/title heading.
- $s - Version (NR)
  Version, edition, etc., information used with a title of a work in a name/title heading.
- $t - Title of a work (NR)
  A uniform title, a title page title of a work, or a series title used in a name/title heading.
- $v - Form subdivision (R)
- $x - General subdivision (R)
- $y - Chronological subdivision (R)
- $z - Geographic subdivision (R)
- $6 - Linkage (NR)
- $8 - Field link and sequence number (R)

111 - Heading—Meeting Name (NR)

An established meeting name used in a name, name/title, or extended subject heading in established heading records or an unestablished meeting name used in these types of headings in reference records.

Indicators

- First - Type of meeting name entry element
  0 - Inverted name
  The meeting name begins with a personal name in inverted order.

1 - Jurisdiction name
The entry element is a jurisdiction name under which a meeting name is entered.
2 - Name in direct order

- Second - Undefined

  # - Undefined

Subfield Codes

- $a - Meeting name or jurisdiction name as entry element (NR)
  A name of a meeting or a jurisdiction name under which a meeting name is entered.
- $c - Location of meeting (NR)
  A place name or a name of an institution where a meeting was held.
- $d - Date of meeting (NR)
- $e - Subordinate unit (R)
  The name of a subordinate unit entered under a meeting name.
- $f - Date of a work (NR)
- $g - Miscellaneous information (NR)
  A data element not more appropriately contained in another defined subfield.
- $h - Medium (NR)
  A media qualifier used with a title of a work in a name/title heading.
- $k - Form subheading (R)
- $l - Language of a work (NR)
  The name of a language(s) used with a title of a work in a name/title heading.
- $n - Number of part/section/meeting (R)
  A number designation for a meeting entered under a corporate name or for a part or section of a work used with a title in a name/title heading.
- $p - Name of part/section of a work (R)
  A name designation of a part or section of a work used with a title in a name/title heading.
- $q - Name of meeting following jurisdiction name entry element (NR)
  The name of a meeting that is entered under a jurisdiction name contained in subfield $a.

- $s - Version (NR)
  Version, edition, etc., information used with a title of a work in a name/title heading.
- $t - Title of a work (NR)
  A uniform title, a title page title of a work, or a series title used in a name/title heading.
- $v - Form subdivision (R)
- $x - General subdivision (R)
- $y - Chronological subdivision (R)
- $z - Geographic subdivision (R)
- $6 - Linkage (NR)
- $8 - Field link and sequence number (R)

130 - Heading—Uniform Title (NR)

An established uniform title used in a title or extended subject heading in established heading records or an unestablished uniform title used in these types of headings in reference records.

Indicators

- First - Undefined
  # - Undefined
- Nonfiling characters
  0–9 - Number of nonfiling characters

Subfield Codes

- $a - Uniform title (NR)
- $d - Date of treaty signing (R)
- $f - Date of a work (NR)
- $g - Miscellaneous information (NR)
  A data element not more appropriately contained in another defined subfield.
- $h - Medium (NR)
  A media qualifier.
- $k - Form subheading (R)

- $l - Language of a work (NR)
- $m - Medium of performance for music (R)
- $n - Number of part/section of a work (R)
- $o - Arranged statement for music (NR)
- $p - Name of part/section of a work (R)
- $r - Key for music (NR)
- $s - Version (NR)
- $t - Title of a work (NR)
  A title-page title of a work.
- $v - Form subdivision (R)
- $x - General subdivision (R)
- $y - Chronological subdivision (R)
- $z - Geographic subdivision (R)
- $6 - Linkage (NR)
- $8 - Field link and sequence number (R)

148 - Heading—Chronological Term (NR)

A chronological term used as a heading in an established heading record, an established heading and subdivision record, a traced or untraced reference record, or a reference and subdivision record.

Indicators

- First - Undefined
  - # - Undefined
- Second - Undefined
  - # - Undefined

Subfield Codes

- $a - Chronological term (NR)
- $v - Form subdivision (R)
- $x - General subdivision (R)
- $y - Chronological subdivision (R)

- $z - Geographic subdivision (R)
- $6 - Linkage (NR)
- $8 - Field link and sequence number (R)

150 - Heading—Topical Term (NR)

An established topical term used in main or extended subject headings in established heading records or an unestablished topical term used in these types of headings in subdivision, reference, or node label records.

Indicators

- First - Undefined
  # - Undefined
- Second - Undefined
  # - Undefined

Subfield Codes

- $a - Topical term or geographic name entry element (NR)
- $b - Topical term following geographic name entry element (NR)
- $v - Form subdivision (R)
- $x - General subdivision (R)
- $y - Chronological subdivision (R)
- $z - Geographic subdivision (R)
- $6 - Linkage (NR)
- $8 - Field link and sequence number (R)

151 - Heading—Geographic Name (NR)

A geographic name used as a heading in an established heading record, an established heading and subdivision record, a traced or an untraced reference record, or a reference and subdivision record.

Indicators

- First - Undefined
  # - Undefined

- Second - Undefined

  # - Undefined

Subfield Codes

- $a - Geographic name (NR)
- $v - Form subdivision (R)
- $x - General subdivision (R)
- $y - Chronological subdivision (R)
- $z - Geographic subdivision (R)
- $6 - Linkage (NR)
- $8 - Field link and sequence number (R)

155 - Heading—Genre/Form Term (NR)

A genre or form term used as a heading in an established heading record, an established heading and subdivision record, a traced or an untraced reference record, or a reference and subdivision record. The term may consist of more than one word.

Indicators

- First - Undefined

  # - Undefined

- Second - Undefined

  # - Undefined

Subfield Codes

- $a - Genre/form term (NR)
- $v - Form subdivision (R)
- $x - General subdivision (R)
- $y - Chronological subdivision (R)
- $z - Geographic subdivision (R)
- $6 - Linkage (NR)
- $8 - Field link and sequence number (R)

180 - Heading—General Subdivision (NR)

A topical, form, or language term used as a heading in a subdivision record.

Indicators

- First - Undefined
  - # - Undefined
- Second - Undefined
  - # - Undefined

Subfield Codes

- $v - Form subdivision (R)
- $x - General subdivision (R)
- $y - Chronological subdivision (R)
- $z - Geographic subdivision (R)
- $6 - Linkage (NR)
- $8 - Field link and sequence number (R)

181 - Heading—Geographic Subdivision (NR)

A geographic name or term used as a heading in a subdivision record.

Indicators

- First - Undefined
  - # - Undefined
- Second - Undefined
  - # - Undefined

Subfield Codes

- $v - Form subdivision (R)
- $x - General subdivision (R)
- $y - Chronological subdivision (R)
- $z - Geographic subdivision (R)
- $6 - Linkage (NR)
- $8 - Field link and sequence number (R)

182 - Heading—Chronological Subdivision (NR)

A chronological term used as a heading in a subdivision record.

Indicators

- First - Undefined
  - # - Undefined
- Second - Undefined
  - # - Undefined

Subfield Codes

- $v - Form subdivision (R)
- $x - General subdivision (R)
- $y - Chronological subdivision (R)
- $z - Geographic subdivision (R)
- $6 - Linkage (NR)
- $8 - Field link and sequence number (R)

185 - Heading—Form Subdivision (NR)

A form or genre term used as a heading in a subdivision record.

Indicators

- First - Undefined
  - # - Undefined
- Second - Undefined
  - # - Undefined

Subfield Codes

- $v - Form subdivision (R)
- $x - General subdivision (R)
- $y - Chronological subdivision (R)
- $z - Geographic subdivision (R)
- $6 - Linkage (NR)
- $8 - Field link and sequence number (R)

BIBLIOGRAPHIC DATA

The 6XX fields (with the exception of field 653, which is used for uncontrolled index terms) in bibliographic records contain subject headings or access terms that are constructed according to established subject cataloging or thesaurus-building principles and guidelines. The standard list or authority file used is identified by the value in the second indication position of each 6XX field or by the MARC 21 source code contained in subfield 2 that is used in conjunction with value 7.

600 - Subject Added Entry—Personal Name (R)

A subject added entry in which the entry element is a personal name.

Indicators

- First - Type of personal name entry element

  0 - Forename
  1 - Surname
  3 - Family name

See the description of the first indicator under field 100 .

- Second - Thesaurus
  The thesaurus or authority file from which the heading came.

  0 - Library of Congress Subject Headings
  The subject added entry conforms to and is appropriate for use in the *Library of Congress Subject Headings* (LCSH) and the Name authority files.
  1 - LC subject headings for children's literature
  The subject added entry conforms to the "AC Subject Headings" section of the *LCSH* and is appropriate for use in the LC Annotated Card Program.
  2 - Medical Subject Headings
  The subject added entry conforms to the NLM authority files.
  3 - National Agricultural Library subject authority file
  The subject added entry conforms to the NAL subject authority file.
  4 - Source not specified
  The subject added entry conforms to a controlled list that cannot be identified by another defined value or by a code in subfield $2.
  5 - Canadian Subject Headings
  The subject added entry conforms to and is appropriate for use in the *Canadian Subject Headings* and the NLC authority files.

6 - Répertoire de vedettes-matière
The subject added entry conforms to and is appropriate for use in the *Répertoire de vedettes-matière* and the NLC authority fields
7 - Source specified in subfield $2

Subfield Codes

- $a - Personal name (NR)
- $b - Numeration (NR)
- $c - Titles and other words associated with a name (R)
- $d - Dates associated with a name (NR)
- $e - Relator term (R)
- $f - Date of a work (NR)
- $g - Miscellaneous information (NR)
- $h - Medium (NR)
  A media qualifier.
- $j - Attribution qualifier (R)
  Attribution information for names when the responsibility is unknown, uncertain, fictitious, or pseudonymous.
- $k - Form subheading (R)
- $l - Language of a work (NR)
- $m - Medium of performance for music (R)
- $n - Number of part/section of a work (R)
- $o - Arranged statement for music (NR)
- $p - Name of part/section of a work (R)
- $q - Fuller form of name (NR)
- $r - Key for music (NR)
- $s - Version (NR)
- $t - Title of a work (NR)
- $u - Affiliation (NR)
- $v - Form subdivision (R)
- $x - General subdivision (R)
- $y - Chronological subdivision (R)

- $z - Geographic subdivision (R)
- $2 - Source of heading or term (NR)
  Code from: *MARC Code Lists for Relators, Sources, Description Conventions*
- $3 - Materials specified (NR)
- $4 - Relator code (R)
- $6 - Linkage (NR)
- $8 - Field link and sequence number (R)

See the descriptions of subfields $a, $b, $d, $e, $f, $g, $l, $n, $p, $q, $t, $u, and $4 under field 100.

610 - Subject Added Entry—Corporate Name (R)

A subject added entry in which the entry element is a corporate name.

Indicators

- First - Type of corporate name entry element
  See the description of the first indicator under field 110 .

  0 - Inverted name
  1 - Jurisdiction name
  2 - Name in direct order

- Second - Thesaurus
  The thesaurus or authority file from which the heading came.

  0 - Library of Congress Subject Headings
  The subject added entry conforms to and is appropriate for use in the *Library of Congress Subject Headings* (LCSH) and the Name authority files.
  1 - LC subject headings for children's literature
  The subject added entry conforms to the "AC Subject Headings" section of the *LCSH* and is appropriate for use in the LC Annotated Card Program.
  2 - Medical Subject Headings
  The subject added entry conforms to the NLM authority files.
  3 - National Agricultural Library subject authority file
  The subject added entry conforms to the NAL subject authority file.

4 - Source not specified
The subject added entry conforms to a controlled list that cannot be identified by another defined value or by a code in subfield $2.
5 - Canadian Subject Headings
The subject added entry conforms to and is appropriate for use in the *Canadian Subject Headings* and the NLC authority files.
6 - Répertoire de vedettes-matière
The subject added entry conforms to and is appropriate for use in the *Répertoire de vedettes-matière* and the NLC authority fields
7 - Source specified in subfield $2

Subfield Codes

- $a - Corporate name or jurisdiction name as entry element (NR)
- $b - Subordinate unit (R)
- $c - Location of meeting (NR)
- $d - Date of meeting or treaty signing (R)
- $e - Relator term (R)
- $f - Date of a work (NR)
- $g - Miscellaneous information (NR)
- $h - Medium (NR)
  A media qualifier.
- $k - Form subheading (R)
- $l - Language of a work (NR)
- $m - Medium of performance for music (R)
- $n - Number of part/section/meeting (R)
- $o - Arranged statement for music (NR)
- $p - Name of part/section of a work (R)
- $r - Key for music (NR)
- $s - Version (NR)
- $t - Title of a work (NR)
- $u - Affiliation (NR)
- $v - Form subdivision (R)
- $x - General subdivision (R)

- $y - Chronological subdivision (R)
- $z - Geographic subdivision (R)
- $2 - Source of heading or term (NR)
  Code from: *MARC Code Lists for Relators, Sources, Description Conventions*
- $3 - Materials specified (NR)
- $4 - Relator code (R)
- $6 - Linkage (NR)
- $8 - Field link and sequence number (R)

See the descriptions of subfields $e, $f, $l, $p, $t, $u and $4 under field 100 and subfields $a, $b, $c, $d, $g, and $n under field 110 .

611 - Subject Added Entry—Meeting Name (R)

A subject added entry in which the entry element is a meeting name.

Indicators

- First - Type of meeting name entry element
  See the description of the first indicator under field 111 .
  - 0 - Inverted name
  - 1 - Jurisdiction name
  - 2 - Name in direct order
- Second - Thesaurus
  The thesaurus or authority file from which the heading came.
  - 0 - Library of Congress Subject Headings
    The subject added entry conforms to and is appropriate for use in the *Library of Congress Subject Headings* (LCSH) and the Name authority files.
  - 1 - LC subject headings for children's literature
    The subject added entry conforms to the "AC Subject Headings" section of the *LCSH* and is appropriate for use in the LC Annotated Card Program.
  - 2 - Medical Subject Headings
    The subject added entry conforms to the NLM authority files.
  - 3 - National Agricultural Library subject authority file
    The subject added entry conforms to the NAL subject authority file.

4 - Source not specified
The subject added entry conforms to a controlled list that cannot be identified by another defined value or by a code in subfield $2.

5 - Canadian Subject Headings
The subject added entry conforms to and is appropriate for use in the *Canadian Subject Headings* and the NLC authority files.

6 - Répertoire de vedettes-matière
The subject added entry conforms to and is appropriate for use in the *Répertoire de vedettes-matière* and the NLC authority fields

7 - Source specified in subfield $2

Subfield Codes

- $a - Meeting name or jurisdiction name as entry element (NR)
- $c - Location of meeting (NR)
- $d - Date of meeting (NR)
- $e - Subordinate unit (R)
- $f - Date of a work (NR)
- $g - Miscellaneous information (NR)
- $h - Medium (NR)
  A media qualifier.
- $k - Form subheading (R)
- $l - Language of a work (NR)
- $n - Number of part/section/meeting (R)
- $p - Name of part/section of a work (R)
- $q - Name of meeting following jurisdiction name entry element (NR)
- $s - Version (NR)
- $t - Title of a work (NR)
- $u - Affiliation (NR)
- $v - Form subdivision (R)
- $x - General subdivision (R)
- $y - Chronological subdivision (R)
- $z - Geographic subdivision (R)

- $2 - Source of heading or term (NR)
  Code from: *MARC Code Lists for Relators, Sources, Description Conventions*
- $3 - Materials specified (NR)
- $4 - Relator code (R)
- $6 - Linkage (NR)
- $8 - Field link and sequence number (R)

See the descriptions of subfields $f, $g, $l, $p, $t, $u, and $4 under field 100 ; subfields $c and $n under field 110 and subfields $a, $e, and $q under field 111 .

630 - Subject Added Entry—Uniform Title (R)

A subject added entry in which the entry element is a uniform title.

Indicators

- First - Nonfiling characters

  0-9 - Number of nonfiling characters
  A value that indicates the number of character positions associated with an initial definite or indefinite article at the beginning of a uniform title field that are to be disregarded in sorting and filing processes.

- Second - Thesaurus
  The thesaurus or authority file from which the heading came.

  0 - Library of Congress Subject Headings
  The subject added entry conforms to and is appropriate for use in the *Library of Congress Subject Headings* (LCSH) and the Name authority files.

  1 - LC subject headings for children's literature
  The subject added entry conforms to the "AC Subject Headings" section of the *LCSH* and is appropriate for use in the LC Annotated Card Program.

  2 - Medical Subject Headings
  The subject added entry conforms to the NLM authority files.

  3 - National Agricultural Library subject authority file
  The subject added entry conforms to the NAL subject authority file.

4 - Source not specified
The subject added entry conforms to a controlled list that cannot be identified by another defined value or by a code in subfield $2.

5 - Canadian Subject Headings
The subject added entry conforms to and is appropriate for use in the *Canadian Subject Headings* and the NLC authority files.

6 - Répertoire de vedettes-matière
The subject added entry conforms to and is appropriate for use in the *Répertoire de vedettes-matière* and the NLC authority fields

7 - Source specified in subfield $2

Subfield Codes

- $a - Uniform title (NR)
- $d - Date of treaty signing (R)
- $f - Date of a work (NR)
- $g - Miscellaneous information (NR)
- $h - Medium (NR)
  A media qualifier.
- $k - Form subheading (R)
- $l - Language of a work (NR)
- $m - Medium of performance for music (R)
- $n - Number of part/section of a work (R)
- $o - Arranged statement for music (NR)
- $p - Name of part/section of a work (R)
- $r - Key for music (NR)
- $s - Version (NR)
- $t - Title of a work (NR)
  The title-page title of an item.
- $v - Form subdivision (R)
- $x - General subdivision (R)
- $y - Chronological subdivision (R)
- $z - Geographic subdivision (R)

- $2 - Source of heading or term (NR)
  Code from: *MARC Code Lists for Relators, Sources, Description Conventions*
- $3 - Materials specified (NR)
- $6 - Linkage (NR)
- $8 - Field link and sequence number (R)

See the descriptions of subfields $f, $g, $l, $n, and $p under field 100.

648 - Subject Added Entry—Chronological Term (R)

A subject added entry in which the entry element is a chronological term.

Indicators

- First - Undefined
  - # - Undefined
- Second - Thesaurus
  The thesaurus or authority file from which the heading came.
  - 0 - Library of Congress Subject Headings
    The subject added entry conforms to and is appropriate for use in the *Library of Congress Subject Headings* (LCSH) and the Name authority files.
  - 1 - LC subject headings for children's literature
    The subject added entry conforms to the "AC Subject Headings" section of the *LCSH* and is appropriate for use in the LC Annotated Card Program.
  - 2 - Medical Subject Headings
    The subject added entry conforms to the NLM authority files.
  - 3 - National Agricultural Library subject authority file
    The subject added entry conforms to the NAL subject authority file.
  - 4 - Source not specified
    The subject added entry conforms to a controlled list that cannot be identified by another defined value or by a code in subfield ∃2.
  - 5 - Canadian Subject Headings
    The subject added entry conforms to and is appropriate for use in the *Canadian Subject Headings* and the NLC authority files.
  - 6 - Répertoire de vedettes-matière
    The subject added entry conforms to and is appropriate for use in the *Répertoire de vedettes-matière* and the NLC authority fields

7 - Source specified in subfield $2

Subfield Codes

- $a - Chronological term (NR)
- $v - Form subdivision (R)
- $x - General subdivision (R)
- $y - Chronological subdivision (R)
- $z - Geographic subdivision (R)
- $2 - Source of heading or term (NR)
  Code from: *MARC Code Lists for Relators, Sources, Description Conventions*
- $3 - Materials specified (NR)
- $6 - Linkage (NR)
- $8 - Field link and sequence number (R)

650 - Subject Added Entry—Topical Term (R)

A subject added entry in which the entry element is a topical term.

Indicators

- First - Level of subject

  # - No information provided
  0 - No level specified
  The level of the term could be determined but is not specified.
  1 - Primary
  The term describes the main focus or subject content of the material.
  2 - Secondary
  The subject term describes a less important aspect of the content of the material.

- Second - Thesaurus
  The thesaurus or authority file from which the heading came.

  0 - Library of Congress Subject Headings
  The subject added entry conforms to and is appropriate for use in the *Library of Congress Subject Headings* (LCSH) and the Name authority files.

1 - LC subject headings for children's literature
The subject added entry conforms to the "AC Subject Headings" section of the *LCSH* and is appropriate for use in the LC Annotated Card Program.

2 - Medical Subject Headings
The subject added entry conforms to the NLM authority files.

3 - National Agricultural Library subject authority file
The subject added entry conforms to the NAL subject authority file.

4 - Source not specified
The subject added entry conforms to a controlled list that cannot be identified by another defined value or by a code in subfield $2.

5 - Canadian Subject Headings
The subject added entry conforms to and is appropriate for use in the *Canadian Subject Headings* and the NLC authority files.

6 - Répertoire de vedettes-matière
The subject added entry conforms to and is appropriate for use in the *Répertoire de vedettes-matière* and the NLC authority fields

7 - Source specified in subfield $2

Subfield Codes

- $a - Topical term or geographic name entry element (NR)
- $b - Topical term following geographic name entry element (NR)
- $c - Location of event (NR)
- $d - Active dates (NR)
  The time period during which an event occurred.
- $e - Relator term (NR)
  A term that describes the relationship between the topical heading and the described materials.
- $v - Form subdivision (R)
- $x - General subdivision (R)
- $y - Chronological subdivision (R)
- $z - Geographic subdivision (R)
- $2 - Source of heading or term (NR)
  Code from: *MARC Code Lists for Relators, Sources, Description Conventions*
- $3 - Materials specified (NR)

- $6 - Linkage (NR)
- $8 - Field link and sequence number (R)

651 - Subject Added Entry—Geographic Name (R)

A subject added entry in which the entry element is a geographic name.

Indicators

- First - Undefined
  - # - Undefined
- Second - Thesaurus
  The thesaurus or authority file from which the heading came.
  - 0 - Library of Congress Subject Headings
    The subject added entry conforms to and is appropriate for use in the *Library of Congress Subject Headings* (LCSH) and the Name authority files.
  - 1 - LC subject headings for children's literature
    The subject added entry conforms to the "AC Subject Headings" section of the *LCSH* and is appropriate for use in the LC Annotated Card Program.
  - 2 - Medical Subject Headings
    The subject added entry conforms to the NLM authority files.
  - 3 - National Agricultural Library subject authority file
    The subject added entry conforms to the NAL subject authority file.
  - 4 - Source not specified
    The subject added entry conforms to a controlled list that cannot be identified by another defined value or by a code in subfield $2.
  - 5 - Canadian Subject Headings
    The subject added entry conforms to and is appropriate for use in the *Canadian Subject Headings* and the NLC authority files.
  - 6 - Répertoire de vedettes-matière
    The subject added entry conforms to and is appropriate for use in the *Répertoire de vedettes-matière* and the NLC authority fields
  - 7 - Source specified in subfield $2

Subfield Codes

- $a - Geographic name (NR)
- $v - Form subdivision (R)

- $x - General subdivision (R)
- $y - Chronological subdivision (R)
- $z - Geographic subdivision (R)
- $2 - Source of heading or term (NR)
  Code from: *MARC Code Lists for Relators, Sources, Description Conventions*
- $3 - Materials specified (NR)
- $6 - Linkage (NR)
- $8 - Field link and sequence number (R)

653 - Index Term—Uncontrolled (R)

An index term added entry that is not constructed by standard subject heading/thesaurus-building conventions.

Indicators

- First - Level of index term

  # - No information provided
  0 - No level specified
  The level of the term could be determined but is not specified.
  1 - Primary
  The term describes the main focus or subject content of the material.
  2 - Secondary
  The subject term describes a less important aspect of the content of the material.

- Second - Undefined

  # - Undefined

Subfield Codes

- $a - Uncontrolled term (R)
- $6 - Linkage (NR)
- $8 - Field link and sequence number (R)

654 - Subject Added Entry—Faceted Topical Terms (R)

A topical subject constructed from a faceted vocabulary.

Indicators

- First - Level of subject

  # - No information provided
  0 - No level specified
  The level of the term could be determined but is not specified.
  1 - Primary
  The term describes the main focus or subject content of the material.
  2 - Secondary
  The subject term describes a less important aspect of the content of the material.

- Second - Undefined

  # - Undefined

Subfield Codes

- $a - Focus term (R)
- $b - Non-focus term (R)
  A term other than that considered the focus.
- $c - Facet/hierarchy designation (R)
  The designation used by the thesaurus specified by the MARC code contained in subfield $2 to identify the facet/hierarchy for each term contained in subfields $a and $b.
- $v - Form subdivision (R)
- $y - Chronological subdivision (R)
- $z - Geographic subdivision (R)
- $2 - Source of heading or term (NR)
  Code from: *MARC Code Lists for Relators, Sources, Description Conventions*
- $3 - Materials specified (NR)
- $6 - Linkage (NR)
- $8 - Field link and sequence number (R)

655 - Index Term—Genre/Form (R)

Terms indicating the genre, form, and/or physical characteristics of the materials being described. A *genre term* designates the style or technique of the intellectual content of textual materials or, for graphic materials, aspects such as vantage point, intended purpose, or method of representation. A *form term* designates historically and functionally specific kinds of materials distinguished by their physical character, the subject of their intellectual content, or the order of information within them. *Physical characteristic* terms designate historically and functionally specific kinds of materials as distinguished by an examination of their physical character, subject of their intellectual content, or the order of information within them.

Indicators

- First - Type of heading

  # - Basic
  0 - Faceted

- Second - Thesaurus
  The thesaurus or authority file from which the heading came.

  0 - Library of Congress Subject Headings
  The subject index term conforms to and is appropriate for use in the *Library of Congress Subject Headings* (LCSH).
  1 - LC subject headings for children's literature
  The subject index term conforms to the "AC Subject Headings" section of the *LCSH* and is appropriate for use in the LC Annotated Card Program.
  2 - Medical Subject Headings
  The subject index term conforms to the NLM subject authority file.
  3 - National Agricultural Library subject authority file
  The subject added entry conforms to the NAL subject authority file.
  4 - Source not specified
  The subject index term conforms to a controlled list that cannot be identified by another defined value or by a code in subfield $2.
  5 - Canadian Subject Headings
  The subject index term conforms to and is appropriate for use in the *Canadian Subject Headings* that is maintained by the National Library of Canada.
  6 - Répertoire de vedettes-matière
  The subject index term conforms to and is appropriate for use in the *Répertoire de vedettes-matière.*
  7 - Source specified in subfield $2

Subfield Codes

- $a - Genre/form data or focus term (NR)
- $b - Non-focus term (R)
- $c - Facet/hierarchy designation (R)
- $v - Form subdivision (R)
- $x - General subdivision (R)
- $y - Chronological subdivision (R)
- $z - Geographic subdivision (R)
- $2 - Source of term (NR)
  Code from: *MARC Code Lists for Relators, Sources, Description Conventions*
- $3 - Materials specified (NR)
- $5 - Institution to which field applies (NR)
- $6 - Linkage (NR)
- $8 - Field link and sequence number (R)

656 - Index Term—Occupation (R)

An index term that is descriptive of the occupation reflected in the contents of the described materials.

Indicators

- First - Undefined
  - # - Undefined
- Second - Source of term
  - 7 - Source specified in subfield $2

Subfield Codes

- $a - Occupation (NR)
- $k - Form (NR)
- $v - Form subdivision (R)
- $x - General subdivision (R)
- $y - Chronological subdivision (R)

- $z - Geographic subdivision (R)
- $2 - Source of term (NR)
Code from: *MARC Code Lists for Relators, Sources, Description Conventions*
- $3 - Materials specified (NR)
- $6 - Linkage (NR)
- $8 - Field link and sequence number (R)

657 - Index Term—Function (R)

An index term that is descriptive of the activity or function that generated the described materials.

Indicators

- First - Undefined
  - # - Undefined
- Second - Source of term
  - 7 - Source specified in subfield $2

Subfield Codes

- $a - Function (NR)
- $v - Form subdivision (R)
- $x - General subdivision (R)
- $y - Chronological subdivision (R)
- $z - Geographic subdivision (R)
- $2 - Source of term (NR)
Code from: *MARC Code Lists for Relators, Sources, Description Conventions*
- $3 - Materials specified (NR)
- $6 - Linkage (NR)
- $8 - Field link and sequence number (R)

658 - Index Term—Curriculum Objective (R)

Index terms denoting curriculum or course-of-study objectives applicable to the content of the described materials. The field may also contain correlation factors indicating the degree to which the described materials meet an objective. Codes assigned to specific objectives in published lists are also recorded in this field.

Indicators

- First - Undefined
  # - Undefined
- Second - Undefined
  # - Undefined

Subfield Codes

- $a - Main curriculum objective (NR)
- $b - Subordinate curriculum objective (R)
- $c - Curriculum code (NR)
  A coded representation of the curriculum objective recorded in subfield $a.
- $d - Correlation factor (NR)
  A statement that identifies the degree to which the described materials correlate to the curriculum objective recorded in the field.
- $2 - Source of term or code (NR)
  Code from: *MARC Code Lists for Relators, Sources, Description Conventions*
- $6 - Linkage (NR)
- $8 - Field link and sequence number (R)

Appendix H

Abbreviations

Library of Congress, *Subject Cataloging Manual: Subject Headings*, appendix A.

Procedures:

1. ***Policy for headings established in the subject authority file***. Generally, do not include abbreviations when establishing new subject headings, except when specifically authorized in this instruction sheet.

2. ***Policy for headings established in the name authority file and used as subject headings.*** When assigning personal, corporate body, or jurisdictional name headings as subject headings, assign them exactly as they appear in name authority records, including all abbreviations.

LC practice:

3. ***Correction of existing records and headings in the subject authority file.*** When an error involving an abbreviation on a bibliographic record is encountered, update the record following standard correction procedures. When an obsolete heading involving an abbreviation is encountered in the subject authority file, change it according to the provisions of H193.

4. ***Form and topical subdivisions with abbreviations***. Many standard subdivisions were formerly abbreviated on LC cards and may still be encountered when working with pre-1970 records. Spell out in full all topical and form subdivisions when assigning headings to new works being cataloged. Use no abbreviations in form or topical subdivisions except **etc.** (cf. sec. 9, below). *Examples:*

$x Description and travel	[*not* $x Desc. & trav.]
$x History and criticism	[*not* $x Hist. & crit.]
$x Periodicals	[*not* $x Period.]
$x Politics and government	[*not* $x Pol. & govt.]
$x Social life and customs	[*not* $x Soc. life & cust.]

5. ***Acronyms, initialisms, etc***. Establish concepts that are known primarily in an abbreviated form as such. Use the form of the abbreviation, acronym, etc., preferred in reference sources. Add a 4XX field with the spelled out form. *Examples:*

150 $a C.O.D. shipments
450 $a Cash on delivery shipments
450 $a Collect on delivery shipments

150 $a DBS/R (Computer system)
450 $a Datenbankbetriebssystem Robotron (Computer system)

150 $a DC-to-DC converters
450 $a Direct current-to-direct current converters

150 $a DDT (Insecticide)
450 $a Dichlorodiphenyltrichloroethane

150 $a MARC formats
450 $a Machine-Readable Cataloging formats

150 $a T-shirts
450 $a Tee shirts

6. ***Ampersands***. Use ampersands in the following situations:

Name headings assigned as subjects. When assigning a name heading established with an ampersand as a subject heading, retain the ampersand. *Examples:*

610 2 $a Black & Decker Manufacturing Company (Towson, Md.)
610 2 $a C.S. Wertsner & Son.
610 2 $a Dow Jones & Co.

Subject headings for named entities. When establishing a subject heading for a proper-named entity tagged 110 or 151, establish it using an ampersand if the name is found only in that form in all sources consulted. Add a 4XX field with the ampersand spelled out as **and**. If the name is found in both a form that uses the ampersand and a form where **and** is spelled out, establish the heading using the spelled out form. Add a 4XX field using the ampersand form. *Examples:*

110 2 $a E & E Ranch (Tex.) *[no other form found]*
410 2 $a E and E Ranch (Tex.)

151 $a Chesapeake and Ohio Canal (Md. and Washington, D.C.)
451 $a C & O Canal (Md. and Washington, D.C.)
451 $a C and O Canal (Md. and Washington, D.C.)
451 $a Chesapeake & Ohio Canal (Md. and Washington, D.C.)

Topical subject headings based on name headings. When establishing a topical subject heading that is based on a name heading that includes an ampersand, retain the ampersand. *Examples:*

150 $a Currier & Ives dinnerware
150 $a Bil & traktor (Firm) Strike, 1978

Do not use ampersands in the following situations:

Topical or form headings or subdivisions. When establishing a form or topical heading tagged 150 (except those based on name headings, as noted above), spell out the word **and**. When establishing or assigning a form or topical subdivision, spell out the word **and**. For example, use **–History and criticism**, not **–Hist. & crit.**

Geographic qualifiers. Spell out the word **and** when it is used to connect two elements in the qualifier of a geographic heading. For example, use **Harding, Lake (Ga. and Ala.)**, not **Harding, Lake (Ga. & Ala.)**.

7. ***Coined plurals.*** Form the plurals of letters and acronyms by adding the lowercase letter **s** without an apostrophe, provided that the resulting construction is clear and unambiguous. *Examples:*

150 $a Biological response modifiers
450 $a BRMs (Biochemistry)

150 $a Threshold limit values (Industrial toxicology)
450 $a TLVs (Industrial toxicology)

8. Dates.

a. Anno Domini; Before Christ. Use the abbreviations **A.D.** and **B.C.**, when appropriate, but only after a specific year or span of years. Add **A.D.** to dates only if the dates in question span both B.C. and A.D. Add **B.C.** to all B.C. dates. If a date span is B.C., add **B.C.** only to the end of the span. *Examples:*

651 0 $a Egypt $x History $y 332-30 B.C.
651 0 $a China $x History $y Han dynasty, 202 B.C.-220 A.D.

b. *[...] century*. Spell out the word **century** in full. *Examples:*

650 0 $a English literature $y 20th century.
650 0 $a Twenty-first century.

c. Circa. Use the abbreviation **ca**. in period subdivisions, placing it before the date to which it refers. *Examples:*

651 0 $a United States $x History $y Colonial period, ca. 1600-1775.
650 0 $a Church history $y Primitive and early church, ca. 30-600.
600 30 $a Hoysala dynasty, ca. 1006-ca. 1346.

d. Names of months. Spell out names of months in full in subject headings and subdivisions. *Examples:*

651 0 $a Bulgaria $x History $y September Uprising, 1944.
600 10 $a Ford, Gerald R., $d 1913- $x Assassination attempt, 1975 (September 5)

Use name headings with abbreviated months if they appear in that form in name authority records. *Example:*

610 10 $a Italy $k Treaties, etc. $g Yugoslavia, 1975 Nov. 18.

9. *Doctor; Doctor of [...].* Use the abbreviation used in the name authority record. *Examples:*

610 20 $a Dr. Williams Library $v Catalogs.
600 10 $a Francis, John, $c Dr. $x Art collections.
600 10 $a Hartmann, Peter, $c Dr. jur. $x Poster collections.
600 10 $a Grant, David, $c M.D.

10. Et cetera. Use the abbreviation **etc.** in headings and subdivisions. *Examples:*

650 0 $a Law reports, digests, etc. $z United States.
650 0 $a Surveying $v Handbooks, manuals, etc.

11. Geographic qualifiers. Most geographic headings are qualified by the name of the larger geographic unit. Jurisdictions that are to be abbreviated when used as geographic qualifiers are listed in H810. *Examples:*

651 0 $a West (U.S.)
651 0 $a Harpers Ferry (W. Va.)
651 0 $a Harry S. Truman Dam (Mo.)
651 0 $a Red River (Tex.-La.)

12. Great Britain. Spell out in full. The abbreviation **Gt. Brit.** is not authorized by *AACR2*. *Examples:*

651 0 $a Great Britain $x History.
[*not* 651 0 $a Gt. Brit. $x Hist.]

650 0 $a Women artists $z Great Britain.
[*not* 650 0 $a Women artists $z Gt. Brit.]

610 20 $a Labour Party (Great Britain)
[*not* 610 20 $a Labour Party (Gt. Brit.)]

610 10 $a Great Britain. $b Royal Navy.
[*not* 610 10 $a Gt. Brit. $b Royal Navy.]

13. Mount; Mountain; Mountains. Spell out in full in subject headings for geographic features. *Examples:*

651 0 $a Fuji, Mount (Japan)

651 0 $a Signal Mountain (Tenn.)
651 0 $a Appalachian Mountains.

Use name headings with abbreviations if they appear in that form in name authority records. *Example:*

610 10 $a Mt. Lebanon School District (Mount Lebanon, Pa.)

14. Mr.; Mrs. Use the abbreviation **Mr.** or **Mrs.** in subject headings for fictitious characters. *Examples:*

650 0 $a Jeffries, Mrs. (Fictitious character)
650 0 $a Moto, Mr. (Fictitious character)

Use name headings with the abbreviations **Mr.** or **Mrs.** if they appear in that form in name authority records. *Examples:*

610 20 $a Mr. A Boys Ranch $x History.
600 00 $a Mr. Lucky. $t Trick dog training.
600 10 $a Downing, Clyde, $c Mrs. $x Art collections $v Catalogs.

15. Numerals.

a. Cardinal and roman numerals. Spell out cardinal and roman numerals. *Examples:*

650 0 $a One (The number)
650 0 $a Three-dimensional display systems.
650 0 $a Zero (The number)

Exception: When reference sources indicate that a numeral in a specific phrase is not normally spelled out, establish and assign the heading in that form. *Examples:*

650 0 $a 35mm cameras.
650 0 $a 4-H clubs.
650 0 $a TRS-80 Model III (Computer)

b. Ordinal numerals. Spell out an ordinal numeral if it is the initial element of a heading. *Examples:*

650 0 $a First communion.
650 0 $a Fourth of July.
650 0 $a Fifteenth century.
650 0 $a Twenty-first century.
650 0 $a Twelfth Avenue (Seattle, Wash.)

Exceptions:

- When reference sources indicate that a numeral in a specific phrase is not normally spelled out, establish and assign the heading in that form. *Example:*

650 0 $a 20th Century Limited (Express train)

- For streets that have numerical names above one hundred, ordinal numerals may be abbreviated. *Example:*

650 0 $a 114th Street (Edmonton, Alta.)

Record ordinal numerals not in the initial position in a heading in the form **1st, 2nd, 3rd, 4th,** etc. *Examples:*

650 0 $a Dacian War, 1st, 101-102.
650 0 $a Dacian War, 2nd, 105-106.
650 0 $a Church history $y 3rd century.
651 0 $a United States $x Social life and customs $y 20th century.

*16. **Saint (including foreign equivalents).*** Spell out in full in subject headings. *Examples:*

650 0 $a Saint Bernard dog.
651 0 $a Saint Lawrence River.
651 0 $a Saint Ninian's Island (Scotland)
600 30 $a Saint John family.

When assigning name headings as subjects, use the headings exactly as they appear in name authority records. *Examples:*

610 20 $a Federal Reserve Bank of St. Louis.
610 20 $a Saint Louis Museum of Fine Arts.
630 0 $a St. Louis post-dispatch.
610 20 $a Eglise de St-Joachim (Saint-Joachim, Québec)
[no period after St]
651 0 $a St. Andrews (Scotland)

*17. **United States.*** Spell out in full in subject headings. *Examples.*

651 0 $a United States $x Economic conditions.
651 0 $a France $x Foreign relations $z United States.
650 0 $a Progressivism (United States politics)
650 0 $a Certificate of Merit (United States Army)

Exception: As a *geographic* qualifier, **United States** is abbreviated **(U.S.)**. *Examples:*

651 0 $a Atlantic Coast (U.S.)
651 0 $a West (U.S.)
650 0 $a Coal Miners Strike, U.S., 1949-1950.
650 0 $a Distinguished Service Cross (U.S.)

When assigning name headings as subjects, use the headings exactly as they appear in name authority records. *Examples:*

610 10 $a United States. $b Congress. $b House.
610 10 $a United States. $b Dept. of Agriculture.

610 20 $a U.S. Army Engineer Topographic Laboratories.
610 20 $a U.S. Nuclear Regulatory Commission.

610 20 $a US Army Military Police School.
610 20 $a US-USSR Joint Symposium on Myocardial Metabolism.

610 20 $a Chemical Center and School (U.S.)
610 10 $a Ryukyu Islands (United States Civil Administration, 1950-1972) .
$b Office of the High Commissioner.

Appendix I

Capitalization

The information presented in this appendix is based on Library of Congress, Cataloging Policy and Support Office, *Subject Cataloging Manual: Subject Headings*, 5th ed., 2000 cumulation (Washington, D.C.: Library of Congress, 2000), appendix B.

Procedures

1. Policy for name headings used as subject headings. When using valid *AACR2* personal, corporate, and jurisdictional names and uniform titles as subject headings, transcribe them exactly as they appear on name authority records, including capital letters as indicated.

2. Policy for subject headings established in the subject authority file. Transcribe existing headings and subdivisions in *AACR2* form exactly as they appear in subject authority records, using capital letters as indicated.

3. Proper nouns and adjectives. Capitalize proper nouns and adjectives in subject headings, subdivisions, or references regardless of whether they are in the initial position. *Examples*:

150 $a !Kung (African people)

150 $a *Naborr (Horse)

150 $a 97 Sen (Fighter planes)

150 $a Tariff on X-ray equipment and supplies

100 0 $a Jesus Christ $x Views on the Old Testament

150 $a Gosannen kassen ekotoba (Scrolls)
450 $a Hachiman Tarō ekotoba (Scrolls)

4. Initial words. Capitalize the first word of a subject heading, subdivision, or reference regardless of whether it is a proper name. *Examples*:

150 $a Teenage boys
450 $a Adolescent boys

150 $a Writing $x Materials and instruments

150 $a Serbo-Croatian language $y To 1500

151 $a Beauce (France)
451 $a La Beauce (France)

151 $a Cévennes Mountains (France)
451 $a Les Cévennes (France)

Exception: When a term is found in reference sources with the initial letter consistently lowercased, establish the heading (or reference) in that form. *Examples:*

150 $a p-adic numbers

150 $a p-divisible groups

150 $a 35mm cameras
450 $a 35 mm cameras

150 $a Three-manifolds (Topology)
450 $a 3-dimensional manifolds (Topology)

5. Capitalization according to reference sources. Capitalize any letter within a heading that appears as such in reference sources. Use this rule in establishing named systems, computer languages, tests, etc. *Examples*:

150 $a 4-H clubs
150 $a Agent Orange
150 $a California Basic Educational Skills Test
150 $a DC-to-DC converters
150 $a DDT (Insecticide)
151 $a IJssel Lake (Netherlands)
150 $a UNIMARC
150 $a PostScript (Computer program language)
150 $a SdKfz 251 (Half-track)
150 $a SP/k (Computer program language)

6. Conjunctions, prepositions, and articles. Do not capitalize conjunctions, prepositions, and the articles **a**, **an**, and **the** and their equivalents in other languages if they are not the first word in the heading, subdivision, or reference. *Examples*:

150 $a Colors in the Bible
151 $a Chesapeake and Ohio Canal (Md. and Washington, D.C.)

Exception: Capitalize **The** if it is the first word in a parenthetical qualifier, or the first word following a comma in an inverted heading. *Examples*:

150 $a Jota (The Serbo Croatian letter)
151 $a Geysers, The (Calif.)

7. ***Inverted headings and subdivisions***. Capitalize the word following a comma that would be in the initial position if the heading, subdivision, or reference were expressed as a phrase in direct word order. Capitalization is especially important to clarify inverted headings. *Examples*:

150 $a Sculpture, Mandingo

150 $a Medicine, Magic, mystic, and spagiric

150 $a Coral Sea, Battle of the, 1942

151 $a United States $x History, Naval

150 $a Measuring instruments
450 $a Instruments, Measuring

8. ***Parenthetical qualifiers***. Capitalize the first word in a parenthetical qualifier, as well as any proper nouns or adjectives within a parenthetical qualifier. Also capitalize the first word that follows a colon within a parenthetical qualifier. *Examples*:

150 $a Chambri (Papua New Guinea people)
150 $a Citizenship as point of contact (Conflict of laws)
150 $a Wu (The Chinese word)
151 $a Thebes (Egypt : Extinct city)

Note: *In the past, certain headings and subdivisions were established with parenthetical qualifiers beginning with lowercased prepositions or with other lowercased words. Continue using and establishing headings of this type in situations where a pattern for their use exists, but do not propose new headings of this type where no previous pattern exists. Example:*

150 $a English language $v Conversation and phrase books (for secretaries)

9. ***Hyphenated compounds***. When capitalizing the first part of a hyphenated compound, capitalize the second part also if it is a proper noun or proper adjective. Do not capitalize the second part of a hyphenated compound if it modifies the first or if the two parts constitute a single word. *Examples:*

150 $a Ecuador-Peru Conflict, 1981
150 $a Sabazius (Thraco-Phrygian deity)

[*but* 150 $a Twelve-tone system
150 $a Twenty-first century]

10. Armed Forces. Capitalize the word **Forces** in the heading **Armed Forces** and in the subdivision **–Armed Forces.** *Examples*:

150 $a Armed Forces $x Civic action
151 $a United States $x Armed Forces $z Foreign countries

11. [...] countries. Lowercase the word **countries** in phrase headings and subdivisions. *Examples*:

651 0 $a Arab countries $x History $y 20th century.
650 0 $a Canary Islanders $z Foreign countries.
651 0 $a Communist countries.
651 0 $a European Economic Community countries $x Economic conditions.

12. Terms attached to dates.

a. Anno Domini; Before Christ. Capitalize the abbreviations **A.D.** and **B.C.** (For details on the use of **A.D.** and **B.C.,** see appendix H, sec. 8.a.). *Example*:

151 $a China $x History $y Han dynasty, 202 B.C.-220 A.D.

b. [...] century. Do not capitalize the word **century.** *Examples*:

150 $a English literature $y 20th century
150 $a Twenty-first century

c. **Circa.** Do not capitalize the abbreviation **ca.** in period subdivisions. *Examples*:

151 $a United States $x History $y Colonial period, ca. 1600-1775

13. Named dynasties. Do not capitalize the word **dynasty**. *Example*:

100 3 $a Achaemenid dynasty, $d 559-330 B.C.

14. Family names. Do not capitalize the word **family**. *Examples*:

100 3 $a Miller family
100 3 $a Pasêk Kayu Sêlêm family

15. Family names with initial particles. Headings for individual families derived from French, Spanish, Portuguese, Italian, German, and Dutch may include the initial particles **De, Du, La, L', Von, Van,** etc. Capitalize initial particles in family names in both headings and references. *Examples*:

100 3 $a Baden family
400 3 $a Von Baden family

100 3 $a De Groot family
400 3 $a De Groote family

16. Named events. Capitalize all significant words in headings, subdivisions, or references that designate named events. *Examples*:

150 $a Watergate Affair, 1972-1974

150 $a Marinette Knitting Mills Strike, Marinette, Wis., 1951

151 $a Harpers Ferry (W. Va.) $x History $y John Brown's Raid, 1859
450 $a John Brown's Raid, Harpers Ferry, W. Va., 1859

151 $a Transylvania (Romania) $x History $y Peasant Uprising, 1784
550 $w g $a Peasant uprisings $z Romania

151 $a China $x History $y Qing Dynasty Restoration Attempt, 1917
450 $a Qing Dynasty Restoration Attempt, China, 1917

Exception: The generic terms in the following subdivisions have, by convention, been lowercased. Continue to follow this convention when establishing new headings for any of these events. Do not, however, propose any new subdivisions to be added to this list.

–[. . .] colony, [date]
–[. . .] conquest, [date]
–[. . .] dynasties, [date]
–[. . .] dynasty, [date]
–[. . .] intervention, [date]
–[. . .] movement, [date]
–[. . .] occupation, [date]
–[. . .] period, [date]
–[. . .] periods, [date]
–[. . .] rule, [date]

Examples:

150 $a Painting, Chinese $y Three kingdoms-Sui dynasty, 220-618
151 $a Lebanon $x History $y Israeli intervention, 1982-1984
151 $a India $x History $y British occupation, 1765-1947
151 $a United States $x History $y Colonial period, ca. 1600-1775

17. Cultural and archaeological periods. Do not capitalize headings for cultural and archaeological periods, except for the initial word. *Examples*:

150 $a Bronze age
150 $a Iron age
150 $a Mesolithic period
150 $a Paleolithic period, Lower
150 $a Stone age

18. Named movements. Capitalize only the initial word of a named movement. *Examples*:

150 $a Anti-Nazi movement

151 $a China $x History $y Reform movement, 1898
150 $a Ecumenical movement
150 $a Gay liberation movement
150 $a Pro-life movement
150 $a Stakhanov movement
150 $a Symbolism (Literary movement)

19. Named schools. Capitalize only the initial word when establishing headings or subdivisions for named schools (i.e., groups of painters, economists, architects, etc., that are under a common local or personal influence producing a general similarity in their work). *Examples*:

150 $a Chicago school of theology
150 $a Classical school of economics
150 $a Marxian school of sociology
150 $a Flower arrangement, Japanese $x Shōgetsudō Koryū school

LC practice:

Some headings of this type have been established with the word ***school*** *uppercased. Change these headings as they are encountered in the subject authority file to the form specified above.*

20. Scientific names of plants and animals. Capitalize only the initial word of the scientific name of a plant or animal, even if subsequent words include proper nouns or adjectives. *Examples*:

150 $a Anguilla japonica

150 $a Litchi chinensis
450 $a Nephelium litchi

150 $a Pinus sibirica
450 $a Pinus cembra sibirica

21. Geographic headings. Capitalize both generic and proper nouns and adjectives in names of places, regions, sites, metropolitan areas, and named geographic and geological features, including coasts, islands, rivers, valleys, watersheds, etc., in English headings or references. For non-English headings and references apply the appropriate capitalization rules according to Appendix A of *AACR2* and reference sources. *Examples*:

151 $a Alaska, Gulf of (Alaska)
151 $a Assateague Island National Seashore (Md. and Va.)
151 $a Atlantic Coast (Canada)
151 $a Beluga Lake (Alaska)
151 $a Boundary Waters Canoe Area (Minn.)

151 $a Dakota Aquifer
151 $a Death Valley (Calif. and Nev.)
151 $a Ionian Islands (Greece)
151 $a McKinley, Mount, Region (Alaska)
151 $a Beijing Metropolitan Area (China)
151 $a Pennsylvania Dutch Country (Pa.)
151 $a Po River Valley (Italy)
151 $a Stone Creek Site (Alta.)
151 $a Tokyo Region (Japan)
151 $a Valley Forge National Historical Park (Pa.)
151 $a Washington Region

151 $a Parco naturale della Maremma (Italy)
451 $a Maremma, Parco naturale della (Italy)
451 $a Parco della Maremma (Italy)

151 $a Tatar Strait (Russia)
451 $a Tatarskiĭ proliv (Russia)

Note: Lowercase the word ***regions*** *in the heading* ***Arctic regions****. Example:*

151 $a Arctic regions $x Aerial exploration

22. Capitalization rules for languages other than English. Use the current, appropriate rules for capitalization for the language concerned when establishing headings and making references. For guidance consult such sources as Appendix A of *AACR2* and reference sources. In cases of conflict, generally prefer the capitalization rule in Appendix A of *AACR2*. *Examples*:

151 $a Tatar Strait (Russia)
451 $a Tatarskiĭ proliv (Russia)
Strait *is capitalized in the English heading* ***Tatar Strait (Russia)*** *in accordance with Sec. 21 above. The Russian word for strait,* ***proliv****, as part of the vernacular UF reference, is lowercased because it appears as such in Russian encyclopedias and because lowercasing is consistent with the capitalization, rules for Russian geographic names in Appendix A of AACR2.*

151 $a Balkan Mountains (Bulgaria)
451 $a Stara planina (Bulgaria)

110 2 $a Hôtel de ville (Marseille, France)
410 2 $a City Hall (Marseille, France)

110 2 $a Neues Rathaus (Leipzig, Germany)
410 2 $a New City Hall (Leipzig, Germany)

151 $a Parc provincial des Laurentides (Québec)
451 $a Laurentides Provincial Park (Québec)
451 $a Parc national des Laurentides (Québec)

Appendix J

Punctuation

Library of Congress, *Subject Cataloging Manual: Subject Headings*, appendix D.

1. Period at the end of a heading. Place a period at the end of a subject heading. *Examples:*

600 10 $a Reagan, Ronald.
650 0 $a Presidents $z United States $v Biography.

Exception: Omit the final period if the final element in the heading is a closing parenthesis, an open date, or a mark of ending punctuation. *Examples:*

650 0 $a Seasonal variations (Economics)
650 0 $a Education $z Washington (D.C.)
651 0 $a United States $x Economic policy $y 2001-
600 10 $a Capote, Truman, $d 1924-
600 10 $a Sienkiewicz, Henryk, $d 1846-1916. $t Quo vadis?

2. Spaces within abbreviations.

Note: *For general guidelines on the use of abbreviations in subject headings, see appendix H of this book.*

a. General rule. Leave no space after any periods within an abbreviation. *Examples:*

650 0 $a C.O.D. shipments.
630 00 $a Bible. $p N.T. $p Matthew.
651 0 $a Egypt $x History $y To 332 B.C.
651 0 $a Washington (D.C.)

b. Initials within a corporate name. Leave no space within adjacent initials where a personal name forms part of a corporate name or part of a subject heading. *Example:*

610 20 $a C.S. Wertsner & Son.

c. Acronyms. Leave no space after letters within an acronym. *Examples:*

650 0 $a DYNAMO (Computer program language)
650 0 $a MARC formats.

d. ***Abbreviations within date spans***. Leave no space after an abbreviation and the hyphen of a date span. *Example:*

651 0 $a China $x History $y Han dynasty, 202 B.C.-220 A.D.

e. ***Space after final period of an abbreviation.*** Leave one space between the final period of an abbreviated term and a word that follows. *Examples:*

650 0 $a C.O.D. shipments.
650 0 $a Breakage, shrinkage, etc. (Commerce)
650 0 $a Church finance $x History $y Early church, ca. 30-600

f. ***Initials in personal name headings***. Leave one space within adjacent initials in personal name headings or in headings for fictitious characters. *Examples:*

600 10 $a Manchester, P. W.
600 10 $a Smith, J. J., $d 1910-
650 0 $a Sheridan, T. S. W. (Fictitious character)

g. ***Abbreviations consisting of more than a single letter***. Leave one space between preceding and succeeding initials if part of an abbreviation consists of more than a single letter. *Examples:*

651 0 $a Charleston (W. Va.)
651 0 $a Adelaide (S. Aust.)
600 10 $a Whitehead, David, $c Ph. D.

h. Ampersands. Leave one space before and after an ampersand. *Example:*

610 20 $a Columbus & Greenville Railway.

LC practice:

3. *Open dates*. Do not add a blank space after an open date that is followed by a $v, $x, or $t subfield. *Examples:*

600 10 $a Wyeth, Andrew, $d 1917- $v Exhibitions.
↑
Do not add a blank space here

600 10 $a Michener, James A. *$q* (James Albert), $d 1907- $t Centennial.
↑
Do not add a blank space here

If an open date is followed by a $k subfield, add a blank space and a comma after the date. *Example:*

400 1 $w nnen $a Woods, Donald, $d 1933- , $k in motion pictures.
↑
Add a blank space and comma here

4. Name headings used as subject headings. Use the same punctuation, capitalization, diacritics, and spacing indicated on valid *AACR2* name authority records. *Examples:*

610 20 $a Eglise de St-Joachim (Saint-Joachim, Québec)
↑
[no period after St]

610 20 $a C.S. Wertsner & Son.

If a name heading ends with a closing parenthesis or mark of ending punctuation other than a period, retain this punctuation before adding the subdivision. *Examples:*

610 20 $a Association of Flight Attendants (U.S.) $v Periodicals.
600 10 $a Sienkiewicz, Henryk, $d 1846-1916. $t Quo vadis? $v Illustrations.

5. Subheadings. Subheadings are used in name headings to designate relationships between units and subunits, and function like subdivisions in subject headings. Like a subdivision, a subheading appears in a separate subfield which is indicated by a delimiter. For this discussion of punctuation, titles in author/title entries are also treated as subheadings. *Examples:*

610 20 $a Yale University. $b Library.
610 10 $a United States. $b Army. $b Chaplain Corps.
600 10 $a Shakespeare, William, $d 1564-1616. $t Sonnets.
630 00 $a Bible. $p N.T. $p Mark.

If the $a subfield includes a parenthetical qualifier, place a period after the parentheses. *Example:*

610 10 $a New York (N.Y.). $b Dept. of Social Services.

6. Use of commas before free-floating terms and phrases. When constructing headings with free-floating terms and phrases based on headings that are inverted or that include a comma not enclosed within a parenthetical qualifier, place an additional comma between the basic heading and the free-floating term or phrase. *Example:*

651 0 $a Rudolf, Lake, Region (Kenya and Ethiopia)
↑
comma added here

Glossary

Items marked with an asterisk (*) are based on Library of Congress, Cataloging Policy and Support Office, *Subject Cataloging Manual: Subject Headings.* 5th ed., 2000 cumulation (Washington, D.C.: Library of Congress, 2000).

AC Program. *See* Annotated Card Program.

***Adjectival qualifier**. A word or phrase used to modify, clarify, or limit the meaning of the noun portion of a subject heading. In a *straight heading,* the word or phrase appears before the noun in natural English-language word order; in an *inverted heading,* the word or phrase appears after the noun and is separated from the noun by a comma. An adjectival qualifier is most commonly used to modify a topic by the name of a specific language, nationality, or ethnic group, as in the headings **English poetry**; **Diplomatic and consular service, Egyptian**; **Mexican American cookery**.

Alphabetical subject catalog. A catalog containing subject entries based on the principle of specific and direct entry and arranged alphabetically. *See also* Alphabetico-classed catalog; Classed catalog; Dictionary catalog.

Alphabetico-classed catalog. A subject catalog in which entries are listed under broad subjects and subdivided hierarchically by topics. The entries on each level of the hierarchy are arranged alphabetically. See also Alphabetical subject catalog; Classed catalog; Dictionary catalog.

Analytical subject entry. Subject entry for part of a work. Also called subject analytic.

Annotated Card Program. A Library of Congress program for cataloging children's materials that differs from regular cataloging by the addition of a summary note and additional subject headings assigned from *Subject Headings for Children's Literature*.

Associative reference. *See* Related term reference.

***Authority file**. A file containing individual *authority records* for established *name headings* or *subject headings* and *subdivisions.*

***Authority record**. A record that contains the established form of a *name heading,* a *subject heading,* or a *subdivision,* a list of cross-references made to the heading or subdivision from alternative or related forms, and a list of sources that justify the established and alternative forms. *See also* Name authority record; Subject authority record.

Biographical heading. *See* Class-of-persons heading.

***Biography**. A narrative work more than 50 percent of which recounts the personal aspects of the life of one or more individuals. **Personal aspects** include such details as the individual's early years, education, marriage and other personal relationships, personal habits and personality, family life, travels, personal experiences and tragedies, last years and death, etc. *See also* Collective biography; Complete biography; Individual biography; Partial biography.

Biography, Collective. *See* Collective biography.

Biography, Individual. *See* Individual biography.

***Broader term reference**. A reference from one *subject heading* to another subject heading that is at a higher level in a hierarchy and is therefore a more inclusive term. Broader term references appear in 5XX fields in *subject authority records,* and are identifiable by the presence of the value **g** in the first character position of the $w control subfield. *See also* Hierarchical reference; Narrower-term reference.

BT. *See* Broader term reference.

Chain. A series of subject terms from different levels of a hierarchy, arranged either from general to specific or vice versa.

***Chronological subdivision**. A subject heading *subdivision* in a $y subfield of a 6XX field that designates a period of time, such as **–1945-1990**, **–20th century**, etc. Also called period subdivision.

Citation order. The order in which elements or facets in a compound or complex subject heading or in a heading with subdivisions are arranged.

Class catalog. *See* Classed catalog.

Class entry. A subject entry consisting of a string of hierarchically related terms beginning with the broadest term leading to the subject in question.

Classed catalog. A subject catalog consisting of class entries arranged logically according to a systematic scheme of classification. Also called class catalog, classified subject catalog, systematic catalog. *See also* Alphabetical subject catalog; Alphabetico-classed catalog; Dictionary catalog.

Classified subject catalog. *See* Classed catalog.

Class-of-persons heading. A heading used with biographies that consists of the name of a class of persons with appropriate subdivisions, for example, **Physicians–California–Biography**; **Poets, American–19th century–Biography**.

Coextensive heading. A heading that represents precisely (not more generally or more specifically) the subject content of a work.

***Collective biography**. A biography of two or more individuals. *See also* Individual biography.

Complete biography. A biography that covers the entire life story of an individual. *See also* Partial biography.

Coordinate system. *See* Postcoordination.

Cross reference. A direction from one term or heading to another in the catalog. *See also* Use reference; Explanatory reference; General reference; Hierarchical reference; Related-term reference; Specific reference.

***Database**. A collection of logically interrelated data stored together in one or more computerized files, usually created and managed by a database management system. The data are encoded, and each file is designed with a high-level structure for accepting, storing, and providing information on demand. Typically, there is a set of definitions for the database that describe its various data elements and a set of codes to identify each element. The database may include the database management software that created the file, or it may include only the data.

Depth of indexing. The degree to which individual parts of a publication are represented in indexing. *See* also In-depth indexing.

Diaries. Registers or records of personal experiences, observations, thoughts, or feelings, kept daily or at frequent intervals.

Dictionary catalog. A catalog in which all the entries (author, title, subject, series, etc.) and the *cross references* are interfiled in one alphabetical sequence. The subject entries in a dictionary catalog are based on the principle of specific and direct entry. The term, when used in reference to the subject entries, is sometimes used interchangeably with the term *alphabetical subject catalog*. *See also* Alphabetical subject catalog; Alphabetico-classed catalog; Classed catalog.

Direct subdivision. *See* Geographic subdivision.

***Directory**. An alphabetical or classified list containing names, addresses, and identifying data of persons, organizations, etc., intended to enable the user to locate and/or contact the individuals or organizations listed.

Duplicate entry. (1) Entry of the same heading in two different forms, for example, **United States–Foreign relations–France**; **France–Foreign relations–United States**. (2) Assignment of two headings to bring out different aspects of a work. Frequently, one of the headings is a specific heading and the other a general (also called generic) heading subdivided by an aspect, for example, **Bluegrasses** and **Grasses–Kentucky** for a work about bluegrass in Kentucky.

***Electronic serial**. A work in a machine-readable format, issued in successive designated parts for an indefinite period of time (that is, it meets the definition of a serial),

Enumeration. Listing precombined subject headings or index terms for compound or complex subjects in a subject headings list or thesaurus. *See also* Precoordination; Synthesis.

Equivalence reference. *See* Use reference.

Exhaustive indexing. The practice of assigning indexing terms or subject headings to represent all significant concepts or aspects of a subject. *See also* In-depth indexing; Summarization.

Explanatory reference. A reference providing explanatory statements with regard to the heading involved. It is used when a simple reference does not give adequate information or guidance to the user.

Facet. Any of the various terms or classes into which a given category in a controlled vocabulary or classification scheme may be divided, for example, division of the class "literature" into language, genre, time period, theme, etc. Each facet contains terms based on a single characteristic of division, for example, poetry, drama, fiction, prose, etc., in the genre facet. *See also* Citation order.

Facet analysis. The division of a subject into its component parts (*facets*). Each array of *facets* consists of parts based on the same characteristic, for example, language *facet*, space *facet*, time *facet*.

Festschrift. A collection of two or more essays, addresses, or biographical, bibliographical, and other contributions published in honor of a person, an institution, or a society, usually on the occasion of a birthday or anniversary celebration.

***Film**. A generic term for any pictorial medium intended for projection, including motion pictures, filmstrips, slides and transparencies, videotapes, and videorecordings.

First-order political division. A geographic unit representing a political division under the national level. The political divisions of countries are known as autonomous communities, cantons, departments, provinces, republics, states, etc. The names of the first-order political divisions of certain countries are used in geographic qualifiers or indirect subdivisions instead of the name of the country.

***Form**. The physical, bibliographical, artistic, or literary nature of a work.

***Form heading**. A type of *subject heading* that expresses what a work **is** (in contrast to what it is **about**), such as **American poetry**, **Law reports, digests, etc.**, **Large type books**, etc.

***Form subdivision**. A type of subject heading *subdivision* that appears in a $v subfield of a 6XX field and that expresses what a work is, such as **–Periodicals, –Juvenile films**, etc.

Free-floating phrase. A phrase that may be combined with a valid heading to form a new heading without establishing the usage editorially.

***Free-floating subdivision**. A subject heading *subdivision* that may be assigned under designated subjects without the usage being established editorially, that is, without a *subject authority record* for the particular *string* being created in the *subject authority file.*

General reference. A blanket reference to a group of headings rather than a particular heading. *See also* Specific reference.

***General see also reference**. A *narrower term reference* made not to specific individual subject headings but to a category of *subject headings* or *subdivisions,* frequently listing one or more individual headings or subdivisions by way of example. General see also references appear in 360 fields in *subject authority records.*

***General see reference**. A *use reference* made not to specific individual headings but to a category of *subject headings* or *subdivisions,* frequently listing one or more individual headings or subdivisions by way of example. General see references appear in 260 fields in *subject authority records.*

Generic posting. The practice of assigning additional headings that are broader than the heading that represents precisely the content of the work.

Geographic heading. A name heading representing a place or an entity closely associated with a place (e.g., a park, a forest, a tunnel, etc.). Also called local subdivision. *See also* Jurisdictional name heading; Non-jurisdictional name heading.

***Geographic qualifier**. The name of a larger geographic entity added in parentheses after the name of a more specific locality or other entity to designate its location, as in the subject headings **Whitney, Mount (Calif.)**; **Gobi Desert (Mongolia and China)**; **Colorado River (Colo.-Mexico)**; **Empire State Building (New York, N.Y.).**

***Geographic subdivision**. A type of subject heading *subdivision* that appears in a $z subfield of a 6XX field and that expresses the name of the place to which the *subject* or *form* of the work, designated in the main part of the heading, is limited. Geographic subdivision may be **indirect**, in which the name of a larger geographic entity is placed in a separate $z subfield before the name of a more specific locality, or **direct**, in which a place name is assigned without the interposition of the name of a larger geographic entity.

Hierarchical reference. A *cross reference* connecting headings on different levels of a hierarchy. *See also* Broader term reference; Narrower term reference; Related term reference.

In-depth indexing. The practice of assigning indexing terms or subject headings to represent individual parts of a publication. *See also* Exhaustive indexing; Summarization.

Indirect subdivision. *See* Geographic subdivision.

***Individual biography**. A biography of one person. *See also* Collective biography.

***Inverted heading.** A heading that consists of a noun modified by an adjective, formulated to place the noun in the initial position followed by a comma and the adjective. *See also* Straight heading.

Jurisdictional name heading. A *geographic heading* representing a political or ecclesiastical jurisdiction. Entities that belong to this category include countries, principalities, territories, states, provinces, counties, administrative districts, cities, archdioceses, and dioceses. Jurisdictional name headings are established in accordance with *AACR2R*.

Juvenile film. A *film* intended for children through the age of fifteen.

Juvenile work. Works intended for children through the age of fifteen (or through the ninth grade).

LCSH. *See* Library of Congress Subject Headings

***Library of Congress Subject Headings.** The printed list of headings produced from the *subject authority file* maintained by the Library of Congress and published annually. The term is frequently abbreviated as **LCSH** and is sometimes used interchangeably with the term *subject authority file.*

Literary warrant. The use of an actual collection of material or body of literature as the basis for developing an indexing or classification system. In the case of LCSH, the literary warrant is the Library of Congress collection.

***Liturgy**. Prayers, rituals, acts, and ceremonies used in the official worship of a religion or denomination, public or private.

Local subdivision. *See* Geographic subdivision.

Model heading. *See* Pattern heading.

Multiple heading. A heading with a modifier followed by a bracketed series of similar modifiers ending with the word "etc.," for example, *Authors, American, [English, French, etc.].* This device was used previously by the Library of Congress to illustrate how a heading may be modified. The practice of establishing multiple headings was discontinued in 1979.

Multiple subdivision. A subdivision that incorporates bracketed terms, generally followed by the word "etc.," for example, **Subject headings–Aeronautics, [Education, Latin America, Law, etc.]**; **Names, Personal–Scottish, [Spanish, Welsh, etc.]**. This device is used to indicate that the same main heading may be subdivided by similar subdivisions suggested by the terms enclosed in brackets may be created.

***Name authority file**. A file containing individual *name authority records.* As used in this manual, this term refers specifically to the name authority file created and maintained by the Library of Congress with contributions from participating libraries.

***Name authority record**. An *authority record* for a *name heading.*

***Name heading**. A heading that is a personal name, corporate name, meeting name, uniform title, or jurisdictional name.

Name-title heading. A heading consisting of the name of a person or corporate body and the title of an item. It is established according to *AACR2R* and used in both descriptive and subject cataloging.

***Narrower term reference**. A reference to a *subject heading* at a lower level in a hierarchy than the term referred from. Narrower term references do not appear in *subject authority records,* but are generated by automated systems as the reciprocals of *broader term references.*

Non-jurisdictional name heading. A *geographic heading* representing an entity other than a jurisdiction. Typical non-jurisdictional name headings include those for rivers, mountains, parks, roads, etc.

Nonprint heading. *See* Unprinted heading.

NT. *See* Narrower term reference.

***Parenthetical qualifier**. A word or phrase placed in parentheses after a heading either to distinguish between two different meanings of an identical term or to clarify the meaning of the heading, as in the subject headings Plates (Engineering); Plates (Tableware); BASIC (Computer program language); Adonis (Greek deity).

Partial biography. A work that presents only certain details of a person's life. *See also* Complete biography.

Pattern heading. A heading that serves as a model of subdivisions for headings in the same category. Subdivisions listed under a pattern heading may be used whenever appropriate under other headings in the same category. For example, **Piano** serves as a pattern heading for musical instruments. Also called model heading.

Period subdivision. *See* Chronological subdivision.

***Periodical**. A publication other than a newspaper that is actually or purportedly issued according to a regular schedule (monthly, quarterly, biennially, etc.) in successive parts, each of which bears a numerical or chronological designation, and that is intended to be continued indefinitely.

Place subdivision. *See* Geographic subdivision

Political qualifier. *See* Type-of-jurisdiction qualifier.

Postcoordination. The representation of a complex subject by assigning separate single-concept terms at the indexing stage and the retrieval of that subject through combining the separate terms at the search or retrieval stage. Also called a coordinate system. *See also* Precoordination.

Precoordination. The representation of a complex subject by means of combining separate elements of the subject in the subject headings list or thesaurus or at the indexing stage. *See also* Postcoordination.

***Proposal**. A suggested new subject heading or a suggested change to an existing heading, submitted by a cataloger in the form of a subject authority proposal record ("sp" record) or a printout of an existing *subject authority record* marked up with proposed changes, for consideration at the weekly subject headings editorial meeting of the Cataloging Policy and Support Office, which is responsible for overall development of the Library of Congress *subject authority file.*

Qualifier. A term (enclosed in parentheses) placed after a heading for the purpose of distinguishing between homographs or clarifying the meaning of the heading, for example, **Jive (Dance)**; **Juno (Roman deity)**; **New York (State)**. *See also* Geographic qualifier; Type-of-jurisdiction qualifier.

Qualifier, adjectival. *See* Adjectival qualifier.

Qualifier, geographic. *See* Geographic qualifier

Qualifier, parenthetical. *See* Parenthetical qualifier

Refer-from reference. An indication of the terms or headings from which references are to be made to a given heading. It is the reverse of the indication of a Use reference and is represented by the symbols UF (used for). See also Use reference.

Reference. *See* Cross reference.

***Reference source**. An authoritative published work or other source of information consulted to determine the appropriate terminology to be used in establishing a *subject heading* and creating an appropriate structure of cross references to and from the heading.

***Related term reference**. A reference from one *subject heading* to another subject heading that is in a different hierarchy. Related term references appear in 5XX fields in *subject authority records,* and are identifiable by the presence of the value **n** in the first character position of the $w control subfield.

RT. *See* Related term reference.

***Scope note**. A note associated with a *subject heading* that provides information about the heading such as its definition, application, or relationship to other headings, in order to enable catalogers to use the heading consistently and users to determine what type of material may be found under the heading. Scope notes appear in 680 fields in *subject authority records.*

***See also reference**. A cross reference leading from one valid heading to another. In the Library of Congress *subject authority file,* a see also reference is in the form of a *broader term reference* (which can generate a *narrower term reference* as its reciprocal), or a *general see also reference.*

***See reference**. *See* Use reference

Specific entry. Entry of a work under a heading that expresses its special subject or topic, as distinguished from an entry for the class or broad subject that encompasses that special subject or topic.

Specific reference. A reference from one heading to another. *See also* General reference.

Specificity. (1) The closeness of match between a term or heading and the document to which it is assigned; (2) where a given term lies within a hierarchy of related terms—whether it is near the top and thus fairly general, or fairly far down and thus quite specific.

***Straight heading**. A heading established in direct, natural language word order. *See also* Inverted heading.

***String**. A term used to refer to the combination of a subject heading and one or more subdivisions. In the context of the MARC 21 format, a string is a 6XX field that has at least one $v, $x, $y, or $z subfield in addition to the $a subfield.

***Subdivision**. The portion of a subject heading *string* that appears in a $v, $x, $y, or $z subfield of the 6XX field and that is used to identify a specific aspect of the main *subject heading,* such as form, subtopic, time period, or place, in connection with the bibliographic work to which it is assigned. *See also* Chronological subdivision; Form subdivision; Geographic subdivision; and Topical subdivision.

***Subdivision record**. An *authority record* for a *subdivision* with the authorized form of the subdivision appearing in a 18X field. The Library of Congress uses subdivision records to control *free-floating subdivisions.*

***Subheading**. The portion of a corporate body name heading that is subordinate to the main heading. In printed or in nontagged displays, subheadings are conventionally separated from main headings by a period and two spaces. In the heading **United States. Congress. House**, for example, **Congress** and **House** are subheadings. In the MARC 21 format, subheadings appear in $b subfields of X10 fields.

***Subject**. The topic treated or matter discussed in a work. What a work is about.

Subject analysis. The process of identifying the intellectual content of a work. The results may be displayed in a catalog or bibliography by means of notational symbols as in a classification system, or verbal terms such as subject headings or descriptors.

Subject analytic. *See* Analytical subject entry.

***Subject authority file**. A file containing individual *authority records* for *subject headings* and *subdivisions.* As used in this manual, the term refers specifically to the subject authority file created and maintained by the Library of Congress and used to produce the publication *Library of Congress Subject Headings (LCSH).* The term is frequently used interchangeably with the terms *Library of Congress Subject Headings* or *LCSH.*

***Subject authority record**. An *authority record* for a *subject heading.*

***Subject heading**. A heading in a 6XX field in a MARC bibliographic record, consisting of either a single element in an $a subfield or of an $a subfield followed by subdivisions in $v, $x, $y, and/or $z subfields, that designates what a work is or what it is about.

Subject-to-name reference. A reference from a subject heading to a name heading for the purpose of directing the user's attention from a particular field of interest to names of individuals or corporate bodies that are active or associated in some way with the field. Except for non-jurisdictional headings, such references are no longer made by the Library of Congress.

Summarization. The practice of assigning indexing terms or subject headings to represent the overall content of a document rather than individual parts of it. *See also* Exhaustive indexing; In-depth indexing.

***Supplementary work**. A separately issued *subordinate* work that continues or complements a previously issued work.

Syndetic device. The device used to connect related headings by means of *cross references*. *See also* Cross reference.

Syntax. The order in which individual vocabulary elements of the language are concatenated to form larger expressions (Svenonius).

Synthesis. The representation of a subject by combining individual terms that are listed separately in a subject headings list or thesaurus. *See also* Precoordination.

Systematic catalog. *See* Classed catalog.

Thesaurus. A list of controlled indexing terms used in a particular indexing system.

***Topical heading**. A type of *subject heading* that expresses what a work is about.

***Topical subdivision**. A type of subject heading *subdivision* that appears in an $x subfield of a 6XX field and that designates a specific aspect, or subtopic, of the main heading other than period, place, or form.

Tracing. An indication of the access points that have been made for a particular cataloging record. These access points include descriptive and subject headings.

Type-of-jurisdiction qualifier. A term (enclosed in parentheses) indicating type of jurisdiction, added to a geographic name in order to distinguish between places of the same name, for example, **Washington (State)**. Also called political qualifier.

UF. *See* Use reference.

Uniform heading. The representation of a given subject by one heading in one form only.

Uniform title. The title by which a work is identified for cataloging purposes. It is established according to *AACR2R* and used in both descriptive and subject cataloging.

Unique heading. The use of a heading to represent one subject or one concept only.

Unprinted heading. A heading that is assigned to cataloging records but not listed in LCSH. Most headings consisting of proper names (including personal and corporate headings) and many music headings are unprinted headings. Also called nonprint heading.

***Use reference**. A reference from a term that is not valid for use as a subject heading to an equivalent term that is a valid heading. Use references are traced in 4XX fields in *subject authority records*.

Bibliography

Aluri, Rao, D. Alasdair Kemp, and John J. Boll. *Subject Analysis in Online Catalogs*. Englewood, Colo.: Libraries Unlimited, 1991.

Angell, Richard S. "Library of Congress Subject Headings—Review and Forecast." In *Subject Retrieval in the Seventies: New Directions: Proceedings of an International Symposium*, edited by Hans (Hanan) Wellisch and Thomas D. Wilson, 143-163. Westport, Conn.: Greenwood Publishing, 1972.

———. "Standards for Subject Headings: A National Program." *Journal of Cataloging and Classification* 10 (October 1954): 193.

Anglo-American Cataloguing Rules. 2nd ed., 2002 rev. Prepared under the direction of the Joint Steering Committee for Revision of AACR, a committee of: the American Library Association, the Australian Committee on Cataloguing, the British Library, the Canadian Committee on Cataloguing, Chartered Institute of Library and Information Professionals, the Library of Congress. Chicago: American Library Association, 2002.

Association for Library Collections & Technical Services, Cataloging and Classification Section, Subject Analysis Committee, Subcommittee on Metadata and Subject Analysis. *Subject Data in the Metadata Record: Recommendations and Rationale: A Report from the ALCTS/CCS/SAC/Subcommittee on Metadata and Subject Analysis*, 1999. Available: http://www.ala.org/alcts/organization/ccs/sac/metarept2.html.

Association for Library Collections & Technical Services, Cataloging and Classification Section, Subject Analysis Committee, Subcommittee on the Revision of the Guidelines on Subject Access to Individual Works of Fiction. *Guidelines on Subject Access to Individual Works of Fiction, Drama, Etc.* 2nd ed. Chicago: American Library Association, 2000.

Austin, Derek. *PRECIS: A Manual of Concept Analysis and Subject Indexing*, 2nd ed., with assistance from Mary Dykstra. London: The British Library, Bibliographic Services Division, 1984.

Balnaves, John. "Specificity." In *The Variety of Librarianship: Essays in Honour of John Wallace Metcalfe*, edited by W. Boyd Rayward, 47-56. Sydney: Library Association of Australia, 1976.

Bates, Marcia J. "Factors Affecting Subject Catalog Search Success." *Journal of the American Society for Information Science* 28 (May 1977): 16-169.

———. "Implications of the Subject Subdivisions Conference: The Shift in Online Catalog Design." In Subject Subdivisions Conference (1991: Airlie, Va.). *The Future of Subdivisions in the Library of Congress Subject Headings System: Report from the Subject Subdivisions Conference*, edited by Martha O'Hara Conway, 92-98. Washington, D.C.: Library of Congress, Cataloging Distribution Service, 1992.

———. "Rethinking Subject Cataloing in the Online Environment." *Library Resources & Technical Services* 33(4) (October 1989): 400-412.

Batty, David. "WWW—Wealth, Weariness or Waste: Controlled Vocabulary and Thesauri in Support of Online Information Access." *D-Lib Magazine* (November 1998). Available: http://www.dlib.org/dlib/november98/11batty.html.

Berman, Barbara L. "Form Headings in Subject Cataloging." *Library Resources & Technical Services* 33(2) (April 1989): 134-139.

Berman, Sanford. *Prejudices and Antipathies: A Tract on the LC Subject Heads Concerning People.* 1993 ed. Jefferson, N.C.: McFarland, 1993.

Borgman, Christine L. "Why Are Online Catalogs Hard to Use? Lessons Learned from Information-Retrieval Studies." *Journal of the American Society for Information Science* 37 (November 1986): 387-400.

———. "Why Are Online Catalogs Still Hard to Use?" *Journal of the American Society for Information Science* 47 (July 1996): 493-503.

Cataloging Service Bulletin 1- , Summer 1978- . Washington, D.C.: Library of Congress, Processing Services.

Chan, Lois Mai. "Alternatives to Subject Strings in the Library of Congress Subject Headings System: with Discussion." In Subject Subdivisions Conference (1991: Airlie, Va.). *The Future of Subdivisions in the Library of Congress Subject Headings System Library of Congress: Report from the Subject Subdivisions Conference*, edited by Martha O'Hara Conway, 46-56. Washington, D.C.: Library of Congress, Cataloging Distribution Service, 1992.

———. "Exploiting LCSH, LCC, and DDC to Retrieve Networked Resources: Issues and Challenges." In *Proceedings of the Bicentennial Conference on Bibliographic Control for the New Millennium: Confronting the Challenges of Networked Resources and the Web*, Washington, D.C., November 15-17, 2000, sponsored by the Library of Congress Cataloging Directorate, edited by Ann M. Sandberg-Fox, 159-178. Washington, D.C.: Library of Congress, Cataloging Distribution Service, 2001.

———. "Library of Congress Subject Headings as an Online Retrieval Tool: Structural Considerations: Paper Presented at the Symposium on Subject

Analysis, 29-30 March 1985, Durham, N.C." In *Improving LCSH for use in Online Catalogs*, edited by P. A. Cochrane, 123-133. Littleton, CO: Libraries Unlimited, 1986.

———. *Library of Congress Subject Headings: Principles of Structure and Policies for Application*. Annotated Version, prepared by Lois Mai Chan for the Library of Congress. Advances in Library Information Technology, No. 3. Washington, D.C.: Cataloging Distribution Service, Library of Congress, 1990.

———. "Still Robust at 100: A Century of LC Subject Headings." *The Library of Congress Information Bulletin* 57(8) (August 1998): 200-201.

Chan, Lois Mai, Eric Childress, Rebecca Dean, Edward T. O'Neill, and Diane Vizine-Goetz. "A Faceted Approach to Subject Data in the Dublin Core Metadata Record." *Journal of Internet Cataloging* 4(1/2) (2001): 35-47.

Coates, E. J. *Subject Catalogues: Headings and Structure*. London: Library Association, 1960. Reissued with new preface 1988.

Cochrane, Pauline A. *Improving LCSH for Use in Online Catalogs: Exercises for Self-Help with a Selection of Background Readings*. Littleton, Colo.: Libraries Unlimited, 1986.

———. "Improving LCSH for Use in Online Catalogs Revisited—What Progress Has Been Made? What Issues Still Remain?" *Cataloging & Classification Quarterly* 29(1/2) (2000):73-89.

Cochrane, Pauline A., and Monika Kirtland. *I. Critical Views of LCSH . . . II. An Analysis of Vocabulary Control in the Library of Congress List of Subject Headings*. Syracuse, N.Y.: ERIC Clearinghouse on Information Resources, 1981.

Conway, Martha O'Hara, and Karen M. Drabenstott. "The Expanded Use of Free-Floating Subdivisions in the Library of Congress Subject Headings System: With Discussion." In Subject Subdivisions Conference (1991: Airlie, Va.). *The Future of Subdivisions in the Library of Congress Subject Headings System: Report from the Subject Subdivisions Conference*, edited by Martha O'Hara Conway, 26-35. Washington, D.C.: Library of Congress, Cataloging Distribution Service, 1992.

Cutter, Charles A. *Rules for a Dictionary Catalog*. 4th ed., rewritten. Washington, D.C.: Government Printing Office, 1904.

Decourt, Eugénio, and Sónia Maria Guerreiro Pacheco. "Subject Access in the Brazilian Library Network BIBLIODATA CALCO." In *Subject Indexing: Principles & Practices in the 90's: Proceedings of the IFLA Satellite Meeting Held in Lisbon, Portugal, 17-18 August 1993, and Sponsored by the IFLA Section on Classification and Indexing and the Instituto da*

Biblioteca Nacional e do LIVRO, Lisbon, Portugal, edited by Robert P. Holley, Dorothy McGarry, Donna Duncan, and Elaine Svenonius, 3-11. München; New Providence, N.J.: K.G. Saur, 1995.

Drabenstott, Karen Markey. "Enhancing a New Design for Subject Access to Online Catalogs: Examination of 2,000 User Queries Extracted from the Transaction Logs of Syracuse University, UCLA, University of Kentucky and the University Of Michigan." *Library Hi Tech* 14 (1996): 87-109.

Drabenstott, Karen Markey, and Diane Vizine-Goetz. *Using Subject Headings for Online Retrieval: Theory, Practice, and Potential.* San Diego, Calif.: Academic Press, 1994.

Drabenstott, Karen Markey, and Marjorie S. Weller. "Failure Analysis of Subject Searches in a Test of a New Design for Subject Access to Online Catalogs: ASTUTE Experimental Catalog Use at Earlham College and the University Of Michigan-Dearborn." *Journal of the American Society for Information Science* 47 (July 1996): 519-537.

Drabenstott, Karen M., Schelle Simcox, and Marie Williams. "Do Librarians Understand the Subject Headings in Library Catalogs?" *Reference & User Services Quarterly* 38(4) (Summer 1999): 369-387.

Dunkin, Paul S. *Cataloging U.S.A.* Chicago: American Library Association, 1969.

Dykstra, Mary. "Can Subject Headings Be Saved?" *Library Journal* 113 (September 15, 1988): 55-58.

———. "LC Subject Headings Disguised as a Thesaurus." *Library Journal* 113 (March 1, 1988): 42-46.

Eaton, Thelma. *Cataloging and Classification: An Introductory Manual.* 4th ed. Ann Arbor, Mich.: Edwards Brothers, 1967.

El-Hoshy, Lynn M., "Charting a Changing Language with LCSH." *Library of Congress Information Bulletin* 57(8) (August 1998): 201.

———. "Introduction to Subdivision Practice in the Library of Congress Subject Headings System." In Subject Subdivisions Conference (1991: Airlie, Va.). *The Future of Subdivisions in the Library of Congress Subject Headings System: Report from the Subject Subdivisions Conference*, edited by Martha O'Hara Conway, 117-129. Washington, D.C.: Library of Congress, Cataloging Distribution Service, 1992.

Ferl, Terry Ellen, and Larry Millsap. "The Knuckle-Cracker's Dilemma: a Transaction Log Study of OPAC Subject Searching: Online Survey of Users Who Access MELVYL from Public Access Terminals in the Libraries of the University of California, Santa Cruz." *Information Technology and Libraries* 15 (June 1996): 81-98.

Frarey, Carlyle J. "Studies of Use of the Subject Catalog: Summary and Evaluation." In *Subject Analysis of Library Materials*, edited by Maurice F. Tauber, 147-165. New York: School of Library Service, Columbia University, 1953.

———. *Subject Headings, The State of the Library Art*, vol. 1, part 2. New Brunswick, N.J.: Graduate School of Library Science, Rutgers—The State University, 1960.

Hanson, J. C. M. "The Subject Catalogs of the Library of Congress." *Bulletin of the American Library Association* 3 (1909): 385-397.

Hayes, Susan. "Enhanced Catalog Access to Fiction: A Preliminary Study." *Library Resources & Technical Services* 36(4) (October 1992): 441-459.

Haykin, David Judson. "Project for a Subject Heading Code." Revised. Unpublished paper, Washington, D.C., 1957.

———. *Subject Headings: A Practical Guide*. Washington, D.C.: Government Printing Office, 1951.

———. "Subject Headings: Principles and Development." In *The Subject Analysis of Library Materials*, edited by Maurice F. Tauber. New York: School of Library Service, Columbia University, 1953.

Hearn, Stephen. "Machine-Assisted Validation of *LC Subject Headings:* Implications for Authority File Structure." *Cataloging & Classification Quarterly* 29(1/2) (2000): 107-115.

Hemmasi, Harriette, and J. Bradford Young. "LCSH for Music: Historical And Empirical Perspectives." *Cataloging & Classification Quarterly 29(1/2) (2000): 135-157.*

Hildreth, Charles R. *Online Public Access Catalogs: The User Interface*. Dublin, Ohio: OCLC, 1982.

Hoerman, Heidi Lee, and Kevin A. Furniss. "Turning Practice into Principles: A Comparison of the IFLA Principles Underlying Subject Heading Languages (Shls) and the Principles Underlying the Library of Congress Subject Headings System." *Cataloging & Classification Quarterly 29(1/2) (2000): 31-52.*

Holley, Robert P. "Report on the IFLA Satellite Meeting 'Subject Indexing: Principles and Practices in the 90's,' August 17-18, 1993, Lisbon, Portugal." *Cataloging & Classification Quarterly* 18(2) (1993): 87-95.

Hulme, E. Wyndham. "Principles of Book Classification." *Library Association Record* 13 (1911): 445-447.

Jouguelet, Suzanne. "Evolution des pratiques d'indexation par sujets en France." In *Subject Indexing: Principles & Practices in the 90's: Proceedings of the IFLA Satellite Meeting Held in Lisbon, Portugal, 17-18 August 1993, and Sponsored by the IFLA Section on Classification and Indexing and the Instituto da Biblioteca Nacional e do LIVRO, Lisbon, Portugal,* edited by Robert P. Holley, Dorothy McGarry, Donna Duncan, and Elaine Svenonius, 64-80. München; New Providence, N.J.: K.G. Saur, 1995.

Kaiser, Julius O. *Systematic Indexing*. The Card System Series, vol. 2. London: Pitman, 1911.

Kirtland, Monika, and Pauline Cochrane. "Critical Views of LCSH Library of Congress Subject Headings: A Bibliographic and Bibliometric Essay." *Cataloging & Classification Quarterly* 1(2/3) (1982): 71-94.

Lancaster, F. W. *Vocabulary Control for Information Retrieval.* 2nd ed. Arlington, Va.: Information Resources Press, 1986.

Larsgaard, Mary Lynette. *Map Librarianship: An Introduction.* 3rd ed. Englewood, Colo.: Libraries Unlimited, 1998.

Library of Congress. *Free-Floating Subdivisions: An Alphabetical Index.* Prepared by Subject Cataloging Division. Washington, D.C.: Library of Congress, Cataloging Distribution Service, 1989- .

———. *Library of Congress Subject Headings.* Washington, D.C.: Library of Congress, 1975- .

———. *Subject Headings Used in the Dictionary Catalogues of the Library of Congress.* Washington, D.C.: Government Printing Office, Library Branch, 1910/1914-1966.

Library of Congress. Motion Picture/Broadcasting/Recorded Sound Division. *The Moving Image Genre-Form Guide.* Compiled by Brian Taves, Judi Hoffman, and Karen Lund. Washington, D.C.: Library of Congress. MBRS, 1998). Available: http://lcweb.loc.gov/rr/mopic/migintro.html.

Library of Congress. Office of Subject Cataloging Policy. *LC Period Subdivisions Under Names of Places.* 5th ed. Washington, D.C.: Library of Congress. Cataloging Distribution Service, 1994.

———. *Revised Library of Congress Subject Headings: Cross-References from Former to Current Subject Headings.* 1st ed. Washington, D.C.: Library of Congress. Cataloging Distribution Service, 1991.

Library of Congress Rule Interpretations. 2nd ed. [Edited by Robert M. Hiatt ; formulated by the Office for Descriptive Cataloging Policy, Library of

Congress]. Washington, D.C.: Cataloging Distribution Service, Library of Congress, 1989- .

Lilley, Oliver Linton. "How Specific Is Specific?" *Journal of Cataloging and Classification* 11 (1955): 4-5.

List of Subject Headings for Use in Dictionary Catalogs. Prepared by a committee of the American Library Association. Boston: Published for the A.L.A. Publishing Section by the Library Bureau, 1895; 2nd ed. rev., 1898; 3rd ed. rev., 1911.

Lopes, Inês "Subject Indexing in Portuguese Libraries: A New Approach with SIPORbase." In *Subject Indexing: Principles & Practices in the 90's: Proceedings of the IFLA Satellite Meeting Held in Lisbon, Portugal, 17-18 August 1993, and Sponsored by the IFLA Section on Classification and Indexing and the Instituto da Biblioteca Nacional e do LIVRO, Lisbon, Portugal,* edited by Robert P. Holley, Dorothy McGarry, Donna Duncan, and Elaine Svenonius, 121-143. München; New Providence, N.J.: K.G. Saur, 1995.

Mandel, Carol A., and Judith Herschman. "Subject Access in the Online Catalog." A report prepared for the Council on Library Resources, August 1981.

Mann, Thomas. "Teaching *Library of Congress Subject Headings.*" *Cataloging & Classification Quarterly* 29(1/2) (2000): 117-126.

———. "Why LC Subject Headings Are More Important Than Ever: The Solution to Some of Researchers' Biggest Problems Is Staring Us Right in Our Faces." *American Libraries* 34(9) (October 2003): 52-54.

MARC 21 Format for Authority Data: Including Guidelines for Content Designation. Prepared by Network Development and MARC Standards Office. Washington, D.C.: Library of Congress, Cataloging Distribution Service, 1999.

MARC 21 Format for Bibliographic Data : Including Guidelines for Content Designation. Prepared by Network Development and MARC Standards Office, Library of Congress, in cooperation with Standards and Support, National Library of Canada. Washington, D.C.: Library of Congress, Cataloging Distribution Service, 1999.

Markey, Karen. *The Process of Subject Searching in the Library Catalog*. Dublin, Ohio: OCLC, 1983.

———. *Subject Searching in Library Catalogs Before and After the Introduction of Online Catalogs.* OCLC Library, Information, and Computer Science Series 4. Dublin, Ohio: OCLC, 1984.

Marshall, Joan K. *On Equal Terms: A Thesaurus for Nonsexist Indexing and Cataloging*. New York: Neal-Schuman, 1977.

Matthews, Joseph R., Gary S. Lawrence, and Douglas K. Ferguson, eds. *Using Online Catalogs: A Nationwide Study*. New York: Neal-Schuman, 1983.

McGarry, Dorothy, and Elaine Svenonius. "More on Improved Browsable Displays for Online Subject Access." *Information Technology and Libraries* 10(3) (September 1991): 185-191.

Medical Subject Headings. Bethesda, Md.: U.S. Dept. of Health and Human Services, Public Health Service, National Institutes of Health, National Library of Medicine, 1960- .

Metcalfe, John W. *Subject Classifying and Indexing of Libraries and Literature*. Sydney: Angus and Robertson, 1959.

Miksa; Francis. *The Subject in the Dictionary Catalog from Cutter to the Present*. Chicago: American Library Association, 1983.

Miller, David P. "Out from Under: Form/Genre Access in LCSH." *Cataloging & Classification Quarterly* 29(1/2) (2000): 169-88.

National Library of Canada. *Canadian Subject Headings*. Ottawa: National Library of Canada, 1978- .

Olson, Hope A. "Difference, Culture and Change: The Untapped Potential of LCSH." *Cataloging & Classification Quarterly* 29(1/2) (2000): 53-71.

Olson, Hope A., and John J. Boll. *Subject Analysis in Online Catalogs*. 2nd ed. Englewood, Colo.: Libraries Unlimited, 2001.

O'Neill, Edward T., and Lois Mai Chan. "FAST (Faceted Application of Subject Terminology): A Simplified Vocabulary Based on the Library of Congress Subject Headings." *IFLA Journal* 29(4) (December 2003): 336-342.

O'Neill, Edward T., and Rao Aluri. *Research Report on Subject Heading Patterns in OCLC Monographic Records*. OCLC Research Report Series OCLC/RDD/RR-79/1. Columbus: Ohio College Library Center, 1979.

O'Neill, Edward T., et al. "Form Subdivisions: Their Identification and Use in LCSH." *Library Resources & Technical Services* 45(4) (2001): 187-197.

Ostrove, Geraldine E. "Music Subject Cataloging and Form/Genre Implementation at the Library of Congress." *Cataloging & Classification Quarterly 32(2) (2001): 91-106.*

Pietris, Mary K. "The Limited Use of Free-Floating Subdivisions in the Library of Congress Subject Headings System: with Discussion." In Subject Subdivisions Conference (1991: Airlie, Va.). *The Future of Subdivisions in the Library of Congress Subject Headings System: Report from the Subject*

Subdivisions Conference, edited by Martha O'Hara Conway, 11-25. Washington, D.C.: Library of Congress, Cataloging Distribution Service, 1992.

Prevost, Marie Louise. "An Approach to Theory and Method in General Subject Heading[s]." *Library Quarterly* 16(2) (April 1946): 140-151.

Principles underlying subject heading languages (SHLs). Edited by Maria Inês Lopes and Julianne Beall, Working Group on Principles Underlying Subject Heading Languages, approved by the Standing Committee of the IFLA Section on Classification and Indexing. München : K.G. Saur, 1999.

Ranganathan, S. R. *Elements of Library Classification.* 3rd ed. Bombay: Asia Publishing House, 1962.

Répertoire de vedettes-matière. Ottawa: Bibliothèque nationale du Canada, 1976- .

Richmond, Phyllis Allen. "Cats: An Example of Concealed Classification in Subject Headings." *Library Resources & Technical Services* 3 (Spring 1959): 102-112.

Salton, G., and C. S. Yang. "On the Specification of Term Values in Automatic Indexing." *Journal of Documentation* 29 (December 1973): 352.

Salton, G., and Michael J. McGill. *Introduction to Modern Information Retrieval.* New York: McGraw-Hill, 1983.

Schweitzer, Alina. "A Balancing Act Between Conformity and Divergence: Subject Access to Library Materials in Canada." In *Subject Indexing: Principles & Practices in the 90's: Proceedings of the IFLA Satellite Meeting Held in Lisbon, Portugal, 17-18 August 1993, and Sponsored by the IFLA Section on Classification and Indexing and the Instituto da Biblioteca Nacional e do LIVRO, Lisbon, Portugal,* edited by Robert P. Holley, Dorothy McGarry, Donna Duncan, and Elaine Svenonius, 16-30. München; New Providence, N.J.: K.G. Saur, 1995.

Shera, Jesse H., and Margaret Egan. *The Classified Catalog: Basic Principles and Practices.* Chicago: American Library Association, 1956.

Shubert, Steven Blake. "Critical Views of LCSH—Ten Years Later: A Bibliographic Essay." *Cataloging and Classification Quarterly* 15(2) (1992): 37-97.

Soergel, Dagobert. *Organizing Information: Principles of Data Base and Retrieval Systems.* Orlando, Fla.: Academic Press, 1985.

Soltani, Poori. "Major Subject Access in Iran." In *Subject Indexing: Principles & Practices in the 90's: Proceedings of the IFLA Satellite Meeting Held in Lisbon, Portugal, 17-18 August 1993, and Sponsored by the IFLA Section on Classification and Indexing and the Instituto da Biblioteca Nacional e do LIVRO, Lisbon, Portugal,* edited by Robert P. Holley, Dorothy McGarry, Donna Duncan, and Elaine Svenonius, 94-108. München; New Providence, N.J.: K.G. Saur, 1995.

Stone, Alva T. "The *LCSH* Century: A Brief History of the *Library of Congress Subject Headings,* and Introduction to the Centennial Essays." *Cataloging & Classification Quarterly* 29(1/2) (2000): 1-15.

Stone, Alva T., ed. *The LCSH Century: One Hundred Years with the Library of Congress Subject Headings System.* New York: Haworth Information Press, 2000. Also published as volume 2, no. 1/2 (2000) of *Cataloging & Classification Quarterly.*

Studwell, William E. *Library of Congress Subject Headings Philosophy, Practice, and Prospects*. New York: Haworth Press, 1990.

———. "The 1990s: Decade of Subject Access: A Theoretical *Code* for LC Subject Headings Would Complete the Maturation of Modern Cataloging." *American Libraries* 18 (December 1987): 958.

———. "On the Conference Circuit: The Subject Heading *Code*: Do We Have One? Do We Need One?" *Technicalities* 10 (October 1990): 10-15.

Subject Data in the Metadata Record Recommendations and Rationale: A Report from the ALCTS/SAC/Subcommittee on Metadata and Subject Analysis. 1999. Available: http://www.govst.edu/users/gddcasey/sac/MetadataReport. html.

Subject Indexing: Principles and Practices in the 90's : Proceedings of the IFLA Satellite Meeting Held in Lisbon, Portugal, 17-18 August 1993, and Sponsored by the IFLA Section on Classification and Indexing and the Instituto da Biblioteca Nacional e do LIVRO, Lisbon, Portugal, edited by Robert P. Holley, Dorothy McGarry, Donna Duncan, and Elaine Svenonius. UCBIM Publications - New Series, vol. 15. München; New Providence, N.J. : K.G. Saur, 1995.

Subject Subdivisions Conference (1991: Airlie, Va.). *The Future of Subdivisions in the Library of Congress Subject Headings System: Report from the Subject Subdivisions Conference,* edited by Martha O'Hara Conway.. Washington, D.C.: Library of Congress, Cataloging Distribution Service, 1992.

Svenonius, Elaine. "Design of Controlled Vocabularies." In *Encyclopedia of Library and Information Science,* edited by Allen Kent. New York: Marcel Dekker, 1990. Vol. 45, Suppl. 10, 82-109.

———. *The Intellectual Foundation of Information Organization.* Cambridge, Mass.: MIT Press, 2000.

———. "LCSH: Semantics, Syntax and Specificity." In *The LCSH Century: One Hundred Years with the Library of Congress Subject Headings System,* edited by Alva T. Stone, 17-30. New York: Haworth Information Press, 2000.

———. "Metcalfe and the Principles of Specific Entry." In *The Variety of Librarianship: Essays in Honour of John Wallace Mercalfe*, edited by W. Boyd Rayward, 171-189. Sydney: Library Association of Australia, 1976.

———. "Unanswered Questions in the Design of Controlled Vocabularies." *Journal of the American Society for Information Science* 37 (1986): 331-40.

Svenonius, Elaine, and Dorothy McGarry. "Objectivity in Evaluating Subject Heading Assignment." *Cataloging & Classification Quarterly* 16(2) (1993): 5-40.

Taube, Mortimer. "Specificity in Subject Headings and Coordinate Indexing." *Library Trends* 1 (October 1952): 222.

Vatican Library. *Rules for the Catalog of Printed Books.* Translated from the 2nd Italian edition by Thomas J. Shanahan, Victor A. Schaefer, and Constantin T. Vesselowsky, and edited by Wyllis E. Wright. Chicago: American Library Association, 1948.

Vickery, Brian C. "Systematic Subject Indexing." *Journal of Documentation* 9(1) (1953): 48-57.

Weinberg, Bella Hass. "The Hidden Classification in Library of Congress Subject Headings for Judaica." *Library Resources & Technical Services* 37 (October 1993): 369-379.

Wilson, Patrick and Nick Robinson. "Form Subdivisions and Genre." *Library Resources & Technical Services* 34(1) (January 1990): 36-43.

Yee, Martha M. "Two Genre and Form Lists for Moving Image and Broadcast Materials: A Comparison." *Cataloging & Classification Quarterly* 31(3/4) (2001): 237-295.

Index

About the Author

LOIS MAI CHAN is Professor of Library and Information Science at the University of Kentucky.